The Ethics of Writing

It was only toward the middle of the twentieth century that the inhabitants of many European countries came, in general unpleasantly, to the realisation that their fate could be influenced directly by intricate and abstruse books of philosophy.

Czesław Miłosz, The Captive Mind

> . . . graves at my command
> Have waked their sleepers, oped and let 'em forth
> By my so potent art. But this rough magic
> I here abjure, and, when I have required
> Some heavenly music, which even now I do,
> To work mine end upon their senses that
> This airy charm is for, I'll break my staff,
> Bury it certain fathoms in the earth,
> And deeper than did ever plummet sound
> I'll drown my book.

The Tempest, V. i.48–57

The Ethics of Writing

Authorship and Legacy in
Plato and Nietzsche

SEÁN BURKE

Edinburgh University Press

For Tom Burke (born 27 January 2000)

© Seán Burke, 2008

Edinburgh University Press Ltd
22 George Square, Edinburgh

Typeset in 11/13 Bembo
by Servis Filmsetting Ltd, Manchester, and
printed and bound in Great Britain by
Biddles Ltd, King's Lynn, Norfolk

A CIP record for this book is available from the British Library

ISBN 978 0 7486 1830 9 (hardback)

The right of Seán Burke
to be identified as author of this work
has been asserted in accordance with
the Copyright, Designs and Patents Act 1988.

Contents

Acknowledgements

I am very grateful to the Arts and Humanities Research Council for funding in 2004 under their Research Leave Scheme whereby one term of leave awarded by the Council is matched by a term granted by the University. In 2001, I was the recipient of the University of Durham's Sir Dernham Christopherson Research Fellowship for Outstanding Scholars Across all Disciplines. These Awards allowed this book and a forthcoming fraternal book on discursive ethics in Levinas and Derrida to crystallise as a substantial research project.

I am also grateful to my former colleagues in the Department of English Studies at Durham: to Timothy Clark for inviting me to contribute to a special issue of the Oxford Literary Review, to David Fuller and Patricia Waugh for organising the lecture series *The Arts and Sciences of Criticism* (and for editing the subsequent publication) and to Patricia Waugh, again, for giving me an open template to contribute to her edition, *Literary Theory and Criticism: A Guide*. I would also like to thank David Fuller for academic guidance, Gareth Reeves for excellent mentorship, Mark Sandy for discussions on Nietzschean scholarship and Christopher Rowe for the opportunity to discuss his exhaustive engagements with the *Phaedrus* in a number of 'face to face' encounters. The academic leadership of Michael O'Neill has been a source of inspiration since the mid-1990s – as to the formative stages of the present work and its forthcoming companion volume – and is still felt, most positively, to this day.

I would also like to thank Peter Finch for inviting me to present the Annual Gwyn Jones Welsh Academy Lecture in April 2003, an experience which was to give considerable heart to the writing of this book. John Drakakis's enthusiasm for my work on authorship led to productive, relevant and enjoyable seminars at Sterling. Thanks also to Kaisa Kurikka and Lea Rojola at the University of Turku for the 2002 conference 'The

Resurrection of the Literary Author?' from which nascent ideas concerning the Nietzschean legacy took shape. As ever, I am grateful to Cairns Craig for cultivating my work through PhD supervision right through to his advocacy of the current book in proposal form. The expression of long-term gratitude is due to Brian Vickers who has (from afar) consistently upheld the integrity of my research as also to Jackie Jones for her discernment, delightful correspondence, unstinting support and steadfast faith in this project. Thanks are also extended to the staff at Edinburgh University Press and to Ruth Willats for insightful editing of the typescript.

In Cardiff, I have benefited from the balanced judgements and wisdom of Dr Sue Williams and Dr Neil Jones, as from regular contact with Cheryl Scammels whose professional encouragements have opened passageways where I saw only impassable paths. My continuing friendship with Sophie Vlacos has involved not only the exchange of books and ideas but weekly meetings for coffee and culture. Timothy Parry commented intelligently on parts of my manuscript and his ever-renewing spiritual commitment to the ethical imperative reminded me of the deeper values that should always motivate theoretical engagements. Albeit in a somewhat different manner, my friends at The Gower Hotel have also played a part in maintaining a balance between theoretical and practical ethics. Lively, enjoyable discussions with the playwright Mark Jenkins, who has exhaustively researched the Marxist legacy, provided a most intriguing meeting point for parallel ethical projects. The production of the typescript itself owed so very much to the intelligent assistance of David Perrins and that of his tirelessly innovative employer at Alpha Omega Publishing.

The completion of this work would not have been possible without the three-generational inspiration and support of my family. The Greek term *boētheia* – registering the central theme of this book – can mean 'succour, support, guardianship, help, assistance'. These and so many more related terms could be used and yet fail to capture the incalculable support of my parents, John and June, and the pleasure in their company that I have experienced since returning to Cardiff. During a period of transition, my sister Tracey, for whom no act of assistance is too much time or trouble, has been a tremendous source of strength; John, in turn, has provided wise, thoughtful guidance. My brother, Kevin has brought much culture and light into this time of composition, while James and Tom have reminded me that writing (like life) can be fun as well as work, a medium of connection rather than a mark of absence.

Sections of the 'Introduction' and 'Conclusion' first appeared in essays I wrote for David Fuller and Patricia Waugh, eds, *The Arts and Sciences of Criticism* (Oxford: Clarendon Press, 1999) pp. 199–216, Patricia Waugh, ed., *Literary Theory and Criticism: An Oxford Guide* (Oxford: Oxford University Press, 2006) pp. 486–96 and are reprinted here by kind permission of Oxford University Press. Substantial parts of Chapter One, Sections Two and Three, were first published as 'The Birth of Writing: Nietzsche, Havelock and Mythologies of the Sign', in the *Oxford Literary Review*, vol. 21 (2000). Passages from Chapter Two, Section Two, initially appeared in the *Journal of the History of the Human Sciences*, vol. 10, no. 3 (1997).

Key to References and Abbreviations

I. REFERENCES

Occasional recourse is made to alternative translations when the references below give rise to ambiguity or debate as pertinent to the themes of this book. The alternative translations are provided in the footnotes only.

All references to the works of Plato are to *The Collected Dialogues of Plato, Including the Letters*, ed. Edith Hamilton and Huntington Cairns, Bollingen Series LXXI (Princeton, NJ: Princeton University Press, 1961). Title, page numbers and letters correspond to the Renaissance translation of Stephanus and are given parenthetically within the text.

All references to Aristotle are to W. D. Ross, ed., *The Works of Aristotle* (Oxford: Clarendon, 1928). Title, page, letter and line references are supplied parenthetically within the text as standardised according to the Berlin Academy edition, *Aristotelis Opera*, ed. Immanuel Bekker, 5 vols (1831–70).

All references to the books of the Bible are to *The Bible: Authorised King James Version with Apocrypha*, ed. with an Introduction and Notes by Robert Carroll and Stephen Crickett (Oxford: Oxford University Press, 1997). Title, chapter and verse(s) are supplied parenthetically within the text.

2. ABBREVIATIONS
Works by Nietzsche

AC   *Twilight of the Idols and The Antichrist*, trans. R. J. Hollingdale (Harmondsworth: Penguin Books, 1968).

ADL   *On the Advantage and Disadvantage of History for Life*, trans. Peter Preuss (Indianapolis: Hackett, 1980).

AOM   *Assorted Opinions and Maxims*, trans. R. J. Hollingdale in HH.

BGE   *Beyond Good and Evil: Prelude to a Philosophy of the Future*, trans. R. J. Hollingdale (Harmondsworth: Penguin Books, 1973).

BT   *The Birth of Tragedy and The Case of Wagner*, trans. Walter Kaufmann (New York: Random House, 1967).

CW *The Birth of Tragedy and The Case of Wagner*, trans. Walter Kaufmann (New York: Random House, 1967).

D *Daybreak: Thoughts on the Prejudices of Morality*, trans. R. J. Hollingdale (Cambridge: Cambridge University Press, 1982).

EH *Ecce Homo: How One Becomes What One Is*, trans. R. J. Hollingdale, reprinted with a new introduction by Michael Tanner (Harmondsworth: Penguin Books, 1992).

GM *On the Genealogy of Morals* and *Ecce Homo*, trans. Walter Kaufmann and R. J. Hollingdale (New York: Vintage Books, 1973).

GS *The Gay Science with a Prelude in Rhymes and an Appendix of Songs*, trans. Water Kaufmann (New York: Vintage Books, 1974).

HH *Human, All-Too-Human: A Book for Free Spirits*, trans. R. J. Hollingdale (Cambridge: Cambridge University Press, 1986).

SE 'Schopenhauer as Educator', trans. R. J. Hollingdale in UM.

SL *Selected Letters*, trans. A. N. Ludovici (London: Soho Books, 1985).

TwI *Twilight of the Idols* and *The Antichrist*, trans. R. J. Hollingdale (Harmondsworth: Penguin Books, 1968).

UM *Untimely Meditations*, trans. R. J. Hollingdale (Cambridge: Cambridge University Press, 1983).

WP *The Will to Power*, trans. Water Kaufmann and R. J. Hollingdale (New York: Random House: Vintage, 1967).

WS *The Wanderer and His Shadow*, trans. R. J. Hollingdale in HH.

Z *Thus Spoke Zarathustra: A Book for Everyone and No One*, trans. R. J. Hollingdale (Harmondsworth: Penguin Books, 1969).

Other Works

EO Jacques Derrida, *The Ear of the Other: Otobiography, Transference, Translation: Texts and Discussions with Jacques Derrida*, trans. Peggy Kamuf and Avital Ronell (New York: Schocken Books, 1986).

ER J. Hillis Miller, *The Ethics of Reading* (New York: Columbia University Press, 1987).

PP Jacques Derrida, 'Plato's Pharmacy', in Jacques Derrida, *Dissemination*, trans. Barbara Johnson (London: Athlone Press, 1981), pp. 61–171. An earlier version of this essay/monograph was published as 'La Pharmacie de Platon' in *Tel Quel* nos. 32 and 33 (1968). The finalised French version is collected in Jacques Derrida, *La Dissémination* (Paris: Éditions du Seuil, 1972), pp. 71–197.

PtP Eric A. Havelock, *Preface to Plato* (Cambridge, MA: Belknap Press of Harvard University Press, 1963).

3. A NOTE ON CITATION

A few brief but intense textual moments are cited more than once in this book. This 'repetition' is neither random nor the product of a prior, programmatic intention. Rather, I saw no reason to gloss or search for an alternative citation when the 'same' sequence of written words spontaneously rejuvenated itself in quite distinct contexts. Iterability, Derrida showed, denotes the impossibility of a pure act of textual repetition. Nietzsche's declaration 'I am one thing, my writings are another' need not vary in form to orientate discussions of textual epistemology, autobiographical subjectivity, or the ethics of authorial responsibility. The phrase 'rephrases' itself with a vitality that dislodges the discretion – if not heresy – of paraphrase. Likewise, the passages describing the intersubjective light of understanding in the *Phaedrus* and the *Seventh Letter* remain entirely illuminating as relating to the inspirational, romantic or spiritual in one context, the scientific, pedagogic or epistemological in another. Socrates' analogy between poetic repetition and the reverberations of a gong (*Protagoras*, 329a) 'sounds' below in diverse surrounds with a resonance that does not return the same.

This approach was typical of the 'close reading' which produced much of the finest critical endeavour of the previous century. Works which return time and again to lines from Hamlet's third soliloquy, or to the close of Keats's great 'Odes', are but choice examples of what is here called 'theme and variation'. With each successive 're-turn' the textual moment(s) gains in resonance, intelligibility, ambiguity, polysemy, 'depth' or range. In a book whose theme is the ethical significance of the preserved word's reappearance in contexts and climes quite alien to those of its original inscription, explicit iterability acquires a certain performative consistency. Borges observed that 'universal history is perhaps the history of the different intonations given [to] a handful of metaphors'. The aim of this work is to reawaken the Socratic anxiety about the orphaned writing opening itself to abusive and sometimes calamitous intonations. Indeed, a barbaric but not inaccurate title for this book would be 'The Ethics of Citationality', dedicated, as the work is, to drawing out just a few of the ethical intonations that can be given to a single sentence 'spoken' through Socrates in Plato's *Phaedrus* (275e) and thus to reiterating the primordial statement of iterability, re-citing the principle of citation.

Prologue: Friedrich Nietzsche in Auschwitz,[1] or the Posthumous Return of the Author

And God had him die for a hundred years and then revived him and said:
'How long have you been here?'
'A day or part of a day,' he answered.

(Koran, II, 261)

We, too, associate with 'people'; we, too, modestly don the dress in which (*as* which) others know us, respect us, look for us . . . But there are also other ways and tricks when it comes to associating with or passing among men . . . for example, as a ghost . . . One reaches out for us but gets no hold of us . . . Or we enter through a closed door. Or after all lights have been extinguished. Or after we have died. This is the last trick of the *posthumous* people *par excellence* . . . this whole subterranean, concealed, mute, undiscovered solitude that among us is called life but might just as well be called death – if only we did not know what will *become* of us, and that it is only after death that we shall enter *our* life and become alive, oh so very much alive, we 'posthumous people'!

(Friedrich Nietzsche, *The Gay Science*, &365)

Nietzsche's story ends as our narration begins. Wheelchair-bound, intermittently lucid, he is, as before, tremulous and peremptory. Cavernous, his eyes retain a rheumy dignity. The void into which he so long gazed would now seem to gaze into him.

It is October 1944, precisely one hundred years after his birth. 'Only the day after tomorrow belongs to me', he recalls writing so many years ago. 'Some are born posthumously [*Einige werden posthum geboren*]' (AC, 114). He remains the weary prophet of his own Second Coming. This afternoon, Alfred Rosenberg will honour his centenary with a speech

---

[1] The title alludes to the essay 'Richard Wagner in Bayreuth', in Friedrich Nietzsche, *Untimely Meditations*, trans. R. J. Hollingdale (Cambridge: Cambridge University Press, 1983).

broadcast to the mothers and fathers of the nation. Even in this era of burgeoning technology, the wireless is still to him a secular miracle, miraculously secular.

He spends the morning retracing a crude, overlong work, resigns himself to its perceived affinities with his own teachings. *Mein Kampf* makes a myth of a country he never owned as his own. He is now in Poland from whose aristocracy he had mendaciously claimed descent. The land is now remarkable for its concentration camps. Richard Wagner, whom by turns he worshipped and despised, has even provided the strident musical accompaniment to this movement in history. Is Wagner a man, he had asked himself, or is he not rather a disease (CW, 155–6)? Over time, the question had reverted upon the questioner. Some eleven years ago his intolerable sister Elisabeth had orchestrated a grand reception in Munich for Adolf Hitler. That same year, the author of the Turinese letter known as *The Case of Wagner* felt the thrill and disquiet of a destiny foretold. 'When we call "*Heil* Hitler!" to this youth,' a Berlin professor had written, 'then we are greeting at the same time Friedrich Nietzsche with that call.'[2] Subsequent events may have taught him that the only *Übermensch* known to the Third Reich is that 'coldest of all cold monsters', the State (Z, 75).

Cheap and tendentious anthologies of his aphorisms abounded throughout the 1930s. In Italy, Mussolini took his injunction to 'live dangerously' ('*vivi pericolosamente!*') as a rallying cry of Fascism. Four years later, a book entitled *Nietzsche und der Nationalsozialismus* had forever associated his name with the Third Reich. He was, this dismaying tract declared, 'a great ally in the present spiritual warfare'.[3] Whether he was

[2] Alfred Bäumler, quoted in Jacob Golomb and Robert S. Wistrich, eds, *Nietzsche, Godfather of Fascism?: On the Uses and Abuses of a Philosophy* (Princeton, NJ and Oxford: Princeton University Press, 2002), p. 5. This welcome collection of essays continued a line of interrogation that stretches back more than fifty years. We should not tire of this question, particularly when it is addressed at a high level of scholarship and with the benefit of contemporary theoretical and historicist sophistication. The issue of a philosopher's responsibility for the posthumous effects of his text stretches as far back as Plato's *Phaedrus* (275d–e) and was put into resonant twentieth-century context by Sir Karl Popper in a work composed while the implications of the Nietzschean (mis)appropriation by the Nazi propaganda machine remained unclear. Contemporary thought urges that we should not be allowed to forget Auschwitz, especially at a time when its unrepresentable horrors are passing from living memory. Nonetheless, and despite the commendable nature of this volume, one cannot but suspect some malformation in the very question itself. What is the 'Godfather' *per se*, if not a figure uneasily suspended between the progenitor, the benign overseer, the appointed guardian, the one who – stationed always in a rescuing proximity – always arrives when all familial ties are sundered by death, departure or disavowal?

[3] Heinrich Härtle, *Nietzsche und der Nationalsozialismus* (Munich, Eher: Zentralverlag der NSDAP, 1937).

surprised, infuriated or indifferent that the concept of 'politics' had, as he predicted, 'become completely absorbed into a war of spirits, all the power structures of the old society [having] been blown into the air' (EH, 97) we will never know. Defenceless before its publishers and purchasers, his discourse succumbed to endless reconfigurations. Not one, but legion, he realised that the happy soul of *Daybreak*, the poet of *Zarathustra* who on the heights of Sils Maria dreamt himself '6,000 feet above man and time', the melancholic of 'The Wanderer and His Shadow' and the clear-sighted genealogist of morals had been compressed into a single image: that of the 'aristocratic radical', a hypersensitive twenty-three-year-old photographed in full Prussian military outfit. He often had cause to ponder this image, the haunted eyes behind pince-nez spectacles, the young philologist resolutely upright, sword in hand. He had not disliked military service and proved himself an excellent horseman, but a serious fall relieved him of liability to serve. How odd, he reflected, that it was also on his birthday, 15 October 1868, that he was discharged from the army. Just a week earlier, he had found his thoughts turning from Wagner and Schopenhaueur to the Cross, death and the tomb.

Lunch was a sacrificial, interrupted feast. How he detests the *table d'hôte*. It would give the spirit heavy feet – the feet of English women. Altogether better is the cuisine of Piedmont. A single glass of wine was for him enough to make life a Vale of Tears. Water sufficed. He would live by flowing fountains such as were found in Nice, Turin, Sils Maria. Meal over, he relaxes in the hospitality room. Through the window a ray of sunlight recalls him to the point of slumber. He luxuriates in a delicious idleness such as had crept over him on that 'perfect day' in 1888 when he 'buried his forty-fourth year . . . was entitled to bury it'. Unanswerable, rhetorical, the question still hovers: '*How should I not be grateful to my whole life?*' (EH, 7).

At three o'clock he turns on the wireless. 'In a truly historical sense,' Rosenberg's alien voice intones, 'the National Socialist movement eclipses the rest of the world, much as Nietzsche, the individual, eclipsed the powers of his times.'[4]

Later, with perfunctory attendance, he is wheeled out in a mild autumn afternoon. He again bears privileged witness to the *Selektion*. A woman amongst many, ashen not grey, is beyond words or plea. She looks on him as if on vacancy. God, he had said, died of pity for the world. Did

---

[4] Alfred Rosenberg, quoted and translated in Golomb and Wistrich, *Nietzsche, Godfather of Fascism?*, from the *Marbacher Kataloge: 'Das 20. Jahrhundert. Von Nietzsche bis zur Gruppe 47'*, ed. B. Zeller (Deutsche Schillergesellschaft Marbach a. N., 1980) p. 20.

he now feel vindicated, or was he ready to die of the very pity he deplored? He had truly written in blood, in letters even the blind can see. His pages were now the destiny of people and nations. Were these children, these wanderers and elderly but ciphers to be erased by the will-to-power?

The afternoon air carries familiar, acrid smoke. He is amidst the cat-astrophe he augured. *Amor fati* and eternal return: these two concepts exact the heaviest demand. Does he now love his fate? He beholds 'the crisis without equal on earth' of which he spoke in *Ecce Homo*. Will his knowledge in 1944 repeat the form of his foreknowledge in 1888? Does he love his fate so much as to will its return eternally? He had described eternal return as Zarathustra's 'abysmal thought'. What more abysmal thought than the eternal return of Auschwitz? 'This is your fate, Friedrich Nietzsche, this is your eternal life!' He had proclaimed the death of God. Had God not died today or yesterday, here in Auschwitz-Birkenau?

In a listless mid-afternoon, he draws from a greasy opium pipe, scans the pages of his *Gay Science*. Scarce does he discern anything of gaiety or science, joy or wisdom. He alights awhile on the aphorism that had sealed his signature, secured his fame. 'Whither is God?' he had had his 'Madman' ask:

> '*We have killed him* – you and I. All of us are his murderers. But how did we do this? How could we drink up the sea? Who gave us the sponge to wipe away the entire horizon? What were we doing when we unchained the earth from its sun? Whither is it moving now? Whither are we moving? Away from all suns? Are we not plunging continually? Backward, sideward, forward, in all directions? Is there still any up or down? Are we not straying as through an infinite nothing? Do we not feel the breath of empty space? Has it not become colder? Is not night continually closing in upon us? Do we not need to light lanterns in the morning? Do we hear nothing as yet of the noise of the gravediggers who are burying God? Do we smell nothing as yet of the divine decomposition? Gods, too, decompose. God is dead. God remains dead. And we have killed him . . . who will wipe this blood off us? What water is there for us to clean ourselves? What festivals of atonement, what sacred games shall we have to invent? Is not the greatness of this deed too great for us? Must we ourselves not become gods simply to appear worthy of it? There has never been a greater deed; and whoever is born after us – for the sake of this deed he will belong to a higher history than

all history hitherto . . . This tremendous event is still on its way, still wandering; it has not yet reached the ears of men . . . This deed is still more distant from them than the most distant stars – and yet they have done it themselves. . . .' [O]n the same day the madman forced his way into several churches and there struck up his *requiem aeternam deo*. Led out and called to account, he is said always to have replied nothing but: 'What, after all, are these churches now if they are not the tombs and sepulchres of God?' (GS, 181–2)

★

Between the tombs and sepulchres of the dead God evoked in *The Gay Science* and the torture camps and gas chambers of Auschwitz, we pose a question that is imponderable in its simplicity: 'How, amidst, the Holocaust, would Nietzsche have felt?' Shown the layout of the Gulag archipelago, we can imagine Karl Marx protesting 'That is not what I meant at all', before moving on to further, impenitent works. The judges of Jean-Jacques Rousseau might rule that his pastoral philosophy made the Terror and thence Napoleon Bonaparte possible. Charles Darwin could be summoned as a witness for the prosecution or defence in a trial and trail of the eugenics movement. Niels Bohr, Werner Heisenberg and Julius Robert Oppenheimer were destined to see – without foreseeing – the mushrooming consequences of their work. Nietzsche, we might think, is an unfortunate gambler in the lottery which Bernard Williams called 'moral luck'.[5] If the argument 'no Hitler, no Holocaust' holds, then Nietzsche's reincarnation at Auschwitz would be the result of a stalled carriage at Sarajevo and a young, mentally ill Austrian failing to gain a degree at art school.

In recalling Nietzsche to Auschwitz, though, we ask of him no more than Nietzsche asks of us: namely, that we love our fate (*amor fati*), affirm whatever shapes our outcomes, or whatever our outcomes shape. That Nietzsche did not intend National Socialism – that nothing could have been further from his mind – does not close the issue of responsibility. He wrote as he would have his philosophers of the future live: dangerously. He did not take care to explain himself; he mystified, propounded an esoteric teaching, mixed poetry with philosophy, elevated his discourse to prophetic status. He courted aberrant readings, yet recalled all to the authorial signature. 'How lightly one takes the burden of an excuse upon

---

[5] Cf. Bernard Williams, *Moral Luck* (Cambridge: Cambridge University Press, 1981), pp. 20–39.

oneself, so long as one has to be responsible for nothing. But I am accountable.'[6] His doctrine of *amor fati* leaves no scope for remorse or regret and must encompass an individual's legacy as well as his lifespan. 'Nothing that happened at all can be reprehensible in itself,' Nietzsche told us: '. . . one should not want to eliminate it: for everything is so bound up with everything else, that to want to exclude something means to exclude everything: a reprehensible action means: a reprehended world' (WP, 165).[7] Accordingly, Nietzsche could not will things otherwise, could not wish that he had written differently or not written at all. Everything that happens in his name returns to his name. In the forever eerie closing section of *Ecce Homo* ('Why I am a Destiny'), this voice of everyone and no one declares:

> I know my fate. One day there will be associated with my name the recollection of something frightful – of a crisis like no other before on earth, of the profoundest collision of conscience, of a decision evoked *against* everything that until then had been believed in, demanded, sanctified. I am not a man, I am dynamite . . . With all that I am necessarily a man of fatality. For when truth steps into battle with lie of millennia we shall have convulsions, an earthquake spasm, a transposition of valley and mountain such as has never been dreamed of. The concept politics has then become completely absorbed into a war of spirits, all the power-structures of the old society have been blown into the air – they one and all reposed on the lie: there will be wars such as there have never yet been on earth. Only after me will there be *grand politics* on earth. (EH, 96–7)[8]

---

[6] Nietzsche deemed it fit to capitalise the statement of accountability in a letter written à propos of *Thus Spoke Zarathustra* in the summer of 1883. '*Wie leicht nimmt man die Last einer Entschuldig[ung] auf sich, so lange man nichts zu verantworten hat. ABER ICH BIN VERANTWORTLICH)*'. NF, Juni–Juli 1883, in *Kritische Gesamtaugabe, Wekre*, ed. Giorgio Colli and Mazzino Montinari (Berlin and New York: Walter de Gruyter, 1967) 7/1: 383. Interestingly, Geoff Waite chooses this citation as the penultimate citation in his compendious and, one would hope, now classic work *Nietzsche's Corps/e: Aesthetics, Politics, Prophecy, or the Spectacular Technoculture of Everyday Life* (Durham, NC: Duke University Press, 1995), p. 395.

[7] Naturally, reference to any edition of the *Nachlass* raises issues of ethics and legacy which contemporary scholarship has yet to resolve. However, this entry, written in the spring of 1888, is in absolute accordance with the interconnected doctrines of *amor fati* and eternal return which Nietzsche was still in the process of developing. It also resonantes productively with the closing section of *Ecce Homo* and in no manner betrays editorial distortion.

[8] Given the 'fatality' of this passage, it seems proper to cite the no less authoritative translation of Walter Kaufmann: 'I know my fate [*Ich kenne mein Los*]. One day my name will be associated with the memory of something tremendous [*Ungeheures*] – a crisis without equal on earth, the most profound collision of conscience [*Gewissens-Kollision*], a decision [*Entschiedung*] that was conjured up against everything that had been believed, demanded, hallowed so far . . . It is only beginning with me that the earth knows great politics [*grosse Politik*]'. Friedrich Nietzsche, *Ecce Homo*, trans. Walter Kaufmann (New York: Random House: Vintage Books, 1969), pp. 326–7.

There are numerous responses that can be made to this extraordinary textual moment in a single moment of attention by one and the same reader. A visceral irritation can be provoked by the sheer self-regard of a human being claiming for himself the role of a destiny, an abreaction that will subsequently consolidate itself with the biographical fact of Nietzsche's megalomania at the time of writing and his impending mental collapse. There is also a romantic response – perhaps no less visceral – which takes the form of an appalled exultation, a feeling of being in the presence of a dark sublime. How uncannily prescient are these words, the romantic will say, how exact in predicting that the name will be '*associated*' with the cataclysm and its 'memory'. The cynic in the reader's soul may also suppose that the author of the passage followed a gambler's instinct, a long shot which if it came in could be replayed as destiny. In 1888, Nietzsche's work languished in obscurity: *Beyond Good and Evil*, his prelude to a philosophy of the future, had sold a mere twenty-six copies. The presumed Nietzschean wager would run on something like the following lines: 'If my work rises from obscurity, if the evident fault-lines in the European order become cataclysms, if the instinct for power triumphs again over pallid ideals such as democracy, then my tempestuous "rhetorics", my iconoclasm, my critiques of pity, piety and the good should prove tinder for the incandescent spirits of the great warmongers, the zealots of a new order. There is enough of blood, of domination, of mastery, will and cruelty, of my role as the Antichrist who splits the history of Europe in two, for me to appear as the prophet of this new order, of these "wars the like of which have never been seen on earth". Where else would the new spirits look for justification than to I who alone among intellectuals decided the debate between arms and letters in favour of the former?' Driven by ill-health, and suspecting that the time left to him was short, the cynic would see this 'Nietzsche' as making a last throw of the dice in his titanic struggle for recognition.

The close of *Ecce Homo* poses a problem for those who have sponsored Nietzsche in his post-war recuperation as a serious philosopher, even to the extent of wishing that 'Why I am a Destiny' could be taken out of the textual system that we know as 'Nietzsche'.[9] It belongs, they imply, to the body of his writings but not to his *oeuvre*, his canonical work as philosopher and philosophical critic of culture. The category or unity of discourse represented by the authorial *oeuvre* is thus subordinated to a standard of value and decorum. Here we encounter a significant decision

[9] Cf. as but one example amongst many of the 'philosophically recuperated Nietzsche', Arthur C. Danto, *Nietzsche as Philosopher* (New York: Columbia University Press, 1965).

in any ethics of authorship and discourse: similar decisions are made in regard to juvenilia and works of old age, when senility and dementia constitute biographical contexts.

Any work of criticism involves some level of editing and abridgement, but becomes questionable when made canonical or axiological: 'What is a Destiny' is not incoherent, as are some of Nietzsche's last letters. If ethical judgement is the order of the day, equal weight should be given across the entire range of the intelligible work. At another extreme, the Nazis produced anthologies and selections from Nietzsche's texts which emphasised the nationalistic, warriorlike, militaristic, and the few statements that could – by no means unproblematically – be construed as promoting anti-Semitism. That the latter procedure amounts to a desecration, travesty and mutilation of the body 'Nietzsche', and that of Kaufmann to the best-intentioned recuperation, only confirms that the higher claim is to respect a field demarcated by a proper name rather than a concept, an *ethos* rather than *logos* of reading. 'What is a Destiny' is transparently of a piece with other of Nietzsche's writings, as too with his anxious relationship to legacy. It harmonises with his insistence that '[o]nly the day after tomorrow belongs to me' and that '[s]ome are born posthumously'. As Derrida says, it gives us 'to understand that we shall read the name of Nietzsche only when a great politics will have effectively entered into play . . . and that the name still has its whole future before it' (EO, 31). The name thus awaits its historical supplementation, will be born posthumously in its textual estate – its texts written 'astride of a grave and a difficult birth' – signed and countersigned in the name of the eternal return. Everything reverts upon the name – all consequences, whether programmed or unintended. The 'wars the like of which have never been seen on earth' cannot be fought in anything other than the Nietzschean name. Unsurprisingly, then, the worthy exercise by which the pro-Semitic statements in his *oeuvre* are weighed against the anti-Semitic, the exhortations to cruelty against the compassionate pathos of distance, the bellicose and bombastic against the delicate psychological insight, takes us no further towards an understanding of Nietzsche's embroilment in the National Socialist programme.

Customary models of causality lead us further from addressing the problem of Nietzsche which consists in restructuring malformed questions such as 'Did Nietzsche cause National Socialism?' or 'Would Nietzsche have approved of the Third Reich?' The very fact that both would certainly be answered in the negative confirms their redundancy, but does not correct the failure of critical intelligence that has allowed such unhelpful approaches to distort inquiry. To counterpoise *Zarathustra* or *Ecce Homo* and Hitler's election as Chancellor of the Third Reich would be to forget more than three decades of European history, the Great War, the Treaty of Versailles, the economic collapse of Germany *entre deux guerres* and the curious destiny by which a deranged, left-wing spy was co-opted by the German Right as a streetcorner speaker and thence rose to the rank of Führer. Even in the absence of such real-world consideration, the very issue of interpretability would complicate the issue of causality beyond use or recognition. The passage from authorial intent to written text to readerly interpretation and thence to implementation and institutionalisation on the plane of history is not one that can be short-circuited by any such apparent truisms as 'Rousseau wrought the French Revolution' or 'Marxist thought led directly to Stalinist Communism'. Vainly would we negotiate the labyrinthine manner in which an imaginative event translates into a text, which creates imaginative possibilities in a reader who creates a further text, which is then used to form an institution, which in turn leads to a concrete event such as a war or revolution and a post-war or post-revolutionary institution or government. Were we to sidestep these forbidding complexities, if text X could be proved to have participated in the shaping of event Y, we would still have to ask how far the production of text X was influenced by biographical circumstance Z and the extent to which the author was exculpable as a subject forged at a certain crossroads of race, milieu and moment.

In *Act and Idea in the Nazi Genocide*, Berel Lang declares that 'to reconstruct in the imagination the events leading up to the Nazi genocide against the Jews without the name or presence of Nietzsche is to be compelled to change almost nothing else in that pattern'.[10] According to Lang, then, the name and invocation of Nietzsche served as no more than a ripple or coruscation on the river of history, an *ad verecundiam* flourish on a flow of events that was neither inspired by nor depended on the philosophy of eternal return, the *Übermensch* and will-to-power. Martin Jay writes in *Fin de Siècle Socialism* that 'while it may be questionable to saddle Marx with responsibility for the Gulag archipelago or blame Nietzsche for Auschwitz, it is nevertheless true that their writings could be misread as justifications for these horrors in a way that . . . John Stuart Mill or Alexis de Toqueville could not'.[11] Jay properly strikes a middle path between culpability and exoneration, between seeing a genetic relation between, say, *Thus Spoke Zarathustra* and the Holocaust or seeing the Nazi

---

[10] Berel Lang, *Act and Idea in the Nazi Genocide* (Chicago: University of Chicago Press, 1990), p. 198.
[11] Martin Jay, *Fin de Siècle Socialism* (New York: Routledge, 1988), p. 33.

propagandists in a simple 'borrow-a-quote' contract with Nietzsche's *oeuvre*. Indeed, Lang's position can be maintained alongside Derrida's insistence that Nietzsche's texts did become embroiled in the Nazi movement so long as one carefully distinguishes between intention and responsibility to see the former as a subset of the latter, whilst recognising that unintended consequences are not necessarily unforeseeable consequences.

In such a reckoning, the issue of the political content of a discourse is primary. Nietzsche wrote on politics in a way that Kant or Mill did not. His writings were tempestuous, and occasionally he followed the false Marxian logic that violent cataclysms in the past both necessitate and determine the form of violent cataclysms in the future.[12] Yet Nietzsche does not advocate revolution in any consistent or systematic fashion and his calls for a transvaluation of values are largely directed toward a re-moralisation and uplifting of the human spirit. We would surely proceed on more direct historical pathways from Rousseau to the French Revolution and the subsequent Terror, from the Marxist *oeuvre* to the commingling of utopian values and real-world atrocities that were to become State Communism. Yet the question of Nietzsche's implication will not be silenced. As Derrida writes: 'One may . . . wonder why it is not enough to say: "Nietzsche did not think that", or "he would have surely vomited this", that there is a falsification of the legacy and an interpretative mystification going on here' (EO, 23–4). It is not only not enough to say that Nietzsche would have been sickened by Nazism, but fictional in that it would require an absolute recantation of the doctrines of the *Übermensch, amor fati*, eternal return, tragic affirmation and those other commitments that encompass the 'constructive' phase of the Nietzschean philosophy. It would involve the erasure of an unprecedented signature and its replacement with the feeling, suffering man, the usurpation by Nietzsche-as-person of Nietzsche-as philosophical-author when the latter is all that can remain, all that is ours to inherit, all that is left for us to work upon. To see this signature in all its onerous singularity we must place it alongside other signatory modes, other forms of contract by which authors establish contexts of interpretation with their readers. Hitler had read very little Nietzsche and was altogether more affected by Arthur Schopenhauer, yet we do not routinely cross-examine *The World as Will and Representation* in terms of its causal relation to National Socialism, still less take Kant seriously as a precursor (despite the

---

[12] Nietzsche 'suggests that the violence essential to the production of a higher type in the past will be equally necessary in the future'. Bruce Detwiler, *Nietzsche and the Politics of Aristocratic Radicalism* (Chicago: University of Chicago Press, 1990), p. 57.

fact that the Nazi propagandists twisted, used and abused his thought to the promotion of German supremacism). However, play has itself turned many a childish day to tragedy, whether registered in the sense of a game, an artwork or a world that is ungoverned by God or truth or moral precept but an open sea for the explorer, a limitless space without horizon for the higher types to create. If Nietzsche did not cause, nor was the god-father of, fascism, why do we still feel a duty to weigh one against another? Partly, it is a case of iterability, of words wandering away from context; partly, too, of the perversions wrought by unsuitable readers, that benighted class of tourists in the realm of culture (*philodoxoi*) who may manifest themselves as villains or gulls. Mainly, though, it is a question of discursive ethics and, in the specific case of Nietzsche, of *amor fati*, tragic affirmation, eternal return, a unique signatory mode.

With Nietzsche, the only sustained attempt at shaping his legacy – apart from the ineffectual esotericism by which he sought to address his true teaching only to an elect of knowledge, and prefaces of uneven quality – takes the form of *Ecce Homo*. Here, though, we behold not so much the man as a confusing summation of his writings and an auto-canonical labour. Bizarre chapters on how to read his previous work build not towards a conclusion or set of parameters, but to an invocation, an impassioned, creative admission that he does not know what he means or how we should read him. Not for nothing is the ultimate chapter enti-tled 'Why I am a Destiny' for it is the work of the future to make his meanings cohere as intention and significance, his writing life having been a provocation rather than a programme, a performance rather than a project. Thus he tells us and himself that he is a violent transformative destiny who cannot be read until he – in his textual afterlife – has become what he is. The text gives us to wonder whether he knew how to read himself, and the repeated incantation 'Have I been understood?' seems as much self- as other-directed. Reviews of his previous publications read as desperate attempts to divine an intentional structure beneath diverse, copious and stormy inspirations. A search for coherence in his *oeuvre* is better rewarded by the failure to cohere than somesuch homogenising concept as will-to-power or the Dionysian; the grand plan is best dis-cerned in the refusal of a plan; the governing intent in the abandon-ment of intent to infinite variety, discursive fecundity. The relations between the deontological and the consequential undergo a peculiar reversal because the former has little to work upon beside an authorial recklessness. True, we might say, Nietzsche did not intend Nazism, so what did he intend?

'What I mean,' Nietzsche can be taken as saying, 'cannot be ascertained from my texts but only from their effects, their noontide, the ushering out of a Christian age and the inauguration of the new epoch of Zarathustra. My meaning, my textual being, my legacy and significance is posthumous; come unto me, you judges and philosophers of the future and find the meaning and true intent of my texts in the wars and aftermaths I foretell; fill up the emptiness of the intentional at this time of writing (1888) with the consequences, influence, legacy and historical realisation of my teaching.' Outcomes become intentions, the name calling to a posthumous incarnation which will fill the inchoate space of the deontological realm with whatever retrospective coherence accrues from the future, the space of teleological judgement; all that is actualised in the mirrors of projected audiences, in social movements, cultural, political and aesthetic transitions. The signature signs itself only in the form of a countersignature. Intention unfurls as desire, will-to-power performs itself in the very discourse that diagnoses will-to-power as the substratum of all existence. 'Marx and Nietzsche . . . have so little to say about the content of a good life,' Bernard Yack notes in *The Longing for Total Revolution*, and asks '[h]ow could such a weak and undeveloped concept of the good life inspire such intense longing?'[13] We might answer that it does so through a textual version of will-to-power, the longing of Marx, Nietzsche and so many others to leave behind their unique impress, to write their names immemorially on the tablets of history. Both aspired to a historical sublime, a world-transformative significance, yearned to see their names writ large beside those of Socrates and Jesus, Plato and Goethe, Shakespeare and Sophocles. More so than the poets, these nineteenth-century *savants* lived in a spiralling *agon*, in the desire to redescribe their predecessors and place themselves at the culmination of the past and the promise of the future, even to the extreme of turning the fragile *pax Europa* into a scene of voicing that is also a murderous stage. And Nietzsche well knows how hazardous is his inspiration, how he puts his readership in jeopardy.[14]

---

[13] Bernard Yack, *The Longing for Total Revolution: Philosophical Sources of Discontent from Rousseau to Marx and Nietzsche* (Berkeley and Los Angeles: University of California Press, 1992), p. 6.

[14] Eloquently developed in the poetics of Harold Bloom, the notion of redescription is philosophically translated in Richard Rorty's *Contingency, Irony and Solidarity* (Cambridge: Cambridge University Press, 1989). Rorty does not, however, give over attention to the violent cultural overturning envisaged by Nietzsche's battle with his elective precursors, nor of the 'dangerous game' he consciously played in a writing which did not innoculate itself within a consistently drawn fictional frame. On the latter theme, cf. Daniel Conway's *Nietzsche's Dangerous Game: Philosophy in the Twilight of the Idols* (Cambridge: Cambridge University Press, 1997), which identifies 'parastrategesis' as a generic term which embraces the range of esoteric (and generally inadequate)

In all cases, though, Nietzsche pledges himself to whatever is spoken in his name. One must distinguish carefully between intention and responsibility in order to see the former as a subset of the latter. An analogy might be drawn between the deed or act of writing and the concept of deed in its customary moral and legal senses. A man or woman who drinks and drives does not usually intend to kill; the intention is only to drive whilst under the influence of alcohol. But that lack of specific intention does not prevent us from holding that person responsible for the death of another. We do have Nietzsche on record stating his intent in writing *Thus Spoke Zarathustra*, an intent which is also an unshackling from any intent: 'To play the great play – to stake the existence of humanity, in order perhaps to attain something higher than the survival of the race.'[15] Chillingly, Nietzsche subordinates the ethical to the aesthetic, humanity to the dream of a 'something higher' (of which we can only surmise that it will be a post-humanity). Since Nietzsche has no sense whatsoever of what will succeed 'man', this is no more than the ambition for his own writings, the fortunes of his own name. It is a throw of the dice, an irresponsibility that carries a grave weight of responsibility. His intention is to play, which – whilst it intends nothing beyond itself carries a weight of responsibility for outcomes, as Nietzsche acknowledges in many places when, curiously, he resembles the reviled Spirit of Gravity in *Thus Spoke Zarathustra*. His signature image system extols all that is light, all that possesses *celeritas*: the *Übermensch* returning on the steps of a dove, those freethinkers of *Human-all-too-Human* who are 'aeronauts of the spirit'; the *nom-de-plume* chosen for the poet of *The Gay Science* which is 'Prince Free-as-a-Bird' (Prinz Vogelfrei). Yet, when it is a matter of accountability, of ethics and morals,

---

devices by which an author (in this case, Nietzsche) attempts to pre-programme posthumous reception. Conway's work, like Waite's, is essential reading for all with an interest in the ethics of writing both in and beyond the case of Nietzsche.

[15] Friedrich Nietzsche, Letter of June/July 1883, in *Kritische Gesamtaugabe, Werke*, ed. Giorgio Colli and Mazzino Montinari, 7/1:386. 'What on earth might this something, this x, be? And at whose expense?' asks Waite in his compendious, ever-rational work, '*Nietzsche's Corps/e* – a work which would seem to have as much pertinence for our times as did Kaufmann's for previous generations of Nietzschean readers. Cf. Waite, *Nietzsche's Corps/e*, p. 259. At the same time, Nietzsche writes to Peter Gast: 'My *Zarathustra*, which will be sent to you in a week or so, will perhaps show you what lofty heights my will has soared. Do not be deceived by the legendary character of this little book. *Beneath all these simple but outlandish words lie my whole philosophy and the things about which I am most in earnest* . . . I know perfectly well that there is no one alive who could create anything like this *Zarathustra*.' Letter to Peter Gast, 28 June 1883, see *SL*, p. 154 (my emphases). The convictions expressed in this letter, particularly those extracted for emphasis, will receive fullest expression in *Ecce Homo* – itself driven in no small measure by the need to draw the world's attention to the epochal significance of *Thus Spoke Zarathustra* – in the penultimate chapter of this volume when we consider Rudolf Carnap's confidence in the protective nature of Nietzsche's choice of a poetic genre to express his *Lebensphilosophie*.

Nietzsche reverts to metaphors of depth and weight. The eternal return, Zarathustra's abysmal thought [*abründlicher Gedanke*], is 'the heaviest demand', and in tying his signature to this nightmarish challenge there is the further obligation upon Nietzsche to love, love his fate, to will and embrace all that returns. Nothing can there be of resignation, still less of protestation, before a fate, a destiny. Nietzsche has signed to this return even as far back as the Dionysus of *The Birth of Tragedy* who affirms life in the midst of all woe, injustice and suffering. Like Marx, the prophet of Sils Maria is obliged to sign not for the content of his work but for its futures. 'Do not all interpretations belong to God?', it is asked, rhetorically, in Genesis (40: 8). Within this schema of posthumous birth, eternal return, *amor fati* and an unprecedented authorial signature, all interpretations belong and return to Nietzsche. Examples of Nietzsche's privileging of all that is aquiline could be multiplied indefinitely. Intriguingly, though, his *nom-de-plume* Prinz Vogelfrei carries heavy connotations of the phrase 'jail bird' and might thereby combine images of freedom and confinement, air and earth, *celeritas* and *gravitas*.[16] A central doctrine of Nietzsche's philosophy is that one must love one's fate even to the extent of willing it to return eternally. One must affirm all that one is, all one has done and all that one is to become. To love one's fate absolutely means also to love one's posthumous fate, one's legacy, the destiny of one's writings, even if they are to become volatile material for National Socialist propaganda, even if they are to be inscribed on the gates of Auschwitz. Nietzsche thus pledges himself to whatever is said or done in his name. His signature (in other words, the contract he establishes with his texts and readerships) thus differs from, say, that of Sir Salman Rushdie in that he holds himself accountable for whatever (mis)readings are made of his work. He admitted his irresponsibility yet signed his name to it, made an ethically responsible acknowledgement of an ethically irresponsible act. Nietzsche courted this risk. He said a joyous 'yes' to whatever might visit or intrude upon his legacy. Like the tragic Greeks, he made no distinction between unintended and unforseeable consequences. Oedipus called himself to his own tribunal, wished as much to answer to the future as he would have the future answer to him. 'On me alone falls responsibility for this deed,' says the King of Thebes. As

---

[16] Examples of Nietzsche's privileging of all that is aquiline could be multiplied indefinitely. Intriguingly, though, his *nom-de-plume* Prinz Vogelfrei (Prince Free-as-a-Bird) carries heavy connotations of the phrase 'jail bird' and might thereby combine images of freedom and confinement, air and earth, *celeritas* and *gravitas*. 'Prinz Vogelfrei . . . refers not only to any Unbearable Lightness of Being, any noble or free thinking. For it is also a legal slogan designating a criminal, a jail bird.' Waite, *Nietzsche's Corps/e*, pp. 393–4. The Spirit of Gravity intrudes at many places, not only in *Thus Spoke Zarathustra*, but in also in his copious letters of the 1880s.

Oedipus instituted a tribunal which would prosecute no other than himself, so Nietzsche accounts not only for the deed but the whole compass of the deed, inadvertent outcomes included. Unlike inconsolable Oedipus, though, Nietzsche said a gleeful 'yes'. With joyous affirmation, he called himself to his own tribunal, wished as much to answer to the future as he would have the future answer to him. It is for these reasons that we take Friedrich Nietzsche to Auschwitz. He bids us do so.

★

Professor Friedrich Wilhelm Nietzsche knows Dr Josef Mengele. At only twenty-three, an ardent Nazi already in 1934, he had shown prodigious scientific potential at the fledgling *Institut für Erbbiologie und Rassenhygiene*. Not long into his thirties, such was the rare combination of research genius, organisational exactitude and discipline embodied in Mengele that Heinrich Himmler appointed him Chief Doctor at the supplementary extermination camp near Auschwitz. Himmler had entrusted him not only with the running of the camp but also with experimenting on its inmates with a view to enhancing fertility so as to increase exponentially the German race. Most prized amongst his scientific interests, though, as he once confided to Nietzsche, is his research on twins. Within just a few weeks of his appointment, his byname amongst inmates is the Angel of Death.

Professor Nietzsche is accommodated on the same corridor as Mengele. Neither man has ever addressed the other by their baptismal names. Nietzsche knows that each morning the doctor shaves exactingly, dons his uniform with pride and strides out in the morning air to preside over the *Selektion*. Does he see in Mengele a representative of the higher species, an aeronaut of the spirit? Or does he see a new incarnation of the instinctually sick, priestly type in this man who is both bureaucrat and technocrat? This man's name has nothing to do with him or his writings. Yet 'Mengele' will always conjure his own name as a cognate. But the philosopher of eternal return had called the bad as well as the good, the unintended as well as the intended to plague the name's destiny. He had decided to take on 'all that came hardest' to him, to bear it again and again in a world without respite or end. Some years earlier, a German Jew had apparently committed suicide in a hotel room at a Nazi border. In his notebooks, the little-known Walter Benjamin had written of 'The Angel of History'. Nietzsche had himself written fabulously of the *Übermensch* returning, like Christ, on the steps of a dove. He felt as though another had pre-empted his thought, felt much as he did on encountering Dostoevsky's formula that 'if God is dead, then everything is permitted'.

Mengele's working day is at an end, but the indefatigable doctor made a show of accompanying his guest of honour through the tentative twilight and its weary ceremony. The professor watches with fathomless eyes. In the oh-so-delicate ears of which he boasted, the word 'angel' took wing above the clamour of history. For 'A – 7113', or Elie Wiesel as once he was once and was to become again, something angelic appeared on the Galician horizon:

> Roll call. SS all round us, machine guns trained: the traditional ceremony. Three victims in chains – and one of them, the little servant, the sad-eyed angel. The SS seemed more preoccupied, more disturbed than usual. To hang a young boy in front of thousands of spectators was no light matter. The head of the camp read the verdict. All eyes were on the child. He was lividly pale, almost calm, biting his lips. The gallows threw its shadow over him . . .
> The three victims mounted together on to the chairs.
> The three necks were placed at the same moment within nooses.
> 'Long live liberty', cried the two adults.
> But the child was silent.
> 'Where is God? Where is He?' someone behind me asked.
> At a sign from the head of the camp, the three chairs tipped over.
> Total silence throughout the camp. On the horizon the sun was setting . . .
> Then the march past began. The two adults were no longer alive. Their tongues hung swollen, blue-tinged. But the third rope was still moving; being so light, the child was still alive. . . .
> For more than half an hour he stayed there, struggling between life and death, dying in slow agony under our eyes. And we had to look him full in the face. He was still alive when I passed in front of him. His tongue was still red, his eyes were not yet glazed.
> Behind me, I heard the same man asking:
> 'Where is God now?'
> And I heard a voice within me answer him:
> 'Where is He? Here He is – He is hanging here on this gallows.'[17]

★

[17] Elie Wiesel, *Night* (London: Penguin Books, 1981), pp. 76–7. For a wonderfully intelligent and compassionate account of the process of *selektion* and execution from a theoretical standpoint, see John Llewelyn, *Appositions of Jacques Derrida and Emmanuel Levinas* (Bloomington and Indianapolis, IN: Indiana University Press, 1995), esp. 130–42. Llewelyn's book also makes a highly important contribution to theoretical studies generally and will be a significant touchstone in the second volume of this work.

That night they dined in a quiet town hotel. Mengele recounted how he had that afternoon assembled an ad hoc orchestra comprising about a hundred inmates. It was to alternate between raucous performances of the *Blue Danube* and the *Rosamunde*. There were technical problems with the crematoria, Mengele explained. That night, the SS were using the grills in the open fields. Mengele had requested a window table. Claiming that fresh air improved the appetite he asked the obsequious waiter to leave the window ajar. Later, he would express his gratification that the music was all that could be heard from the camp.

Professor Nietzsche was ravenous. He did not eat between meals: the stomach works best as a whole. Tea was the succour of mornings alone. Coffee, he knew, produced gloom. Claiming he could not choose what to eat, he ordered all three main courses. The waiter laid out his cutlery as if laying a cryptogram. Its configured message was plain: 'You have broken the history of humanity into two parts: one only lives *before* or *after* you' (cf. EH, 103).

While Mengele and his underling drank the austere wine of Naumberg, he ordered a cup of thick, oil-free cocoa. 'A never so infinitesimal sluggishness of the intestines . . . suffices to transform a genius into something mediocre, something "German"' (EH, 24). Disturbed intestines explained the origins of the Aryan spirit. Mengele ordered soup before the meal! The meat was cut into shreds, the vegetables fatty and flour-coated. Pudding was no more than a paperweight!

The boy's face was nothing remarkable, Mengele declared. Auschwitz-Birkenau, Nietzsche wryly agreed, was the face of a child. The Spirit of Gravity was now heavy upon his stomach, the spirit he had so vehemently denounced in *Zarathustra*. What now of the philosopher's laugh, the joyous dance of the pen? What left of his irony, his distemper or the innocence of a child playing dice with the universe? How different had he not wrought and indulged that 'most multifarious art of style' whereby the poet wears the mask of the philosopher? How different had he kept his 'wicked thoughts' to himself? How different had he left the future undisturbed, his thoughts dying on the air as spoken or unspoken words?

Ever precise, Mengele and his underling accompany the return to Nietzsche's hotel room. 'I am one thing, my writings are another,' Nietzsche recalled writing in *Ecce Homo* (EH, 39). 'Behold the man', were the words of Pontius Pilate to the Roman crucifiers. Was this, his blighted centenary, the hour of Nietzsche's posthumous birth? Here, from this hotel balcony, at what looked like the end of the world and its time? Was he now, finally, the Antichrist, or the Dionysus who counters and countersigns the Crucified One?' – Have I been understood? – *Dionysus against the Crucified*' (EH, 104).

    Someone or something had spoken behind A – 7113. Was it he or He or another or the Angel of History who asked, 'Where is God now?'

Two legends compete as to the final moments of his destiny, the close of his day. The first has him indoors, before a small table. With ritualistic ease, he places the Swastika beside his *Zarathustra*. In the second, prospecting a moon–gladed Galician lake, his hands are clasped round a small crucifix. In both, simultaneously, he dies the deaths of the penitent and apostate.

Introduction: The Responsibilities
of the Writer

> . . . a poet is a light and winged thing, and holy, and never able
> to compose until he has become inspired, and is beside
> himself, and reason is no longer in him . . .
>
> (Plato, *Ion*, 534b)

> Weave a circle around him thrice,
> And close your eyes with holy dread.
> For he on honey-dew hath fed,
> And drunk the milk of Paradise.
>
> (Samuel Taylor Coleridge, 'Kubla Khan')

Like writing, reading so often begins in romance and ends in pragmatism.
On first looking into the *Ion* of Plato or Coleridge's 'Kubla Khan', the
idea of the poet as divinely inspired enthrals. Only later do we recognise
that such celebrations are of a piece with the banishment of the poets.
The line 'weave a circle around him thrice' we either neglect or hazily
register in magical, runic terms. Only on rereading do we discern the
theme of exclusion, of quarantine, the structure by which society simultaneously celebrates and ostracises its artists, only by setting Plato's
Republic beside his *Ion* can we recognise that the very irrationality that
exalts and sets the poet apart also makes the poet accountable to – or
excluded from – a *polis* constructed according to the principles of philosophical rationalism. Hence, the perennial lament of the artist that he is
both shaman and scapegoat, condemned to live inside and outside, at both
the defining, mythopoeic centre yet at the ethical margins of his society.
Such is the paradoxical situation of the artistic vocation: culture demands
an elect to which it grants imaginative freedom, but only at the price of
accountability. Ireland longed for another great novelist, yet castigated
Joyce in his day; Milton, who lived to see the public burning of his books,
has since towered within the English canon; the very class that fêted
Oscar Wilde was to imprison him, then drive him into exile. The artist is

expected to transcend his or her society yet is called to account to that society if the work offends its mores.

During the twentieth century, however, most academics, aesthetes and art lovers would have had us believe the contrary: the writer is beyond ethical recall. A freestanding object, the literary work is independent of its creator and answerable only to itself. Within modernist aesthetics and New Criticism it became a virtual heresy to trace the novel to its author, the cantata to its composer, the sculpture to its sculptor. The work was to be judged in terms of its internal coherence rather than the external motivations for its creation or its subsequent social, political or ethical effects: once woven, the web has no need of a spider. An orthodoxy in classrooms and university lecture halls in the second half of the twentieth century, this approach was to be expressed in France rather more dramatically as 'the death of the author'. The reader became the producer rather than consumer of the text; literature's significance was to be found not in its origins but in its destination, the question 'Who is speaking?' became misleading and redundant.

In a world of textual anonymity, the author would be protected from the effects of the text and the text protected from the effects of its author's life. Authors would not have been persecuted or denied expression by oppressive regimes; female authors would not have felt impelled to adopt male pseudonyms in order to gain a respectful audience. However, in a society in which it mattered nothing who is speaking, the author could sign his or her text without risk. Anonymity is not a value in itself but depends upon context: one and the same person might be in favour of anonymity in the case of a text like the *Satanic Verses* whilst being righteously concerned to identify the author of *Mein Kampf*.

As for protecting the text from its author, the avoidance of reductive *ad hominem* arguments (literally, 'arguments against the man'), by which biographical details are used to discredit the work, would be made impossible. That the Labour politician Tony Benn hailed from a wealthy background does not invalidate his *Arguments for Socialism*, any more than Jonathan Swift's pettiness makes *Gulliver's Travels* a petty book, or Philip Larkin's racism deprives *High Windows* of aesthetic merit. However, it is not the conjunction of authorial life and text which is fallacious but the fact that the life is used to judge rather than contextualise the work. The placement of an author's life beside his work opens a channel of interpretation and inquiry rather than one of evaluation. With the anti-Semitism of Richard Wagner or Nazi affiliations of Martin Heidegger, it is ethically and morally incumbent upon us to ask how a great musician and a great philosopher came to ally themselves with so much that is worst in modernity. Such knowledge is vital in our reconstruction of the relations between art and politics in the epoch of European culture that preceded National Socialism, but should not be over-extended so as to dismiss outright *The Ring* cycle or *Being and Time*. Knowledge of who is speaking is essential to any reconstruction of why ethically troublesome or pernicious discourses came into being at a certain juncture of culture, history, of national and personal circumstance.

Societies are not, in any case, likely to lose interest in who is speaking. The commercial fortunes of biography in our day and age would alone testify to the fact that the demand to retrace a work to its author is virtually as powerful as that to retrace a crime to its perpetrator, a murdered body to its murderer. Furthermore, in the act of publication, the writer, like any ethical agent, implicitly signs a contract with society, and accepts the possibility that a tribunal may one day assemble around the work. Consequently, we will feel justified in holding an author to account where real-world effects are clearly and demonstrably intended by the work, but rare is the case when a text does not generate areas of ambiguity or blind spots. We have also to ask whether misinterpretations can be revisited upon the author's legacy if only to the extent that the author did too little to guard against misinterpretation. Indeed, we would have to ask if such a thing as pure misinterpretation is possible.

I: THE RISK OF WRITING: RESPONSIBILITY AND UNINTENDED OUTCOMES

> On no man else
> But on me alone is the scourge of my punishment.
> (Sophocles, *Oedipus Rex*)

Famously, and with a prescience with which the succeeding century would have surprised even the founder and master architect of dialectical idealism, Hegel identified 'the risk of reason', the inevitable danger that the unfettered idea would run its logical but potentially calamitous course. In an altogether more limited way, our concern here is with 'the risk of writing'. To write is to risk – exponentially – the risk of reason. Whereas an oral teacher can distinguish between those who can benefit from a discourse without abusing its terms, hazarding its outcomes, a written text has no power of selection over its audience, nor can it correct misreadings.

Nathaniel Hawthorne sketched an idea for a short story in which a writer finds that his tale takes on a life of its own: characters act against his designs and a catastrophe ensues which he struggles in vain to avert. Two themes emerge in the template for this never-to-be-written story: first, the confusion of the aesthetic and the everyday plane; second, the degree of responsibility an author should take for the outcomes – unintended as well as intended – of his or her work. *The Sorrows of Young Werther* allegedly inspired numerous impressionable youths to romantic suicide, and we could imagine Goethe striving vainly to avert such catastrophes. In *Frankenstein,* Mary Shelley gave supremely Gothic expression to the anxieties of her time concerning creation running athwart of its creator's control. *The Picture of Dorian Gray* has at its centre a 'dangerous book' (doubtless based on Joris-Karl Huysmans' ultra-decadent *À Rebours*) which exercises a fatal influence upon the protagonist just as the novel was to revert upon its author in the part it played in Wilde's persecution, prosecution, imprisonment, exile, decline and premature demise.

At the political level, Marx could not enter into dialogue with Lenin or Stalin; Rousseau was no more able to question the republican excesses of Saint-Just than Plato was to ask what had become of 'the good beyond being' (*epekeina tês ousias*) in Maoist China. Distant though such examples are, they illustrate how, when a work is caught up in real-world catastrophes, the rarefied notions of artistic and philosophical impersonality implode and authorial intention reasserts itself as an indispensable category in the ethics of discourse.

Some twenty years after French theory had declared the death or irrelevance of the author, academia again showed itself passionately interested in the question 'who is speaking?' upon the revelations of Heidegger's practical involvement with National Socialist politics and the deconstructionist Paul de Man's wartime journalism. It was the Rushdie affair, however, which showed that authorial responsibility retains the passionate interest of culture in general. From all walks of life, people entered into debates which turned on the issues of authorial intention, censorship, the responsibility of the writer, the writer's duty to his own culture, and the limits that should or should not be set upon artistic freedom. In the press, authorial intention became the core concept of many a letter, comment or opinion page. No doubt under pressure from the extreme Maududist reactions in the autumn of 1988, the following year, Ayatollah Khomeini put a grisly and literal twist on the theoretical notion of the death of author: 'the author of the book entitled *The Satanic Verses*, which has been compiled, printed and published in opposition to Islam, the

Prophet and the Koran, as well as those publishers who were aware of its contents, have been sentenced to death'.[1]

Rushdie lived to see that his story 'shaped itself against his intentions'; 'unforeseen events' did occur. A catastrophe – for Rushdie and his publishers – seemed to be in the offing. The ensuing 'real-world' drama could not have been programmed into the composition of *The Satanic Verses*. But does this absolve Rushdie of any responsibility for these unintended outcomes? He was not obliged, as was Scheherazade, to weave fictions on pain of death, nor to choose as his source material 'The Satanic Verses' which centuries of scholarly tradition had zealously protected from public circulation. Nor need he have traded one set of cultural values against another by bringing irony, metafictionality, self-consciousness, etc., into contest with a religion and textual tradition which has not acknowledged mediation as a form of authorial absolution or abnegation of responsibility.[2]

---

[1] The Ayatollah's statement of the fatwa on Valentine's Day 1988, as published in *The Observer*, 19 February 1989. As one admirably concise amongst a great many thoughtful reflections on the 'Rushdie affair' from a postcolonial perspective see Máire Ní Fhlathúin, 'Postcolonialism and the Author: The Case of Salman Rushdie', in Seán Burke, ed., *Authorship: From Plato to the Postmodern: A Reader* (Edinburgh: Edinburgh University Press, 1995), pp. 277–84.

[2] 'The Koran is copied in a book, is pronounced with the tongue, is remembered in the heart and, even so, continues to persist in the centre of God and is not altered by its passage through written pages and human understanding' (Koran, Chapter XIII). The categories of aesthetic, cognitive and ethical are not treated as mutually exclusive in the present work: rather, the argument proposes that the ethical realm can be malignly invaded by mixed discourses which draw from aesthetic resources in the presentation of (supposedly) pure cognitive claims. It is the fluidity rather than fixity of these boundaries that gives rise to ethical concern. In this context, and in presuming to write of the responsibilities of the writer, it is our first duty to concede that this work has commenced by implicating itself in the very writerly irresponsibility that it will henceforth call into question. It has failed to make a responsible contract with its reader. Part-story, with an essayistic interlude, it knowingly flaunts the law of genre. It raises issues relevant to moral philosophy, to deontological and teleological ethics, without itself belonging to philosophy or the genre of philosophical or theoretical commentary. It draws on fictional resources without making positive propositions concerning the issues of intention, consequences, responsibility or the ethical problematic of the afterlife of the written sign. One might even say that it exploits the unbearable catastrophe of Auschwitz in order to capture the reader's intention through the manipulation of arresting imagery. It strongly implies that Nietzsche was irresponsible in allowing *muthos* to overlap with *logos*, and the aesthetic impulse to create values to override the epistemological and ethical challenges of philosophical rigour. At the same time this 'critique' relies on rudimentary devices of the fantastic – the anachronism, the *revenant* – to shape the terms of what should be the most serious debate. The prologue to this work, however, is unlikely to have negative ethical effects. It is not written by one who is or ever will be a cultural authority or even an author in any canonical sense of the term. Against the exploitative charge, one might invoke Adorno's insistence that the categorical imperative of modernity is '[t]hat Auschwitz not be forgotten'. The creation of a fantastic scenario in which Nietzsche is brought face to face with events which were seeking a certain legitimation in his name follows from Derrida's brave assertion that something in Nietzsche's work must have lent itself to this appropriation. Furthermore, the author of the present work may console himself that not only is *The Ethics of Writing* bereft of constructive content, but destined to remain '*non legor, non legar*', or received only within the narrowest and safest of academic confines. Nevertheless, in its 'Prologue', the work enters quite opportunistically into the realm

Rushdie drew attention to the fictional frames, but did so in the knowledge that a fundamentalist audience would not take the 'aesthetic', 'ironic' or hypothetical 'as if' for anything more than get-out clauses allowing an author simultaneously to say and not say, to own and disown the text as it suited the needs of the hour. To this extent, Rushdie declined to put his name to what had been written in his name, wished to be the authoritative reader as well as the writer of a text he freely surrendered from the privacy of an intuition to the publicity of an institution. Society called him back along the ethical path that tracks a text to a proper name, to a person, a biography and set of intentions. That the awful personal consequences for Rushdie are utterly disproportionate (to a Western, liberal consciousness at the very least) when weighed against the supposed 'blasphemies' of *The Satanic Verses* alters nothing in this regard.

Nietzsche did not live to see the words of his Zarathustra – 'Do not drive the hero from thy heart' – inscribed on the gates of Auschwitz. Before those words, at that place, Nietzsche might recall the euphoric, life-affirmative and illness-remittent emotion with which he penned them on the heights of Sils Maria in 1883, little knowing how far and on such terrible winds of history they would migrate. He would certainly remind himself that just as you cannot step into the same river twice, so no pure repetition of an act of writing – no restoration of original context – is ever possible.

Two writers: one living, one dead. One who avowedly writes postmodern fiction; the other who, from what he often called 'the genius of the heart', produced a hybrid discourse still today called 'philosophy'. One author, then, who offended the canons of Islam, the other those of 'humanism'. One who lived in the eye of a media hurricane, the other who raged in utter obscurity throughout his productive life. One who was alive to see the dramatic reception of his texts, the other who died with only a handful of friends to count as a readership. A living author who sought exculpation; a dead author who had called his name to a posthumous reckoning. Yet in both cases writing emerges as fatherless, orphaned at birth, free to reappear in alien contexts, to garner unintended meanings, to have unforeseeable outcomes. Plato's perspective on writing and (ir)responsibility coincides exactly with the postmodern view in lamenting that very authorial dispossession the latter celebrates:

Footnote 2 (*cont.*)
    of the mixed discourse – or aestheticisation of theoretical discourse – which it will question and, of occasion, condemn. It is a responsibility of the writer to acknowledge rather than suppress self-contradiction.

textuality defenceless before its clients, unable to answer for itself, only capable of returning the same form of words in the face of numerous conflicting interpretations, powerless to predict or programme its own audience and reception. The 'risk of writing' gives the question 'Who is speaking?' its perennial urgency. To understand the nature of this demand we need to investigate its origins, which are indeed the very origins of literary criticism. We need also to make an imaginative journey back to a time when literature and ethics were inseparable.

II: THE ORIGINS OF AUTHORIAL AGENCY

Unlike any other discipline, literary criticism arose in hostility to the object of its study. It has a precise moment of origin in Plato's arguments towards the banishment of the poets from the ideal city. In the *Republic*, Plato presents cases of varying persuasiveness against poetry (by which we may understand literature in general). He advances the (in)famous 'copy of a copy' argument (*Republic*, 596b–602c) whereby the artist is an inferior copier of a copyist, one who merely represents a bed which a carpenter has made from a template provided by the ideal form of the bed. More telling are the ethical denunciations of literature for promoting patterns of imitation which are injurious to social order and the psychic development of children – arguments that remain valid today in debates over the pornographies of sex and violence – and for fostering intense emotional identification which involves the audience, readers or auditors in the action in such a way as to preclude rational reflection (an argument which, curiously enough, finds a twentieth-century equivalent in Brecht's theatre and theory of alienation).

To comprehend the urgency and intensity of the *Republic*'s critique, though, we have to remind ourselves that before Plato there were no firm distinctions between myth and truth, imaginative literature and rational thought, ethics and literature. Within primarily oral cultures, literature was not an aspect of cultural knowledge but its repository.[3] With the Homeric poems, Socrates and Plato confronted a tribal encyclopaedia, one that not only constituted a vast reservoir of historical and mythical events, but also served as a guide to mores, attitudes and ethical imperatives. Thus the poetry of oral tradition is not to be seen as recreation, myth

---

[3] The account of the transition from the orality of Homeric Greece to a Greek psyche remodelled by an interiorised literacy in Eric A. Havelock's *Preface to Plato* (Cambridge, MA: University of Harvard, Belknap Press, 1963; henceforth abbreviated as PtP) informs much of our interpretation of the *Republic*. However, its exclusion of the *Phaedrus* is the subject of a sustained critique under the succeeding section heading 'The Birth of Philosophy out of the Spirit of Writing'.

or under an aesthetic aspect, but as the dominant educational resource of its culture. The recitation of the Homeric works served simultaneously as theatre, festival and library. There can be no archive in an oral culture unless certain gifted individuals hold that information in their heads and ritualistically pass it on to another generation, and so on. The consequence of devoting the best minds of a culture to the task of memorisation is to preclude any sustained attempt at abstract thought.

In the two centuries which, according to the technological argument, separated the incorporation of writing and its assimilation as a psycho-noetic resource – from the seventh century BC to the emergence of logical Socratism and Platonic dialogue – writing had liberated the finest minds of Athenian culture from expending their energies in this colossal task of retaining generational, genealogical and historical records through mnemonics and living memory. Thus unencumbered, mnemonic intelligence had become free to become detached intellection. It was now possible to analyse, assess or question the information stored in the artificial and external sign. The external sign created knowledge as object and made mind the subject in relation to that object. Subjective detachment from text as a material object rather than internalised psychic resource – the very precondition of criticism if not of philosophy itself – was made possible by the external sign; like stellar or geological objects, discourse became an observable phenomenon, a preserved object open to philosophical or proto-scientific reflection.

In the oral tradition, on the other hand, subject and object were not differentiated: performers and audience alike simply immersed themselves within the tale and its telling – a species of identification quite the reverse of literary criticism which involves standing back from the work, assessing it as an object of study rather than of direct experience. Only with the cultural assimilation of writing does the notion of subjective autonomy come into being and, correlatively, that of authorial responsibility. Thus when Plato recalls his master in the *Apology*, it is as that primordial literary theorist who asked the poets what they meant by their poems, who called for a rational agent to step out from the shadowy, cave-like world of poetic identification. Socrates was disappointed in his assumption that the authors of these works might provide a rational account of their work. Poets and dramatists had sheltered behind ritual, collective authorship and the doctrine of inspiration which, whilst it dignifies the work with divine status, also relieves the author or poet of any responsibility or initiative in its production:

> It is hardly an exaggeration to say that any of the bystanders could
> have explained those poems better than their actual authors . . . I

decided that it was not wisdom that enabled them to write their poetry, but a kind of instinct or inspiration, such as you find in seers and prophets who deliver all their sublime messages without knowing in the least what they mean . . . (*Apology*, 22b–c)

Plato's Socrates confronted interiorised *logoi* with departed, unknown or intellectually deficient agents. Whether memorised or inscribed, poetic works proliferate in society without a responsible subject who will answer for their shortcomings, explain ambiguities and guard against abuse of their cultural authority. Hence Socrates places the following questions at the centre of subsequent thought: 'Who is speaking?' 'What do you mean by what you say?' 'How can you justify what you say?' 'What are its potential consequences?' A culture in which poetry served to unify knowledge now fragments, becomes compartmentalised: philosophy, history, politics, literature and ethics become separate realms of enquiry. The Socratic practice of asking the poets what they meant thus amounts to enjoining the poet not only to be a reader, a literary critic, of his or her own work, but also to take ethical responsibility for that work.

This imperative is apparent in the *Ion* where Socrates looks to the rhapsodes for an explanation of poetic meaning. Most famous for its celebration of the poet as possessed by a divine madness, the *Ion* is seen to contradict Plato's banishment of the poets in the *Republic*. The romantic reading sees this contradiction as issuing from an unconscious competition between the poet and philosopher in the Platonic psyche: another reading will neutralise the contradiction by seeing Socrates' praise of the poet as ironic. Both readings, however, deny that the poet has any conscious control or interpretative provenance over the work. Whichever way the dialogue is taken, philosophy's claim to be the best judge of poetic meaning is reinforced: the way is thereby paved for the *Republic's* gesture of banishment. In the *Ion*, Socrates does not confront the poet but the bearer of his posthumous word, the rhapsode. Ion lectures on Homer in addition to performing from the *Iliad* and the *Odyssey*, but he shows himself powerless to answer questions, to reconstitute intention, even to offer plausible interpretations of passages from Homer. The discourse entrusted to the rhapsodes is thus unprotected, open to all order of rhetorical abuse, liable to fall into any hands, to reappear on any tongue: the rhapsodes themselves are pseudo-authorities, men without the wisdom to counter (mis)appropriation of poetic content. The argument is clearly not intended as any criticism of Homer: here as elsewhere an anxious debt of influence and admiration is acknowledged (*Republic* X, 595b–c). Nor is Socrates' target 'Ion' himself, but the absence of a tradition, of an heir who could safeguard the Homeric inheritance against misreading. In choosing as Socrates' interlocutor one of the finest rhapsodes – Ion has just won first prize at the prestigious rhapsodic competition in Epidaurus – Plato seeks to show that the authorised legatees of the Homeric *paideia* provide little or no defence against misappropriation. They are not villainous in themselves, but rather poor sentries at the gates of tradition:

> SOCRATES: From both the *Odyssey* and the *Iliad* I picked out for you the passages belonging to the doctor, the diviner, and the fisherman; now you likewise, since you are better versed than I in Homer, pick out for me the sort of passages, Ion, that concern the rhapsode and the rhapsode's art, the passages it befits the rhapsode, above all other men, to examine and to judge.
>
> ION: *All* passages, Socrates, is what I say! (539d–e)

Naturally, the Socratic premise is absurd when considered from an aesthetic point of view: a poetry expert will judge precisely that which is poetic in poetry rather than treat each line as a constative statement. One would not, for example, seek out a veterinarian to consult on a reading of Baudelaire's *Les Chats*, still less a geologist to explain Malcolm Lowry's *Under the Volcano*. In the same spirit, though in heavier tones, the *Republic* reduces the poem to prosaic statement so as to separate out the aesthetic from the cognitive (*Republic*, 393c–394b). Stripped of its tropes, the poetic 'argument' will no longer beguile, capture unwary travellers or offer itself to those who call its authority to their questionable ends. The reduction of the poetic to prose statement serves to separate aesthetic from cognitive and reveals the insufficiency of poetry as an ethical guide.

These strategies will seem absurd and insensitive to us today, yet our response is precisely a measure of their success. The more ridiculous the idea of reducing a poem to a prose statement sounds to us, the more certain we can be that the poetic has been distanced from the constative. In a society which had not arrived at even the provisional Kantian separation of the cognitive, ethical and aesthetic realms, the *Iliad* and the *Odyssey* were taken not only as (Arnoldian) touchstones but as discourses of unquestionable truth and guides to everyday action. Faced with a culture in which Sophocles was elected a general because the people were so impressed by his *Antigone*, Plato's mission to separate the cognitive from the poetic acquires a validity and urgency quite alien to our own sense of the relations between literature and cognitive knowledge. One need only imagine a contemporary situation in which Ezra Pound's *Cantos* had become the dominant educational resource of the twentieth century to find some sympathy with this Socratic/Platonic anxiety.

Plato was not the first to criticise the hold of the poets over Greek consciousness: both Heraclitus and Xenophanes (though a poet himself) had challenged the concept of poetic authority. But Plato's extensive concern with the effect of poetry on its audience, its potential contribution to the spread of false wisdom, reveals an ultra-civilised determination to treat discourse as an ethical act of the sternest significance. The Socratic practice of asking the poets what they meant – of demanding an alternative syntax – amounts to enjoining the poet not only to be a reader, a literary critic of his or her own work, but also to take ethical responsibility for that work. In this regard, the Socratic interrogation constitutes a clear demand that poets sign their texts in the full sense of signing for the future, for misreading, for unintended meaning. Only by separating out the personality of the poet from the content of the poem, by enforcing a critically reflective distance between person and poem, can Plato ensure that the artificer takes as much responsibility for the artifice as a parent for its child. In this moment of interrogation, literature is demystified, finds itself accountable to philosophical ethics and the modern conception of the author as a rational agent comes into being.

Dialogue decisively consolidates this ethical ambition, this immense 'modernisation' of knowledge. The method of question and answer *in the presence of the speaker or author of the text* is necessary to ensure that context is perpetually reanimated and explicated anew. Eluding the fixities of poetic or scribal words, dialectical *logoi* seek to ensure that discourse cannot proceed from ear or eye to the psyche without understanding having been achieved. In this way alone can we have the assurance that discourse is an ethically responsible act rather than a dangerous abandonment.

This ethical concern connects with the critique of writing in the *Phaedrus*. Here Plato addresses the afterlife of a written work, the problems that writing poses to the future by travelling without a fixed destination, by exceeding the field in which an author can oversee its reception. Although poetry is not specified in the main argument, there are clear connections between Plato's distrust of the poets and his distrust of written discourses in general. Written words like paintings are mute; when you ask a question of them, they do no more than repeat themselves (*Phaedrus*, 275d). Of poetry, the *Protagoras* complains: '[n]o one can interrogate poets about what they say' (347e). Writing is ethically troublesome in the same manner as poetry. In the *Apology*, Socrates says of the poets he has questioned: 'the very fact that they were poets made them think that they had a perfect understanding of all other subjects, of which they were totally ignorant' (22b–c). In its myth of writing as a divine gift refused, King Thamus of the *Phaedrus* puts writing in the same case: 'it is no true wisdom that you offer your disciples, but only its semblance (*doxan*), for by telling them of many things without teaching them you will make them seem to know much, while for the most part they know nothing, and as men filled, not with wisdom (*anti sophōn*), but with the conceit of wisdom (*dox-osophoi*), they will be a burden to their fellows' (*Phaedrus*, 275a–b).

In a culture of writing, texts will fall into the hands of the ill-befitted without the benefit of a teacher's wisdom or the tutelary presence of their authors. The concern is clearly ethical in that the spread of false wisdom will have a malign effect on the social order. Where the speech situation allows the dialectician to monitor the reception of his discourse, writing

> drifts all over the place, getting into the hands not only of those who understand it, but equally of those who have no business with it; it doesn't know how to address the right people, and not address the wrong. And when it is ill-treated and unfairly abused it always needs its parent (*patros*) to come to its help (*boētheia*), being unable to defend or help itself. (*Phaedrus*, 275e)

The scruple itself is simple and severe. Whereas an oral teacher can distinguish between those who can benefit from a discourse without abusing its terms, a written text has no power of selection over who receives its words. The written word can mutiny against its subject's intentions. Like poetry, writing is defenceless before misreading: it is incapable of discriminating between those who understand (*tois epaïousin*) and those who do not. The *Phaedrus* thus militates against writing in what would seem to be a universal manner. The validity of this perhaps paradoxical passage and its import for twentieth-century theories of intention, interpretation, hermeneutics, authorship and textual ethics will be the main concern of this work. What will follow through here – and in a second volume on discursive ethics in Levinas and Derrida – might well be taken as a prolonged meditation on *Phaedrus*, 275d–e.[4]

---

[4] Given that *Phaedrus*, 275e is the very first statement on iterability, it is tempting to take consolation in the unrelenting recourse that this work will make to these few, inexhaustible words expressed by or through Socrates. A scholar of infinite patience might trace their reappearance in essayistic, hermeneutic or academic works of the twentieth century. Our argument suggests that these words on iterability are indefinitely reiterable. The inaugural definition of that curious discursive property that, following Derrida, we now refer to as 'iterability' may itself prove the most renewable of statements. On the self-referential paradox of Plato here writing against writing, see Mary Margaret Mackenzie, 'Paradox in Plato's *Phaedrus*', *Proceedings of the Cambridge Philological Society* n.s. 28 (1982), pp. 64–76.

A subsidiary theme will be the connection between the critique of writing in *Phaedrus* and that of literature in Books II, III and X of the *Republic*. The *agon* into which Plato's Socrates entered with the poets will also be considered with reference to the work of the *Ion*, and scattered Socratic remarks in the *Apology* and the *Protagoras*. The thought of modernity opened the space of poeticised, romanticised and grandly narrativising philosophy, embracing a creative or ontogenetic mission first heavily marked in the work of Rousseau and the German Idealists. A postmodern standpoint which has been called to wage war on totality and to reject grand narrative, the present work argues, increases the responsibility of the author to protect his or her discourse against dangerous or catastrophic misinterpretations. Such protective measures include respect of an ethics of signature, genre, of the cadre, the *parergon* and the contract which is established with the contemporaneous reader and the posthumous readerships which will carry forward the codicillary amendments to the textual estate.

Alan Megill, in his excellent *Prophets of Extremity*, uses the word 'aestheticism' to describe the ontogenetic tendency or indeed 'crisis' arising from the disintegration of Enlightenment thought. Rather than just denoting attempts within the philosophy of art to define the aesthetic as an autonomous sphere or irreducible mode of knowledge, the word can describe the movement from within philosophical and theoretical thought towards an aesthetic description of reality which is yet propounded from within 'philosophy' or 'theory'. Nietzsche's famous *dictum* 'it is only as an *aesthetic phenomenon* that existence and the world are eternally *justified*' (BT, 52) might stand as one talismanic formulation of this drive. Discerning this common tendency or 'drive' in the work of Nietzsche, Heidegger, Foucault and Derrida, Megill writes:

> Looking at these thinkers together, one is struck by how they are all peculiarly aesthetic, or 'aestheticist' in their sensibility . . . As it is usually employed, the word aestheticism denotes an enclosure within an enclosure within a self-contained realm of aesthetic objects and sensations, and hence also denotes a separation from the 'real world' of nonaesthetic objects. Here, however, I am using the word in a sense that is almost diametrically opposed to its usual sense . . . not to the condition of being enclosed within the limited territory of the aesthetic, but rather to an attempt to expand the aesthetic to embrace the whole of reality.[5]

---

[5] Alan Megill, *Prophets of Extremity: Nietzsche, Heidegger, Foucault, Derrida* (Berkeley and Los Angeles: University of California Press, 1985), p. 2.

If not an *enantioseme*, 'aestheticism' is at least amphibolous. This book wholeheartedly endorses Megill's concept of 'aestheticism' as the philosophical impulse become mythopoeic, but here the idea of art as an enclosed sphere will be given the strong ethical sense of a responsible contract made from and between author and reader. With fulsome gratitude to the description of the phenomenon Megill identifies as 'aestheticism', our use of the word will be both more traditional and also on occasion extended to indicate an ethical caution that the imaginative advertises itself as a caveat against sedulous readers or even authors who incline to superimpose the ideal upon the real, the dream upon the destiny of societies or nations. The fictional, dramatic or poetic 'frame' will be seen as an ethical guardrail against inept, abusive or malign misreadings. The insistence of a work on its provisional, hypothetical or imagined nature will be seen as an ethically responsible gesture made by the author. Such would not be to collapse the distinction between literature and philosophy but to recommend that works of indeterminate generic status such as the *Phenomenology, The Communist Manifesto, Thus Spoke Zarathustra, Creative Evolution,* Heidegger's 'Letter on Humanism' or *Civilisation and its Discontents* ally themselves with the great imaginative works of world literature rather than lay claim to philosophical or scientific status.

Our construction of the case of Nietzsche accords with Megill's, of his analysis of the prophet of Sils Maria's 'cosmogonical poetry' and the 'onto-poetic historicism' which Heidegger inherited. It also repeats, in a modest but supplementary fashion, Derrida's reading of the Nietzschean legacy, his construction of a posthumous fate, his tragic and reckless irresponsibility with the destination of his writings. The sole addition we make to Derrida's *The Ear of the Other* will be to emphasise the ethical dangers of subordinating the epistemological to the aesthetic.

Though he was by no means oblivious to the question of writing – the subject of *Ecce Homo* is writing or what the name 'Nietzsche' names rather than the man who bore it – Nietzsche did not produce a critique of writing, and took no discernible stance on the speech-writing issue at a philosophical or logocentric level, and so his work is not approached in the same manner as that of Plato and Levinas. Rather, he is taken as exemplary of the issues of legacy raised at *Phaedrus,* 275e. In 'the case of Nietzsche', writing wanders away from its author to take on a life of its own with an astounding, coruscating and often disturbing vitality such as has not been witnessed in the estate of any philosopher before or since. Furthermore, though it anticipates the poststructuralist dismantling of self-present meaning and the disruptive work of metaphor in the text of philosophy, Nietzsche's celebration of the Dionysian phenomenon allies itself with the dark oralism of the pre-Socratics, the participatory lifeworld of thaumaturgical rituals, the dissipation of individual consciousness in pre-literate 'performance' and collective immersion in the work of art – themes which will make Heidegger seem perhaps more an inheritor of the Nietzschean estate than will be the judgement of posterity, many posterities. *Thus Spoke Zarathustra* constitutes a formal complement to this contradictory relation to the declamatory and inscribed in its reliance upon and simultaneous repudiation of Biblical orality and Platonic dialectic, its interleaving of parable, poetry and song. In the generic sense, the title of the spellbinding 1882 work would say it all (*The Gay Science with a Prelude in Rhymes and an Appendix of Songs*) were Nietzsche's other subtitles not also so revelatory: *A Book for Everyone and No One, The Idle Hours of a Psychologist, Prelude to a Philosophy of the Future* and *A Book for Free Spirits*. Ambivalent and contradictory in his assessments of art and literature, Nietzsche would nonetheless incline towards the poetic in the ancient quarrel through his subordination of the classical epistemological project to the creative will. Furthermore, *The Birth of Tragedy* – the most influential of his works in the first half of the twentieth century – belongs perhaps beside *Preface to Plato* and 'Plato's Pharmacy' in the great defences of poetry. The argument that Socratic rationalism as it contaminated the work of Euripides destroyed the pre-conceptual pessimism of strength that gave such magnificent depth and power to Aeschylus and Sophocles, taken alongside his chronologically valid (but logically dubitable) observation that mankind thought in images before in concepts, reverses exactly the priorities of Plato and Levinas, and amounts to a reconfiguration of post-Christian modernity that would be a restoration of the values (if not the pre-literacy) of the oralist lifeworld of Homeric and pre-Socratic Greece. The relationship of these themes to the work of Eric Havelock will be considered in the second section of Chapter 1.

The names of Plato (at least that of the author of *Republic*), Hegel, Marx and Freud could also be added to Megill's list of the high-canonical prophets of extremity. As it is, the dangerous combination of ostensibly philosophical or scientific claims and aesthetic presentation through redemptive narrative – *muthos* masquerading as *logos*, or philosophical statement gathering force from the techniques of epic or prophetic genres – can only be implied throughout this work. This project took shape in the conjunction of Sir Karl Popper's *The Open Society and its*

Enemies, Jacques Derrida's *The Ear of the Other* and Alan Megill's *Prophets of Extremity.*[6] The absence of Nietzsche from Popper's work, understandable given the time of its writing, seems nonetheless to warrant separate study.

In his relation to aestheticism, our approach to Derrida will differ from Megill's in that we will offer a particular and doubtless partial construal of his work as a disentropic way of reading aestheticism which 'deconstructs' the 'real-world' implications of speculative philosophy whilst also drawing attention to its dangers. His arguments concerning the implication of the Nietzschean signature in National Socialism is perhaps the major impetus to writing this work: indeed a theoretically informed

---

[6] We hope to take forward something of the spirit of Popper's critique of Plato, Hegel and Marx into a more linguistically sensitive and theorised era. See Karl Popper, *The Open Society and its Enemies,* Volume I: *The Spell of Plato,* Volume II: *The High Tide of Prophecy: Hegel, Marx, and the Aftermath* (London: Routledge & Kegan Paul, 1945). To recast *The Spell of Plato* and *The High Tide of Prophecy* through a theorised ethics of writing presented a significant challenge whereby the intemperate liberalism of Popper's approach could be cancelled while affirming the continuing moral relevance of assessing authorial acts in terms of their historical outcomes. Extending analysis in modernity from Hegel and Marx to Nietzsche raised the compelling legacies and reception histories of Freud and Heidegger. Such a critical project would have required a team of authors and scholars drawn from numerous disciplines if the theme of the dangerous discourses of modernity was to be assayed with even a modicum of competence. Borges tells of a man who dedicated his life to painting the universe only to find, at day's close, that he had only succeeded in outlining the features of his own face. Such immodest ambitions are perhaps the prerequisite for the most humble offerings and these impetuses helped refine a reading not of the dangerous discourses of speculative thought and their unethical conflation of *muthos* and *logos,* but of two cardinally irenic texts – *Phaedrus* and *Totality and Infinity* – which call into question the propriety of the written word, and writing as potentially violent remainder. Regarding Derrida, no reading of his work is offered in these pages, nor in the second volume. The perspectives taken on the *Phaedrus, Ecce Homo, Totality and Infinity* and *Otherwise than Being* are all refracted through, respectively, 'Plato's Pharmacy', *The Ear of the Other,* 'Violence and Metaphysics' and 'At this Moment in this Text Here I Am'. 'Plato's Pharmacy' and *The Ear of the Other* are not subjected to reading since our readings proceed directly from these texts. We do not do justice to Derrida (can one ever do so?) in using his work towards our ultimately liberal-conservative ends in which deconstruction figures as an expansive, disentropic neutralisation of the real-world claims of speculative philosophy, as a way by which we can continue to read the works of Hegel, Nietzsche, Marx, Freud and Heidegger, whilst being aware, as good readers, that we enter a realm of 'truth effects' which should never again be taken for 'truths' with potentially catastrophic possibilities for the lives of millions, as translated onto the plane of political history. In *The Death and Return of the Author* we offered an interesting but partial and exorbitant reading of Derrida's relationship to authorship: here we try not to make amends for this but to acknowledge that, more than any other twentieth-century philosopher, the late, much lamented and properly mourned Algerian *savant* has, more than any other, led us towards intelligent reading. In this work, particularly its second volume, the boundless corpus of Derrida exhibits the professional scepticism of analytic philosophy and the work of logical positivism without effecting an absolute reduction or dismissal of the text of speculative philosophy. Countervailingly, in drawing out his ethical relation to the Hellenic/Hebraic issue, to Eurocentrism and the epochal hegemony of the Graeco-Christian *logos,* we hope to make a relatively original case for the actively radical ethical intervention of Derrida against a tradition which has marginalised a Judaic interpretative tradition emanating from Maimonides and his radicalisation of Levinas's thought, which took messianic eschatology beyond its phonocentric impasse to the great ethical achievement of *Otherwise than Being.*

rewriting of Popper's *The Open Society and its Enemies* from a Derridean perspective was the original intention of this work, which would also call upon the logical positivist insistence that metaphysical and speculative philosophy should be proffered and received not as *philosophia propria* but as *lebenphilosophie*. Popper's intemperate liberalism would then have been tempered by a rereading of Vaingher's *The Philosophy of As If* in terms of an ethical guardrail, an indispensable and morally incumbent cadre, *parergon* and a contractual obligation on any author who would use the resources and terminology of philosophy in order to depart from or transcend rational foundations.[7] *The Ethics of Writing*, then, offers itself as a 'shadow of the original conception': these prospects for reading have instead guided our approach to Plato and Nietzsche. They remain largely in the background but will be revisited at the close, and reopened in the second volume on the ethical thematics of writing in Levinas and Derrida. By way of contemporary ethical debates within critical theory, we commence the main argument by (re)turning not to Plato but to modernity's construction of the great Athenian. Our imperative is not to discredit the epistemological or metaphysical significance of 'his' *Phaedrus*, but to reflect upon its construction for the thought just prior to the millennium and to draw out its implications for what we are calling 'the ethics of writing'.

★

Why, then, the ethics of writing rather than of authorship? The latter would, after all, represent a positive development from the restoration of the author as a discursive category which not only survived but posed a specific set of challenges to theoretical redescription. On the logically and chronologically prior assurance that authorship asked the question of theory simultaneously with the question itself, its unique instantiation of intention, responsibility, duty, obligation, foreseeable and unforeseeable outcomes, its powerful association with the general moral category of the deed would more than justify but actively require re-examination for a critical era in which the ethical has transcended the cognitive and

---

[7] See Hans Vaihinger, *The Philosophy of As If: A System of the Theoretical, Practical and Religious Fictions of Mankind*, trans. C. K. Ogden (London: Routledge & Kegan Paul, 1924). Heidegger's fiduciary appeal to a mysterious poetry of being only accessible to the pre-Socratics, to a few poets (Hölderlin, in particular) and the extremely ambiguous ethical status of the pious philosopher himself will be discussed in Volume II in the context of Levinas's promulgations – very different in aims, though indistinguishable in their audacious claim to write beyond the limits of representation – of a language that exceeds the concepts and resources of traditional philosophy.

aesthetic as the highest faculty of adjudication in the humanities and social sciences.[8]

The main title indicates a concern with responsibility for the medium in which an author works as raised by the orality/literacy debate in North American universities. The idea of authorship was not taken on its own terms in light of the consequences for individual creativity of textuality refracted through an oralist, typographic or latterly digitalised milieu. Further, the 'death of the author' was haphazardly embroiled with the speech/writing issue first as it came to attention in continental philosophy. In the high tide of bewilderment with which Derrida's work was received in Anglo-American universities, authorship found itself caught up in a simplistic chain of prejudicial oppositions said to constitute 'the metaphysics of presence'. Grouped with notions of 'presence', the 'transcendental signified', 'voice' and 'speech' as against the derivatives of 'absence', 'indeterminacy' and 'writing', postmodern culture as shaped in large measure by literature departments promulgated an entirely counterintuitive equation of authorship with presence which could have been corrected by consulting a single page of the *Phaedrus* or Derrida's 'Signature, Event, Context'. When Roland Barthes declared that 'writing is the destruction of every voice, of every place of origin . . . that neutral, composite, oblique space where our subject slips away, the negative where all identity is lost, starting with the very identity of the body writing', or Michel Foucault that discourses might 'circulate in a pervasive anonymity', the poststructuralist view of writing as radical dispossession revealed itself as a restatement of the Socratic wisdom that writing drifts all about the place, in the absence of its father or author.[9] The only difference between the poststructural and the Socratic depiction of writing is that the former celebrates what the latter abhors.

In seeking here to talk of 'The Ethics of Writing: Authorship and Legacy', authorship is given not as a mark of presence but of the absence attendant upon allowing words to take on a life and destination beyond

---

[8] Many would hold that scientific discoveries, too, should come under the sway of the ethical: one and the same person may well be in favour of applications of the findings of stem-cell research whilst being absolutely opposed to the militaristic development of further nuclear technologies. The themes of this book bear on this issue, but its analysis lies beyond our compass for two distinct reasons. First, the writer of this work has not been trained in science; second, the question of the relationship between authorial acts and scientific innovations requires independent studies in and of itself at the levels of theory and practice.

[9] Roland Barthes, 'The Death of the Author', in Roland Barthes, *Image-Music-Text*, trans. and ed. Stephen Heath (London: Fontana, 1977), pp. 42–8: p. 42; Michel Foucault, 'What is an Author?' *Language, Counter-Memory, Practice: Selected Essays and Interviews*, ed. Donald Bouchard, trans. Donald Bouchard and Sherry Simon (Ithaca, NY: Cornell University Press, 1977), pp. 113–38: p. 138.

the originator's compass or recall – *logoi* decapitated, yet mobile, 'rider-less', in the part-title of Sylvia Plath's poem. Derrida makes this connection with the utmost lucidity in 'Signature, Event, Context':

> For the written to be the written, it must continue to 'act' and to be legible even if what is called the author of the writing no longer answers for what he has written, for what he seems to have signed, whether he is provisionally absent, or if he is dead, or if in general he does not support, with his absolutely current and present intention or attention, the plenitude of his meaning, of that very thing which seems to be written 'in his name' . . . This essential drifting, due to writing as an iterative structure cut off from all absolute responsibility, from *consciousness* as the authority of the last analysis, writing orphaned, and separated at birth from the assistance of its father, is indeed what Plato condemned in the *Phaedrus*. If Plato's gesture is, as I believe, the philosophical movement par excellence, one realises what is at stake here.[10]

The idea of authorship, as opposed to its construction as counter-ideal, derives from the separation of speaker from sign that writing enforces. Writing is already implicit as concept in the memorised text – memorisation sunders the sign from the original scene of articulation – but only the actual practice of writing can crystallise this deferral as the discursive practice of authorship. The oral poem cannot guarantee its preservation in the precise form of words decided by its author(s). In the vast majority of cases, writing permits an author to abandon or publicise his work in the form which he last intended it to assume. In *all* cases, writing enables a subject self-consciously to craft his work to a posthumous destination. Authorship graphically supplements mortality: it is predicated on departure, absence and death. On this widespread misreading of Plato, Derrida and Derrida's 'Plato's Pharmacy', it was assumed that authority is invested in the idea of speech as presence, while writing is associated with a dissemination which undoes univocity. The spoken is seen as monologic; the written as voiceless, plural, anti-authoritarian. Although but one term in this opposition, writing – when registered *qua* writing – is seen to undo the very binarism of which it is a constituent. Authorship is returned to an absence from which it never departed. This arc of return is superfluous: such readings deconstruct Plato's text only through inverting the priorities of the *Phaedrus*. The rejection of authorship as a logocentric category, as a transcendental signified within a metaphysics of presence, rested upon

---

[10] Jacques Derrida, 'Signature, Event, Context', in Derrida, *Margins of Philosophy*, trans. Alan Bass (Brighton: Harvester Press, 1982), pp. 309–30: p. 316.

a counterintuitive association of 'authorship' with *presence* metonymically registered as 'voice'. Naturally, any such presence can be at most supplementary given that the corollary absence of the author is the precondition of writing and authorship whose coming into being may be said to be coeval. The question of whether authorship can be said to precede writing or vice versa is very much open. Once naively thought of as naming the first great author of the Western canon, 'Homer' does not name a biographical subject but two epic poems of uncertain date. A central aim of the present work is to contest the association of authorship with presence in the full sense of that term and to reinforce the essential graphicity of authorship. Its origin stirs not in the union but the separation of subject and sign identified for the first time in the *Phaedrus*. The closer affinity of writing with the less humanistic term signature – which adverts more closely to the ethical in the sense of contractual obligation, the assumption of responsibility – suggested this displacement of presence and indeed the subdivision of authorial acts into discrete textual acts over a lifetime which we will raise or imply throughout.

The title of this work, it goes without saying, alludes to J. Hillis Miller's *The Ethics of Reading*.[11] Although the original inspiration stemmed from adjacent rereadings of *The Ear of the Other* and *The Open Society and its Enemies*, the work was decisively encouraged by the emergence of the ethical theme from deconstruction and the Anglophone discovery of Levinas which owes so much to the admirable endeavours of Robert Bernasconi and Simon Critchley in the late 1980s. The latter's *The Ethics of Deconstruction* is an indispensable reference point for any contemporary discussion of textual ethics; in turn, it inspired Robert Eaglestone to construct the contemporary debate in terms of an opposition between a thematic Martha Nussbaum and a textualist Hillis Miller rethought through the very distinct challenge of a Levinasian criticism.[12] Our concerns are quite remote from those of Nussbaum, in which literature is construed as

---

[11] J. Hillis Miller, *The Ethics of Reading* (New York: Columbia University Press, 1987). Hereafter referenced in the main text by the abbreviation ER. In treating of the ethics of writing we are obliged to remain within the realm of 'textual ethics', but in our equation of 'authorial acts' with 'deeds' in the more traditional ethical sense, it is our aim to approach the borderline at which an act of inscription translates into ethically serious consequences at the social, historical, institutional and political levels. It is beyond our compass to discuss ethics *qua* ethics. On contemporary philosophical ethics, see Bernard Williams, *Ethics and the Limit of Philosophy* (London: Fontana, 1985), a work whose distinction between ethics and morality is presupposed throughout the present work and the succeeding volume treating of ethics and voice in Levinas and Derrida. On 'textual ethics', a lively account is given in Jay Bernstein, *The New Constellation: The Ethical-Political Horizons of Modernity/Postmodernity* (Cambridge: Polity Press, 1991).

[12] Cf. *Re-Reading Levinas*, ed. Robert Bernasconi and Simon Critchley (London: Athlone, 1991) and Simon Critchley's invaluable, *The Ethics of Deconstruction: Derrida and Levinas*, second edition

a specialised arena in which moral issues and dilemmas are represented as invitations or indeed imperatives to philosophical reflection: indeed, the genitive in 'the ethics of writing' does not propose itself as double in the manner of 'the ethics of reading'.[13] Thematic ethical criticism has a distinguished lineage, stretching back through F. R. Leavis and Matthew Arnold in the English critical canon.[14] The *locus classicus* of such reading remains Hegel's analysis of Sophocles' *Antigone* as the competition between equally valid but partial moral claims and their sublation, synthesis or uplifting (*aufhebung*) – in this case the principle of absolute right as embodied in Creon versus individual rights as represented by the eponymous heroine and their resolution in ethics as the recognition of both the universality of law and the recognition of subjective freedom.[15] Were literary thematics

(Edinburgh: Edinburgh University Press, 1999). For a construction of the ethics of reading debate in terms of readings of Hillis Miller, Martha Nussbaum and Emmanuel Levinas, cf. Robert Eaglestone, *Ethical Criticism: Reading after Levinas* (Edinburgh: Edinburgh University Press, 1997). On the contexts of this debate, see Martha Nussbaum, *The Fragility of Goodness: Luck and Ethics in Greek Tragedy and Philosophy* (Cambridge: Cambridge University Press, 1986) and *Love's Knowledge: Essays on Philosophy and Literature* (Oxford: Oxford University Press, 1990). The reader will naturally be drawn back to the long tradition of moral criticism, particularly as produced in England. As with Hillis Miller, Nussbaum's criticism focuses on the novel as the genre most suited to the representation of moral and ethical dilemmas. Her main focus in the work of Henry James, though as she would freely admit, there are very few novels that would not admit of such a pattern of reading: the apparent cowardice of *Lord Jim* or the supposed transcendence of human-all-too-human values made by Kurtz are good examples of works where a moral aberration is presented from numerous competing ethical perspectives. Dramatic literature invariably centres on moral conflict and, as our few modest remarks on Hegel's reading of *Antigone* will suggest, tragedy from Shakespeare to the modern day can be read from the vantage of equally valid but partial ethical claims working themselves through the conflict of central protagonists.

13 'Does the ethical act *of* the protagonist inside the book correspond to the ethical acts the reading of the book generates outside the book?', Hillis Miller asks, in relation to 'the double genitive in ethics *of* reading' (ER, 2). Whilst we will be concerned with the issue of protagonism and representation – especially in the ancient context of the 'Socratic problem' and Nietzsche's perhaps ironic, certainly canny gauntlet of the 'Zarathustran problem' – we will not wish to lay any particular emphasis on the writing of ethics even as it coincides with the ethics of writing in Plato, Nietzsche, Derrida and, subsequently, Levinas (ethicists, as they are, one and all to varying degrees and in very different fashions). Many interesting puzzles do indeed open when one considers 'the ethics of writing when writing ethics', but such aporetic structures would warrant study in and of themselves.

14 Cf. Matthew Arnold, *Lectures and Essays in Criticism: Complete Words*, Volume III, ed. R. H. Supir (Ann Arbor, MI: University of Michigan Press, 1962); F. R. Leavis, *The Common Pursuit* (London: Chatto & Windus, 1952) and *The Critic as Anti-Philosopher: Essays and Papers*, ed. G. Singh (London: Chatto & Windus, 1982).

15 Should our inclination have been towards this form of criticism, we might extend Hegel's analysis to a complementary competition in the conflict between the written and unwritten law, the former being upheld by Creon against Antigone's appeal to the latter as justifying the burial rights of her brother. The Hegelian reading of *Antigone* proves irresistible in its relation to the *res gestae*, the milieu and the historical moment in which it locates this closing drama of the Sophoclean trilogy. For Hegel, it represents an absolutely critical moment in the journey by which the human mind advances towards ultimate knowledge. Ethics itself, rather than ethical criticism, advances even should one mistrust – as we will throughout – the unverifiable movement of *Geist* towards absolute knowledge. That essential scepticism aside, as a moment of productive and cogent ethical criticism, the Hegelian interpretation is second to none in the history of ethico-literary reading.

our concern here, our focus would not be on the responsibilities of the reader to the literary text but the ethical motivations and probity of the authorial act along with its accountability for social and political outcomes of the work.[16] Besides which, admirable though they are within their own ambitions, twentieth-century reading of ethical thematics in literary works seems a retrogression from the dialectical precedent. Hegel does not merely use *Antigone* as a means to open a discussion of the ethical stakes of the play's central conflict. In his profound reading he both adds a philosophical dimension to the drama that would have been unknowable to Sophocles himself and at the same time advances ethical thought itself by uncovering the dialectical movement in which the ever-pertinent contest between universal law and individual freedom was produced.

To the ethics of reading – as promoted in the name of deconstruction – our preoccupations are somewhat closer in that the work of Derrida is the starting point for the chapters on Plato and Nietzsche, as it will be for the second volume which focuses on Levinas's ethical metaphysics. It is, however, worth noting from the outset the vast difference we perceive between the ethical questions Derrida raises about the posthumous name of Nietzsche in its conjunction with National Socialism or that of Marx with the First and Second International, and Hillis Miller's pedagogic focus on the ethical moment entering 'into the social, institutional, political realms, for example, in what the teacher says to the class or in what the critic writes' (ER, 4).[17] Whereas the proclamation of the death of the author

---

[16] We would, then, be more interested in the degree of responsibility the Victorian novelist took for the potential influence of his or her novel rather than the ethical dilemmas which it weaves into the fabric of its narrative. Questions such as whether Gilbert Osmond, Heathcliff or Dorian Gray or, at the furthest extreme, Des Esseintes might provide disturbed minds with models for self re-creation would be more significant to a study such as this rather than the overall, sophisticated structures of ethical anxiety which the author contrived with cautionary intent. Should literary ethics have been our preoccupation, our questions would be altogether closer to those raised by Plato's Socrates in in Books II and III of the *Republic*.

[17] 'In what I call the "ethical moment" there is a claim made on the author writing the work, on the narrator telling the story within the fiction of the novel, on the characters within the story at decisive points in their lives, and on the reader, teacher or critic responding to the work . . . My assumption, moreover, is that there are analogies among all four of these ethical moments, that of the author, the narrator, the character and the reader, teacher, critic, though what is the basis of these analogies, what *logos* controls them, remains to be interrogated' (ER, 8–9). At the most fundamental level, the present work seeks to focus on 'the moment of the author' and, in a largely propadeutic fashion, to clear the grounds for an interrogation of the ethicity of the moment of inscription: of the categories listed above Miller's *The Ethics of Reading* commendably focuses on 'reader, teacher, critic' but to the complete occlusion of 'the author'. In this sense our study is supplementary and its ethos compatible with the work of the Yale deconstructionist. However, we reserve the right to remain sceptical about certain of Miller's claims and the rather rarefied pedagogic, liberal-humanist construction of ethics within the American campus. On Miller's entirely perplexing claim that de Man's model of reading promises a 'new millenium', see Eaglestone, *Ethical Criticism*, pp. 75–6.

required an agonistic response in the interests of moving towards a newly discovered model which superseded the prevailing dominance of text over commentary – thereby redescribing the anti-authorial movement as a necessarily antithetical movement in a dialectical progression – consideration of the ethics of criticism from the perspective of authorial responsibility is complementary to rather than in conflict with the ethics of reading. The revision of anti-authorial theory did not seek to restore the supposed tyranny of the author, but rather to ensure that one did think to have done with prejudicial hierarchies by a crude reversal of positive and negative poles. In relation to the ethics of reading, no such revision is needed, but rather a complementary or supplementary attention to authorial ethics which is not disputed in ethical criticism but has as yet to emerge as a topic in its own right within contemporary debates.[18]

The Ethics of Reading, in fact, gives us the perfect opportunity to convey the relation in difference of the present work. When Miller says of each reading that 'the reader must take responsibility for it, and for its consequences in the ethical, social and political worlds' (ER, 59), we wish only to mark the difference that what is true of reading here is *a fortiori* true of the act of writing, of the responsibility an author takes for what is publicised – without coercion or in a condition of severe mental illness – in his or her name. This is not to restore a passivity/activity parallel between reading and writing, but only to say that the act of writing at the very least calls to an equal degree of responsibility and ethically attuned responsiveness. Nor is it to say that the ethics of reading and writing can ever be fully distinguished: Plato's argument against the poets in *Republic* is in no small part an affair of the ethics of reading, of the reading of poetry *qua* poetry and in part, with the brutal directness of a logocentric *précis* of the *Iliad* (*Republic*, 393c–394b). What applies to Books II, III and X of the *Republic* applies to the entire movement of the *Ion* and one would not traduce the *Phaedrus* by viewing it as inspired by critical readings of the sophists and contemporary rhetors, the gifted Isocrates in particular. *Ecce Homo*, too, is

---

[18] Implicit in Popper's work of forty years previously, it is to be regretted that *The Ear of the Other* did not promote a general debate on authorial responsibility. On the other hand, is to be regretted further, from our point of view, that *Specters of Marx*, whilst writing at great length and with superlative intelligence about the debt, did not take up the issue of legacy in the more contained terms of the reflection on Nietzsche. For whatever reason, Derrida chose not to ask the question of Marx that he put to Nietzsche, namely, to what extent is the name, the estate, the textual legacy of the *Communist Manifesto, Das Kapital*, etc. implicated in the monstrosities of Bolshevism and the still more poisoned milk that was Stalinism, And how, provisionally, are we to link this to the Hegelian inheritance? Fascinating work though it is on so very many levels, Derrida's response to Marx proved disappointing to this project of establishing the groundwork of an ethics of writing. Cf. Jacques Derrida, *Spectres of Marx*, trans. Peggy Kamuf (London: Routledge, 1994).

in good measure an act of reading, devoting as it does much of its work
to an autocritique – symptom and circumstance of the most agonising
authorial loneliness – of Nietzsche's own writings. One need not go as far
as Harold Bloom's assertion that all writing is a revisionary rereading of a
precursive *oeuvre* to recognise that there is no such thing as writing *sui
generis*. Derrida's unique placement between exemplary reader and the
foremost philosophical author of the latter half of the previous century,
along with his deconstructive rewritings of the texts of speculative philosophy, could be construed as ethical writing *par excellence*, as can the very
different attempts of Levinas to arrive at a purely ethical saying (*le dire*)
which will be the subject of extended discussion in the succeeding book
of this venture into authorial ethics.[19] At all times we acknowledge a
'dependence-in-difference' upon the ethics of reading, which involves a
shift of emphasis, not of ethos. Our recourse to *Phaedrus*, 275d–e is
refracted   through   twentieth-century   theoretical   controversies   and
inevitably takes the first statement of iterability out of a context which can
never be restored. If a circling, sometimes fortuitously spiralling meditation can be deemed an 'approach', then such is the way of this work.
Issues such as whether we are using Derrida to read Plato, Plato to read
Levinas or the *Phaedrus* to read Nietzsche, Levinas, Havelock and
Derrida become increasingly insignificant as the web in which the
Phaedrus and *Republic* have become woven becomes the text itself: 'a web
that envelops a web, undoing the web for centuries; reconstituting it too
as an organism, indefinitely regenerating its own tissue behind the cutting

---

[19] The virtual repetition of the *Phaedrus* in Levinas work will be the starting point for our succeeding volume on ethics and voice in Levinas and Derrida. The aporia within the aporia of citing
writing against writing is most visible in 'The Transcendence of Words', in Emmanuel Levinas, *The
Levinas Reader*, ed. Sean Hand (Oxford: Blackwell, 1989), pp. 144–9, and in the monumental
Totality and Infinity: an Essay on Exteriority, trans. Alphonso Lingis (The Hague: Martinus Nijhoff,
1969). Levinas's Platonism also extends to an antipathy to the artwork which, as in the Platonic
work, is never explicitly connected to the critique of writing. While in a second voulume we will
make every attempt to rise to the radical challenges of Levinas's ethical horizons – and to respect
notions at first arcane in the extreme to non-academics and non-theorists, particularly those cen-
tring on the unethical nature of the copula, and of the ethical necessity of thinking beyond being,
essence or ontology – his work has an attraction for this project which that of Miller and De Man
possesses only obliquely, namely that ethical metaphysics works, albeit otherwise, with issues
common to the history of ethical reflection – viz. duty, irenics, obligation to the other, particularly
in his/her need, suffering or destitution, opposition to egotism and subjective autonomy, the necessity of dialogue and of resistance to authoritarian monologism, of responsiveness and responsibility. With Levinas we are not drawn to *Totality and Infinity*, not only on account of its ethical
propositionality, but also because one of its central themes is the ethics of communication and of
modes of discourse; similarly, *Otherwise than Being* is a central text in this description of the ethics
of writing because it works as much towards ethical writing as to the production of an ethical
system, or rather because, unlike its predecessor, it treats the former as indistinguishable from the
latter.

trace, the decision of every reading' (PP, 63). Theme and variation rather than induction or deduction characterise the mode of reading. We proceed in the hope that the ethical questions raised by the generic and intentional contracts established between author and reader are successively enriched by insistent return to the themes of responsibility for the afterlife of the written sign. The approach to Nietzsche, so very different in kind due to the absolutely irreducible and singular nature of his signature, richly bears out the paradox implicit in the election of any *exemplary* moment.

The word 'approach' describes well the reticence and tentative relationship that any theorist must entertain towards the dialogues of Plato. The Hellenist who has spent the best part of a scholarly life studying the *Phaedrus* will be the first to declare that he or she has only arrived at the best possible construction or construal of this dialogue which is at once so close to contemporary concerns and yet historically so remote, written so very long ago. Perhaps all intentions are beyond recall but those of the founder of Western philosophy who articulates much but not all of his thought through a 'Socrates' who is in part historical figure and textual figuration.

Our approach is therefore through the vantage of twentieth-century debates, and our negotiation of the question of writing takes its bearings from and between two readings which could not be closer to one another and more impenetrable: that of Eric Havelock whose reading of the Platonic philosophy as promoting a rational detachment owes itself to the science of writing, and that of Jacques Derrida who sees Plato as inaugurating the history of logocentrism through the repression of writing outside full speech. The former reading, *Preface to Plato*, is in perpetual flight from the *Phaedrus* in its concentration on the *Republic*; the latter, 'Plato's Pharmacy', virtually *and* vitally inhabits the *Phaedrus* in a reading of unprecedented intensity, but one which does not draw the arguments against the poets into its orbit. Both readers bravely approach Plato in radically different ways and both have allowed a multitude of subsequent theoretical approaches to commence.

The first volume is descriptive in its premonitory account of Plato, but critical of the contradiction generated between the dialogism of *Phaedrus* and the monologic, constructive ambitions of the *Republic*. It is critical too of the arguments of Havelock and the epistemological claims of the technological hypothesis in general. In the section on 'the case of Nietzsche' the work becomes critical in a conventionally ethical sense and applies the principles of Derrida's *The Ear of the Other* to Nietzsche's responsibility for his legacies. 'Plato's Pharmacy' guides the reading of the *Phaedrus* in such a way as to suggest that the influence of Plato on Derrida is only equalled by that of the exhaustive deconstructive monograph on our construction of the Socratic 'dialogue on dialogue'. Aside from lamenting the absence of the direct ethical focus of *The Ear of the Other* in Derrida's writings on Plato, Hegel and Marx, our bearings and indeed moorings are very much within his colossal 'deconstructive' *oeuvre*. Forging a path between the metaphysical implications of the speech/writing opposition and the epistemological transformations Havelock retraces the usurpation of Homeric orality by the science of writing, 'The Ethical Opening' will argue that Plato's concerns about orality and inscription (as with the perennial quarrel between poetry and philosophy) conform to the Kantian distinctions between the cognitive, the aesthetic and the ethical, and likewise instate the latter as the highest court of judgement.

In entitling this work *The Ethics of Writing*, the terms 'ethics' and 'writing' are used more to delimit than to expand a field of inquiry. Their conjunction circumscribes a potentially amorphous and boundless topic: the immense realms of ethical thought and writing in general are confined to a navigable compass. Just as the concept of the author became altogether more animated in and upon the pronouncement of its 'death', so too the ethical implications of the gesture of inscription and its connections to the broader ethical issues of deed and responsibility, text and intention, inception and reception, motivation and context come into dynamic play under the sign of negation. Like authorial theory, whose beginning was in its end, the ethics of writing are never more visible than when – in the dream of an inaudible scene of voicing – philosophy writes itself off the page, and writing continues to write in spite of its notional erasure.

The *force majeure* of two intense readings (Derrida on the *Phaedrus*, Havelock on the *Republic*) is paralleled by Havelock's non-reading of the *Phaedrus* which mistakenly assumes that an argument for the constitutive role of writing in the development of logical Socratism and Platonic dialogue can only proceed by suppressing the *Phaedrus*'s apparent antipathy to inscription. It is then with Derrida's affirmative resolution of the aporetic situation of writing against writing and Havelock's avoidance of the only Platonic dialogue which raises the issue of inscription that we will reopen the textual estate.

In the next chapter, we will work through the extraordinary narrative sustaining Havelock's case that ethics, as detached reflection on the Good, only became possible – along with epistemology and what we still today call 'philosophy' – through the noetic interiorisation of inscription and consequent remodelling of the Greek psyche down no fewer than five generations of privileged, literate and typically Athenian families and communities. In doing so, we will not for a moment lose sight of Plato or Nietzsche and will indeed see the latter's influence as 'the shaping spirit of the imagination' from which *Preface to Plato* emerged. Consideration and critique of Havelock's thesis is necessary groundwork for this project, for here we are confronted neither with the ethics of writing nor the writing of ethics but with writing as the essential precondition of ethics.

That said, academic or theoretical books are not arias or lyric poems which must be experienced sequentially or as a unity. Rarely are they read cover to cover and – given the necessary limits set upon how much one can absorb in a lifetime – a parsimonious approach is often prudent. Hence, it is at least a courtesy, if not a minor responsibility of the writer of academic works, to indicate pathways of selective reading. Those who are happy to proceed upon the assumption that the speech/writing issue in Plato is dependent upon ethical imperatives and have no desire to engage with the orality-literacy thesis of *Preface to Plato* can proceed to Chapter 2 and pick up the theme of legacy independently. Those whose primary orientation is authorship or signature could reopen this book at Chapter 3. Should an interest in the problematics of the Nietzschean legacy be the predominant reason for consulting this work, then scrutiny of the closing pages of Chapter 3 would constitute reasonable preparation for the succeeding chapter on Nietzsche and authorial responsibility. For yet another reader who wishes to engage at an open, abstract and humanistic level with the conflict between discursive freedoms and dangerous discourses, then the concluding chapter, 'Creativity versus Containment', might suffice as a prospect of the general dilemma posed by the emergence of mixed discourses in modernity. Whilst the creation of a discursive 'whole' is an ideal towards which the writer of a theoretical book should aspire, it is also his or her duty to accept what Nietzsche says of the error of philosophers: 'The philosopher believes that the value of his philosophy resides in the whole, in the building; posterity discovers in it the bricks which are then often used for better building' (AOM, &201). What is true of the philosophical edifice or system can only be *a fortiori* the case with secondary literature of the kind proffered here.

1

The Ethical Opening

Farewell and believe. Read this letter now at once many times
and burn it. So much for these matters.

(Second Letter, 314c)

DOCUMENT INSERT: 12/21/59. Field Report: Pete
Bondurant Kemper Boyd, 'For Forwarding to John Stanton.'
Marked: <u>KB – BE CAREFUL HOW YOU TRANSMIT
THIS. KB.</u> Sorry this report Stanton wanted is late. I don't like
writing things down, so cross out what you want and get it to
him. Make sure Stanton destroys it.

(James Ellroy, *American Tabloid*)

I: SPEECH AND WRITING: THE APORIA

The anxieties expressed in this double exergue are those of a writing
construed in the simple sense of 'sensitive' information intended for dissemination to a very small circle of hand-picked initiates. This pairing is
partly intended to show how little has changed in this regard in the
twenty-five centuries that have elapsed since the cultural assimilation of
writing in Socratic Greece. Written in the 1990s, James Ellroy's *American
Tabloid* is a factional account of the covert operations that surrounded
the assassination of John F. Kennedy. This time span – 1959 to November
1963 – saw the composition and publication of *Totalité et Infini*, and the
'completion' of Derrida's monumental review essay 'Violence et métaphysique: Essai sur la pensée d'Emmanuel Levinas' – a response which
in its perspicuity, detail and length is both unprecedented in the history
of written discourse and raises the genres of both 'essay' and 'review' to
an inconceivable, literally vertiginous height – for publication in two
consecutive 1964 issues of the *Revue de métaphysique et moral*. In
September 1963, Levinas published 'Le Trace de L'Autre', the essay
which marked a pronounced linguistic turn in his vision of ethical

metaphysics.[1] This essay was to give Derrida considerable pause, though he had no time to incorporate his response into the fabric of 'Violence and Metaphysics'. As we shall argue in the second volume of this project, it was during the autumn of 1963 and at the intersection between the replication of Socrates' arguments against writing in the *Phaedrus* in *Totality and Infinity* and the seemingly antithetical notion of the trace, that the great deconstruction of logocentrism took shape in Derrida's mind, passing through the monumental triad of works published in 1967 and the *coup de grâce* of the following year, the 'return to source', published as 'La Pharmacie de Platon' in two issues of *Tel Quel*. The discomposure produced between these two displaced Jewish intellectuals who had settled in Paris and made phenomenology the starting point for their philosophy was to produce both the grammatological project and Levinas's redefinition of ethical metaphysics according to *archē-writing* rather than speech as the trace that God leaves in the movement of alterity. As we will modestly trace in the succeeding book, this textual encounter, which was to deepen into a profound friendship, allowed both to affirm a Maimonidean inheritance that broke with the morally regrettable precursive 'presence' of Martin Heidegger. This period also saw the publication of Marshall McLuhan's *Guttenberg Galaxy* in 1962 and the completion, in April of that year, of Eric Havelock's *Preface to Plato*. Something akin to a communications revolution announced itself in the massive international attention that McLuhan's work attracted.[2] In Paris and in North America two traditions were taking shape which centred on the speech/writing or orality/literacy debate as the axial point at which a culture of poetic identification was usurped by a

---

[1] Emmanuel Levinas, *Totalité et Infini: Essai sur l'extériorité* (The Hague: Martinus Nijhoff, 1961). Jacques Derrida, 'Violence et métaphysique: essai sur la pensée d'Emmanuel Levinas', *Revue de Métaphysique et de Morale* (1964), no. 3 (pp. 322–54) and 4 (pp. 425–73). Emmanuel Levinas, 'La Trace de l'autre', *Tijdschrift voor Philosophie* (September 1963), pp. 605–23. This nexus of texts will be our central focus in the succeeding volume on discursive ethics. The 'encounter' between these philosophers, we will argue, goes beyond the conventional notion of a linguistic turn in Levinas's ethical metaphysics to encompass the very point of departure for the great grammatological project of the 1960s.

[2] Marshall McLuhan, *The Guttenberg Galaxy: The Making of Typographic Man* (London and Toronto: Routledge, 1962). Naturally the work of McLuhan has considerable bearing on any discussion of writing as technical apparatus. However, theoretical reflections on the ethics of writing and of genre as refracted through debates on the *Phaedrus* and the *Republic* are our focus and Havelock offers a dedicated and influential theoretical reading on the role of writing in the evolution of the Platonic work. The same applies, in a very different way, to our dependence upon (rather than privileging of) Derrida's 'Plato Pharmacy'. Though this chapter uses the orality–literacy issue in its contradiction with the Derridean critique as a way of opening the ethical foundations of the competition between speech and writing, we are not presenting a work *on* orality and literacy. That we have recourse, at times, to the work of Ong and others is dictated by its relevance to Havelock's arguments in *Preface to Plato*.

detached, logocentric rationalism which during a jagged history finally came to dominate Western thought from the Enlightenment to the postmodern era. Both implicitly drew parallels between the twentieth-century preoccupation with the question of language and the philosophical transformation that took place in fifth-century BC Athens. These traditions – so close and yet so impenetrable – would not come into productive communication until the closing years of the previous century.[3] In the broadest terms, the thematic of speech and writing was addressed in metaphysical and grammatological terms in France; in the American tradition, the argument was primarily technological and merged with the debates concerning hypertext and digitalisation in the 1980s and 1990s. In radically different ways, all had to commence by addressing the status of writing within Plato's *oeuvre*, and the aporia generated by the fact that the first great philosophical author had denounced writing in writing.[4]

The denunciations of writing in the *Phaedrus* and the *Seventh Letter* are of a very different nature from that made in the *Second Letter* as cited above, and not only because the latter is of questionable authenticity. Nor again solely because the former works are as much positive celebrations of the blessedness of the ideal speech situation – in which the interanimate *logos* passes between teacher and pupil in an epiphanous moment of dialectical understanding – as they are condemnations of the absence of the reader from the scene of inception and of the author from the scene of reception. With the *Second Letter*, as with the citation from *American Tabloid*, there is no positive value attached to voice-as-presence, but only an anxiety over writing's inability to discriminate between those very few to whom the author intends to communicate and those very many before

---

[3] A pivotal work here is *Technologies of the Sign*, the title of volume 21 of the *Oxford Literary Review* (2000). This volume opened a fertile space of communication between the continental and North American, the deconstructive and technological. Edited by Timothy Clark and Nicholas Royle, it did not seek to harmonise but rather promote dialogue between the adjacent but incommunicative reflections on orality/literacy and speech/writing.

[4] Much of this interest is governed by canonicity. Why otherwise should a protest that declares itself within the very media against which it protests strike us as so very significant? If we wish, for example, to gain a wide audience for an anti-democratic polemic it will be within democratic mechanisms that our polemic is registered. Again, were the Internet bombarded with intelligent invective against the Internet, the self-refutation would probably be noted with the same goodnatured lassitude we might today reserve for Dada-anti-Dada or a silent symphony. In itself, this species of contradiction would seem routine, of little weight. The contradiction as we shall explore in the Conclusion and in the second volume of this work is also a wonderfully exploitable resource for philosophical redescription. Nietzsche, Heidegger, Havelock, Levinas and Derrida, in very different ways, seek to garner significance for their work by placing it at the point of transition between a poetico-oral pre-Socratism and a graphic Platonism, both as the opening of the rationalist *epistēmē* and as the moment at which discursive media underwent a profound transformation.

whom he or she would remain resolutely silent. Hence, there is no contradiction in this pre-philosophical precaution between the medium and
the message: incorporated within the very message is the injunction to
memorise its content whilst erasing its existence as an object in the world.
Both advocate their own destruction by a certain recipient, a designated
addressee. They stand in lieu of direct oral communication with a designated interlocutor and wish to entrust the given message to the discernment of the addressee in terms of any subsequent transmission. It may be
that the message is to expire with the addressee or that the latter is in
contact with a small number of initiates who are in turn able to carry
forward its content with extreme vigilance. In any event, the text itself is
under no circumstances to be allowed to persist in its written form. That
the *Second Letter* survives is a breach of its author's intent (no matter who
that author might be) – either a direct betrayal or the product of care-
lessness on the part of the recipient.

The *Phaedrus*, on the other hand, at no point suggests its own destruction as writing once its 'messages' or 'truths' have been interiorised. Despite
its unparalleled preoccupation with issues of audience, reception, legacy,
the dangers of unmonitored dissemination, the selection of suitable souls
for dialectical instruction and the problem of writing being unable to
choose its clients or defend itself against misinterpretation in the inevitable
absence of the author from the scene of reception, the dialogue makes no
destinational provisions, sets no pre-emptive limits on its circulation, or uses
a narrow vocabulary to ensure that it is intelligible to a restricted class of
initiates only, nor again does it use cryptographic or hermetic textual
strategies (as will Maimonides and others) to guarantee that only those
with a certain level of *gnosis* will be able to penetrate and choose wisely
among its many 'meanings'. Plato's only indication of an intended readership or audience is the address to the *philosophoi*, or 'lovers of wisdom', to
whose class will be admitted authors who have demonstrated before the
dialectical tribunal their ability to defend their writings with a wisdom in
excess of that displayed by the writings themselves. Everything suggests
that, at the very literal level of the pleonasm, the dialogue was written for
posterity. We might perhaps conjecture that its circulation was intended to
be limited to the Academy, and that it might form the 'manual' basis for
philosophers to construct oral demonstrations of the inferiority of the
written word, but there is no question that the *Phaedrus* was destined to
persist – beyond its author's lifetime.

The dialogue is, then, at first scrutiny in full performative contradiction with itself. If Plato endorses Socrates' judgement that it is not with

serious intent that a man of wisdom will write in 'water' or 'that black fluid we call ink' (*Phaedrus*, 276c), then he is manifestly declaring that the demonstration of the inferiority of the written word is itself non-serious, the fruits of a pastime, and not to be taken seriously. Thus the entire text is merely playful, including its denunciation of writing. If the injunction is to be taken seriously, then we must presuppose that Plato is either blind to the fact that he is writing or grants a status to his own text which transcends the condition of textuality as stipulated in the dialogue. The performative contradiction, or self-referential paradox, is one we might be tempted to dismiss. Certainly, the intelligibility and the force of the arguments made for dialogic speech over writing are not compromised in themselves by the fact that they are inscribed: indeed, to cancel their validity on such grounds would seem an invalid operation akin to the *ad hominem* fallacy. Using the medium of communication by which a philosophical argument is promulgated to discredit the argument would seem scarcely more justifiable than to dismiss the ontological argument for God's existence upon discovering that St Anselm or René Descartes had been *sub rosa* atheists. On the other hand, we are obliged to ask why Plato allowed such a contradiction to pass unregistered and unremarked in the dialogue. The hypothesis that Plato was unaware that he was writing as he was writing the *Phaedrus* is so absurd as not even to intrude upon the most insensitive critical work on the dialogue: furthermore, it would lead back into the long and scandalously lax presumption that the *Phaedrus* is a badly composed dialogue whose defects are to be explained by placing it among the first works of an inconceivably juvenile mind or at the close of the canon and the commencement of its author's senility. It is indeed greatly to the credit of 'Plato's Pharmacy' that Derrida puts these assumptions forever to rest, arguing for 'a rigorous, sure, and subtle form', for the magisterial poise of a demonstration which 'affirms itself and effaces itself at once, with suppleness, irony, and discretion' (PP, 67). To presume that Plato was aware of the aporia is not only consistent with what we always and everywhere experience as his genius as a philosopher and a writer, but also ensures the ever-invigorating, never exhausted provocations of this dialogue which can be read on so many sophisticated planes of irony, self-reflexivity and even – following Derrida – 'playfulness'. It also begins to explain why in the latter half of the twentieth century – which has simultaneously witnessed the collapse of grand narratives and a resurgence of interest in language and hermeneutics comparable only to the scholastic era – we take the aporetic situation of Plato's writing against writing so very seriously, perhaps more so than the establishment of the ideal commonwealth. The sophistications of the dialogue suggest a tension and a dynamism in the founding work of Western rationalism which elevates Plato's dilemma concerning the movement of culture from an oral to a written archive above the vacillations of his contemporaries. Like the minstrel Parmenides who was also a primordial syntactician, or the historical Socrates who defied the oral lifeworld of the poets via an unwavering commitment to oral methods, or Alcidamas and Isocrates who both denounced writing in the medium of writing, Plato's discourse might otherwise seem to be but one amongst many in its ambivalences at this crossing.[5] The contradiction resonates because it was

---

[5] Plato's work is by no means alone in its self-contradiction at this cultural juncture: indeed, 'writing against writing' became almost a 'mini-genre' as the *tekhnē* of writing became incorporated at the highest level into Athenian culture. Though the figure of Janus could look on the past and future with equipoise, the rhetors and philosophers of classical Greece were discomposed at the threshold between the tradition of the spoken word and the prospect of a culture of writing. Gorgias, Acidamas and Isocrates all extolled living speech in writing (see R. P. Sprague, ed., *The Older Sophists*, Columbia: University of South Carolina Press, 1972). Whether of authentic Platonic authorship or not – the latter being more likely – the *Second Letter* certainly represents the cultural and intellectual anxieties of the transition which Socrates expressed in the *agora*, and Plato represented in his acts of transcription and dialogic 'authorship'. Like the discussion itself, literature on the authenticity of the Platonic letters is expansive. Nineteenth-century scholarship typically assumed the letters to be forgeries *tout court*. Wilamowitz-Moellendorff upset this consensus by declaring the *Seventh* and *Eighth Letters* to be genuine, and early in the twentieth century Hackforth's discriminations served to orient the debate in the English-speaking world as follows: 'we may hold five of the Platonic epistles genuine, viz., iii, iv, vii, viii, xiii . . . we must reject five, viz., i, ii, v, vi, xii . . . the remaining three, ix, x and xi, must be left doubtful.' R. Hackforth, *The Authorship of the Platonic Epistles* (Manchester: Manchester University Press, 1913), p. 188. Bluck provided a detailed survey of research in the first half of the twentieth century, which suggests widespread agreement that the *Seventh Letter* as genuine. Richard Stanley Harold Bluck, *Plato's Life and Thought* (London: Routledge & Kegan Paul, 1949). We will then, with qualification, invoke the *Seventh Letter* as genuine; recourse will be made to the *Second Letter* only in so far as it constitutes a pertinent cultural document rather than a constituent of the Platonic *oeuvre*. For a relatively recent formulation of the case against including the *Seventh Letter* in the Platonic canon, see Ludwig Edelstein, *Plato's Seventh Letter, Philosophia Antiqua* vol. XIV (Leiden: E. J. Brill, 1966), especially pp. 76–85, where the argument against authenticity is pursued in the specific context of the repudiation of writing. Quite the contrary argument can be found in Paul Friedländer, *Plato 1: An Introduction*, 3 vols, trans. Hans Meyerhoff (London: Routledge & Kegan Paul, 1958), pp. 236–45. Letters, of course, have a very different status from texts written with publicity in mind. Most letters are intended to remain in the semi-private sphere of an exchange restricted to two individuals: thus the sender of the *Second Letter* will instruct the receiver to interiorise the content but to destroy its visible remainder, the pages of the communication. A text written from publication which descries writing is clearly in considerably greater contradiction than a letter which disowns writing on the grounds of its tendency to promote unmonitored circulation and perdurance; thus we could not hold that the author of the *Second Letter* is in contradiction to any comparable extent to the author of the *Phaedrus*. For related but somewhat different reasons, Isocrates is not strictly in an aporetic situation when he writes to Philip: 'I do not fail to realize what a great difference there is in persuasiveness between discourses which are spoken and those which are to be read, and that all men have assumed that the former are delivered on subjects which important and urgent while the latter are composed for display and personal gain. And this is a natural conclusion; for when a discourse is robbed of the prestige of the speaker, the tones of his voice, the variations which are made in the delivery, and, besides, of the

the one by which the founder of Western metaphysics refused to find himself constrained. It is therefore an issue of signature, of authority and of *oeuvre*. For many, too – no less for a traditional commentator such as Paul Friedländer than for a Derrida or Havelock – this contest between two modes of communication has become the question of philosophy's coming-into-being, the tension through which the dominant categories of our thought evolved.[6]

Once opened, virtually all who confront the aporia seek to resolve its tension. Even Derrida, whose work flourishes in its relentless patience with such aporia, and who insists upon the banality of the aporia (PP, 112), moves in 'Plato's Pharmacy' towards a resolution which makes good its promise at the outset that 'the *Phaedrus* . . . in its own writing, plays at saving writing' (PP, 67). At other extremes, Diogenes Laertius explains away the contradiction by consigning the dialogue to Plato's juvenilia, whereas an early twentieth-century theory assumed it was produced in dementia. There is even a neo-Platonist treatise which fancifully declares that Plato was imitating the deity in providing two writings, that which is unwritten (the Book of Nature) and that which is written (the Books of Scriptures).[7] Many philosophers and Platonic commentators have even resorted to the feeble strategy of calling on our gratitude that Plato bypassed his qualms about the propriety of writing, that he proceeded to write his dialogues anyway and via the injunction *tua res agitur*.[8] Still

---

Footnote 5 (*cont.*)

   advantages of timeliness and keen interest in the subject matter; when it has not a single accessory to support its contentions and enforce its plea, but is deserted and stripped of all the aids which I have mentioned; and when someone reads it aloud without persuasiveness and without putting any personal feeling into it, but as though he were repeating a table of figures – in these circumstances it is natural, I think, that it should make an indifferent impression upon its hearers. And these are the very circumstances which may detract most seriously also from the discourse which is not presented to you and cause it to impress you as a very indifferent performance . . .' Isocrates, 'Letter to Philip', trans. George Norlin in *Isocrates I*, Loeb Classical Library (London: William Heinemann Ltd, 1928), pp. 262–3.

[6] 'Addressing others through his written work, words alone – even the clearest and most glowing words – would have seemed to him ineffective without the living embodiment . . . Thus he must have made Socrates the most powerful force in his written work because he could not in any other way determine the necessary relationship between "speaker" and "discourse"; because it seemed to him that only in this way could education and struggle, research and construction, festival and death, in short "philosophy" become audible.' Friedländer, *Plato 1: An Introduction*, p. 132.

[7] 'A Neoplatonic treatise refers to the aporetic dilemma presented by the fact that while the master in the *Phaedrus* spoke so disparagingly about writing, he still considered his own works as worthy of being written down. As a solution, it is proposed that he also tried to follow the deity in this respect. Just as the deity created both the invisible and what is visible to our senses, so he, too, wrote down many things and transmitted other unwritten' (ibid., 124). The 'solution' is fanciful to say the least.

[8] A thoughtful manner of negotiating this contradiction is provided by Rowe: 'the treatment of writing is presented in the context of what is, in dramatic terms, a *conversation* – and a conversation, moreover, which at least since the end of Socrates' second speech seems to have been a perfectly

others will see here the contest between poet and philosopher in Plato, between *muthos* and *logos* in his discourse, or between Solon and Socrates in his psyche. As would be expected, the category of irony is often used to domesticate the aporetic situation. One can imagine that the *Phaedrus* is presenting itself in meta-theatrical terms by having Socrates speak out against Plato's betrayal of the oral method in a delicate moment of self-ironising on Plato's part: the same constellation, however, can also recommend readings which tend to psychoanalyse Plato in terms of his guilt in betraying the Socratic *ethos*, a tendency which can be discerned in even the most respectful readings, such as Derrida's, which sees Plato as writing 'out of Socrates' death' and thereby involved in a double parricide involving both Socrates and the primal fatherhood of Parmenides (*Sophist*, 241d–242a; PP, 163–4).[9]

The most radical proponents of the quasi-solutions offered by ironic readings will see the emphasis on writing-as-play as a further play on Plato's part in which his own repudiation of writing is to be seen as pastime, as non-serious; a reading which gains some support from the light, teasing and ludic quality of many of the exchanges between Socrates and Phaedrus and the atmosphere of festivity which pervades the dialogue. Further ironising possibilities are realised by the complexities of the Platonic/Socratic signature, the set of Socratic statements being at most a subset of the corpus of Platonic convictions: such a resolution has been attempted but must founder if one is to accept the authenticity of the *Seventh Letter* and more deeply still if the caveats of the *Second Letter* are admitted into the *oeuvre*. More interestingly, if one accepts the relative posteriority of the *Phaedrus*, one can see the irony in historical terms, as the dialectician ventriloquising his own justified anxieties concerning the Academy's neo-Pythagorean misreadings of his work, a process which

respectable example of dialectic in action. On this basis we might want to argue that the *Phaedrus* itself, or part of it, will be exempted from Socrates' criticisms and if the *Phaedrus*, why not other dialogues too, in so far as they illustrate the principles of dialectic? But the failings identified in the written composition in general – that it always says the same thing, and cannot answer questions or defend itself – seems to belong no less to the written dialogue. If it may possess internal movement of a kind, it still remains statuesquely silent in relation to the reader. Some small confirmation that this is also Plato's view on the matter is provided by the fact that at the end he makes Socrates describe the discussion of speech and writing too as having been an "amusement", the very term he has just associated with writing (278b). But more importantly, this is how the *Phaedrus* as a whole clearly reads . . . the dialogue illustrates its own theory of writing as play, just as Socrates' second speech, within the dramatic context itself, illustrates the same theory as extended to cover the set rhetorical piece.' C. J. Rowe, *Plato: Phaedrus* (Warminster: Aris & Phillips, 1986).

[9] In fact, Derrida invokes the enthralling picture of a double parricide, 'a violent eruption against the venerable paternal figure of Parmenides' and of a writing which may be taken as 'written *from out of the death of Socrates*' (PP, 163).

had begun during Plato's own lifetime. Others will seek to heal the breach by claiming that one cannot pronounce against writing without having written, without having known what it is to write. Just as only one who has imitated can grasp the difference between a Form and the copy of a Form, so only a devotee who has also been a logographer is placed to assert the superiority of the oral procedure.

One might also contend, with some reason, that Plato could not in principle, as in practice, promote dialectic as a changeless discourse, even if words were not like flux in their attempt at grasping the eternal world of being: on such an argument Plato's greatest reservation about writing would be that its very immobility, its durability, might provide a grotesque parody of the immutable realm of *eidos*. Thus, while Plato willed Socratism, dialectic and the whole inexhaustible and immense achievement to survive, he did not wish it to perdure in a form that forbade accountability, question and answer. Inside the dialogues, then, within the frames – but not in the controlling, editing, selecting, in the logography through which they have been entombed – is represented the fluidity, the essence of *logos-zōon*, the animation by which these Athenian exchanges might be ideally and endlessly renewed as plasticity, as ongoing process.[10] On such a reading, the act of writing dialogues, like all art for Oscar Wilde, is a lie against time but one which somehow grasps at a truth beyond time. Such a reading may take succour from the *Republic* in so far as the critique of imitation proceeds from someone who produces both the works themselves and their copies (*Republic*, 597e). As Friedländer inclines, invoking the *epekeina tês ousias* central to the highest metaphysical aims of the *Republic*:

> we are perhaps not entirely untrue to his spirit if we interpret, in a preliminary way, the meaning of his written work according to the model of the world of appearances, which, to be sure, is only a *copy* of the eternal forms, but a copy of *eternal forms*, though afflicted with all the limitations of transitory existence, yet, to the eye which has learned to see, pointing toward eternal being and toward what is beyond being.[11]

In a somewhat similar spirit, a mimetic gambit is possible. The dialogic form is preserved in the form of a conversation: it thereby duplicates the image of the living word, of question and answer, of the crucial Platonic concept of knowledge as processual, as the ever-moving, ever-renewing

---

[10] For a splendid 'defence' of the written yet ever mobile, dialogic and ascending circles of knowledge to be derived from the *Phaedrus*, see Robert Cushman, *Therapeia: Plato's Conception of Philosophy* (Chapel Hill, NC: University of North Carolina Press, 1958).

[11] Friedländer, *Plato I*, pp. 124–5.

exchange between the sincere souls of the master and the *ephebe* in pursuit of *alētheia*. This would be an argument of the early Gadamer, who stressed that Plato's dialogues should be read as actual speech situations, discussions in which each of the participants has concerns and beliefs peculiar to him-or-herself. For Gadamer, any reading which seeks to detach dialogic statements from their illocutionary and perlocutionary contexts fails to embrace the quality of those statements themselves: 'it does not seem at all reasonable to me to study Plato primarily with an eye to logical consistency . . . [t]he real task can only be to activate for ourselves wholes of meaning, contexts within which a discussion moves – even when its logic offends us'.[12] However, such arguments run aground on the fact that the contradiction, like writing in its unchanging, unresponsive words, remains as long as the dialogues *remain*, even should they do so as dramatic illustrations of the living process of dialogic exchange, of knowledge as process. And not only do the dialogues remain, but as drama they play themselves again in a strangely static, unresponsive and statuesque form, in the very image of ancestral silence, in the monumental immobility of the painted work via which Plato's Socrates launches against writing one of his many arguments by analogy.[13] One might indeed proceed more carefully by disclaiming the necessity of mimetic consistency between message and medium: we would scarcely, to take an extreme example, condemn an equation in physics for failing to move in the manner it describes. A discourse is not invalidated for failing to perform what it recommends and we might hear Socrates with a different ear, as he speaks out of the dialogues, in a protreptic key. We could then take his words in the *Phaedrus* as a *prooimion* to a social practice of discourse which would happen in society as it had in that *elenchus* of the marketplace practised by the historical Socrates.

Worthy and enlightening as they are, all approaches of this sort deal only with the performative contradiction in Plato's discourses on writing. The fact that the *Phaedrus* and the *Letters* use the very medium they disown obscures the subtlety of the case against inscription; a case which, quite apart from being inscribed itself, does not outlaw or repudiate writing as such.[14] Such readings do not take account of the more fruitful

---

[12] Hans Georg Gadamer, *Dialogue and Dialectic: Eight Hermeneutical Studies on Plato*, trans. P. Christopher Smith (New Haven, CT and London: Yale University Press, 1980, p. 5).

[13] Similarly, in a less lofty analogy, Socrates will call into account the unresponsive nature of poets by comparing their 'answers' to those of a bell which, when struck, reproduces the same sound (*Protagoras*, 329a).

[14] Acknowledging that he owes much to the work of Cushman, Fish nevertheless provides the most articulate and succinct arguments for the harmonisation of written form and dialectical

contradictions which are of a thematic or philosophical nature; to wit, the disjunction within the Platonic *oeuvre* by which Plato will write against writing in the *Phaedrus* and *Letters* II and VII, but will pronounce emphatically in favour of writing as he elaborates the theories and prescriptions of his *Laws*. This contradiction will underlie the proposed argument that Plato's ideas about speech and writing form twin aspects of a consistent ethical programme which has little to do with either the *phonē* or inscription as such. Along the way we will occasionally reopen the aporia, particularly when deeper subtleties and layers of textual significance in the *Phaedrus* come into view. We will also address the issue of writing against writing in terms of the ironic distance opened between Plato as author and Socrates as protagonist or when other aspects of what is traditionally called 'the Socratic problem' bear upon the argument. Naturally, the 'contradiction' will also be given new life in the curious figure of the 'aporia within the aporia' (which we will explore in a forthcoming fraternal work) whereby Levinas extols the writing against writing of the *Phaedrus* (274b–277a) in his own writing against writing, and does so not to guard against the dangers of inscription but for unmediated, face-to-face communication as the model for a transcendent ethics of discourse.

Whilst the two readings we will interleave do not take an ethical stance on Plato's ideas on speech and writing, they succeed in raising the issue to an unprecedented level of dignity and attention in the history of philosophy. Published within six years of each other, Havelock's *Preface to Plato* and 'Plato's Pharmacy' construe the speech/writing issue in terms of an immense Platonic *agon* whose aims are no less than control of the *epistēmē*, of the future of knowledge and discourse itself. Havelock reads Plato (through the *Republic*) as a champion of the techniques of abstract reflection promoted by the interiorisation of the word, while Derrida follows the *Phaedrus* in his complexity of its attempts to uphold the idea of self-presence embodied in the dialectical *logos*. For Derrida this inaugural logocentric argument is read as 'philosophy played out in the play between two kinds of writing' in spite of the fact that 'all it wanted to do was to distinguish between writing and speech' (PP, 149). Both readings

Footnote 14 (*cont.*)

   imperative: 'To read the *Phaedrus* is . . . to use it up; for the value of any point in it is that it gets *you* (not any sustained argument) to the next point, which is not so much a point (in logical demonstrative terms) as a level of insight. It is thus a self-consuming artificactm a mimetic enactment in the reader's experience of the Platonic ladder in which each rung, as it is negotiated, is kicked away.' Stanley Fish, *Self-Consuming Artifacts: The Experience of Seventeenth-Century Literature* (Los Angeles and London: University of California Press, 1972), p. 13. However, what is true of the *Phaedrus* is certainly not the case with the *Republic*, and it on this contradiction or hinge that our argument concerning the ethics of Platonic writing commences.

resolve the aporia according to complementary radicalisms which have contrary starting points. We might, for more than convenience, schematise their relation as (i) Plato's attempt to uphold speech as *logos* in the birth of philosophy (Derrida); and (ii) *logos* upheld as interiorised writing in philosophy's agonistic emergence from the oral life-world (Havelock). Derrida's argument elegantly displaces the aporia by seeing Plato's distinction between the *logos-zōon* of speech and the abandoned trace of inscription as the distinction between two writings: the 'good' writing of dialectics on the one hand, and the 'bad' writing of lifeless inscription, *sungrammata*, on the other (PP, 149). As Derrida says: 'the *Phaedrus* is less a condemnation of writing in the name of present speech than a preference for one sort of writing over another, for the fertile trace over the sterile trace . . .' (PP, 149). Furthermore, while Derrida's position leaves no room for Plato's antagonism with the oral lifeworld of memorised poetry (and indeed, on one reading at least, 'Plato's Pharmacy' can be construed as the latest in a long, distinguished and ever more convoluted lineage of defences of poetry), Havelock's insistence that the science of dialectic is allied with writing forces him to avoid the denunciations of writing altogether.

Both Havelock and Derrida affirm the speech/writing issue as the founding of the *epistēmē*: Derrida's argument is metaphysical; Havelock's argument is epistemological – patterns of supplementarity as well as those of conflict open up between them. However, where Derrida argues for Plato as a self-undoing champion of orality, of the spoken *logos*, Havelock sees Plato as the beneficiary, often unwitting, of the science of writing: while Plato understands *logos* as animate and self-present, on Derrida's reading dialectics understands *logos* as abstraction from presence, immediacy according to Havelock.[15] Both also postulate blindness on Plato's part to the significance of writing: Derrida sees Plato as unaware that dialectic is a super-sophisticated form or ruse of writing; Havelock sees Socrates (if not Plato) as blind to the chirographic origins of the new techniques of detached reflection which made dialectic possible. Derrida shows himself keenly aware that writing is aligned with morality, mores

---

[15] For Havelock, *logos* is rational detachment; it is not animate but rather renders objects to refection. Derrida, on the other hand, reflects that Plato wishes to establish *logos* as pure, integrated, creatural vitality: '*Logos*, a living animate creature, is thus also an organism that has been engendered. An organism: a differentiated body proper, with a centre and extremities, joints, head, and feet. In order to be "proper", a written discourse ought to submit to the laws of life just as a living discourse does' (PP, 79). It is tempting, though oversimplifying, to suggest that the difference between these constructions of what Plato denoted by *logos* is that between the *Republic* of Havelock and the *Phaedrus* of Derrida.

and the social order (PP, 74), but the mission he sets himself is to track the *Phaedrus* in the mythic, anthropomorphic and familial metaphors by which the emergence of philosophy as *logos* establishes itself. For Havelock, philosophical ethics (as reflection on mores, customs, duties, as distinct from and bringing into being 'applied ethics'), only became possible when writing disencumbered culture from memorising ethical content, thus allowing abstract reflection on the ethical as such. However, ethics in this sense became possible only as one category of thought amongst so many others, on Havelock's thesis, and his attention is given to the epistemological revolution brought about by the technology of the preserved word, rather than its ethical consequences. In arguing a path between these two positions, the burden of this argument will be to demonstrate that Plato is not hostile to speech or writing *per se*, nor is his discourse *allied* – at a conscious or unconscious level – with the virtues of either medium. What follows will therefore attempt to restore the ethical, which is also to say, the prosaic.

Our argument in the next section follows a simple critical and revisionary trajectory in seeking to amplify the ethical inclinations of *Preface to Plato* whilst cancelling the epic, narrative cast in which they are presented. We will also call into question the probity of a thesis on speech and writing which neither addresses the *Phaedrus* nor locates itself in relation to the philosophy of language whilst defending the central claim that the evolution of a written archive was a necessary if insufficient condition of the subjective detachment from newly apprehended 'objects' of knowledge which characterises Western rationalism. Similarly, though less critically, we will follow 'Plato's Pharmacy' in its scrupulous attention to the textual intricacies and the play of hitherto unrecognised philosophemes in the *Phaedrus*, whilst emphasising an ethical drive beneath the metaphysical determinations of the dialogue. That this ethicised reading of writing's status of remaining was suggested by *The Ear of the Other* (in which the *Phaedrus* goes unmentioned) and 'Signature, Event, Context' is both beside and very much to the point in the sense that we are not proposing any assessment of Derrida's work, but rather taking our bearings from certain aspects of that immense *oeuvre* whose horizons are perhaps today only just beginning to present themselves to our comprehension.[16]

---

[16] Derrida may have presumed this connection so obvious as not to warrant mention. On the other hand, he may well have wished to confine his discussion of the dangers of writing remaining within the specific context of the case of Nietzsche, thus discouraging any revisitation of the general question of writing. 'Otobiographies', let us not forget, was given as a paper which was to launch 'Roundtable' discussions on autobiography and translation.

Against Havelock's suppression of the *Phaedrus* (in its ostensible contradiction with *Preface to Plato*'s thesis that the cultural assimilation of writing made the Socratic and Platonic revolution possible), we contend that the contradiction should be strenuously confronted, both as a matter of intellectual integrity and because the anti-oralist case as applied to the poets is ultimately compatible at an ethical level with the discussion of the dangers of written discourses, and writing *per se*. We will then continue to steer an ethical middle ground between the (on our view) overstated metaphysical orientations of the otherwise extraordinarily intense 'Plato's Pharmacy' and the thought-provoking but insecure epistemological claims of *Preface to Plato*.

In making this clearing however, it will be necessary to detach the claims of Havelock's technological hypothesis from the grand narrative in which it is artfully presented. This will involve demonstrating, in the first instance, that Havelock's epic story of the victory of logical Socratism over the older tragic and Homeric lifeworld of ancient Greece is a retelling of *The Birth of Tragedy* for an era preoccupied with the question of language. Just as Nietzsche's first work made an incalculably greater contribution to the literary and artistic culture of the early twentieth century than it did to either aesthetics or classical studies, so *Preface to Plato* belongs alongside the great genetic histories of early modernity. As we will argue, *The Birth of Tragedy* and *Preface to Plato* both tell the story of the origins of poetic and cognitive language without considering the paradoxical assumption that language can relate its own origins. The Havelockian revision consists in putting language in the foreground of his genetic history but in such a way as to propel rather than inhibit narrative dynamics. Where the overtly mythopoeic aims of modernism tended to appropriate the Nietzschean mythology in terms of psychic structures, Havelock has reconfigured one and the same myth in a manner superficially tempered by the linguistic turn. Within a postmodern world which, following Adorno and Lyotard, has rejected the aestheticisation of history and genetic narratives, Havelock created the space for a post-war myth of origins whereby the *agon* between rationalism and irrationality can renew itself as a contest of communicative media. What this says for the fortunes of the orality–literacy debate remains unclear, but from the point of view of aesthetics and literary theory, Havelock's ingenious, forever productive, narratively brilliant, pedagogically indispensable but ultimately depthless revisionism demonstrates the impoverishing effect of superimposing linguistic terms onto categories initially developed in the realm of consciousness while those categories are not offered to sustained

interrogation. So far from taking analysis deeper into problems of signi-
fication, meaning and reference, the technological hypothesis serves to
bypass complexities raised in literary theory and the philosophy of language. The oralist position, this work will contend, is a short-cut to thinking about language and an (albeit beguiling) eclecticism which buries
epistemological questions under a welter of historical, anthropological
and psychological speculation. For this reason, *Preface to Plato* belongs
more to the beginning than to the end of modernity. When one further
considers that Nietzsche's myth of the origins of logical consciousness
replays oppositions formulated by the German Idealists, then Havelock's
hypothesis reveals itself as a most belated romanticism, one which
owes more to the old opposition between the sensuous and the intelligible than to the twentieth-century linguistic turn.[17] This is not to say that
Havelock's theory is without significance to contemporary thought, but
that its significance depends on our overestimation of 'the somewhat
trivial opposition of speech and writing' to the history, ethos and objects
of philosophy.[18] Stripped of its enchantments, patiently 'declared', as it
were, we will attempt to demonstrate, Havelock's work enlightens the
dialogue on writing even as his work on Platonic writing writes the
Phaedrus out of its history and his story.

II: THE BIRTH OF PHILOSOPHY OUT
OF THE SPIRIT OF WRITING

> . . . if the poet should conceal himself nowhere, then his
> entire poeticizing and narration would have been accom-
> plished without imitation. And lest you may say again that
> you don't understand, I will explain to you how this would
> be done. If Homer, after telling us that Chryses came with
> the ransom of his daughter and as a supplicant of the
> Achaeans but chiefly of the kings, had gone on speaking not
> as if made or being Chryses but still as Homer, you are aware
> that it would not be imitation but narration, pure and simple.
> It would have been somewhat in this wise. I will state it
> without metre for I am not a poet. The priest came and
> prayed that to them the gods should grant to take Troy and
> come safely home, but that they should accept the ransom
> and release his daughter, out of reverence for the god and
> when he had thus spoken the others were of reverent mind
> and approved, but Agamemnon was angry and bade him

---

[17] Bowie, for example, argues that *The Birth of Tragedy* retrogresses from the insights of the Idealist
and Romantic philosophers. See Bowie, *Aesthetics and Subjectivity*, pp. 219–27.
[18] Jacques Derrida, *Points . . .: Interviews, 1974–1994*, ed. Elisabeth Weber, trans. Peggy Kamuf et al.
(Stanford, CA: Stanford University Press, 1995), p. 198.

> depart and not come again lest the sceptre and the fillets of
> the god should not avail him. And ere his daughter should be
> released, he said, she would grow old in Argos with himself,
> and he ordered him to be off and not vex him if he wished
> to get home safe. And the old man on hearing this was fright-
> ened and departed in silence, and having gone apart from the
> camp he prayed at length to Apollo, invoking the appellations
> of the god, and reminding him of and asking requital for any
> of his gifts that had found favour whether in the building of
> temples or the sacrifice of victims. In return for these things
> he prayed that the Achaeans should suffer for his tears by the
> god's shafts.
>   It is in this way, my dear fellow, I said, that without imita-
> tion simple narration results. (*Republic*, 393c–394b)

The exquisitely concise 'Funes the Memorius' – narrated in just over
seven pages – and the insistently pedagogic *Preface to Plato* are both mir-
acles of twentieth-century storytelling. Composed astride two decades,
both works betray the inspiration of Nietzsche's *On the Advantage and
Disadvantages of History for Life*, in particular the extraordinarily beautiful passage in which he evokes the overwhelming flux within which the
pre-conceptual mind must have been immersed (ADL, 10).[19] Borges's
'Funes' is incapable of forgetting: he cannot gather a species under a
genus, an experience under a concept. He was, as Borges – curiously
placing himself by a narratological as well as authorial signature – writes,
'almost incapable of ideas of a general Platonic sort'. Hence, he is incapable of imposing a subjective order upon the immense, indeed acutely
intense, variegation of everyday life, cannot recognise himself as a
subject in relation to an object of knowledge. All of which is to say that
Funes can never become a 'self' in the modern sense of this reductive
but psychological and existential 'concept'. Rather, poor, ever-assailed
and pre-mathematical, 'Funes' is a site of innumerable and entirely
unconnected events (here one might perceive, in Borges's story, a further
influence, that of David Hume, who argued what a Heraclitean frag-
ment implied, that the self is but a 'consecution of sensations').[20] Not
only was it difficult for Funes 'to comprehend that the generic symbol

---

[19] This connection between Borges's 'Funes', Havelock's depiction of the preliterate mind and the
Nietzschean precedent is made by Edmundson in a work which is generally pertinent to the ethics
of writing considered under a generic aspect. See Mark Edmundson, *Literature Against Philosophy,
Plato to Derrida: A Defence of Poetry* (New York: Cambridge University Press, 1995).

[20] We say pre-mathematical, but Funes may indeed have been no less disabling supra-arithmetical:
'In place of seven thousand thirteen, he would say (for example) *Máximo Pérez*; in place of seven
thousand fourteen, *The Railroad*; other numbers were *Luis Melián Lafinur, Olimar, sulphur, the reins,*

dog embraces so many diverse individuals of diverse size and form: it bothered him that the dog at three fourteen (seen from the side) should have the same name as the dog at three fifteen (seen from the front)'. Still more disturbing is his inability to recognise 'Funes' as denoting the continuity of a psychological or spiritual identity. He cannot comprehend the most rudimentary sense of a bodily continuity: 'His own face in the mirror, his own hands, surprised him every time he saw them . . .' In relation to 'the self', his condition produces, in inverted aetiology (i.e. total recall as opposed to the desuetude and eventual disappearance of recall), the tragic condition of Alzheimer's disease. With typical, indeed singular economy and inimitable fluency, the story encapsulates the notion that the abstraction made possible by philosophical reflection is the *sine qua non* of the notion of selfhood, even should the latter be Apollonian illusion, or the great Humean fiction of Western philosophy. 'To think is to forget differences, generalise, make abstractions. In the teeming world of Funes, there were only details, almost immediate in their presence.'[21]

Havelock, on the other hand, presents his tale as classical history, philological discovery and philosophical dissertation. Over some 300 intensely readable pages, he argues that the pre-literate intelligence was denied the possibility of abstract reflection because the finest minds of the culture were necessarily charged to memorising the cultural archive, especially as expressed in the Homeric and Hesiodic epics. The majestic, but questionably scholarly scope of his project, we shall argue, derives from the acknowledged debt to Milman Parry's brilliant scholarly case that Homeric poetry was not the product of singular authorship, that the two great epics were memorised generation by generation and that successors added culturally significant moments within the narrative templates.[22]

Footnote 20 (*cont.*)

> the whale, the gas, the cauldron . . . In place of five hundred he would say *nine* . . . I tried to explain to him that his rhapsody of incoherent terms was precisely the opposite of a sequence of numbers. I told him that saying 365 meant saying three hundreds, six tens, and five ones, an analysis which is not found in the numbers, *The Negro Timoteo* or *meat blanket*. Funes did not understand me, or pretended not to understand me.' Jorge Luis Borges, 'Funes the Memorious', trans. James E. Irby, in Jorge Luis Borges, *Labyrinths*, pp. 87–95: pp. 93–4. Furthermore, Hume's theoretical proposition that what we call a self is a mere consecution of sensations is, for Borges's imagined Funes, a lived experience: 'it bothered him that the dog at three fourteen (seen from the side) should have the same name as the dog at three fifteen (seen from the front). His own face in the mirror, his hands, surprised him every time he saw them' (ibid., pp. 93–4).

21 All the above citations are from ibid., pp. 93–4.

22 All participants in the oralist debate acknowledge a debt to Milman Parry's brilliant and scholarly case that Homeric poetry was not the product of singular authorship, but that the two great epics were memorised generation-by-generation and that successors added culturally significant moments within the narrative templates. Cf. Milman Parry, *l'Epithète traditionelle dans Homère*

Parry's realisation was forged through his dual realisation that the poems exhibited overwhelmingly more preliterate mnemonic devices than are to be found in any work of unquestionably graphic authorship. In a culture which has readapted itself to the *tekhnē* of writing – much as we have adapted to the computerised, hypertextual and digital requirements of the previous decades – the nature of the work produced is evidence that the writer had proceeded in the unchecked security of a mental concept translating (with relative ease and without the mediation of the voice) to a written sign. The initiator(s) of the *Iliad* and *Odyssey* – 'Homer' as we denote this 'individual'[23] – worked intensely under the pressures and necessity of memorisation. The oral preservation of the work could only be ensured through recitation from an older to a gifted and considerably younger elite – from father (*patros*) to offspring (*ekgona*), master to *ephebe*, from sapient teacher to outstanding, ultra-receptive pupil. The inheritors of the epic works would be chosen not only for their capacity for attention and demonstrable comprehension of the ethics, ethos and necessity of retaining a cultural archive through and around dramatic narrative. Over many years – in the living present and 'face to face' – the belief of the elected inheritors of the oral tradition in the value of the

---

(Paris: Société d'Éditions 'Belle Lettres', 1928). Parry's work, as collected and collated by his son Adam, was published as *The Making of Homeric Verse: The Collected Papers of Milman Parry*, ed. Adam Parry (Oxford: Oxford University Press, 1970). Along with the daring work of Havelock and Walter J. Ong, SJ, this case was complemented by Alfred B. Lord, *The Singer of Tales* (Cambridge, MA: Harvard University Press, 1960). Lord's admirably succinct essay 'Homer, Parry and Huso', published in *AJA* 53 (1948), pp. 34–44, was doubtless an inspiration to an emergent generation of 'radical' classical scholars. Working within this tradition, whilst discovering a significant, distinctive voice, Havelock renders an entirely cogent reading of this return of Chryseis to her father's burial site (*Iliad*, 1: 15ff.: Plato's prosaic reduction of this epic moment is given in the long epigraph which opens this section). It functions, he argues convincingly and with transparent conviction, as a narrative device. Exploiting this irresistible theme of the return to a site of mourning, 'Homer' produced – with unrecoverable skill – an ironically enlivened and therefore memorable history of significant cultural practices and technological innovation: 'The most striking example as furnished in the first book of the *Iliad* is that of seamanship, a craft central to Greek civilisation at all periods. The poet's narrative is so composed that opportunity is provided for a safe voyage. The girl, if she is too restored to her father's shrine, must be transported on shipboard. This becomes the occasion for recapitulating some standardised operational procedures' (PtP, 81). The procedures for disembarkation, as itemised with strict fidelity to the *Iliad*, are described by Havelock as follows: 'First you reach harbour, second furl sail, third lower the mast, fourth row to the beach, fifth anchor the stern in deep water, sixth get out the (by the bow), seventh get the cargo out, eighth disembark the ship. This is how you dealt with any ship under given circumstances, not just Chryseis' ship . . . The bard is not governed by the economies of dramatic art as we understand the term. He is at once a storyteller and a tribal encyclopaedist' (PtP, 83). For the passage in the discussion see *Iliad*, 432ff; for the fuller account of Havelock's trenchant argument for the encyclopaedist impulse as expressed in the Homeric work, cf. PtP, 81–4.

[23] For a thorough account of the historical, scholarly and interpretative issues that surround this most curious of proper names, see Barbara Graziosi, *Inventing Homer: The Early Reception of Epic*, Cambridge Classical Studies (Cambridge: Cambridge University Press, 2002).

poetry thus preserved would be sternly tested. Thereby the elders would do their utmost to ensure generational continuity with particular attention to the sincerity with which the younger generation would guard against perversion of the mnemonically preserved word.[24]

In the pre-Socratic or tragic age of the Greeks, the elected *ephebe* would be expected to show a facility for esotericism as a safeguard against wilful and exploitative or ignorant misinterpretation. Required also would be a constant vigilance that utilised dramatic, memorable events in the works. Such moments would perforce be exploited as opportunities to interweave no less than one of the following: genealogical records, historical accounts, the reiteration of essential mores and rules of proper ethico-tribal conduct and the recounting of significant technological innovation. In terms of the latter, the recounting of shipbuilding and of the proper procedures of seamanship – a technological achievement of which pre-Socratic Greece was justifiably most proud – could not be threatened by cultural evanescence, consigned to the airwaves or left solely in the minds of the elders who might soon surrender to amnesia, senescence or death. This phenomenon is, of course, most (in)famously evinced by the Homeric catalogue of ships. Such evidence – supported convincingly from other sources – led to the realisation that the *Iliad* and the *Odyssey* were the work of multiple authorship, and that their composition was for the most part oral. The work was redacted, revised and ultimately inscribed many generations subsequent to its inspiration as 'finished form' (a relatively modern, idealistic and highly questionable notion most pronounced in the high aestheticism of modernity, as also in some of the founding principles of the New Criticism and earlier organicist approaches to the literary work). As with many of the Biblical texts, the process of initial (oral) composition, of memorisation, word-of-mouth transmission down the generations, of inscription, review and redaction would proceed over anything between 50 and 500 years (viz. the 'JEPD' formula for the evolution of Genesis).[25] The 'completion' of the work should with more accuracy be described as its inscription, the process of which would

---

[24] Isaiah will be considered at some length in the second volume of the present work in the context of Levinas's notion of the *oeuvre* as generosity reciprocated by radical ingratitude. Levinas's neglect of this work and his resistance to Biblical works of inspirational prophecy will be considered in the light of his privileging of the Mosaic works of commandment: traditional though such a hierarchy might be, Levinas's commitment to philosophical dialogism set beside his preference for Hebraic prescription will be used to open a reading of his often self-contradictory ethic of discourse.

[25] Literature on the historical fragmentation, co-authorship and redaction of the Bible is dizzyingly voluminous. A lucid discussion is provided in R. E. Friedman, *Who Wrote the Bible?* (London: Jonathan Cape, 1988).

doubtless involve modification, reorganisation and addition by the redactors/writers themselves. Hence the bewilderment, to a modern consciousness, of the shifts from narrative to catalogues of ships, etc. altogether analogous to the movements in Genesis and many other works of the Old Testament between myths and narratives of iconic and often entertaining cast. That the perennially engrossing story of Jacob wrestling with an angel so as to be renamed 'Israel', in the birth of a still most troubled nation, should conclude with the injunction that people of Jewish faith should abstain from eating meat from the inner thigh of the animal (Genesis 24: 24–32) remains entirely bizarre to a literate mindset: 'Therefore the children of Israel eat not of the sinew which shrank, which is on the hollow of the thigh: because he touched the hollow Jacob's thigh in the sinew that shrank' (Genesis 32: 32). A dietary injunction as the conclusion of a dream-like narrative cannot but strike the modern reader as peculiar in the extreme: similarly, the virtually unreadable Homeric records of navigational history or the Biblical genealogies, we must suppose, proved every bit as invaluable to an oral culture as they are unbearable to a modern 'literary' consciousness. The only question which outstands, and may do for all time, is whether the episodes of extreme beauty in the Homeric and Biblical pandects were motivated by the necessity of preserving cultural memory or whether the engrossing imaginative acts were later exploited as points at which the orally preserved history of the Greek and Hebraic worlds could be most effectively intercalated.

Only with the cultural assimilation of a written archive, actualised on Havelock's argument between its arrival as *tekhnē* in seventh-century BC Athens and the late fifth-century world of the Socratic interrogation and Platonic inscription, did the distinction between a subject and an object of knowledge become possible. Havelock's explanation of the Platonic case against poetic identification or immersion in the work, his connection of a culture dominated by *muthos* with one which redefined itself according to detached, rational reflection, at last begins to forge a pedagogic opening for a more positive reflection on *Republic*. Along such lines, one can begin at least to make the case for the separation of the aesthetic and cognitive under the sign and guidance of the ethical. Poetic identification, essentially liturgical in nature, precluded the emergence of science and its progenitor in the form of an anti-mythopoeic *logos*. The emergence of detached, proto-scientific reflection was, some twenty-five centuries ago, a boon rather than bane to the evolution of a society based on provisionally rational foundations. The restructuring of the social order

upon the detached intelligence rather than upon the poetic or thaumaturgical might convince, along with the idea that the separation of aesthetic experience into a relatively autonomous realm made art as
recreation preferable to poetry as politicisation. Rational individuation
rather than artistic participation comes to make sense as the culturally and
ethically *desideratum*. On ethical lines, the relative reassurances of logocentrism suit a harmonious society altogether better than the perpetual
an-archy of ritualistic immersion and thaumaturgy.

As invaluable to the opening of a reading as (we shall contend) it is catastrophic to its close, *Preface to Plato* nonetheless has a unique place in
any discussion of the ethics of writing in that its argument insists that
only with writing did ethical reflection come into being: the rhapsodic
world of ancient Greece kept alive the mores and practical precepts of
proper ethical conduct – much as did the commandments received by
Moses at Sinai – but only with the separation between subject and sign
that writing facilitates was the mind thus disencumbered to analyse the
underlying principles or philosophical status of ethics *qua* ethics or 'ethicity', to question rather than subordinately accept the strictures of nor-
mative ethics, to ask the epistemological and ethical question of ethics.
The significance of this cultural transformation which occurred betwixt
Socrates and Plato meant that an ethical *logos* entered into the Western
epistēmē for the first time. The ethics of writing thence was not even the
writing of ethics as such, but the graphic opening of ethics itself. Writing
is the non-epistemological opening of epistemology; the non-ethical
opening of ethics. The pre-literate mind could lay down ethical precepts,
Havelock argues, but never enquire into the 'ethics of ethics', meta-ethics
or ethicity. Even the joyous ethico-social reconciliation at the close of the
Eumenides and hence of the *Oresteia* of Aeschylus, one must assume, would
constitutes for Havelock a memorisable ethical moment rather a higher-
level ethical reflection.

Havelock's argument makes for the most elegant reading of Plato's
arguments against the poets and art generally. His explanation of Plato's
antipathy to identification with the work of art has something of the sat-
isfactory nature of the solution to the riddle of the Sphinx or Fermat's
Last Theorem. The imaginative leap captivates in its arresting simplicity.
An oralist culture obliges its finest minds to preserve tradition through
the colossal task of memorisation and reinforcement through regular, rit-
ualised performances of the Homeric epics. The evolution of a technology of inscription allowes for the development of a written, external
archive which frees the intellect from this colossal labour and allows for

critical reflection which was hitherto precluded by the impossibility of simultaneous memorisation and analysis. The incantatory, paeideutic spell lifts; philosophy, literary criticism and the revolutionary quest of *logos*, having become possible, are realised in Socrates and Plato when writing is fully interiorised within the Greek psyche. Accordingly, philosophy defines itself against the old, oralist, poetic lifeworld, which is now condemned as an ignorance, condemned as that of the mythic cave-dwellers who take illusory patterns for reality. The culture of Homeric and Dionysian Greece is enjoined to emerge from the darkness of oralist participation into the light of philosophical subjectivity or the intelligible sun. Quite literally the opposite of the ideals of organic unity, the injunction that we murder to dissect and the aestheticist notion that the acme of art is achieved when the reader, auditor or spectator experiences a feeling of absolutely 'oneness' with the work, Plato would have us maintain critical detachment from the artistic experience. The work becomes an object of knowledge; its recipient, the critical, sceptical subject; poetry, words on the page rather than enrapturing, musical experience. Rather than enter into any 'experience' of the artistic world, the responsible ethical subject scrutinises that world. The cultural assimilation of a written archive allows for the founding principle of philosophical, dialogic and dialectical epistemic: a subject is detached from an object of knowledge. In what follows we will find much to admire in Havelock's reading of the *Republic*, much to question in his ultimately counterintuitive suppression of the *Phaedrus*, and much to occasion scepticism in his presentation of Greek culture divided according to an asymmetry that comforts the author every bit as much as it would feign to discomfort the reader.[26] With regard to the latter, we encounter the notion of a 'world picture' which we will encounter time and time again. In a very different context, and as a poetic philosopher as dependent upon the notion of the rupture between a Socratic Greece and a preceding culture of hidden poetic wisdom, Heidegger is perfectly placed to observe this totalising notion, this dramatic and simplifying account of 'unity through division':

> The expressions 'world picture of the modern age' and 'modern world picture' both mean the same thing and both assume something

---

[26] The juncture between a pre-Socratic poetry and logical Socratism serves as a revolutionary place from which an extreme author can speak to his own times, its horizon and beyond. We will witness the exploitation of this transitional scene of voicing in Schiller, Schelling, Nietzsche, Heidegger and others in the succeeding work on Levinas and Derrida. On the theme of the return to the pre-Socratic, excellent orientations are provided in Alan Megill, *Prophets of Extremity: Nietzsche, Heidegger, Foucault, Derrida* (Berkeley and Los Angeles: University of California Press, 1985), especially pp. 1–25.

that never could have been before, namely, a medieval world picture and an ancient world picture. The world picture does not change from an earlier medieval one into a modern one, but rather the fact that the world becomes picture at all is what distinguishes the essence of the modern age.[27]

The logical extension of Heidegger's remark is that a picture of any world is impossible. Just as the modern age cannot stand outside its own horizons to capture its world picture, so too any attempt to envisage the medieval or ancient world involves a totalising operation alien to those worlds. Attempts to construct a world picture of ancient Greece have been recurrent in modernity and tend to assign generative power to certain oppositions which realise themselves in historical, philosophical and anthropological contexts. Such discourses are inevitably prey to recuperation as projections of their own cultural moment in so far as their generalising and generative ambitions leave problems of origin unresolved. Relying on diagetical, mythopoeic or dramatic force, they generally take the form of grand narratives in which 'history and interpretation coincide, the common principle that mediates between them being the genetic concept of totalisation'.[28]

Preface to Plato does not court any association with the Hegelian plotting of historical development, nor with the speculative, highly imaginative tradition which extents from German Idealism at least as far as to the Heideggerian (re)construction of early Greek thinking as a primordiality which contemporary thought should recapture. Rather it claims to belong within – even as it radicalises – a patient, scholarly succession, reaching as far back as Diels's search for the *ipsissima verba* of Greek literature, a quest that was paralleled in Biblical studies by Bultmann's form criticism.

Amongst its primary precursors, the text insists, are the works of Milman Parry on the oral provenance of Homeric verse and Nilsson's hypothesis that early Milesian publication was of an oral character. Such research, Havelock avows, was the wellspring of his groundbreaking theory that philosophy was born in the warfare between archaic orality and emergent literacy (PtP, vi–xi). In relation to that oralist-literalist tradition, Havelock's work has been revolutionary. From a quiet, unspeculative area of classical scholarship which sought to distinguish

---

[27] Martin Heidegger, *The Question Concerning Technology and Other Essays*, ed. and trans. William Lovitt (New York: Harper Row & 1977), p. 130.

[28] Paul de Man, 'Genesis and Genealogy (Nietzsche)' in his *Allegories of Reading: Figural Language in Rousseau, Nietzsche, Rilke and Proust* (New Haven, CT: Yale University Press, 1979), pp. 79–102: p. 81.

written from unwritten traditions, the orality–literacy debate has elevated itself into a theory which purports to explain the origins and structure of both poetry and rational consciousness. Although Walter Ong has said that '[t]here is no "school" of orality and literacy' and that '[k]nowledge of orality–literacy contrasts and relationships does not normally generate impassioned allegiances to theories', the last quarter of a century has witnessed an explosion of orality–literacy reinterpretations of the classical, medieval and Renaissance eras, many of which take a distinctly heuristic form.[29] Claims so far-reaching have been made for its cultural and intellectual influence that orality–literacy interpretation can recently take a curiously teleological and redemptive turn in proclaiming the oral dynamics of liturgy as 'the consummation of philosophy'.[30]

Though often disowned, Havelock's *Preface to Plato* has been the touchstone of this transformation. A prodigiously eclectic work, it draws on insights derived from philology, history, anthropology and psychology in its picture of a Greek society divided against itself. Havelock's theory also overlaps with literary theory and aesthetics and makes its own resonant contribution to the ancient quarrel between poetry and philosophy. This all-encompassing scope allied to a technological determinism gives Havelock's theory the cast of a grand narrative. Joseph Margolis, for one, remarks that Havelock's 'account belongs to the genre of nineteenth-century theories of social and cultural evolution'.[31]

This section scrutinises the seemingly unique relation of Havelock's work to both the preceding oralist tradition and to an era of theory which has treated grand narratives with vigilant scepticism. It also argues that the epic scope of *Preface to Plato* derives from the unacknowledged influence of Nietzsche's *The Birth of Tragedy*. The similarities between the two projects are clear and virtually schematic. Both works are dialectical in cast, forge imaginative and interdisciplinary syntheses, and identify Socrates as the figure in whom a cataclysmic break is made between poetic irrationalism and epistemological rationalism. The two texts exhibit a preference for grand generalisation over empirical or analytical precision and are enlivened by agonistic narrative, ventriloquism, performative prose and a novelistic gift for entering into the conflicted psyches of the major protagonists at the great turning point in the culture

---

[29] Walter J. Ong, *Orality and Literacy: The Technologizing of the Word* (London: Methuen, 1982), pp. 1–2.
[30] Cf. Catherine Pickstock, *After Writing: On the Liturgical Consummation of Philosophy* (Oxford: Blackwell, 1998).
[31] Joseph Margolis, 'The Emergence of Philosophy', in Kevin Robb ed., *Language and Thought in Early Greek Philosophy* (La Salle, IL: The Monist Library/The Hegeler Institute, 1989), pp. 228–43: p. 230.

of ancient Greece. Their reception histories also have arresting parallels: treated as disreputable within classical studies, they have been influential on adjacent discourses and have spoken eloquently to succeeding generations of literary theorists and aestheticians.

In retracing Havelock to Nietzsche, this phase of argument is not concerned with literary influence, or with proposing the young Nietzsche as an oralist *avant la lettre*. Rather, it argues that Havelock attempts – and fails – to revise the rudimentary Nietzschean dialectic in linguistic terms, and that this failure suggests the relative inadequacy of the technological thesis to the metaphysical and epistemological problems of language as addressed in the more sophisticated forms of literary theory. Beginning with an account of the logocentric impasse in which *The Birth of Tragedy* becomes mired, the section also shows how Havelock's determination to demythologise the traditional view of Greek culture succeeds only in generating its own contemporary myth of origins. More quietly, as the spectacular site of a non-reading, the suppressed *Phaedrus* comes, virtually of its own accord, to read the text on speech and writing from which it has been expelled.

Nietzsche's first major work was originally entitled *Socrates and Greek Tragedy* [*Socrates und die Griechische Tragödie*].[32] Many might think that this title does more justice to a text which is altogether stronger on tragedy's decline than its nativity. Nietzsche was to retain and revise the concept of the Dionysian, but rejected its interplay with the Apollonian as a belated variation on Schopenhauer's redescription of the perceived world at an intersection of *die Wille* and *die Vorstellung*. 'It should have *sung*, this "new soul" – and not spoken!' Nietzsche was later to exclaim, regretting that 'he obscured and spoiled Dionysian premonitions with Schopenhauerian formulations' (BT, 20; 24). Still later he declared that the book 'smells offensively Hegelian' (EH, 78). He could also have pointed to the influence of Schelling, Schiller, et al., on his dialectical construction of the Apollonian and Dionysian.[33]

Nevertheless, even when considered apart from its dialectical interplay with the Apollonian, the Dionysian can scarcely be recuperated as

---

[32] Friedrich Nietzsche, *Socrates und die Griechische Tragödie: Ursprüngliche Fassung der Geburt der Tragödie aus dem Geiste der Musik*, ed. H. J. Mette (Munich: Beck, 1933). Only when he added the panegyric to Wagner and the theme of cultural rebirth in Germany did Nietzsche adapt the title. All references will be made to Friedrich Nietzsche, *The Birth of Tragedy and The Case of Wagner*, trans. Walter Kaufmann (New York: Vintage Books, 1967) and are supplied parenthetically within the text with the abbreviation BT.

[33] See 'Attempt at a Self-Criticism' (BT, 17–27) and the chapter in *Ecce Homo* on *The Birth of Tragedy* (EH, 78–83).

a compelling category in this early presentation. Introduced as an aesthetic mode deriving from the non-imagistic art of music, it swiftly becomes the substratum of all experience, a pan-universal principle imbued with quasi-metaphysical and ontological status. Nietzsche invokes the Dionysian as an 'art impulse . . . of nature', which bursts 'forth from nature herself, without the mediation of the human artist . . . as intoxicated reality which . . . seeks to destroy the individual and redeem him by a mystic feeling of oneness' (BT, 38).

When Nietzsche comes to identify the counterforce that destroyed the healthy pessimism of tragic culture and identifies it as Socratism, we might expect the text to ground its thesis more securely. However, the work fails to find convincing or precise terms for this cultural shift: 'Dionysus had already been scared from the tragic stage, by a demonic power speaking through Euripides. Even Euripides was, in a sense, only a mask; the deity that spoke through him was . . . an altogether newborn demon, called *Socrates*' (BT, 82). Behind Euripides lies Socrates, behind the aesthetic reflection is the epistemological shift to rationalism. And yet Socrates will also show himself to be a mask: 'the enormous driving-wheel of logical Socratism is in motion, as it were, behind Socrates and . . . must be viewed through Socrates as through a shadow' (BT, 89). Even when Nietzsche warns that the text 'must not draw back before the question of what such a phenomenon as that of Socrates indicates' (BT, 92), he does so not to search for what lay behind the Socratic phenomenon but forward to contemplate the possibility of an aesthetic Socrates for nineteenth-century Germany. Just as the Dionysian has no *fons et origo*, so Nietzsche has no words for the force behind Socratism beyond saying that 'in its unbridled flood it displays a natural power such as we encounter to our awed amazement only in the very greatest instinctive forces' (BT, 88).

In this sense, the cultural thesis of *The Birth of Tragedy* comes very close to degenerating into prosopopoeia or a crude allegorical battle between the wildness of woods and the order of the city, between (in Schellingian spirit) the inebriated god and the sober Athenian. In order for the cultural thesis to be persuasive, Socratism must derive from more than Socrates: the rise of rationalism and the decline of tragedy must be explained by more than the accident of a man of genius arriving at a particular historical juncture. The text is prepared neither to follow transcendental arguments nor to confront the *regressus ad infinitum* of causes behind causes. To this extent, Nietzsche's text does not present us with a quest of origins of the force of the Rousseauian work and constitutes a slighter entry in the logocentric encyclopaedia. Despite its phonic bias,

The Birth of Tragedy avoids productive contradictions arising from an obsessive pursuit of origins. Rather, it forestalls the originary regression by means of whatever pseudo-conceptuality and ostensible closure might be embodied in the 'primordial'. Overwrought appeals to 'the primordial contradiction and primordial pain in the heart of the primal unity' (BT, 55) cover over the hollow that is presented as generative presence.[34]

Yet, despite its philosophical unintelligibility, *The Birth of Tragedy* is not a project that theory or aesthetics seems willing to disclaim outright.[35] The sense of a profound cultural contest between tragic *muthos* and Socratic *logos* remains palpable even though we can never be satisfied with the Dionysian as a principle *per se*, as a 'pure cry of primordial pain' or by a 'Socratism' which simply irrupts into Hellenic history like a Wagnerian 'nature force'. *The Birth of Tragedy* remains both spellbindingly close to revealing something 'essential' to Greek culture and yet unpersuasive. Nietzsche was certainly onto something, we feel, yet quite what that 'something' is, or what terms we might use to describe it, neither reader nor author seems able to discern. Paul de Man has suggested that a 'great deal of evidence points to the likelihood that Nietzsche might be in the grip of a powerful assumption about the nature of language', and certainly the question of language is implied in the text's recourse to articulation and the *principium individuationis*.[36]

The Dionysian is presented as an experience prior to both articulation and individuation: like music it is 'a sphere which is beyond and prior to all phenomena' (BT, 55). Thus, while music connects tragic drama to a chthonian, preverbal state of undifferentiated being, it also serves to halt the interrogation of origins. Melocentrism relieves the text of the need properly to work through its logocentric assumptions: '*language*, as the organ and symbol of phenomena, can never by any means disclose the innermost heart of music' (BT, 55). While the question of origins is displaced onto music, the generative assumptions the text makes about language can never be clarified. Nietzsche perhaps realised as much in amending the title to *The Birth of Tragedy, Or: Hellenism*

---

[34] Here Nietzsche's depiction of the Dionysian belongs altogether more with mystical appeals to the ineffable than to philosophical aesthetics or even a superficially coherent metaphysical scheme. In attempting to write of a time before time or an experience prior to individuated experience, he can only draw upon poetic and incantatory resources. 'The argument relies on an ontology of "creative natural powers" which Nietzsche claims can only function properly in a culture unified by mythology.' Andrew Bowie, *Aesthetics and Subjectivity from Kant to Nietzsche* (Manchester and New York: Manchester University Press, 1990), p. 225.

[35] Ibid., pp. 55–6; 82–3; 220–2.

[36] De Man, 'Genesis and Genealogy (Nietzsche)', p. 87.

and Pessimism.[37] In the 1886 'Attempt at a Self-Criticism' (appended to *The Birth of Tragedy* some fifteen years after its composition), he proclaimed that 'practically everything in this field remains to be discovered and dug up by philologists' (BT, 20). He could not have foreseen how literally the twentieth century would respond to this injunction. Nor could he anticipate that the problematic analogy drawn in *The Birth of Tragedy* between 'genetic movements in history and semiological relationships in language' would issue as the guiding but, on our argument, disorienting principle of an oralist-literalist theory of culture.[38]

III: DIONYSIAN ORALITY VERSUS SOCRATIC 'INSCRIPTION'

> . . . the Greeks, as long as we lack an answer to the question 'what is Dionysian?' remain as totally uncomprehended and unimaginable as ever. (BT, 20)
>
> Just as Parmenides . . . remained a minstrel attached to the oral tradition, yet defiantly struggling to achieve a set of non-poetic syntactical relations and an unpoetised vocabulary, so Socrates remains firmly embedded in oral methodology, never writing a word as far as we know, and exploiting the give and take of the market place, yet committing himself to a technique which, even if he did not know it, could only achieve itself completely in the written word and had indeed been brought to the edge of possibility by the existence of the written word. (PtP, 303)

Havelock sought to answer Nietzsche's question by combining a technological theory of language with discoveries made by classical scholars and philologists in the early part of the twentieth century. Without invoking Nietzsche by name, *Preface to Plato* explains the preverbal mystery of the Dionysian in terms of an oral synthesis. Nietzsche's 'community of unconscious actors' (BT, 64) evolved in response to a preliterate imperative to memorise significant moments in the history of Hellenic culture. *Mousike*, ecstatic participation and the dissolution of personal consciousness were essential components of a mimesis now taken as hypnotic and precritical. It is described in virtually identical terms by Havelock as 'identification by which the audience sympathises with the performance' (PtP, 159). Nietzsche had written of this phenomenon that in

> the Dionysian dithyramb man is incited to the greatest exaltation of all his symbolic faculties; something never before experienced

---

[37] Nietzsche determined on this title in the context of the second edition of 1886. More mundanely, the elimination of 'music' from the title may well be the consequence of his personal and intellectual alienation from Richard Wagner.

[38] De Man, 'Genesis and Genealogy (Nietzsche)', p. 102.

struggles for utterance – the annihilation of the veil of *màyà*, oneness
as the soul of the race and of nature itself. The essence of nature is
now to be expressed symbolically; we need a new world of symbols;
and the entire symbolism of the body is called into play, not the mere
symbolism of the lips, face and speech but the whole pantomime of
dancing, forcing every member into rhythmic movement. (BT, 40)

What Nietzsche said of the Dionysian dithyramb can be effortlessly trans-
posed to the propaedeutic spell cast by the minstrel upon his audience.
Hence Havelock:

[The minstrel] sank his personality in his performance. His audience
in turn would remember only as they entered effectively and sym-
pathetically into what he was saying and this in turn meant that they
became his servants and submitted to his spell. As they did this, they
engaged also in a re-enactment of the tradition with lips, larynx and
limbs, and with the whole apparatus of their unconscious nervous
system. The pattern of behaviour in artist and audience was therefore in some important respects identical. It can be described
mechanically as a continual repeating of rhythmic doings. (PtP, 160)

Such moments of blithe, almost guileless rewriting abound in *Preface to
Plato* and could be adduced to call into question the supposed originality of Havelock's thesis. The role of Attic tragedy in reconciling the community to itself, to nature and the cultural past could with stronger
reason be asserted of Homeric epic when the latter is comprehended as
a tribal encyclopaedia, a repository of historical deeds, mores and practical wisdom. Likewise, the Socratic counterforce (which Nietzsche identified but failed to conceptualise) can be redescribed in the technological
context with no greater demand upon Havelock than that he rephrase
The Birth of Tragedy to present the divisive event that was logical Socratism
as the product of the remodelling of the Greek psyche consequent upon
the noetic assimilation of writing. The dramatic story of the ancient
quarrel between poetry and philosophy can be retold by simply placing
the concepts of oralism and literacy behind the mythicised antagonists
'Dionysus' and 'Socrates'. Nietzsche was correct to divine a Socrates who
regarded tragedy as 'unreasonable, full of causes apparently without
effects, and effects apparently without causes' (BT, 89), but lacked the
terms to retrace this hostility to the separation of a subject from an
object of knowledge consequent upon widespread literacy. Nor was he
placed to see the philosophical determination – fully realised in Plato's
Republic – to devise an educational programme based on literate *logos*
rather than oral *muthos*. 'Logical Socratism', Havelock realised, marked not

only the decline of tragic poetry but the technological triumph of literacy. The Nietzschean account now revealed itself as a brilliant but stratospheric attempt to trace a cultural crisis in ideological rather than technological terms. From this purview, *Preface to Plato* succeeds in rescuing Nietzsche's text from metaphysical incoherence by anchoring its narrative frames to a deterministic account of cultural transformation.

Great poets, Eliot tells us, do not borrow, they steal. Havelock declines to acknowledge the Nietzschean precedent.[39] This gesture resonates, albeit as the product of an antithetical motive, with the suppression of *Phaedrus* which we will discuss below. No doubt mindful of the scepticism with which the sweeping claims of *Preface to Plato* would be met, he claims respectable scholarly and philological sources for his work. Quite against the speculative tenor of Nietzsche's dialectic, the technological argument will purport to ground itself in empiricist methodology. 'Direct evidence for mental phenomena,' Havelock is quick to announce, 'can lie only in linguistic usage' (PtP, vii). However, a tension between the empirical and speculative, between the evidential foundations and grand designs of *Preface to Plato*, becomes apparent from the outset. Plato wrote only once in clear and unequivocal favour of writing, and then in the specific case of law-making (*Laws*: X, 891a). Moreover, in the *Phaedrus*, Plato has been traditionally taken to argue against the incorporation of writing into rationalist culture. One can only assume that it is with conformity to this literal reading that Havelock dedicates just one sentence of *Preface to Plato* to the only dialogue which considers writing *per se* (i.e. the *Phaedrus*) and ensures that this sentence is embedded in the midst of copious footnotes (PtP, 56, n. 7).[40]

In a 1966 review, Friedrich Solmsen draws attention to the suppression of the *Phaedrus*. He also alerts the reader to the 'exaggerated and

---

[39] Only in the context of a chapter entitled 'The Oral Composition of Greek Drama' does Havelock mention Nietzsche and then in a most off-hand manner: 'Nietzsche for one argued that high classic tragedy did indeed die for cultural reasons, but his observation [is] grounded in causes which were perceived in his day to be ideological, not technological, a matter of changing dispositions of the mind, not of mere communication.' Eric A. Havelock, *The Literate Revolution in Greece and Its Cultural Consequences* (Princeton, NJ: Princeton University Press, 1982), p. 266. Later in this chapter the Nietzschean influence becomes plain, along with the weakness of Havelock's revision of *The Birth of Tragedy*. Talking of the diminution of the tragic effect, Havelock relays the Nietzschean schema, but attributes the falling off to a newly discovered *bookishness* in Euripides: 'What [Euripidean tragedies] progressively lose is their role as the carriers of the cultural tradition. The re-enactment of the *ethos* of an oral community through words, melody and dance had been their original reason for existence, one which under conditions of increasing literacy they were bound to lose.' Ibid., p. 312.

[40] The *Phaedrus* is mentioned on six occasions in *Preface to Plato*, each time in the footnotes. Aside from the single sentence in which it is dismissed as 'conservative' and 'illogical' (which we shall discuss below), the reference is nowhere connected with the theme of writing (c.f. PtP, 34 n. 7, 53 n. 7, 55 n. 15, 56 n. 17, 253 n. 44, 275 n. 34).

overdramatised presentation' of Havelock's work, its cavalier approach to evidence, its intention to fill out 'a pre-established scheme' and dependence on 'antecedent commitments'.[41] Naturally, it can never be proved that the Nietzschean framework constitutes an 'antecedent commitment', but in adopting an identical narrative scheme, Havelock cannot admit evidence of continuities between Plato and pre-Socratic culture, still less the liminality of a dialogue which questions the philosophical worth of replacing the spoken with the written word. Even were the *Phaedrus* read as a philosophical defence of Plato's own practice of writing, the text would still affirm productive continuities between the new rationalist culture and the oral culture which it allegedly sought to supplant. The Socratic fear that writing fosters the unmonitored dissemination of knowledge – one which does not constitute an argument against writing *per se*, but is certainly concerned to place limits and controls over its modes of existence and circulation – links Plato to the oral lifeworld, and indeed to any culture at the tense crossover from orality to literacy. This misgiving abounds in the ancient world and is expressed from the Torah to the New Testament, from pre-Socratism to patristics, and persists even in that most textually sophisticated of medieval scholars, Maimonides. In the face of the ethical dangers of writing, Plato certainly wishes to preserve the generational continuity of knowledge as it was passed from father to son, teacher to pupil, and so seeks to achieve a synthesis between the pre-literate *paideia* and epistemological rationalism. To confess the Janusian nature of the *Phaedrus* and thereby Plato's attachment to the oral transmission of knowledge would undermine the dramatic scheme of the oralist position, and that of *Preface to Plato* in particular. Havelock, therefore, cannot treat 'Socrates' or 'Plato' as syntheses of that which came before. This commitment leads to a refusal of the conventional picture of philosophy as evolving from an Ionian line through Parmenides and Heraclitus, a refusal which in turn jeopardises the *a fortiori* claim that writing was only assimilated jaggedly and by degrees into Attic culture. From there Havelock is forced to make the twin claims that the 'pre-Socratics' were incapable of conceptual thought and that conceptual thought itself depends solely for its existence on writing. One begins to suspect that the narrative interest generated by the 'Socratic rupture' is sustained only at the expense of a thoroughgoing investigation of historical, epistemological and linguistic dilemmas.

---

[41] Friedrich Solmsen, 'Review of *Preface to Plato*', *American Journal of Philology*, vol. LXXXVII, no. 1 (1966), pp. 99–105: pp. 103, 105.

It is, for example, ontologically immodest to say that Socrates' capacity for abstract thought depended *solely* on the development of the faculty of rational detachment radically expanded through the emergence of an objective written archive when the influence of the Greek sciences of geometry and arithmetic must at least provide equal if not competing evidence. One can allow that emergent literacy consolidated this epistemic shift without assigning to interiorised writing a monocausal status. Arthur W. H. Adkins says with stronger – if unspectacular – reason that the pre-Socratics 'developed a philosophical language quickly: not, so far as extant fragments suggest, by thinking directly about the deficiencies of existing language for their purposes, but by engaging in philosophical thought'.[42] Indeed, in so far as philosophical reflection might have a primal moment, it must occur in the transition from observed fact ('the sun is dark') to the explained fact ('solar eclipse').[43] The question 'why?' is posed because the observed fact lacks intelligibility and therefore suggests a lacuna in knowledge. This interrogation is available to preliterate cultures and is characteristic of pre-Socratic thought. Here Havelock's thesis would gain in resonance if it were prepared to share and surrender a portion of the ground it has claimed: in this instance, through arguing that writing allowed for a hitherto inconceivable formalisation of scientific habits of thought which were nonetheless developed independently of assimilated writing. Havelock's insistence that conceptual thought was impossible before Socrates rests on an uneasy combination of speculative and philological claims. The absence of the verb 'to be' (*einai*) in preliterate Greece, he claims, precluded conceptual thought. The oral mind, he says, cannot

> use the verb to be as a timeless copula . . . Kantian imperatives and mathematical relationships and analytic statements of any kind are inexpressible and also unthinkable. Equally an epistemology which can choose between the logically (and therefore eternally) true and the logically (and eternally) false is also impossible . . . Hence all 'knowledge' in an oral culture is temporally conditioned, which is another way of saying that in such a culture 'knowledge' in our sense cannot exist. (PtP, 182)

Clearly, the philological evidence is stretched too far here, and Havelock's analysis of the image-making powers of the Homeric psyche betrays his own conflation of abstract and conceptual thought. The capacity of the

---

[42] Arthur W. H. Adkins, 'Orality and Philosophy', in Robb, *Language and Thought in Early Greek Philosophy*, pp. 207–27: p. 224.
[43] I am here indebted to a paper given by Patrick Byrne on Aristotle at the Thinking Through History Conference, *British Society for the History of Philosophy*, University of Leeds, 1998.

preliterate mind for imagistic thinking involved conceptual mediation in its perception of similarity amongst variety regardless of whether the resultant associations have the abstract qualities of the Platonic epistemology.[44] Here Havelock's linguistic determinism leads him into oversimplifications of the relationship between concept and sign and raises the question of how deep is the oralist commitment to engage with language at an epistemological level.

Indeed, one searches Havelock's *oeuvre* in vain for a position on the cognitive status of language. Certainly, Havelock is committed (i) to an empiricist position in his conviction that analysis of language-use is the only means of reconstructing thought from a given historical period, and (ii) to the idea that the noetic horizons of culture are determined by linguistic media. However (i) cannot tally with (ii) for if thought becomes inextricable from language, then language cannot provide distinct empirical evidence for the quality and composition of thought. In so far as one can derive a theory of language here, it seems that if language does not fully determine thought, it at least circumscribes its horizons. Havelock's technological theory of the triumph of *logos* over *muthos* begins to look like little more than a literal execution of the Wittgensteinian apothegm that the limits of one's language are the limits of one's world, with the crucial difference that an epistemological (and also agnostically mystical) statement has been converted into an historical and cultural principle of ethnography.

Furthermore, the contention that the preserved word is the precondition of abstract thought is not argued in Havelock's text but relies on a loose analogy between the technological process of abstracting or exteriorising text from the stream of speech and the epistemological process of abstracting an object from a subject of knowledge: a preliterate diagram, for example, would satisfy the latter without any dependence upon the former. In the absence of any substantial argument or secure evidential foundation, Havelock would appear to be doing little more than graft the terms 'oral' and 'literate' onto sweeping dialectical frames of *The Birth of Tragedy*. Certainly, the terms orality and literacy begin to seem less like technological determinants than quasi-ontological categories and no more adequate to the distance and irrecoverability of Attic culture than the candidly mythopoeic terms 'Dionysian', 'Apollonian' and 'Socratic'. One need only consider how easily detachable are the terms 'oral' and 'literate' from the argument of Havelock's text to suspect superimposition.

---

[44] This point is well made in Dallas Willard, 'Concerning the "Knowledge" of the Pre-Platonic Greeks', in Robb, *Language and Thought in Early Greek Philosophy*, pp. 244–53.

Many of the central tenets of *Preface to Plato* – the influence of memorisation on the form and content of archaic literature; the dating of the
invention of the Greek alphabet and of the transition from oral to literate
dynamics; the contention that the precise prose of Aristotle would have
been impossible in Homeric Greece – can be upheld without affirming
that conceptualisation and literacy are coeval. Indeed, *Preface to Plato* would
retain many of its most compelling insights without the epistemological
thesis: we would be presented with (i) a productive extension of the arguments of *The Birth of Tragedy* to the mimetic qualities of Homeric epic; (ii)
an evolved picture of the Dionysian experience in terms of *mousike*, participation and memorisation; and (iii) a plangent rereading of the *Republic*
as an educational programme. From this perspective, Havelock would
seem to distort his Nietzscheanism via the technological thesis. The contrary assessment would see the gradualism of the technological argument
sacrificed to the Nietzschean schema. Both assessments confirm the
incompatibility of genetic history and serious meditation on language.

Havelock is indeed inspired in seeing the connection between philosophy and writing, as also in his understanding of the *Republic*'s argument
against the poets as concerned not with poetry *qua* poetry, but as the
dominant educational resource of society and as one whose oralist lifeworld demanded a collective immersion which precluded detached
reflection on knowledge. He would, however, have done better to see the
interiorisation of writing in a more gradual fashion rather than as occurring cataclysmically with dialectic, emphasising the liminality of Plato and
his Socrates, as transitional figures between the oralist lifeworld and the
decreasing dependence upon the voice as occurring in the texts of
Aristotle. Such a position could have allowed for the attachment of Plato
to oral methods of teaching, whilst proceeding with theoretical support
from the *Sophistical Refutations*, as also from the very fact of the immense
body of writing offered without dialogic mimicry by Aristotle.[45] In

---

[45] Werner Jaeger, *Aristotle: Fundamentals of the History of his Development*, second edition, trans. Richard
Robinson (Oxford: Clarendon, 1948), pp. 168ff. See also Joseph Owens, *The Doctrine of Being in
the Aristotelian Metaphysics*, second edition (Toronto: Institute of Medieval Studies, 1963), especially
pp. 174–7, where he argues that Aristotelian teachings were peripatetic not only in name but in
principle, viz. their written form served not merely as final statements but as prompts to further
and higher levels of collective intellectual apprehension. Neither observation, though, is incompatible with our suggestion that the Aristotelian works had advanced the interiorisation of writing
by adopting the structure of scientific demonstration without incorporating dialogue as a generic
component. No one worthy of the name of philosopher or lover of wisdom has to this day insisted
that his or her works constitute a 'last word': Wittgenstein is only a most memorable twentieth-
century exemplar of the conviction, held by 'true lovers of wisdom', that a body of writing is only
a prompt or dispensable ladder on the way to ever-higher levels of philosophical reflection.

the Aristotelian work, furthermore, there is no perceived threat to the development of philosophy from the poetic lifeworld: it is a measure, perhaps, of the diminished hold of the poets over the *epistēmē* achieved by the *Republic* that Aristotle felt the philosophical confidence to produce a defence of poetry against his master's gestures of banishment, one in which poetry is found to be closer to the epistemological and metaphysical ideals than is history, in that it partakes more of the universal than of the particular. Still further, the dispassionate, unadorned, scientific prose with which Aristotle defends poetry suggests the assimilation of writing is altogether more convincing than Plato's passionate, often metaphorically driven polemic against the poets.

Along such a path, Havelock could have retained the force of his central insights without the genetic and historical distortions into which his monocausal determinism drives the argument of *Preface to Plato*. He could also have given equal weight to the ethical issues surrounding speaking and writing, whilst seeing the cultural assimilation of writing as one factor amongst others which collaborated to make possible the emergence of philosophy in Hellenic Athens. Many of these revisions would have flowed directly from a real engagement with the actual discussions of speech and writing in Plato's *oeuvre*, for, in the final analysis, it is not Havelock's determination to sacrifice philosophical coherence to narrative intrigue, but the refusal to meet the challenges of the *Phaedrus* which destines *Preface to Plato* to epic failure.

In *a Preface to Plato* whose argument is that philosophy 'could only achieve itself completely in the written word and had indeed been brought to the edge of possibility by the existence of the written word', the suppression of the dialogue on *eros*, rhetoric, speech and writing is scandalous, particularly when it takes place in a footnote which assumes what is to be demonstrated in declaring that Plato's 'preference for oral methods was not only conservative but illogical, since the Platonic *epistēmē* which was to supplant *doxa* was being nursed to birth by the literate revolution' (PtP, 56, n.17). Clearly, an admission that Havelock is unwilling to countenance the problematic of writing *as raised in Plato's corpus*, this gesture vitiates the claim that the orality–literacy thesis takes the form of dispassionate, disinterested enquiry. That both Havelock and Walter Ong were ideally placed to open the text of the *Phaedrus* in this manner makes its suppression seem like an act of intellectual bad faith, an impression that is only strengthened when we consider that even in an article entitled 'The Orality of Socrates and the Literacy of Plato', Havelock desists from any accommodation of the only Platonic dialogue to take the relationship between writing and oralism as its theme.[46] For his part, Ong opens the aporia only to close it in the same sentence:

> the relationship between Homeric Greece and everything that philosophy after Plato stood for was, however superficially cordial and continuous, in fact deeply antagonistic, if often at the unconscious rather than the conscious level. The conflict wracked Plato's own unconscious. For Plato expresses serious reservations in the *Phaedrus* and the *Seventh Letter* about writing, as a mechanical, inhuman way of processing knowledge, unresponsive to questions and destructive of memory, although, as we now know, the philosophical thinking Plato fought for depended entirely on writing.[47]

To thus neutralise the conflict by assigning it to the unconscious of an 'individual' we call Plato in the process of repudiating that very technology which fortifies his thought is a problematically modern and – for Ong – uncharacteristically facile gesture. Why should Plato be the subject of psychoanalytic scrutiny in terms of 'buried trauma' over a theme and a tension that so preoccupied him at a most literal, even a most lived level, of a theme and a tension that speaks not only through the *Phaedrus*, the *Second* and *Seventh Letters*, but through the *Protagoras* and his *Laws*? We might indeed be very suspicious of the claim that an unconscious of any kind is at work here, be it cultural or individual: in the former case, because we know how much explicit effort was expended in Plato's day on this opposition, not only by the dialectician himself but also by Isocrates in his 'Letter to Philip' and by Alcidamas in his 'Against the Authors of Written Speeches'; in the latter, because of the little that we do know of Plato's life for certain is that he endlessly confronted the problems of writing, memory and orality whether in the labour of transcribing the spoken discourses of the historical Socrates or, in the work of maturity, composing dialogues which moved further and further from the Socratic *ipssisima verba*.[48] Indeed, we can be sure that the work belongs to

---

[46] See Eric A. Havelock, 'The Orality of Socrates and the Literacy of Plato: With Some Reflections on the Historical Origins of Moral Philosophy in Europe', in Eugene Kelly, ed., *New Essays on Socrates* (Boston, MA: University Press of America, 1984), pp. 67–93. This resistance to the *Phaedrus* is not peculiar to *Preface to Plato*, but is maintained throughout Havelock's corpus. See, for example, *The Literate Revolution in Greece and its Cultural Consequences* (Princeton, NJ: Princeton University Press, 1982); *The Muse Learns to Write: Reflections on Orality and Literacy from Antiquity to the Present* (New Haven, CT and London: Yale University Press, 1986).

[47] Ong, *Orality and Literacy*, p. 24.

[48] Indeed, if we accept the conventional mapping of the Socratic problem, then Plato's entire adult life would describe an unparalleled trajectory in terms of the written word and its relation to speech. From the aporetic dialogues in which the fractures and inconclusiveness of immediate exchange are evident, through to the refinement of actual speech situations from memory but with an attempt at literary structure and abridgement, through to the middle-to-late dialogues which

the middle-to-late period of Plato's career and that it was among the last in which 'Socrates' figures as the main protagonist.

The tensions in Ong's position are visible in emotive and hyperbolic language: we do not know that the philosophical thinking of Plato depended partly let alone entirely on writing; nor do we know that Plato experienced any conflict; still less might we assume that it – or anything else – '*wracked* Plato's own unconscious'. Indeed, were we forced to infer an authorial attitude from the *Phaedrus*, the presumption of a serene, ironic perspective – quite in contrast to the hurried, passionate metaphysical arguments against art in *Republic* X – would seem altogether more consistent with a Plato writing against writing through the Socratic representation, the figure of Socrates. It would, after all, be the height of absurdity to suppose that Plato was unaware that he was writing, or in the grip of an intense trauma, as he wrote – or rather, artfully composed – the festive dialogue. One could psychoanalyse Plato, to be sure, in terms of his guilt in betraying the Socratic commitment to spoken discourse in the very act of that discourse's commemoration; and in so doing one could produce an interpretation whose contours would be no less suggestive than engrossing on a narrative plane, rather akin to the casting off of Falstaff by a Prince Hal now ruthlessly readied for office. One could produce a reading, a psychobiographical drama of sorts, which might take particular note of the fact that only in that dialogue from which Socrates is altogether absent (even as a silent auditor) – the *Laws* – does Plato affirm the virtues of writing. One could do all these things playfully, fancifully or *ex hypothesi*, 'as if': but not (as above) in the manner of a factual proposition. At first glance, one is predisposed to assume the greater integrity in a confrontation of the aporia, but a moment's reflection reveals that it adds entities – in this case a Platonic unconscious on the rack – beyond necessity. Furthermore, it implies that we who live some two-and-a-half millennia hence have greater access to a Platonic psyche than whoever its bearer may have *been*. Just as impertinently, in attributing the aporia to unconscious disorganisation, or the uncanny organisation of an unconscious which only the art of an analyst purports to reconstruct, Ong's

Footnote 48 (*cont.*)

bear comparison with the work of novelists and dramatists who have taken their cues from a witnessed exchange but have crafted the material towards an aesthetically satisfying form, through to the literary artistry of the *Phaedrus* and the continuous prose of the closing sixty-two Stephanus pages of the *Timaeus* (supposedly enounced eponymously), no author of any other time could have found himself more consciously engaged with the evolution of the genre of writing. Besides which, the assumption that the adoption of writing 'wracked Plato's unconscious', whilst unverifiable, would be hard-pressed to account for the serenity of the *Phaedrus*, the text in which this supposed 'technological parricide' would be confronted in all its traumatic resonance.

position threatens indirectly to restore the older and persistent view – stretching from Diogenes Laertius into the early twentieth century (cf. PP, 66–7) – that the *Phaedrus* was an ineptly constructed dialogue.

Indeed, Havelock's estimation that Plato's preference for oral methods is not only conservative but illogical in that it does not fit the scheme of *Preface to Plato* seems the lesser of two distortions. One could hypothesise unconscious motivations, a psyche ravaged by technologies of detachment and the living word, but only without considering the possibility that Plato was no less an enemy of the spoken as the written, and no less a champion of both; that is to say, without considering that Plato upheld the virtues of writing where he saw the defects of speech and wished to attenuate the dangers of writing by imposing upon inscription the ethos of speech. Which is again to say, that nowhere and never is Plato talking about *speech* or *writing per se* but is using them, as indices of another problematic: as hints or pointers towards concerns that are no less than those of the future of discourse, knowledge, society and justice. The path through the impassable in terms of speech and writing therefore resides in refusing to take the terms 'speech' and 'writing' in any metaphorical, metaphysical or even literal sense, and in seeing the spoken and the inscribed as forces within a greater economy, an economy which, we shall argue, is first and last that of the ethical organisation of knowledge. From this point of view, there is no incoherence or contradiction – still less any labour of an unconscious – in Plato's ideas about speech and writing.

'Only a blind or grossly insensitive reading could indeed have spread the rumour that Plato was *simply* condemning the writer's activity' (PP, 67) declares Derrida of the tradition of Diogenes Laertius as continued in Schleiermacher. He could, though, have been referring to what we are calling the non-readings produced by Havelock and Ong. In declaring that Plato in the *Phaedrus* is not only conservative but illogical, Havelock would have done better to use the terms in a self-assessment. He is 'conservative' in abiding by the uncritical assumption that the dialogue is reacting against the incorporation of writing into Greek culture, 'illogical' in failing to recognise that it is by no means in contradiction with the deep thesis of *Preface to Plato*. Even if Plato were condemning writing, his reliance on metaphors drawn from the order of inscription to describe ideal speech testifies more certainly to the cultural assimilation of writing than does his *agon* with the poets in *Republic*. Secondly, in submitting writing to scrutiny from so many different vantages – epistemological, cultural, ethical, metaphysical – and in seeking to set limits on its cultural remit and accessibility, the *Phaedrus* is implicitly responding to its revolutionary potential.

Indeed, so far from constituting a conservative dismissal of the new technology, the dialogue is seeking to harness its potential to dialectical philosophy: by stipulating who should and who should not read, in stressing that authors of written compositions should apply to the Socratic tribunal and present themselves as do graduate students to *viva voce* examinations or defences, the *Phaedrus* is seeking to seize control of the technologies of communication, both spoken and written. These two decisive refutations of Havelock's position can be made even before one questions the assumption that Plato is antipathetic to writing. When the *Phaedrus* is actually opened, read for the first time in this manner, Havelock's position is revealed as counterintuitive in the extreme. Obviously, measurement of Havelock's theory against the *Phaedrus* would be a first step towards righting the wrong in *Preface to Plato*'s suppression of the most crucial work in the evidential base. Indeed, this dialogue provides irrefutable testimony to the liminality of Plato and his Socrates in the cultural assimilation of writing. The process is at work in and through the dialogue, but it has still decades to wait for its full assimilation – that is to say, for writing to be undertaken without the fears expressed in the dialogue whose form itself represents this compromise between the preserved word and its attempt to preserve or imitate the fluidity of living speech – with the monumental writerly corpus produced in the name of Aristotle which, even if certain works such as the *Metaphysics* were redacted from notes by his students, proceeds in independence of dialogic frames and without oralist residue or nostalgia in published form. Moreover, *Phaedrus* marks, as well as any document of the time, the actual moment when writing begins to be exteriorised in the Greek psyche – and it does so at the very apogee of the apparent argument against writing, that is to say the moment at 276a when Socrates describes the ideal speech of which written discourse can be fairly called an image or shadow (*eidōlon*).

IV: THE INTERNAL SCRIBE AND THE ATHENIAN LEGISLATOR

It is quite some time into the discourse on the inferiority of the written word before Socrates makes the positive case for spoken communication or instruction. He does so in a statement which is clearly metaphysical and epistemological. It occurs immediately after the recognition that writing – unlike speech whose author is at hand to ensure selection of audience and to correct abusive or unfair interpretations – is unable to discriminate between suitable and unsuitable readers and cannot come to its own assistance. Socrates would appear to endorse fully the views expressed by the king in the myth of writing as a gift refused. The final

point concerning the ill-effects on society of the rise of a class of readers
who believe that they have attained wisdom from writing without the
benefit of proper instruction and the objections to the atrophying effects
on natural memory go unchallenged by Socrates: further still, the king's
words are scored as prophetic utterance (*Phaedrus*, 275b), though there is
no conceivable evidence to suggest that Plato as author endorses or stands
at an ironic or even sceptical remove from these words.[49] Socrates adds
the point that truth stands without need of an author and that writing
can only serve to remind the reader of what he or she already knows.
Prior to the criticism that writing lacks the auto-attendance of speech,
Socrates has briefly conjoined writing and painting in ontological terms
as unresponsive and as having only the appearance of life. Nothing up to
this point has suggested that the issue is to be treated *more metaphysico*.[50]
Nor do Socrates' points emerge as a chain of logical entailment: though
thought-provoking, they do not seem to be building towards a conclusion. He would appear, rather, to be working up an inventory of the negative social effects of the inscribed word. Hence, the Socratic *logoi* at
276a – which raise mere *logoi* to the realisation of ideal *logos* – represent
a curious return to the metaphysical heights from which, despite the
fascinating discourses on rhetoric and the proto-scientific procedure of

---

[49] In a relatively recent translation containing much charming ancillary material, Stephen Scully
schematises the standpoints taken towards Platonic endorsement of King Thamus' rejection of the
written word according to three fundamental modalities: 'Many say Thamus' distrust applies
equally to all writing, even if Plato tries to mitigate the failings of the written word by imitating
oral speech in his dialogues. But imitation it remains. Others think Plato is being ironic. The work
of the philosopher is paradoxical: he seeks the truth which is fixed and stable (like writing), but
the love of and search for wisdom is forever evolving, (like living speech), a paradoxical union perfectly captured by Plato's invention of the dialogue form. A third view latches onto a phrase that
describes spoken dialectic as "written" in the soul (276a; cf. 278a). This metaphoric slip reveals how
Plato the writer cannot escape from the language even when he tries to discuss the superiority of
the spoken word.' Cf. Stephen Scully, *Plato's Phaedrus: A Translation with Notes, Glossary, Appendices,
Interpretative Essay and Introduction* (Newburyport, MA: Focus Philosophical Library, 2003),
pp. 97–8. We would propose a fourth negotiation which does away with the notion of an intent
which cannot sustain itself in position three: such a position, that of 'Plato's Pharmacy' in carica-
ture, continues to uphold Plato's identification with the regal interdiction even and especially as
it fails to sustain itself without recourse to metaphors drawn from the order of inscription. Rather,
we would argue that the situation whereby the king speaks through a Socrates who has purportedly invented the myth which has been written by Plato involves an abyssal scene of 'voicing'
which remains forever undecidable. Over the succeeding chapters and volume II on Levinas and
Derrida we will also tentatively suggest the possibility that Plato is bidding farewell to the Socratic
experience and the dialogic imperative towards a monologic form of writing as culminating in
the *Laws*. As such, the *Phaedrus* can be read as a glorious and generous farewell to the inspirational
figure of Socrates and his method of question and answer.

[50] We are here treating metaphysics in a traditional, somewhat restrictive fashion. Derrida does in fact
make a very strong and original case for the underlying metaphysical work attending the distinction
between *mnēmē* and *hupomnēsis*, one which we by no means dispute. This issue does not, however,
bear upon the 'ethics of writing' in our focus upon legacy rather than natural and artificial memory.

collection and division, the dialogue has desisted since the famous peroration to divine madness from which even Socrates himself distances
himself.[51] Immediately upon the deprecation of writing as lacking the
ability to defend itself, as a discourse unprotected by the ethical and epistemological value of authorial auto-attendance, Socrates says what Plato
knows that the historical Socrates believed or, rather, what a distant,
writerly Plato would have him 'say':

> SOCRATES: But now tell me, is there another sort of discourse, that
> is brother to the written speech, but of unquestioned
> legitimacy (*adelphon gnēsion*)? Can we see how it orig-
> inates, and how much better and more effective it is
> than the other?
>
> PHAEDRUS: What sort of discourse have you now in mind, and
> what is its origin?
>
> SOCRATES: The sort that goes together with knowledge, and is
> written on the soul of the learner (*hos met'epistēmēs
> graphetai en tēi manthanontos psuchēi*), that can defend
> itself (*dunatos men amunai beatōi*) , and knows to whom
> it should speak and to whom it should say nothing.
> (*Phaedrus*, 276a)

Indicating how speech can defend itself and select its audience, the
ethico-pragmatic account of the shortcomings of writing is converted
into a powerful eulogy to the nature of dialogic communication. The pro-
tectionist arguments and those concerning natural memory make for the
fluency of this shift in philosophical register and have laid down the precepts of ethical and practical wisdom admirably for this rise to the metaphysical level of reflection, but the transition remains both plangent and
unexpected. Just as the earlier arguments have been 'commonsensical', as
it were, articulated at a level of deceptively straightforward cast, so
Socrates will return to this 'down-to-earth' form of discussion when he
drops register at 276d to talk of writing as a pastime, a recreation (*paidia*),
a 'store of refreshment' and a boon to the etiolated powers of recall that
can so often accompany old age. For the moment, though, at 276a,
through the words implanted in the 'mouths' of Socrates and Phaedrus,
the dialogue remains at its apogee of metaphysical contemplation, and for

---

[51] As Socrates is quick to say of his peroration that 'some of its language was perforce poetical'. He
asks for pardon from the god of love (*Phaedrus*, 257a) and refers, somewhat apologetically, to his
speech a full eight pages later: 'we painted, after a fashion, a picture of the lover's experience, in
which perhaps we attained some degree of truth, though we may well have gone astray . . .'
(*Phaedrus*, 265b).

once it is given to the 'youthful' *ephebe* to close this phase of exchange: 'Do you mean the discourse of a man who really knows (*tou eidotos logon*), which is living and animate (*zōnta kai empsukhon*)? Would it not be fair to call the written discourse only a kind of ghost (*eidōlon*) of it?' (276b).

Phaedrus is no Callicles, rarely does more than cue responses from Socrates and bow to the superior wisdom of his elder. However, this passage is written with a suggestive fluency which suggests very strongly a continuous chain of authorial or Platonic reflection, one that will allow Phaedrus to articulate at a level of *gnosis* which has thus far been the exclusive preserve of Socrates. At this point there is nothing to suggest any ironic distance between Socrates and Plato or Plato and what the *Phaedrus* says. From Socrates' association with an older oral culture (the authorities of the temple of Zeus) at 275b, to the unresponsiveness of art and the distinction between worthy and unworthy recipients of writing – everything, as we hope to show, between this moment and the myth of writing must have been of mounting interest to Havelock. His argument itself depends not on the weak sense of writing as external marks on a page, but on what we shall refer to as the strong sense of writing: its assimilation into and transformation of the very Greek psyche itself. Yet, Havelock's stops in his tracks with King Thamus' caveat that writing will have deleterious effects on natural memory. Viewing the very development of the Greek notion of soul or psyche in the context of the transition from the memorised archive to the growth of subjective detachment consequent upon the assimilation of writing, Havelock has this to say: 'At some point before the end of the fifth century before Christ, it became possible for a few Greeks to talk about their souls as though they had selves or personalities which were autonomous.' He adds:

> Scholarship has tended to connect this discovery with the life and teaching of Socrates and to identify it with a radical change which he introduced into the meaning of the Greek psyche . . . In fact . . . *Our present business is to connect this discovery with that crisis in Greek culture which saw the replacement of an orally memorised tradition by a quite different system of instruction and education, and which therefore saw the Homeric state of mind give way to the Platonic. For this connection the essential documentation lies once more in Plato* himself and more specifically in his *Republic*. (PtP, 198–9: my emphases)

However, this connection has not been made on the basis so much of 'essential documentation' derived as from a dazzling interpretation made of *Republic*. The dialogue does indeed have much to say concerning poetry as a discourse which is unsuitable as an educational resource and as one which actively impedes the development of an epistemology in which the subject of knowledge is detached from the object of knowledge. That the basis of poetry in an orally memorised tradition is ultimately responsible for its culture of uncritical immersion and identification rather than the separation and detachment required of philosophical knowledge is a hypothesis which finds trenchant if implicit support in the *Republic*. However, the dialogue provides no documentation whatsoever regarding the speech/writing issue and the place of oral methods of instruction in the educational apparatus of the ideal commonwealth. The contested *Seventh Letter* aside, the *Phaedrus* is the only dialogue in which Plato provides documentation as to his view of writing and, whether fortuitously or deliberately, the documentation is raised in direct connection with the emergent notion of the soul or autonomous personality. The documentation is essential to any consideration of Plato's philosophy of discourse and nowhere more so than to the project of *Preface to Plato*.

First, the notion of 'writing on the soul' does not just occur as a metaphor of the moment. It reappears in the dedicated conclusions that Socrates draws at 277d–278e as an issue to which the entire discussion has been dedicated and as one that has been brought to an undisputable resolution: 'lucidity and completeness and serious importance belong only to those lessons on justice and honour and goodness that are expounded and set forth for the sake of instruction, and are veritably *written in the soul of the listener*' (278a: my emphasis). Secondly, it forms the basis for a subsequent distinction drawn between two forms of writing: serious writing, on the one hand, which is 'written in the soul of the listener', and the non-serious in which an author writes in 'that black fluid we call ink' (*Phaedrus*, 276c). The former contains words and truth which 'can defend both themselves and him who planted them' (277a), whilst the latter leaves behind 'words that can't either speak in their own defence or present the truth adequately' (276c).

In his argument that writing was only gradually assimilated into the Greek psyche some 200 years after its introduction as an exterior resource, Havelock has already distinguished two forms of writing. The difference between writing as external marks, signs on a page and interiorised writing is central to Havelock's position and it is to be regretted that *Preface to Plato* leaves it largely to the reader to demarcate (what we shall call) the 'weak' and the 'strong' senses of writing. The weak writing adverts to writing as still subservient to voice in the form of transcribed

speech, writing on tablets, inventories, genealogies, autobiographical
pastime (*paidia*), memoranda and so on – the preserved word as *tekhnē*.
The strong sense refers to writing as interiorised, independent of the
phonē, as inextricable from thought and not relying on the assistance of
the voice. This transition is noted memorably for his milieu by Augustine
in the collective astonishment provoked in Milan by Ambrose's habit of
silent reading as the definitive mark of a truly interiorised writing in
which the channel has opened between signifier and signified or mental
concept without the mediation of the voice.[52] This distinction, which
Derrida radicalises according to the metaphysical distinction between the
'good' and 'bad' writing as he sees the distinction working in *Phaedrus*,
and which we shall shadow in terms of ethical and unethical writing, suggests the interiorisation of writing in the Socratic/Platonic philosophy
on which Havelock's argument depends absolutely. Its eradication from a
project which insists on the 'essential documentation which lies once
more in Plato' demonstrates the intensity of this most spectacular non-
reading. One can only assume that, driven by the originality of his reading
of *Republic*, Havelock felt that he could not sacrifice momentum to the
patience required to disentangle the terms of this complex opposition and
the manner in which Plato repositions dialectical philosophy in relation
to this ethically redescribed field of speech, writing, communication and
knowledge.

What is the difference between interiorised writing and undertaking to write in water (*en hudati grapsei*) or 'that black fluid we call ink'
(276c)? Between writing in the soul and those written words that are
like seeds sown for eight days' growth at the festival of Adonis?[53] Why
should writing, arraigned as it is for remaining, now be associated with
evanescence, a discourse both transitory and in transit? What is this

---

[52] 'When [Ambrose] was reading, his heart perceived the sense, but his voice and tongue were silent
. . . [T]he need to preserve his voice, which used easily to become hoarse, could have been a very
fair reason for silent reading. Whatever motive he had for his habit, this man had a good reason for
what he did.' St Augustine, *Confessions*, trans. Henry Chadwick (Oxford: Oxford University Press,
1991), VI iii (3), pp. 92–3. We know, of course, that Augustine was to more than master the art of
silent reading, but the autobiographical recollection reveals that the interiorisation of writing, i.e.
the passage from inscribed sign to mental concept without the mediation of the voice, had a long
and jagged history. As the *Confessions* indicate, by the close of the fourth-century AD – even among
the Milanese intellectual elite – writing was still considered to be a prompt to vocalisation rather
than a literature in our modern sense.

[53] Hackforth says, utilising this image by which Socrates distinguishes between the sensible and
foolish farmer: 'a reader tends, Plato thought, to imagine that he can absorb wisdom quickly, by
an almost effortless perusal of written words; but what is so absorbed is something neither solid
nor permanent (hence the comparison to "the gardens of Adonis") . . .' *Plato's Phaedrus*, ed. with
an introduction and commentary by R. Hackforth (Cambridge: Cambridge University Press,
1952), p. 194.

writing compared to those *logoi gegrammetoi* which are motionless, impassive, rigid, obdurately remaining like the features of a portrait? Why should writing be moving and unmoving at the same time; at one time unresponsive and cadaverous and another living, remaining, engraved on that most lasting of surfaces, the soul of the auditor or learner?[54]

Dialectic refuses to see itself as an exterior trace, remaining as *logoi en bibliois*, in spite of Plato's unprecedented effort to ensure its preservation in what for Socrates is a potentially calamitous fall from presence, auto-attendance, to affirm dialectic in the *tekhnē* through which it has travelled into our hands over approximately two-and-a-half millennia. The affirmation of fixity, 'finalisation' *en bibliois*, would in itself be a calumny of *eidos*, an *ersatz* representation of the ultramundane permanence of the Ideas. So far, indeed, from regarding itself as a doctrine, a catechism, a fixed arrangement of words, dialectic tenders itself as an ever-changing, ever-renewing inquiry, a process of constant and collective rephrasing, of interrogatory revision which can only be surely pursued in *ad hominem* conversation. This dialogism reflects Plato's systematic distrust of the definitive, of the *manual*, of the textbook prescription and the pre-emptive conclusions to which such statuesque media can give rise. The Socratic *elenchus* demands that achieved discourse be put through the treadmill of question and answer, counter-argument and attempted refutation so as to avoid the monologic and unilateral transmission of knowledge from author to reader in written discourse, from performer to auditor in the tradition of memorised poetry. As the many aporetic dialogues attest, properly philosophical discourse is prepared to defy the canons of argumentative form, to close abruptly and with incertitude if genuine resolution has not been possible. Quite apart from establishing themselves as

---

[54] This strangely counterintuitive association of writing with the image of flux, of impermanence – of the ever-changing water into which the ever-changing Heraclitean subject will never take a self-same step – belongs to a Greek tradition older than Plato. We might think of Antigone's rebuff to Creon when challenging the inscription, the statute with the 'immutable unwritten law'; of the immense significance given to the unwritten law in the *Agamemnon* of Aeschylus; of Xenephon's *Memorabilia*. One may think of the great tradition of the unwritten in Greek culture of the laws that are given to men and women before words, but one could also argue that it is the difference between interior writing and external marks – between those traces that remain visible and that indelible substance which is forever engraved on the soul, between the writing which is not interiorised by the receiver and that former writing which has been interiorised that is the underlying issue here. The concept of unwritten law maintained civic status throughout the fifth century BC. For cultural references to the concept of unwritten laws, see Rosalind Thomas, *Literacy and Orality in Ancient Greece* (Cambridge: Cambridge University Press, 1992), pp. 68, 135, 145, 147. The theme of the unwritten in general is also recurrent in Greek literature. Cf. Aeschylus, *Prometheus Bound*, 789, *The Suppliant Maidens*, 179, *The Eumenides* 276; Sophocles, *The Women of Trachis*, 683, *Philoctetes*, 1325. It is also recurrent in the Bible: see, e.g. Jeremiah 31: 33, Isaiah 8: 16 and its later and most emphatic reiteration in II Corinthians 3: 1–3.

texts to be cited or even mimed, the dialogue for the most part offer pedagogic exercises, blueprints, guides of a practice to be imitated rather than a discourse to be cited; as models rather than monuments of dialectical practice, as living discourse (*logos-zōon*) which will persist as form/*mnēmē* rather than statement from one generation to the next. One finds such a view maintained at least as late into the dialogic *oeuvre* as *Sophist* (260a).

Vain though they would prove to be, in its attempts at such legacy dialectic had to oppose writing which would render the word wanton, ungovernable, promiscuous. 'Interiorisation' is the governing concept in that the internal habits of thought fostered by the new technology are to be encouraged, whilst its exterior manifestations – its propensity to travel, to wander, to abandon itself to an endlessly availability in terms of who picks it up and who discards it – are to be interdicted. Havelock's interiorisation thesis would derive substantial support rather than be weakened by the *Phaedrus*: the very thesis of interiorised writing is contained within the ostensible repudiation of writing. One can also see how the play of the 'good' and the 'bad' writing diagnosed by Derrida could be harmonised with the difference between interiorised and externalised writing, the workings of a cognitive apparatus and the wanderings of the unruly, even delinquent sign. Interiorised writing is here made – in this very passage between Socrates and Phaedrus – the foundation of the *epistēmē* in its distinction from the exterior writing – dead or half-living marks on the page. Writing will be a spectre only if not properly interiorised, and it is for this reason that dialectic proposes itself as *the* guarantor of a truly assimilated technology of abstract reflection. Hence when Plato will write outside the dialogic form – and not only in his youthful composition of literature which legend tells us he was to consign to ashes – he will proclaim such work exiguous once its *alēthinos logos* has been distilled from the discourse and internalised by its recipient. The *Seventh Letter* is in full conceptual – if not necessarily authorial – concordance with the *Phaedrus*:

> The study of virtue and vice must be accompanied by an inquiry into what is false and true of existence in general and must be carried on by constant practice throughout a long period, as I said in the beginning. Hardly after practicing detailed comparisons of names and definitions and visual and other sense perceptions, after scrutinising them in benevolent disputation by the use of question and answer without jealousy, at last in a flash understanding of each blazes up, and the mind, as it exerts all its powers to the limit of human capacity, is flooded with light. (*Seventh Letter*, 344a–b)

This understanding is neither speech nor writing so understood, and has nothing to do with externalities such as voice or pen and paper: it is interiorised writing, the psychic apparatus of abstract thought, of detachment, of *alētheia*. It is a discourse of recognition in which articulation and reception are one and the same in terms of both cognition and temporality. As Socrates declares of detached reflection in the *Philebus*: 'when . . . experience writes what is true, the result is that true opinion and true assertion spring up in us, while when the *internal scribe* that I have suggested writes what is false we get the opposite sort of opinions and assertions' (*Philebus*, 39a: my emphasis; cf. *Theaetetus*, 191 *et seq.*).

An internal scribe: one can only wonder why Havelock showed such diffidence before the issue of the 'spoken' methods of Socrates. A scribe also who is capable not only of truth but of writing falsehood into the psyche. Such 'writing on the soul' is not presented as the agent of *alētheia*: cutting both ways, its discourse does not represent the attempt to instil the presence of *eidos* as Derrida, for his part, has claimed. Indeed, when Derrida argues that Plato borrows from the image of what he wishes to erase, the very metaphor of that which he longs to possess, when he describes ideal speech in terms borrowed from the order of inscription, it is because Plato has already distinguished interiorised writing from the manifestation, the copy, the marks on a page; he has distinguished that which is written on the soul from that in stone, or sand or in water. But the form *en tēi psuchēi* is not given by Plato or Socrates as the presence of *eidos* or even as the self-undoing attempt towards such presence. Plato's Socrates has identified interiorised writing as possession, as psychic and spiritual holding, but he has not asserted it as the metaphysical guarantee of *alētheia* or even as anything trustworthy in such terms: nothing in Socrates' words above can tell us what falsehoods may abound from the internal scribe, but it is clear that the only safeguard against such bedevilments resides in the public process of dialectic, the discrimination between truth and falsehood, not within the interior resources of the individual but by way of dialogic *elenchus*. The value of interiorisation – taken here, across the corpus and in the *Phaedrus* most especially – resides precisely in its insulation from misreading, from wanton dissemination, from ethical distortion, from its capacity not to be reproduced in the present, but to be re-presented to a dialectical forum, a forum which distils truth from falsehood and rewrites wisdom into the soul of the speaker.

The idea of a 'writing on the soul' does not promote a supposed autonomy of the rational subject since the auditor or learner is essential to the process not only in the *Phaedrus*, but also in the *Seventh Letter*. Writing in the soul is first and foremost concerned to ensure the safe passage of intention by monitoring discursive uptake in the presence of the discourser, but it works transversally to ensure that he who speaks frees his discourse and thoughts from error and falsehood. Thus the distinction between the good writing and the bad writing is one of the ethics of reception. We can draw Havelock and Derrida together through a 'dialectical trace' which denotes interiorised writing and a non-dialectical trace which remains as exterior, spectral marks that dangerously survive to be taken up and possibly misconstrued by those who have not been educated to read with a dialectician's vision, spectres to which Derrida gives the honorific name 'pathbreaking writing' (PP, 154) and Plato condemns as a shadowy but disruptive remainder, a principle of textual excess with the potency to inflict untold damage on society. The force that divides the two traces, the two writings, is thus always ethical and always negatively charged to safeguard against the discourse of truth falling into the hands of those who will pervert it, take it away from the speaker's meaning in a world where the speaker is absent or dead and – in either case – unable to correct misreception. The exterior sign which wanders, fructifies where one does not want it to, is the bad writing which carries its own name. A writing which can monitor its own reception – reception being the key issue, over and above orality and the technologies of writing – carries the name of 'speech'. Everything is invested in the forum which responds to the discourse and the interrogations made of the speaker. It is the public processing of discourse rather than any supposed coincidence of thought and expression that dictates the *Phaedrus*'s preference for the dialectico-oral method. The inclinations the *Phaedrus* makes towards speech derive solely from the concern with correct and responsible audience uptake. If speech is to be privileged, it is solely for its capacity to select the recipients of its discourse, to silence itself when the audience seems inappropriate or to mould its presentation to suit a competent and responsible gathering. Indeed, the *Phaedrus* censures the voice or *phonē* in its poetic-thaumaturgical-participatory properties in terms entirely consonant with Havelock's reading of Plato's cultural agon. Not long after Socrates steps back in embarrassment from his moment of inspiration in the peroration to the divine madness of the lover, he warns of how men can lose their sober senses, become immersed and expire in the collective *ecstasis* of song (*Phaedrus*, 259c).

The stakes of the discussion are indeed epistemological in Havelock's terms just as they bear on the metaphysical in Derrida's, but the majority of concerns expressed by *Phaedrus* are ethical, matters of safeguarding the social order. Plato's opposition to writing and to oral culture are twin strategies within a consistent programme: to win the *paideia* for the dialectical forum, the Academy, whilst ensuring that dialectic ensures a worthy and elite continuity by means of instruction in the presence of the master(s). Plato resists both orality and writing in their untrammelled forms and yet welcomes the resources of both media which assist his revolutionary ethical and educational programme for transforming knowledge. The aporia – if indeed it is finally such – stems not from confusion, or from unconscious motivation and inner conflicts, but from Plato's subordination of the speech/writing issue to ethical imperatives.

Thus when it is a question of making laws, Plato is prepared to speak in defence of writing and to promote in the very immobility, the very unresponsiveness that he has seemingly condemned in writing and memorised speeches and poetry. Laws function in the ethical order, in the second-best state, when the old Plato, in the ruins of his Ideal Republic, realised that ethical norms must be established by some more practical, rudimentary and direct method. *Nomos* being a very distant approximation of *eidos*, the statutes of ethical behaviour are translated by the *philodoxoi* down to the masses and to those whom the *Republic* (475–80) calls the 'men of opinion' (*philodoxoi*). They are unresponsive, inflexible, they refuse question and answer precisely because they are prescriptions and their audience is already decided in advance. Laws are not to be read, only to be obeyed. The *Statesman* had declared as much ('there can be no claim to possess wisdom greater than the wisdom of the laws' (299c)) even before Plato has the Athenian say very near the start of his the *Laws*:

> no young man shall raise the question which of them all are what they should be and which are not, but that all should agree, without a dissonant voice, that they are all god-given and admirable, flatly refusing a hearing to anyone who disputes the point, while if an older man has any reflections to make, he must impart them to a magistrate of his own age, when none of the younger men are by. (*Laws*, 634d–e)

Everything is here in the starkest contrast to the dominant interpretation of the *Phaedrus*. The central dialogic principle of question and answer, of alteration and revision on the basis of intelligent disputation, is now revoked. And this for the reason that Plato does not conceive of laws as amenable to interpretation, to reading. Only those latter and etiolated equivalents of the *philosophoi* and guardians, those elected, ratified lawgivers (*nomothetai*) and magistrates are permitted to question, interpret,

adapt or modify the laws: 'The one certain touchstone of all is the text of
the legislator (*ta tou nomothetou grammata*). The good judge will possess the
text within his own breast as an antidote against other discourse, and thus
he will be the state's preserver as well as his own' (*Laws*, 957d). Thus the
law will be interiorised as writing by the law-giver, but must be preserved
for the masses in the form of prescription. Such is true also of those who
will be elected, like guardians, to a position where they can interpret or
alter the law through 'instruction by repeated conferences' (*Laws*, 968c):
'the student himself will not discover which of his studies is relevant until
scientific knowledge of the subject has found a settlement in his soul'
(968d–e).

Hence Plato works from the assurance that laws cannot fall into the
wrong hands: careful instruction supervised by the elders is supposed to
ensure that they will never be misprised or perverted by irresponsible and
incompetent interpreters. It is on this very assurance that their written
form is declared desirable. That nothing will prove further from the truth
in legal history is beside our point, which is merely to show that discursive media are nothing in themselves to Plato when divorced from the
ethics of reception. The Athenian later makes the matter every bit as
peremptory as it is clear:

> I could not direct our curator of law and minister of education to
> a better standard than, or bid him do better than instruct his school-
> masters to teach it to their pupils, and also if in his researches he
> should light upon connected and similar matters in the verse of our
> poets, in our prose literature, or even in the form of simple unwrit-
> ten discourse of the same type as the present, by no means to neglect
> it, *but get it put into writing*. (811d–e, my emphasis)

The very condition of writing as *scripta manent*, the idea of remaining elsewhere so reviled by Plato, the idea of the rigidly inscribed – all this is
allowed if the ethical dangers of misreception are cancelled. Clinias will
later gain the Athenian's unqualified assent when he declares that the
written law will provide a permanent repository, beyond question, accessible to all and timelessly applicable: 'legal enactments, once put into
writing (*en grammasi tethenta*) remain always on record as though to challenge the question of all time to come' (*Laws* X, 891a).

All that was condemned by the *Phaedrus* is here commended. Laws are
allowed to exist in the very same imperious silence before questioning
that makes written words akin to paintings. Books of law may return the
same answer over and over again, they may remain as repetition of the
same, escaping the fluidity of the iterable, the plasticity that Plato so

praised in oral methods. The entire Platonic epistemology and metaphysics is thus prepared to bend when it is a case of the ethical organisation of society and when the perils of wanton circulation are cancelled.
Ethical considerations thus govern the speech/writing issue: speech is no
more the spoken than writing is the inscribed. Their distinction is significant only where the destinations of discourse provide a *fundamentum
divisionis*; there is no more an epistemology than a metaphysic at the core
of Plato's reflections on the media of discourse – rather, a pragmatism of
near-cynical cast presides over the speech/writing issue. Naturally, the
objection has and will doubtless again be made that to establish connections between Plato as dialectician, ethicist and lawmaker amounts to a
virtual category error. Paul Friedländer is determined to establish a firm
hierarchical discrimination here:

> Strictest observance of the laws is the second-best journey when the
> best is impossible. If ignorant people presume to live without a
> law, this would truly be a bad copy of that pure wisdom which, in
> the ideal state, makes written laws superfluous. Here the contrast
> between the two greatest Platonic writings on the state becomes
> apparent: the *Republic* constructs the kind of state in which true
> wisdom prevails and which, therefore, does not need laws; the *Laws*,
> proceeding along a 'second way' since the first, the way 'for gods and
> sons of gods', cannot be realised, is designed to preserve the struc-
> ture of this second-best state through the strictest rules.[55]

In terms of discursive media, though, both works attest to the preservation of the ideal state and its second-best 'supplement' through preservation in the written word. Moreover, it is within the hiatus between those
who possess genuine wisdom and those who are ignorant that the ethical
demand arises, a hiatus which is apparent in the *Phaedrus's* opposition of
suitable and unsuitable readers, of men who possess wisdom and those
who only possess conceit of wisdom and one which carries very heavy
connotations of the need for censorship. Similarly, it relates to the distinction between the *thursus*-bearers who are many and the mystics who
are few, as to the *Republic's* delineation of *philosophoi* (travellers in the
realm of truth) and *philodoxoi* (tourists in the realm of illusion). Between
the tribunal established by the *Phaedrus* and the *Republic's* banishment of
the poets, the work of legislation is already underway, especially in so far
as it bears on the dissemination of discourses and knowledge. The lacunae
between the metaphysician and the legislator is precisely the space of

---

[55] Friedländer, *Plato I*, p. 116.

ethical discrimination with which both Plato and his Socrates found themselves preoccupied when confronting the social effects of suitable and unsuitable readers, of poetic authority, of sophistical and rhetorical discourses.

Indeed, if it does not dissolve altogether, the aporia descends into triviality when the phonocentric and the disseminative are distributed in ethical terms since the good and bad writings are themselves distinguished in terms of their mode of circulation in society: on the side of the good writing we have the oral method of dialectic and the chirographic making of laws; on the side of the bad we find oral poetry, oratory, sophistic testaments, perhaps even those letters which bear the name 'Plato'.

Viewed through the primacy of the ethical, the counter-case that Plato was rejecting the oral traditions has also to be severely qualified in terms of a societal vision that does not align itself with, but cuts across, discursive media. To see Plato as an inveterate enemy of the oral culture, as wishing to establish dialectic *ab initio*, does no justice to the elegance of his *agon* with the poets. The institution of dialectic is actually concerned to incorporate elements of the oral culture into its ethos and method. At that mysterious and unrepeatable borderline between speech and writing, a cultural passover so unique that dialectic and its favoured genre of dialogue could only have come into being *between* Socrates and Plato, we cannot expect an absolute decision between competing *lexia*, but must hold more plausible a distribution of forces, a preservation of the positive values of the spoken situation which cancels all in the face-to-face communication which enforces participation and loss of critical agency. In both the ethos and the very genre of dialogue itself, a synthesis is achieved between the oral traditions and an emergent rationality dependent *in part* on the *tekhnē* of writing. We should perhaps expect near-paradox of the sort which will be developed here: namely that the Platonic arguments against writing as *tekhnē* constitute the strongest claims for writing as *epistēmē*.

First, one can easily make the argument that so far from jeopardising Havelock's thesis, the denunciations of writing actually consolidate the argument for writing's decisive interiorisation with Socrates and Plato. The primary concern of the middle and late dialogues is not to oppose writing but to establish dialectic as the discourse of knowledge and education. To this end, Plato wishes to claim the educational forum from the Homeric poets and the Athenian tragedians so as to transform a culture in which ecstatic communion took precedence over critical communication. So far from championing oral methods that owe their ethos to the Homeric world, Plato's promotion of dialogic form is in fact concerned to guard against the dangers of ordinary speech situations, orations, hortatory or suasive speech and the fervours, the *enthusiasmos*, of poetic performance. The oral method of dialectic is quite the antithesis of the enthusiastic loss of self, the enraptured communion of poet and audience fostered by Homeric and rhapsodic tradition. This is itself the argument of the *Ion*:

> [The Muse] first makes men inspired, and then through these inspired ones others share in the enthusiasm, and a chain is formed, for the epic poets, all the good ones, have their excellence not from art, but are inspired, possessed and thus they utter all these admirable poems. So it is also with the good lyric poets; as the worshiping Corybantes are not in their senses when they dance, so the lyric poets are not in their senses when they make these lovely lyric poems. (*Ion*, 533e–534a)

Plato wishes to replace what Socrates of the *Ion* refers to as the magnetic chain which unites audience to rhapsode to poet to muse by the dispassionate interaction of critical minds in the presence of a dialectical master.[56] Interaction is to be preserved in a way that is neither reactionary, atavistic nor simply residual: interpersonality and (limited) audience effects are retained, but as rational discussion, enlightened participation and not as *mania*, unreflective performance. The oral/Homeric precedent advises Plato of the dangers of uncritical response: hence he will insist on a rational forum of question and answer, rephrasing, revision, elucidation, which is designed to guard against the tendency to arrive at premature conclusions or the illusion of knowledge created by rhapsodic renditions, dramatic resolutions and the written script – all media whose truth-claims have not been publicly processed. One can see that such a forum whereby knowledge submits to *elenchus* is quite in keeping with Havelock's thesis, whilst one remembers to construe interiorised writing as a psychic, cognitive and epistemological transformation rather than as a simple, external technology of paper, hand and ink.

The genre of dialogue itself attests to Plato's liminality in this regard: a half-way house between the philosophical dissertation and the poetic or dramatic performance, indeed a prototype of the philosophical novel, it is also poised between oral and written modes of expression, between

---

[56] For a relevant reading of the *Ion* and the most original work on *enthusiasmos* of the last few decades, see Timothy Clark, *The Theory of Inspiration: Composition as a Crisis of Subjectivity in Romantic and post-Romantic Writing* (Manchester: Manchester University Press, 1997).

living conversation and *scripta manent*, between seeking to preserve the speech situation and eliminating its shortcomings, between (in Derrida's terms) phonocentrism and dissemination. Antagonistic to both Homeric orality and the circulation without reserve of graphic discourse, dialogue strives to synthesise the public realm of reception embodied by speech and the private habits of dispassionate, isolated intellection associated with the advent of writing. In this sense, drama not only provided Plato with another antagonist in his struggle for control of the pedagogic apparatus of Athenian society but also suggested possibilities for communicative exchange that consolidated his warfare with the oral *paideia*. In the dramas of Aeschylus and especially those of Sophocles, Plato would have witnessed a forum devoted to the resolution of conflicting ethical claims – Attic tragedy supplied the representation if not the epistemological reality of a dialogism which was always impossible in the rhapsodic performance. Thus Plato could take the model of drama, strip it of its aesthetic and narrative qualities, much as he would aspire to strip poetry of its metaphors, and – taking the methods of the historical Socrates as his lead – arrive at the perfect for(u)m for the adjudication of ethical issues and the interactive pursuit of truth.

Secondly, Plato is concerned to preserve for dialectic the generational continuity embodied in the poetic *paideia* seen as 'a corpus of semi-consistent mores transmissible as a corpus from generation to generation' (PtP, 175). There is much to suggest that he aimed to remodel the oral *paideia* on dialogic principles of abstract analysis, thereby incorporating the paternal succession of the *paideia* whilst cancelling rememorisatation. A disseminative writing is a threat to this continuity: writing is unable to monitor its audience and to determine an elect who are suitable for dialectical instruction. Thus while Plato wishes to cancel the authority of the poetic *paideia*, he would preserve its proto-technological means of discursive transmission. 'The recital by parents and elders,' Havelock observes of the pre-philosophical educational programme, 'the repetition by children and adolescents, add themselves to the professional recitations given by poets, rhapsodes and actors. The community has to . . . reinforce [the tradition] in the collective memory of a society where collective memory is only the sum of individuals' memories, and these have continually to be recharged at all age levels' (PtP, 44). Hence Plato's father to son metaphor in the *Phaedrus*, as also the numerous references to generational continuity throughout his work (cf. *Protagoras*, etc.). Writing is anthropomorphised as illegitimate, deviant, outside the process of generation: one can read the complexities of Derrida's reflections on paternity in Plato from the rather simpler vantage of the enshrinement of filial transmission in the archaic process of paideutic instruction. Plato wishes to uphold generational descent from master to *ephebe* in the transmission not of a text, a storehouse, a repository, a memorised tradition, but of a method of critical thinking, a set of axioms from which legitimate conclusions can be drawn collectively and processually without those premature illusions of understanding promoted by writing (*Phaedrus*) or recitation of speeches or poems (*Phaedrus, Republic, Protagoras*). We might here think of the *Phaedrus* when it defines legitimate thoughts as those which bear fruit in others according to a slow process of interpersonal exchange, revision, correction, leading to the eventual interiorisation of the method by which *alētheia* is attained – a process not dissimilar to the training given in arithmetic and geometry during Plato's day.[57] We might also think, in another key, of that pure poetry expressed through Diotima's nonetheless philosophical reflection on generation, on procreancy of the spirit, words which – in line with the parental images of the *Phaedrus* – transpose the joys of begetting children to those of fostering thought.[58]

From father to son, from parent to daughter, from master to *ephebe*, from elder to adolescent, from *patēr* to *ekgonos*, the techniques of abstract reflection are to be nurtured by bonds of paternal affection from one generation to the next: hence it is regarded as the most impious, if necessary, gesture to break with the Parmenidean unity of being, to challenge the paternal pronouncement (*tōi patrikōi logōi*).

Dialectic certainly wishes to supplant the irrationalism of the oral lifeworld in its epistemological aims but retains its model of animate, interpersonal education. The abstract reasoning allowed by writing is to be preserved, but in accordance with an ethos of oral exchange, legacy

[57] Arithmetic and geometry are, of course, to the fore of the educational curriculum of the *Republic*.

[58] '[T]hose whose procreancy is of the body turn to woman as the object of their love, and raise a family, in the blessed hope that by doing so they will keep their memory green, "through time and through eternity". But those whose procreancy is of the spirit rather than the flesh – and they are not unknown, Socrates – conceive and bear the things of the spirit. And what are they? You ask. Wisdom and all her sister virtues; it is the office of every poet to beget them, and of every artist whom we may call creative. Now, by far the most important kind of wisdom . . . is that which governs the ordering of society, and which goes by the names of justice and moderation. And if any man is so closely allied to the divine as to be teeming with these virtues even in his youth, and if, when he comes to manhood, his first ambition is to be begetting, he too, you may be sure, will go about in search of the loveliness – and never of the ugliness – on which he may beget. And hence his procreant nature is attracted by a comely body rather than an ill-favoured one, and if, besides, he happens to on a soul which is at once beautiful, distinguished and agreeable, he is charmed to find so welcome an alliance. It will be easy for him to talk of virtue to such a listener, and to discuss what human goodness is and how the virtuous should live – in short to undertake the other's education' (*Symposium*, 208e–209c). The association of these words is by no means novel: Hackforth actively encouraged it more than half a century ago. See *Plato's Phaedrus*, trans. R. Hackforth, p. 64.

through spoken and generational descent. The face-to-face transmission which was in Homeric times the indispensable condition of cultural continuity, of the survival of knowledge and discourse, is for Plato no longer just a means of knowledge's preservation, but an ideal, of its nurture, its inheritance, its truth-bearing legacy.

Thirdly, *the arguments that Plato uses against poetry are the very arguments he uses against writing*. Plato's criticisms of the poetic *paideia* turn on the fact that, like the written sign in the *Phaedrus*, the poem of Simonides in the *Protagoras* or the rhapsodic rendition in the *Ion*, the memorised poem cannot explain itself: like writing, like painting, it keeps repeating itself over and over again, it cannot vouch for its author's intentions, nor can it monitor its own reception. Repetition, unresponsiveness, rigidity, the refusal of question and answer, the lack of an alternative syntax are used to discredit both oral and written modes of expression. An existing culture of orality and a premonitory culture of writing are dismissed with the same weapons and in virtually the same stroke: everything, in short, which is not dialectic. Memorised speeches, too, fall under this *coup de grâce*. Being learned 'by heart' and presented not as a dialogue of the speaker with himself, still less with his audience (who, like those assembled for the rhapsodic recitals, are denied any responsorial share in the performance), those speeches which are inscribed via *hypomnēsis* rather than *mnēmē*, which are recalled for their words rather than their *logos*, partake equally in the lifeless, mute rigidity of the written word regardless of whether they have been memorised from a script or interior composition. Having listened 'spellbound' to a speech made by Protagoras, Socrates declares:

> It is true that if a man talked on these matters with any of our popular orators, he might possibly hear similar discourses from Pericles or some other proficient speaker, but if one asks any of them an additional question, like books they cannot either answer or ask a question on their own account. Ask them the smallest thing supplementary to what they have said, and like a gong which booms out when you strike it and goes on until you lay a hand on it, so our orators at a tiny question spin out a regular Marathon of speech. (*Protagoras*, 329a–b)

Writing, memorised speeches, dramatic performances, paintings, sculptures and memorised poetry are all condemned as rigid in contrast with the plasticity of the dialogic form. Indeed, for all that its sights are trained on the banishment of the poets, the *Republic* itself declares in Book Nine: 'speech is more plastic than wax and other such media' (588d). All non-dialectical genres are condemned as repetitive and tautological –

taken in this context to denote (i) intellectual stagnancy; (ii) the inability to contextualise reception; or (iii) the absence of an alternative syntax, an *allos logos* in which they could be expressed. Plato damns writing in so far (and, we shall see, only so far) as it shares those defects of intellection fostered by the oral *paideia*, defects to be corrected by the *via media* of dialogue and the higher way of dialectic. By charging writing with a similar corruption of *mnēmē* as that required by oral memorisation, he can extol dialogue and dialectic over the emergent *tekhnē* of writing and the archaic *muthos* of Homeric poetry.

Writing is vilified by the king for its propensity to corrupt natural memory. However, one should also acknowledge that oral poetry is interdicted in terms of its corruption of intellect and memory (*Republic*, 595b). Learning by rote is itself anathema to dialectic and Plato will always favour the calculative: arithmetic and geometry, disciplines which replace inconceivable labours of memory, are among the first areas of dialectical instruction. The realm of Platonism is antagonistic to memorisation as such, in each and every case. Socrates himself has no use for the particular; his thought is always organised *per genera* rather than *per species*: to him a tree is not significant in itself but only as a genus. We witness, as but one example, the princely sarcasm which Socrates displays towards Hippias in the *Greater Hippias*:

HIPPIAS: . . . I can repeat fifty names after hearing them once.
SOCRATES: I am sorry, I quite forgot about your mnemonic art. Now I understand how naturally the Lacedaemonians enjoy your multifarious knowledge, and make use of you as children do of old women, to tell them agreeable stories. (285e–286a)

In his quest of *eidos*, Plato himself is always seeking the one, the archetype under which all detail can be made significant only in its share of the Form, its *metechein*: not only in its poetic use, but in any manifestation, parataxis will be the enemy of *mnēmē* of the Form, of rationality. Hence the good memory is that which alerts us to generality (*mnēmē*) and not to the 'Funesian' wealth of insignificant detail (*hypomnēsis*): abstraction from experiential content and not recall of the multiplicity of experience form the basis of the Platonic *epistēmē* and its warfare against the oral, memorised tradition.

Whether one treats the insistence on reflective agency as inseparable from the emergence of writing as a technology of preserved communication or sees this movement as a cultural *agon* with the sophists, it is clear that the crises everywhere facing Plato are crises of discourse.

Should writing be instrumental in the collapse of the Athenian ethos or a complication added to an already jeopardised ethos, Plato is nonetheless concerned to evolve an ethic of agency applicable to poets, law-givers, speechwriters and men of writing. That *doxa* not circulate in the guise of *epistēmē*, dialectic dreams its kingdom as one in which all ethically pertinent discourses submit to rational enquiry. The Socratic–Platonic *elenchus* is designed as the machine by which discursive acts are evaluated, distilled, purged of supposition, refined or rejected. Underlying this aspiration we find not simply a cultural will-to-power but an ultra-civilised determination to treat discourse as an ethical act of the sternest significance.

When indeed one registers that misology is misreading, then the primary mission of Platonism is given as the work of discursive purification. The bounding of the discursive by the ethical links any number of dialogues which deal with sophistics, poetry, rhetoric, law-giving, states-manship, as also of those *Letters* (II and VII) on the margins of the Platonic *oeuvre*. Whether dealing with rhetors such as Lysias, sophists such as Gorgias and Protagoras, rhapsodes like Ion, with Homer or Simonides, whether looking to the future of his own texts or envisaging the reception of others, Plato treats discourse, indeed the very possibility of discourse, with an authoritarian vigilance that shocks us today in the case of poetry, that makes the treatment of writing as play shake with trepidation and stark irony in the *Phaedrus*. In this determination – one scarcely absent from a Stephanus page of his work – a cultural shift of great moment is registered. Discourse comes to bear an ethical and culturally defining significance within the Socratic–Platonic universe comparable to the devastation visited on the Atreus, the fates of Prometheus or Oedipus for the epic poets and Attic dramatists. Prior to Plato, Greek society concerned itself more with the actions rather than the words of men, having yet to discover that unity of *logos* and *ergon* so characteristic of the Doric world-view. The civic, religious and legal code of Athenian society had been structured almost entirely in terms of things done (*dromena*) rather than things said (*legomena*). Perhaps impelled also by the fate of Socrates who fell to a writ of impiety (*graphē asebeias*) on the basis of what he had said to the youth of Athens, Plato may well have sought to give as much weight to *legomena* as to *dromena*, to specify discourse as an ethical act under the guidance of philosophy rather than under the haphazard conditions by which his master was condemned to death by the dicasts.

The two repudiations, that of writing and that of poetry, are introduced through the figure of corruption: in Book X of the *Republic*, poetry is condemned on the ground that it corrupts intellect; in Thamus's rejection of the god's gift, writing is first rebuked for corrupting memory. That these claims are potentially circular — memorisation corrupts intellect; writing depletes memory; writing corrupts intellect — does not seem to be lost on Plato. Presumably with this in mind, he proceeds to delineate between two those two memories, *mnēmē* and *hypomnēsis*, which (as mentioned above) will become the good and the bad writings respectively delineated in 'Plato's Pharmacy' (PP, 149).

It is, then, as false memory that Plato can arraign not only writing and sophistics, as Derrida argues, but also the oral tradition itself. Memorisation is equated with defective discourse be it written or spoken — hence the conjunction of speechmakers and books in the passage from the *Protagoras*. Indeed, once we accept the obvious association of *hypomnēsis* with writing, sophistics, oratory/rhetoric and memorised poetry/rhapsodic rendition, then the entire constellation of Plato's *agon* is given as something other than the warfare between speech and writing. On assurance of this association — agreement would not seem difficult here — the attacks on orality and writing appear as unified elements of a strategy designed to elevate dialectic to the master discourse of educational, knowledge and ethics.

What Derrida identifies as the 'affinity between writing and *muthos* created by their common opposition to *logos*' (PP, 145, n. 69) can be taken as an affinity of their coincidental resistance to dialectic: a resistance which derives from a common investment in rigid, unresponsive practices of *hypomnēsis*. Writing is thus opposed for the same reasons as preliterate poetry, for its repetition, its promotion of *hypomnēsis* associated with particularity, its unresponsiveness, its silence before questioning, its changeless words. While the metaphysical and the epistemological can be read in a most enlightening manner into this critique, its primary orientation, as we shall continue to argue, is towards the evolution of an ethics of discourse.

2

The Ethics of Legacy

Why did Socrates compare himself to a gadfly? Because he
only wished to have ethical significance. He did not wish to
be admired as a genius standing apart from others, and fundamentally, therefore, make the lives of others easy, because they
could then say 'it is all very fine for him, he is a genius'. No,
he only did what every man can do, he only understood what
every man can understand. Therein lies the epigram. He bit
hard into the individual man, continually forcing him and irri-
tating him with his 'universal'. He was a gadfly who provoked
people by means of the individual's passion, not allowing him
to admire indolently and effeminately, but demanding his self
of him. If a man has ethical power people like to make him
into a genius, simply to be rid of him, because his life expresses
a demand.

(Søren Kierkegaard)[1]

One would not immediately associate the question 'Who speaks?' with
Plato's Socrates whom we remember for impersonal questions such as
'What is the Just?' 'What is the Good?' Yet, the demand for a speaker or
author to give a further account of what has been said or written in his
name is central to the Socratic elenchus, to his insistence that an oral or
written text give a further account of itself in a public forum. The Socratic
mission involves the ethical demand of its interlocutor that Kierkegaard
describes. This modernising notion of responsive and responsible agency
is ethical rather than epistemological in its first concern since Plato and
the historical Socrates are united in their determination to protect society
from the damaging effects of discourse circulating with absent or deficient agents. However, the structure of ethical accountability which Plato
demands of discourses varies according to their epistemological status.

[1] Søren Kierkegaard, *The Journals of Søren Kierkegaard 1834–54*, trans. Alexander Dru (London:
Fontana/Collins, 1958), pp. 154–5.

Whilst Plato will not insist on an ethics of agency in the case of mathematics, his concern to identify a responsible agent for poetic discourse will be pronounced to the point of banishing the poets from his Ideal State whilst (for, it is often forgotten, the poets, like writers, may submit applications to the dialectical court or its representatives at the gates of the *polis*) *muthos* remains ungoverned by a rationally responsive subjectivity. This phase of work does not seek to endorse or dispute the Platonic distinction between subjective modes, or to favour or even accredit a scientific impersonality, but merely to describe the productive conflicts and occasional contradictions produced within dialectic's aspiration to impersonal truth and its dependence on an intersubjective model of rational inquiry. Throughout we will bear in mind that striving towards objectivity is not tantamount to claiming objectivity – an error, perhaps, more common among the opponents than the proponents of science – whilst treating the model of scientific detachment as one subject position among others.

Beginning with a consideration of the ethical status of the oral method, this chapter will then consider the central issue of how Plato might discriminate between suitable and unsuitable readers of a discourse. The next chapter will analytically counterpoise the oral and graphic signatures *more Aristotelico* as also in a general ethical meditation, before renewing the question of agency as it reflects dialectic's uncertain status as a discourse stranded between its own determinations of science and *muthos*. Whilst this chapter will show how dialectical orality is ethically consistent, the next will uncover epistemological weaknesses produced by the conversational method. In this process we will witness how Plato drew an era dominated by oral *ethos* into one characterised by a literate ethics whilst taking note of the manner in which dialectic unfolded in resistance to the new cultural space of authorship which it had itself created. This resistance, it will be argued, produced not only the first account of the ethics of discursive transmission but an analysis of the relation between signatory and discourse of such sophistication that subsequent thought has yet to register its continuing import.

In seeing this identification of discourse as an ethical act, as the movement of the Socratic–Platonic *oeuvre*, one can privilege the *Phaedrus* only by showing how the issue is uniquely theorised as the critique of writing. Important in this regard, the *Republic* nonetheless serves to analyse the impact of discourse within a particular ethico-political framework rather than to reflect on the ethics of discursive transmission in and for itself. The *Phaedrus*, in refusing to specify what discourses and readers it has in mind when distinguishing the suitable from the unsuitable (275e), generalises to the point of meta-ethical reflection on the circulation of spoken and written compositions. It also reflects on the practice of dialectic itself and ceaselessly questions those very frames in which the exchanges of Socrates and Phaedrus are held.

The very setting of the text is enigmatic, doubled and eerie in its self-reflexivity. The conversation is set against the very technology without which it would have evaporated into the Athenian afternoon. A moment of exquisite irony (in the Romantic sense[2]) is achieved wherein dialectic turns to look at itself, to reflect upon and justify its very existence. In so doing, it looks incalculably further than its own method and towards issues that must detain anyone with a concern for the ethics of discursive transmission. That all order of problems and pseudo-problems accrue to this account, that the *Phaedrus* refuses to distinguish between speech and writing in anything like the manner in which it purports to, compromises the ethical import of this text not one whit.

Treating the Platonic canon as a conceptual field without worrying too much about the relative dating of the dialogues, we can see the *Phaedrus* as occupying a liminal position between the early and middle, or 'Socratic', dialogues, and the later work. There is a movement within the *oeuvre* away from the seeming spontaneity of the Socratic exchange, the open discussion guided by reason and question and answer, that casual hermeneutics of the *agora*. Institutional constraints, censorship, strict monitoring of audience, the rigidities of the Academy inscribe themselves in accordance with the swerve away from Socrates, from the aporetic dialogue to the sterner, more lapidarian and authoritative Plato of the *Republic*, the *Statesman*, the *Sophist* and the *Laws*. Indeed as 'Socratic dialogue' develops into 'Platonic dialectic', as *aporia* is increasingly replaced by more and more violent *euporia*, as the interrogative gives way to the prescriptive and Plato's work solidifies into an institutional discipline, so the figures of defence, censorship and self-consciousness encroach into the very dialogues themselves. As the *oeuvre* increases, so it becomes preoccupied with itself, with its fortification, integrity, future and legacy. The destination of the *oeuvre* writes itself within the *oeuvre* itself, much as it

---

[2] Romantic irony is here specified to indicate that self-reflexivity in general is at issue rather than that particular ironic reading which sees the *Phaedrus* as deliberately programming Socrates to articulate the precise opposite of Plato's 'true' beliefs about writing. It is, of course, anachronistic to apply the term to a classical text, but it best describes the detachment and split in the writing subject when his text and *topos* force him to adopt a transcendental neutrality above and beyond the irreconcilable contradictions it has generated.

would for Marx and Freud. It also dictates a change in form, from the aporetic structure of the 'Socratic' dialogues to the thetic organisation evident in many of the later works whose presentation is only nominally dialogic.

The *Phaedrus* finds itself between the two phases: the relaxation and easy optimism of the early and middle periods is evident, but it is now tempered with a rhetoric of exclusion, boundary, defence. Accordingly, the discourse on writing acts as a summation and justification of dialectic and the dialogic form which it chose for its unfolding: it looks back to the epistemological achievements of the form as well as forward to the threats posed to its integrity by the new *tekhnē* of writing. New questions and new worries are confronted. The ideal speech situation of the earlier dialogues is threatened by forces from without. Given that for Socrates and Plato the value of a discourse or speech lies not in its source but in its destination – an audience in whose image the very work should be constructed – how might the philosopher model his *logoi* on the spectre of an anonymous or posthumous readership? Could the writer ever establish sincerity among readers who live after him? The *Phaedrus* thus marks a conceptual, if not historical, borderline between the 'Socratic Plato' and the 'Old Plato' of the *Statesman*, *Sophist* and the *Laws*. It celebrates an age of oral exchange, of *elenchus*, the sociable pursuit of wisdom in and towards *aporia*, which is to a point in and towards innocence. At the same time, the dialogue registers the passing of this age, takes its stand at the crossing into a world dominated by written signs, finished form and continuous discourses. We might witness here the giving way of an epoch in which the acquisition of knowledge was plastic, social, conversational to a culture where one teaches *oneself*, where learning is impersonal, solitary, achieved through an act of silent reading.

So far from the idea of speech denoting consciousness as authority – as was often assumed in the early reception of continental theory, and in particular of the rigid and inaccurate pedagogic framework of 'the metaphysics of presence' through which Anglo-American academics attempted to comprehend, domesticate and thereby drastically distort Derrida's work – Plato's text affirms the conversational ideal as the undoing of authority: antipathetic rather than favourable to interiority, the dialogic method is designed precisely to repudiate the hegemony of individual consciousness. *Logos* is not tied to the speaker that discursive intent be upheld; rather the coincidence of speech and speaker is valued in so far as it enables intention to be challenged by the Socratic *elenchus*.

Two considerations clarify the extent to which the 'received' deconstruction of the *Phaedrus* operates with a falsifying account of the play of
speech and writing in Plato's text and also Derrida's actual reading:

1.   It is not speech (as a *logos* present to the individual) but *dialogic
     speech* that Plato opposes to writing. Only dialogue can escape
     discursive unilateralism: Plato calls this unilateralism 'writing'
     in the *Phaedrus*, but also 'speeches' and 'poems' in the *Protagoras*.
     Oratory or orally delivered poems are equally rigid produc-
     tions if their subjects are unavailable or incapable of respond-
     ing: 'if one asks any of them an additional question, like books
     they cannot either answer or ask a question on their own
     account . . .' (*Protagoras*, 329a).

2.   In the changeless form of its *logoi*, writing promotes those
     properties such as fixed intention and monologic completion
     which have been associated with presence, and specifically an
     authorial presence. Plato objects to writing precisely insofar as
     it replicates unquestioned authorial intentions: unresponsive,
     potentially dogmatic, immune to dialectical interrogation, the
     written word is condemned for its monologic propensity.

Plato distinguishes between good and bad speech in such a manner
that the latter finds itself in the place of a repudiated writing. Enigmatic
on first inspection, this textual economy becomes entirely coherent if one
registers how the *Phaedrus* is governed by the opposition between monologic and dialogic discourse. Socrates' first objection to writing specifies
its unresponsive and monologic nature:

> The painter's products stand before us as though they were alive, but
> if you question them, they maintain a most majestic silence. It is the
> same with written words: they seem to talk to you as though they
> were intelligent, but if you ask them anything about what they say,
> from a desire to be instructed, they go on telling you just the same
> thing for ever. (*Phaedrus*, 275d)

All discourse which offers itself to debate, to question and answer, is
approved in Plato's text in the same movement by which all unresponsive,
univocal communications are condemned. These latter discourses will
include both writing and non-dialogic speech. As we will see later, the
dominance of the monologic/dialogic opposition will also explain how it
is that the *Phaedrus* by no means decides against inscription but favours a
writing which is made dialogically answerable to philosophy. The *Phaedrus*
will thus be read as a text at the crossing – one whose writing, whose art,
bids farewell to the Socratic experience even as it celebrates the dialogic

achievements of the master.[3] In locating the *Phaedrus* along a borderline between transcription and authorial inscription, we will follow the trajectory conventionally mapped as 'the Socratic problem', a textual figure in which the subordination of scribe to protagonist is reversed in tandem with the progression through aporetic (early), hypothetical (middle) and prescriptive (late) dialogues.[4] Although no interpretation of the play of speech and writing in the *Phaedrus* can ever be more than speculative, this approach allows the condemnation of writing to be acknowledged *alongside* the text's existence as written form. According to such a reading, the contest of speech and writing need not be registered as a 'full-blooded antimony',[5] nor will it be necessary to see Plato as everywhere ironising Socrates' words via a covert defence of his own practice of philosophical writing.[6] Rather, in arguing from the opposition between monologic and

---

[3] Given its relatively late dating in the Platonic *oeuvre*, and independently of whether it was composed before or after the *Republic* (in which Socrates has become indistinguishable from the programmatic drive of the 'dialogue'), his subsequent withdrawal as a significant dialogic figure in the latter dialogues and his ultimate disappearance in the *Laws*, the *Phaedrus* can be read as homage to the master of question and answer in the living present. The numerous identifications of Socrates with an older, oral and thamaturgical culture – his praise of the prophetesses at Dodona, his rebuke to the modish Phaedrus for his belief in the chirographic figure of an 'author', the reference to his possession by a 'divine sign', and the unbridled inspirational cast of his peroration to the divine madness of the lover – could be read with consistency as an admission on Plato's part that he had given himself over to the modern tendency of an authorial practice which drew its crucial influences from the oralist past but was, with the highest respect, dissociating himself from the spoken method. The basis of an argument for this liminal nature of the *Phaedrus* – and its crucial swerve from the precursor – need not proceed merely from the text's exploration of the relationship between speech and writing and contemporary claims that it bridges the middle and final phases of Plato's dialogic production. The introduction in the *Phaedrus* (265d–266b) of the method of collection (*synagōgē*) and division (*dihairēsis*) – implicit but not stated as such in the *Republic* (cf. Richard Robinson, *Plato's Earlier Dialectic*, Ithaca, NY: Cornell University Press, 1941, p. 169) allows us to affirm a model of liminality which supports the claim that the *Phaedrus* belongs to a later phase of Plato's career and the assertion of its transitional nature as retrospect. Along such a path one would not seek to contest the seemingly antithetical judgements of either Gadamer (who affirms continuity throughout the *oeuvre* in this respect) or Robinson (who respects the flexible nature of dialectic in Plato's work). 'Socrates' leading in discussion, his "guiding" talk as the earlier dialogues portray it, and the dialectic of *dihairēsis* presented in the later dialogues, have the identical purpose.' Hans Georg Gadamer, *Dialogue and Dialectic: Eight Hermeneutical Studies on Plato*, trans. P. Christopher Smith (New Haven, CT and London: Yale University Press, 1980), p. 122; 'The fact is that "dialectic" had a strong tendency in Plato to mean "the ideal method", *whatever that might be*' (Robinson, *Plato's Earlier Dialectic*, p. 74).

[4] In this later phase, Socrates becomes first taciturn, then mute, only to disappear from the stage altogether when Plato turns his attention to law-making. On a construal of the 'Socratic problem' which runs somewhat against the suppositions of this article, see Gregory Vlastos, *Socratic Studies* (Cambridge and New York: Cambridge University Press, 1994). Vlastos would deny the liminality of the *Phaedrus*: on his view, the earlier dialogues are Socratic whilst those of the middle and late periods should be thought of as unmediatedly Platonic.

[5] Cf. Mary Margaret Mackenzie, 'Paradox in Plato's Phaedrus', *Proceedings of the Cambridge Philological Society* XXVIII (1982), pp. 64–76.

[6] Cf. Ronna Burger, *Plato's* Phaedrus: *A Defence of a Philosophic Art of Writing* (Alabama: University of Alabama Press, 1980).

dialogic discourses, we can register the force of the Socratic objections to writing without implicating Plato in the performative contradiction of writing a text which outlaws writing. Just as the work distinguishes *good* from *bad* speech, so too the text can be read as counterpoising a good and a bad inscription, particularly since what the text specifies as 'things spoken' (*legomenon*) should for the most part be taken as 'things *written* or said'.[7]

The issue of 'who speaks' will inform the analysis according to two modes of its asking. First, as an ethical demand for accountability and retrospective explication. Taken in its simplest sense, the question 'Who speaks?' affirms that a text is not sufficient to itself and needs to be supplemented by another text or statement. Such interrogation is central to the Socratic resistance to the autonomy of either the text or its subject (*Ion*; *Apology*, 21b–23b). Secondly, the question will be explored and utilised in terms of the unique authorial situation of the dialogues, works that are signed in the uncanny space between a Socrates who 'speaks' and a Plato who 'writes'.

In the complicities and contests of the Socratic and Platonic signatures, the concept of authorship comes into being as a category which derives not from the spoken *logos* and presence but rather from writing, from the monologism which the split of subject from statement promotes. This will involve reconstructing the ethical aspirations of the method of question and answer before analysing its decisive reconfiguration in terms of a body of writing which anxiously came to regard itself as writing, a work of dialogic representation which evolved into a creation all of its own. In order to do the slightest justice to this immense discursive movement, we need to follow the ethical imperative that drove the Socratic interrogation in order to register how the massive transformation from the early aporetic dialogues to the final works of Plato involved a gradual replacing of dialogue as representation of a speech situation to dialectic as the origins of a cultural space of authorship which has perdured down some twenty-five centuries.

I: THE ETHICS OF QUESTION AND ANSWER[8]

The so-called 'Socratic' dialogues embody a kind of ideal speech situation which the *Phaedrus* serves to formulate. The conditions identified by

---

[7] As relevantly observed in Rowe, *Plato's Phaedrus*, pp. 194–5 (my emphasis).

[8] The phrase 'question and answer' is intended to isolate a substantial subset of Platonic dialogues characterised by the procedure of *elenchus*. Thus although the *Phaedrus* is not an elenctic dialogue in Vlastos's sense, the activity of the answerer is still vital to its unfolding. For the seminal account of the Socratic *elenchus*, see Vlastos, *Socratic Studies*, pp. 29–37. Robinson to whom we are very grateful for his sustained account of the Socratic elenchus, surprises

Habermas as necessary to such a situation – 'understanding, symmetry of conditions for all participants, sincerity and exclusion of all force except that of the better argument'[9] – are all present in the Socratic dialogues. Indeed, one can read certain statements made by Habermas as restatements of Socratic practice:

> [communicative rationality] . . . carries with it connotations based ultimately on the central experience of the unconstrained, unifying, consensus-bringing force of argumentative speech, in which different participants overcome their merely subjective views and, owing to the mutuality of rationally motivated conviction, assure themselves of both the unity of the objective world and the inter-subjectivity of their lifeworld.[10]

Such would serve as a most appropriate characterisation of the aims of Socratic discussion. The dialogic speech situation not only seeks to counter each of the negative exigencies which Habermas details, but names the respective tendencies. First, it opposes rhetoric for which subjective viewpoint is a court of appeal rather than an obstacle to *epistēmē*. Secondly, it seeks to eliminate sophistics whose orientations tend away from any affirmation of unity in the objective world. Thirdly, it avoids eristic disputation which overtly seeks victory in argument rather than mutuality arising from the rational pursuit of *alētheia*.

Beyond the Habermasian model, dialectical scruples are altogether more attentive to the boundaries, the borders of the speech situation, both in terms of contemporaneous threats and the afterlife of the discourse achieved in the enclosed situation. In the form of dialogic exchange, Plato seeks to eliminate all possibilities of misreception, to protect discourse against ethically problematic outcomes. Hence the stress in both the *Phaedrus* and the very practice of Socratic dialogue is not solely upon the

---

Footnote 8 (*cont.*)

this reader at least when he writes: 'It is useless to look for sufficient reasons for the Platonic doctrine that the supreme method entails question-and-answer, because there are none. The presence of this doctrine in Plato cannot be explained as a logical conclusion but only as a historical phenomenon . . .' Robinson, *Plato's Earlier Dialectic*, p. 86. Whilst strictly speaking there may not be sufficient reasons for the insistence on question and answer, the doctrine is not historically produced if we understand by that an unconsciousness or want of agency on the part of the author. To the contrary, the interpersonal ethos is rigorously systematised, made into a discursive ethic: this is the work of *Phaedrus* 274–8, which must be taken as much as a schema for and a skeletal theorisation of dialectical practice as a discourse on speech/writing. It would seem that Robinson did not take cognisance of the ethical claims that motiviate this Socratic–Platonic justification of the oral ethos of question and answer.

[9] This useful summary of Habermas's conditions for successful argumentation is taken from Adi Ophir, *Plato's Invisible Cities: Discourse and Power in the Republic* (London: Routledge, 1991), p. 185.

[10] Jürgen Habermas, *Theory of Communicative Action* (Boston, MA: Beacon Press, 1984), p. 101.

self-presence of intention – *pace* a certain theoretical tradition[11] – but on the facility of dialogue and dialectic for allowing intention and reception to work together, for allowing one to feed into the other. *Dianoeisthai* – the word Socrates uses for what is intended, meant or thought in a poem (*Protagoras*, 341e; 347a) – can refer either to the cognitive process by which a writer or speaker intends or to the truth claims embodied in the speech or writing,[12] claims whose veracity can only be established by question and answer, i.e. intersubjectively and in the process of reception. How far Plato himself intends is a matter of forbidding complexity, but intention itself is never a category in its own right within the dialogic movement: to see an isolated authorial intention there is to read our own preoccupations (positive or negative) with interiority into a text and a culture which regards discourse as a public affair. So far from looking forward to Cartesian self-presence, or to the reveries of those solitary walkers through modernity such as Schopenhauer or Nietzsche, the Platonic *oeuvre*, altogether more than its Aristotelian successor, insists that dialectical practice cannot be pursued by the free-standing subject.[13] Any degree of intention embodied in discourse would both derive from and belong to the communal structure established in the dialogic exchange. There is no question of discourse originating *ab ovo* in an individual, nor of any individual being empowered to direct his own discourse in a tele-ological fashion: only through question and answer can a discourse find itself organised as a *telos* which is an intention not of the speaker but of truth. The Socratic insistence that a poet, speaker or writer states his intention is a demand that intention enter a forum in which it does not hold absolute sway over discourse but is only one factor amongst others that presents itself to scrutiny via *elenchus*. Socrates wishes to draw inten-tion into the process of reception so that a discourse greater than the orig-inal text or statement may be collectively produced: both the autonomy of an authorial intention and the semantic autonomy of the text are to be resisted by a procedure which incorporates the original statement as a starting point for an ongoing and communal inquiry. Fixity is to be every-where resisted, either in the form of an intention imposed upon a text or

---

[11] In contesting the notion that the speaker's presence guarantees intention, Derrida ascribes to Socrates/Plato a confidence in the self-presence of intention which their words do not seem to support. Cf. Jacques Derrida, 'Signature, Event, Context', in his *Margins of Philosophy*, trans. Alan Bass (Brighton: Harvester Press, 1982), pp. 309–30: p. 316.

[12] On *dianoeisthai* and its relation to poetic intention, see Nickolas Pappas, 'Socrates' Charitable Treatment of Poetry', *Philosophy and Literature*, vol. 13, no. 2 (October 1989), pp. 248–61: p. 256.

[13] One notes how Havelock's thesis of the literate revolution giving birth to an autonomous subject would need to be radically recast in order to accommodate the oral and communal preferences of the Socratic/Platonic philosophy. See PtP, pp. 197–214.

in the changeless nature of written words: both categories belong to a monologism which Socrates would ceaselessly dialogise. Intention is an important category within discursive ethics but only in so far as it is responsive and accountable. Discourse is ever unfinished; hence it can possess an intention, but never a final one.

The Socratic starting-point, in any number of the earlier dialogues, does not take the form of a specific goal but a general will to search for the truth.[14] Socrates often presents himself as a man without a thesis, without knowledge, without a genius in Kierkegaard's sense, without a discourse: he asks to be taken as an enquirer armed only with the method and ethical imperative of *elenchus*. Neither intention nor reception assumes the status of a fixed or governing category but contributes to a process which aims at a truth beyond an individual point of view. The pre-eminence of the Socratic viewpoint is not directive but exploratory. In the early and middle dialogues, Socrates does not claim foreknowledge but the gift of inquisition.[15] Socratic dialogue seeks rather to shorten the shadows that fall between the discursive intention, the discursive act and discursive reception. This is not to deny the importance of intention as a category within the dialogic movement, but to show how it is processed and distilled in the very act of exchange: reception is fed back into the discourse so as to remodel or redirect the aims of that discourse and to encourage its rephrasing so as to reduce attendant ambiguities. Dialogue thus establishes a structure whereby reception may be monitored through dual and complementary strategies. First, it allows *selection of the audience* so that discourse may be (a) crafted to the dispositions of its auditors; and (b) refused to an audience considered potentially unsuitable. Secondly, it provides a means to evaluate audience uptake and eliminate misreception whether it arises from confused intentions on the part of the speaker or misreading of his intentions on the part of his listeners. The situation is similarly structured with regard to accountability. The speaker identifies himself, in the very act of speaking, as the promulgator of a doctrine or point of view, as the responsible agent of the discourse: he is enjoined thereby to take account

---

[14] Naturally the claim that Socrates has covert intentions can be made as part of a challenge to the famous Socratic *doctra ignoratio*. The view that the claim to ignorance is a ruse, albeit well-intentioned, has been developed in Norman Gulley's *The Philosophy of Socrates* (London: Macmillan, 1968). The contrary position that the Socratic disavowal of knowledge is genuine has been defended more recently in Terence Irwin, *Plato's Moral Theory* (Oxford: Clarendon, 1977), pp. 39–40. Whichever position one takes on the debate, it is clear that intention is so little privileged a category in the Socratic procedure as to be either absent or disguised.

[15] Notable exceptions here would be the *Gorgias* in which Socrates speaks in uncharacteristically evangelical tones, and the *Republic* where the drive of the dialogue is generally thetic.

of his doctrines, to register and bow to inconsistencies unearthed by *elenchus*, to defend and make good his propositions and to submit them to dialectical scrutiny before they can lay claim to being true descriptions, definitions, etc. At the same time, the speaker is spared the negative effects of accountability which arise in written discourse or didactic speechmaking by being presented with the opportunity to acquit himself publicly of: (i) false inferences made from his discourse; and (ii) falsity within his discourse. The question-and-answer method thus sets a scene quite alien to writing whereby expeditious retractions may be made by the promulgator of a discourse. Society is thus protected from ill-conceived discourse in the same gesture by which the speaker is protected from public malformation or violation of his or her discourse.

The interrogatory method thus serves an epistemological aim in concert with this attempt to restrain discursive transmission. Dialogic method builds in resistance to pre-emptive conclusions by its intersubjective processing of discourse. Inquisitional ethics refine the flow of thought by (i) providing regular obstacles to its unfolding; (ii) raising difficulties which the discourse might otherwise obfuscate or circumvent; and (iii) installing a regular and spontaneous principle of *refutatio* which is not guaranteed by the continuous treatise. In this resistance to monologic completion the form and *ethos* of Platonic–Socratic dialogue could not be further removed from Hegelian dialectic.[16] Although Hegel preserves the process of refinement through contradiction in his depiction of historical change as a discussion of the *Geist* in and with itself, the Hegelian conversation is finished within these frames, within the covers of its own text, its own history. Whilst the Hegelian play of thesis and antithesis preserves the movement of *elenchus* from a lower to a higher ground of consistency, the insistence on a realisable end-point within the system means that dialectical history is simply left the task of applying the final letters of a textual eschatology which its own logic of history has already supplied. The dialectic of world history does not submit to its own interrogation; nor is any other mind empowered to challenge the mind that has perceived this movement of *Geist*.

In this sense, Hegelian dialectic will always exemplify that form of nineteenth-century optimism which privileges the answer over the question, indeed formulates the question in the expectation of its answer. Such a prioritising of the answer over the question precludes open debate in that the system only invites dissent from outside the system,

---

[16] For a sharply critical distinction between Platonic and Hegelian dialectic, see Hans Georg Gadamer, *Hegel's Dialectic* (New Haven, CT: Yale University Press, 1976), pp. 3–34.

which is to say, outside the terms in which debate about the system might be possible: the terms of its language game are different from – if not indeed incommensurable with – those of a rational forum. Dialogue here arises in terms of an exteriority which has already been defined by the system itself: whereas Socratic dialogue will call its antagonists to itself, Hegelian dialectic makes contradiction its own truth, a confirmation of its own unresponsive dominance over the system. The forms of any such contradiction are already established within the system, always lie in the past which the system has already determined. The subject of Hegelian philosophy is always solitary, untraceable, absent from any courtroom or conference, guiding the dialectical process through history rather than being immanently and dialogically engaged in a particular moment of its unfolding. Whilst Hegel took many of his inspirations from the late dialogue *Parmenides*, nothing could be further from the Socratic practice of question and answer than the unresponsive predestination of *Geist* and its supposedly 'authorless' articulation in dialectical idealism.

Whether compared to the Hegelian philosophy or to any form of monologic discourse, the question-and-answer method works as a safeguard against precipitate judgements, the closing of a system of thought. So far from being an abstract organon, or reducible to a body of maxims or chrestomathy, dialectic as dialogue, as question and answer, encourages abstract thought but in the discontinuous, vital and inter-animating medium of inquisitive conversation. Rather than providing a fund of propositions, it fosters an activity of mind and thereby seeks to avoid iterability in an ever-renewing process. It also establishes a principle of discursive economy whereby logical lacunae are addressed in the act of composition rather than by the wasteful practice of a long treatise or book being challenged by another long treatise or book. The field of knowledge would thus remain uncluttered by exiguous material and the central problems of philosophy allowed to emerge with clarity. In this manner the Socratic dialogue resists the specious concept of 'written' authority. Neither is authority invested in the individual – on the basis, say, of a canon of reputable work – but in reasoning in the living present, in *dianoia*. In this sense, an immediate channel of speaking subject to audience might be seen to work against authority from fossilisation, to nullify that wide temporal gap between pronouncement and reception which, for example, was fallaciously to confer the status of unimpeachable judgement on classical authorities in the medieval era.

The structure is repeated, doubled; secure and consistent if indeed beyond practical realisation. Underlying its every manifestation is a concurrent suspicion of interiority (in the sense of individual or solitary intention) and exteriority (in so far as it denotes indiscriminate publication). A realm is established between the private and public spheres, a place neither of interior consciousness nor of widespread dissemination. The possibilities of unchecked and anti-social discourse are attenuated, along with the potential chaos of manifold readers producing manifold texts. Both as event and in terms of its theorisation in the *Phaedrus*, the Socratic dialogue forbids a private intuition to translate immediately into a public inscription. The abrupt transition from the interiority of authorial consciousness to that unchecked publicity marked by publication in print cultures is so foreign and yet so enigmatically close to this Socratic world as it justifies itself in the *Phaedrus*.

In dialogic form, the *Phaedrus* reflects upon the centrality of the conversational method to the epistemological as well as ethical and pedagogic aims of the Socratic–Platonic philosophy. Over the course of four Stephanus pages, the *Phaedrus* has identified a cluster of concerns which must bear on any attempt to establish an ethical foundation. So far from simply reflecting an historical or culturally determined preference, the method of question and answer is at the core of the Platonic theory of knowledge in so far as such a theory prescribes how knowledge must be communicated as well as acquired. With altogether more subtlety than the *Apology*, the *Phaedrus* serves as the summation of the achievement. of the Socratic life. Over the course of four Stephanus pages and in a seemingly throwaway or non-serious spirit – Socrates refers to the discussion as a pastime, game or play (*pepaisthō*: 278b) – the *Phaedrus* identifies a cluster of concerns which must bear on any attempt to establish an ethical framework for discursive acts. Some of the positive features of the method of question and answer may be enumerated as follows:[17]

(i)   accountability;
(ii) ethical constraints on circulation;

[17] This list might be augmented by collation with Stanley Fish's tabulated comparisons between dialectical speech and rhetorical writing in his *Self-Consuming Artifacts: The Experience of Seventeenth-Century Literature* (Los Angeles and London: University of California Press, 1972), pp. 19–20. The interrogation of Protagoras in this dialogue – one of the few instances in which dialectic deals with an absent author (one might even say that the situation is a *locus classicus* of written words being incapable of defending themselves, and always needing the rescuing presence of the father of *logoi*) – is a clear example of the severity with which Socrates and Plato would prevent the proliferation of unnecessary discourses. Disregarding the textual surfaces of Protagoras's *Truth* (whatever they may indeed have been), its central proposition alone is taken to task and found wanting by Socrates (*Theaetetus* 161c et seq.; 171a et seq.). Drastic though this may seem, it has contemporary relevance in a culture of academic over-publishing and the award of doctorates for theses which proceed from an initial premise which does not hold up to rational scrutiny.

(iii)   personal pedagogic relations;

(iv)   the opportunity to assess reception and the moral probity and competence of the discursive participants;

(v)   clarification of discourse and its intention: the incorporation of individual intention within a broader quest of understanding reality, the Just, the Good;

(vi)   an open-ended rather than pre-emptive discursive structure which discourages intellectual complacency by challenging opinion, dogma and the illusion of closure created by the fixity of the written text;

(vii)   the opportunity to establish worthy legatees;

(viii)   resistance to spurious (and often 'written') authority;

(ix)   a setting for 'on-the-spot' or punctual retraction or modification of claims;

(x)   collective responsibility for discursive production;

(xi)   a processual rather than proclamatory model of discourse;

(xii)   resistance to summary/secondary publicity;

(xiii)   a principle of discursive and noetic economy whereby the fundamental tenets of a discourse are considered independently of their textual presentation;

(xiv)   establishment of a realm *between* the private and public spheres, one neither interiorised nor disseminative.

Resistance to monologism undergirds these protocols: the text censures 'writing' only in so far as it shows itself incapable of responding to dialogic questioning. The process by which truth is achieved is also the process which confounds potential misreception. Guarantees that discourse has been understood are not only achieved by the seemingly negative practice of *elenchus* which clears false assumptions from the auditor but also via the more positively termed *maieusis* which draws forth knowledge from the *ephebe* himself. Comparing himself to the midwife in those very famous words to Theaetetus, Socrates makes it apparent that the delivery of truth belongs to the same movement which aborts falsehood. This proposition – no more than the merest tautology in epistemological terms – becomes an intriguing strategy when viewed from the perspective of the ethics of reception:

> My art of midwifery is in general like theirs; the only difference is that my patients are men, not women, and my concern is not with the body but with the soul that is in travail of birth. And the highest point of my art is the power to prove by every test whether the offspring of a young man's thought is a false phantom or instinct

with life and truth. I am so far like the midwife that I cannot myself give birth to wisdom . . . (*Theaetetus*, 150b–c)

Although Socrates' practice may sometimes contradict this characterisation – as it does in the *Gorgias* and *Republic* – it does splendid justice to the avowed aims of his method. Socrates is insufficient without an interlocutor; his interlocutor is only productive in the presence of his dialectical guide. Not only does *maieusis* deliver knowledge from the auditor's soul, it also separates the wheat from the tares in that soul, by determining what is stillborn from those insights that are alive, that are the legitimate children (*Phaedrus*, 278a–b; *Symposium*, 209a) of that soul. 'Accept then', Socrates enjoins Theaetetus:

> the ministrations of a midwife's son who himself practices his mother's art, and do the best you can to answer the questions I ask. Perhaps when I examine your statements I may judge one or another of them to be an unreal phantom. If I then take the abortion from you and cast it away, do not be savage with me like a woman robbed of her first child. People have often felt like that toward me and been positively ready to bite me for taking away some foolish notion they have conceived. They do not see that I am doing them a kindness. They have not learned that no divinity is ever ill-disposed toward man, nor is such action on my part due to unkindness; it is only that I am not permitted to acquiesce in falsehood and suppress the truth. (*Theaetetus*, 151b–d)

The 'negative' work of *elenchus* is also the 'positive' work of *maieusis*; it is the moment of attendance whereby knowledge comes forth without any danger of misreception, either in the soul of the speaker or those of his auditors.[18] It ensures absolute lucidity in the communication between the signatory and countersignatory, seals a moment in which 'ignorance of what is a waking vision and what is a mere dream image of justice and injustice, good and evil . . .' (*Phaedrus*, 277d–e) has been dispelled. The truth it reveals has been written on the soul of the *ephebe*, writes itself from the soul of the *ephebe*: therein is the dream of dialectic. The epistemological purity of the discourse is vouchsafed according to the same method which protects society from the overspill of malformed discourse, or malformation in audience uptake of true discourse.

---

[18] This binarism of the negative *elenchus* and the positive *maieusis* is open to challenge on many fronts. On the relation, see Robinson, *Plato's Earlier Dialectic*, pp. 87–8. Robinson regards both procedures as destructive. On the other hand, the present work sees *elenchus* as tending towards the positive, a thesis we will develop in the concluding chapter.

Underlying all these categories is the form of contract between author and reader, speaker and auditor, by which the former acts as a philosopher and psychologist and ensures the appropriateness, the competence of his discourse's beneficiaries and legatees. This relation might be described as a structure of oral signature and oral countersignature wherein a discourse must write itself through the master to pupil and be rewritten back to the master. In the form of such a dialectico-oral signature, a signature which is also a countersignature, which signs itself again and again under a plethora of names – 'Socrates' and 'Plato' to start with, but also those imagined but unforeseen pupils into which the primary signature has been written – the *Phaedrus* seeks to domesticate and encompass the entire ethical problematic of discursive transmission: of a discourse's reception, appropriation, its legacies and the pedagogic relations established between its subject and audience. Once it has witnessed its own safe transmission and the establishment of a worthy legacy, the signature may then erase itself, the master may depart, in the assurance of autonomous truth; a truth which will carry the signature forward in itself, in its sons and brothers, who bear the name and the name's genius under names of their own. For what survives the master is the son of his thought in the form of ensouled truth brought to maturity by *dianoia*: *logos* may in its turn father fresh *logoi* or be developed beside its siblings as ensouled truth in its father's tutees.[19]

The ambition is breathtaking: not only does dialectic seek to bring all discourse under its protection and judgement, it also aspires to secure its own future. What the *Phaedrus* dreams is a text and a tradition that can project its destinies from within its own resources, a work from which chance and historical change are excluded, one whose reconstruction can only take place in the apodeitic mirror of its construction. Through a lineage established exclusively on the basis of question and answer, Plato's Socrates seeks to ensure a failsafe structure of legacy whereby the fruits of discussion are carried forward into a future from which the master has

---

[19] Within the family scene of dialectical inheritance, the *logoi* are cast in the relation of filial dependence. When dispossessed of the primary father, the *logoi* are made wards of the dialectical pupils. The interpersonal succession involved in dialectical instruction is thus one of instruction in the art of parenthood – from the 'natural' father to the 'adoptive' parent. As Derrida has shown us: 'One could say anachronously that the "speaking subject" is *father* of his speech. And one would quickly realise that this is no metaphor, at least in the sense of any common, conventional effect of rhetoric. *Logos* is a son, then, a son that would be destroyed in his very presence without the present attendance of his father. His father who answers. His father who speaks for him and answers for him. Without his father, he would be nothing but, in fact, writing. At least that is what is said by the one who says: it is the father's thesis. The specificity of writing would thus be intimately bound to the absence of the father' (PP, 77).

absented himself. As such, dialogue hopes to rule out the distortions that attend a fixed form of words, those spectres of counter-legacy, revisionism and misappropriation which haunt the unresponsive text. Whilst the truths towards which dialectic aspires are – like the *eidē* – static, the quest of those truths is mobile, plastic, re-phraseable. Hence the womb of dialectical *logoi* is never in winter but fertilises its seeds, guarantees increase and immortality (*Phaedrus*, 277a). Legacy, in its movement through time, its movement through mortal frames, its overriding of death, moves invulnerable to time, mortality, vicissitude: it carves a channel through the future wherein it cannot be assailed, misinterpreted. Though insulated and unique as a temporal event, the dialogic scene of instruction wishes to be repeatable in essence according to a model of legacy, of continuity no less magical than procreation itself. Analogous to the genetic extension of the self through posthumous time, dialectical wisdom strives to renew itself in a form which continues without repeating, replicates without reduplication:

> lucidity and completeness and serious importance belong only to those lessons on justice and honor and goodness that are expounded and set forth for the sake of instruction, and are veritably written in the soul of the listener, and . . . such discourses as these ought to be accounted a man's own legitimate children – a title to be applied primarily to such as originate within the man himself, and secondarily to such of their sons and brothers as have grown up aright in the souls of other men . . . (*Phaedrus*, 278a)

The master, the founder, continues in his offspring; his heirs repeat him without repeating his words, execute his will without its words. The claim is astonishing. It answers questions no one would dream to ask. How can a discourse which only articulates itself in the present perdure? How can a wisdom which forbids repetition replicate itself without, at some level, repeating itself? How can a discourse survive its author without opening itself to misappropriation? How might a text or a tradition thus programme its own future, make its destinies predictable within its own resources?

Whereas one can envisage a set of mathematical axioms travelling through history with a degree of security, to assert as much for a body of philosophical work would seem egregiously counterfactual. The work of a pure science such as that achieved by Euclid might surrender its axioms to the future without risk of significant distortion. How, on the other hand, might a text or tradition such as dialectic avoid the fate of misreading which a Thomas More or Charles Darwin so dreaded (in his

anxious 'Prefaces' to *The Origin of Species*) and – albeit with a bitter irony –
Nietzsche was to embrace in calling all interpretations to return eternally
to his name which came to its bearer to indicate not a person so much as
a destiny?[20] The question that the *Phaedrus* raises explicitly in terms of all
other texts also makes itself heard throughout Plato's *oeuvre*, as the question of its own future, its own claims to truth and scientificity. It is also a
question that strikes a clear if unaccustomed note of gravity even for us,
even today in that the legacy presents itself as an ethical discrimination
between those who are fitted to take up the text that falls into their hands
and those who are not: which is to say that ethical misreading, the risk of
writing, is the very condition of legacy's existence. How Plato envisages
such misreading will be the topic of the following section.

II: SUITABLE AND UNSUITABLE READERS

It was the dream itself enchanted me
Character isolated by a deed
To engross the present and dominate memory.
Players and painted stage took all my love
And not those things that they were emblems of.

(W. B. Yeats, 'The Circus Animals' Desertion')

Like Socrates, Jesus taught only by word of mouth. He wrote but once,
and in response to the Pharisees as they gathered to stone the adulteress:
'Jesus stooped down, and with his fingers wrote on the ground, as though
he heard them not' (John 8: 6). These words – inscribed we assume in dust
or sand – were neither recorded nor seen. He also enjoined his followers
to 'Give not that which is holy unto the dogs, neither cast ye your pearls
before swine, lest they trample them under their feet, and turn again and
rend you' (Matthew 7: 6).

If not an injunction against writing, these words are the sternest rec-
ommendation that the gift of *logos* is not to be given indiscriminately.[21]

---

[20] The distinction between the scupulous safeguards Sir Thomas More took to ensure that his *Utopia* would not be open to dangerous translations onto the plane of historico-political institutions and the cavalier disregard Nietzsche displayed towards his legacies, is repeated within a single *oeuvre*, that of Plato. On the one hand, the *Phaedrus* is overtaken with the issue of responsible dissemination and maintains the dialogic ideal; on the other, his *Republic* is monologic, authoritarian and neglects to build generic bulwarks against its implementation as a model for totalitarian ideologies.

[21] Writing itself would deprive the apostles of that power to discriminate between the worthy and unworthy recipients of a discourse: one might even see the development of a New Testament canon as an act of apostasy similar to one made by Plato's textualisation of Socratic orality. Prior to Christianity, writing was rarely seen as a medium by which the power of an institution might be increased: from the time of Plato, through to the Middle Platonists, writing was seen to threaten the authority of the Academy. For a thorough account of the indirect Platonic tradition, see John Dillon, *The Middle Platonists: A Study of Platonism 80 B.C. to A.D. 220* (London: Duckworth, 1977).

Two centuries later, Clement of Alexandria deemed that writing a book is analogous to leaving a sword in the hands of a child. The Lord, Clement says, did not 'disclose to the many what did not belong to the many'. Rather, he taught by word to 'the few he knew that they belonged, who were capable of receiving and being moulded according to them'. The divine truths are therefore 'entrusted to speech not to writing . . .'.[22] The Platonic echoes scarcely need to be underscored. The fear expressed is one that runs through Antiquity (and accounts in no small part for its investment in all order of esoteric practices) and is that discourse may be perverted, turned against its author and the institution to which he belongs. Beyond direct recrimination, the bringing of author and institution into disrepute, there is the further danger that misread intentions will have a malign influence on the future development of society. The matter is put somewhat less prescriptively in the *Seventh Letter*. Referring to supposedly 'unwritten doctrines', the author of the letter attests:

> If I thought it possible to deal adequately with the subject in a treatise or a lecture for the general public, what finer achievement would there have been in my life than to write a work of great benefit to mankind and to bring the nature of things to light for all men? I do not, however, think the attempt to tell mankind of these matters a good thing, except in the case of some few who are capable of discovering the truth for themselves with a little guidance. In the case of the rest to do so would excite in some an unjustified contempt in a thoroughly offensive fashion, in others certain lofty and vain hopes, as if they had acquired some awesome lore. (341d–342a)[23]

This preoccupation with the afterlife of a written discourse is clearly ethical, although, as is so often the case in Plato, the ethical and the epistemological are closely entwined. Those who know will know without benefit of writing and need only a modicum of dialectical guidance; those who do not know will never know – the *lexis* of writing being unable to foster the *logoi* of thought. Writing cannot be beneficial to either class: exiguous in the case of the wise (*philosophoi*), it can only be pernicious when rendered unto the unwise or seeming wise (*doxosophoi*). It will

---

[22] Clement of Alexandria, *The Writings of Clement of Alexandria*, trans Rev. William Wilson, *Ante-Nicene Christian Library: Translations of the Church Fathers, Down to A.D. 325*, eds Rev Alexander Roberts and James Donaldson, vol. 4 (Edinburgh: T. and T. Clark, 1867), p. 356.

[23] The *Seventh Letter* is here invoked as representative of the ancient suspicion of writing in general rather than as a constituent of the Platonic *oeuvre*. The issue of its authenticity is not to the point in this particular context: one might cite Isocrates, Alcidamas or Gorgias to similar, if less sophisticated effect.

provide the latter with a means to falsify true doctrine or apparently to
validate false doctrine. Positive terms being absent, the negative ethical
effects of the spread of false wisdom weigh the case in favour of speech.[24]

The *Phaedrus*, however, is not nearly so decisive. An overt distinction
between suitable and unsuitable readers is drawn. Although embedded in
repudiations of writing, Socrates' words at 275e4 identify the 'right
people', those who understand (*tois epaḯousin*) and can derive some benefit
from written words. Furthermore, just as the statement of impersonality
was adumbrated by the rejection of Tisias's authority, so the earlier words
on rhetoric form a pre-philosophical rehearsal of the concern with reception at 275d–e: epideictic rhetoricians are enjoined to craft their speeches
on the model of the souls of their auditors. The serious rhetorician:

> will classify the types of discourse and the types of soul, and the
> various ways in which souls are affected, explaining the reasons in
> each case, suggesting the type of speech appropriate to each type of
> soul, and showing what kind of speech can be relied on to create
> belief in one soul and disbelief in another, and why. (*Phaedrus*, 271b)

Discourse once again is modelled on its audience. An irresponsible
rhetorician will assume unanimity of reception and thus fail to separate
suitable from unsuitable recipients of his speech. The rhetorician with his
eye on the higher pursuit will not only make this separation but will allow
each class of reader, each disposition of soul, to determine the content and
style of the discourse it receives. In the last speech before taking up the
speech/writing question, Socrates declares that 'unless the aspirant to
oratory can on the one hand list the various natures amongst his prospec-
tive audiences, and on the other divide things into their kinds and embrace

---

[24] Friedländer again defends writing as essential for a society in which all have not risen to a state of
gnosis: 'in the second-best state, fallible men may need the aid of the written word. True poetry of
the soul comes through a god-like communication with the eternal. But when the inspiration is
not present, preserved discourses may give some direction to education . . . Besides their role in
education, written laws can help guide the state in its ordinary functions . . . The state described
by the *Laws* lacks the absolute order of the world set up by the *Republic*. The Athenian knows that
heretical discourses have been scattered through the realm. The legislator himself must propose
counterarguments. Thus towards the end of his life, Plato begins to recognize that a wise man must
fight error by some more direct method.' Paul Friedländer, *Plato 1: An Introduction*, 3 vols, trans.
Hans Meyerhoff (London: Routledge & Kegan Paul, 1958), pp. 397–8. As we contended towards
the close of the last chapter, though, the distinction between the author of the *Laws* and of the
dialogues is unwarranted if our terms remain strictly ethical. There may well be a certain loss of
metaphysical faith, of the optimism expressed in the *epekeina tês ousias*, but awareness of the need
to protect against human fallibility. Moreover, the *Ion*, the *Republic*, the *Phaedrus* and other dialogues share the Athenian's knowledge that 'heretical discourses have been spread through the
realm' and have all, in different and effective manner, proposed counterarguments. Indeed, the
direct methods have already been developed in the trials of writings, sophistics and poetry prior
to their crystallisation in the *Laws*.

each individual thing under a single form, he will never attain such success as is within the grasp of mankind' (*Phaedrus*, 273d–e). The opposition between the competent and incompetent auditor/reader does not supervene on the section demonstrating the inferiority of the written word: it has been a preoccupation carefully structured into the dialogue itself.

Nevertheless, to ask who are the 'suitable' and 'unsuitable' readers demarcated in the *Phaedrus* may on first inspection seem redundant, a false trail.[25] The threat of misreading could come from anywhere. Danger arises from the simple fact of writing being abroad in a culture. The unsuitable reader may arise in his or her encounter with the text of truth, an innocent who may misprise the discourse of *alētheia*. Equally, the unsuitable reader may be found among those vulnerable who take the texts of sophistry for true discourse. In the form of the sophist, there is the unsuitable reader who pillages epic authority to advance mere opinion; there is also the unsuitable author who weaves deceptive tracts from such citation and with the persuasive power of citationality in general. Discourse must therefore be bound within a very small group of dialectical adepts who are trained and accredited in an interpersonal forum. In this manner, the author of a discourse may dispense with the task of limiting publication to an acceptable readership: besides its practical impossibility, such a procedure would not fulfil the requirements of *elenchus*, of limiting discursive transmission and reception to the here and now. Members of a very small elite are to be made the sole inheritors of *logos*: the oral format precludes the masses from any access to the conclusions reached by dialectical discussion. Dialectical method acts as a containment; the oral forum as the boundary separating the common world from the *sanctum sanctorum*, a ring of fire that keeps the ill-befitted at bay.

Along such lines, we might then identify the unsuitable readers with the masses (*demos*) and infer, almost by means of synecdoche, that the *Republic*'s resistance to the mob playing any part in determining the

---

[25] I have used the terms 'suitable' and 'unsuitable' readers for reasons of concision and after Walter Hamilton's translation of this passage. Hackforth translates 'those who understand it and those who have no business with it . . . the right people and . . . the wrong'; Rowe renders the phrase as 'those who know about the subject and those who have nothing at all to do with it . . . those it should address and those it should not . . .'; Nehamas and Woodruff translate the words as 'those with understanding [and] . . . those who have no business with it . . . those to whom it should speak and to whom it should not'; recently, Scully proposes 'those who understand as well as those who have no business reading it'. See *Phaedrus and the Seventh and Eighth Letters*, trans. Walter Hamilton (Harmondsworth: Penguin Books, 1973); *Plato: Phaedrus*, trans. C. J. Rowe (Warminster: Aris and Phillips, 1986); *Plato: Phaedrus*, trans. Alexander Nehamas and Paul Woodruff (Indianapolis, IN and Cambridge: Hackett, 1995), Stephen Scully, *Plato's Phaedrus* (Newburyport, MA: Focus Philosophical Library, 2003).

organisation of society acquires its pendant in the *Phaedrus*'s fear that discourse too might become a public and democratic possession. The truths of dialectic, therefore, are to be expounded in a public arena which is also the theatre of a very select privacy. One might also enlist to this claim the *Gorgias*. Socrates declares that while he is in love with the truth, Callicles is in love with the masses (*demos*). Towards the start of the dialogue, in words used of the 'crowd' that repeat (and yet, as we shall see, crucially deviate from) the depiction of the unsuitable readers in the *Phaedrus*, Socrates rebukes Gorgias:

> SOCRATES: Well, you said just now that a rhetorician will be more
>   persuasive than a doctor regarding health.
> GORGIAS: Yes, I said so, before a crowd.
> SOCRATES: And before a crowd means among the ignorant, for
>   surely, among those who know, he will not be more
>   convincing than the doctor. (*Gorgias*, 459a)

What is true here of oratory will be more gravely the case with written words (*logoi gegrammenoi*) which are still more resistant to public questioning than the texts of demagogic delivery. While literate cultures have devised numerous means to limit discursive circulation (from the adoption of specialised vocabularies, the institution of clergies, the quasi-secular and belated nineteenth-century adventure of instituting a clerisy, to name but a few)[26] the Socrates of the *Phaedrus* will act – right up to the end-point of the discussion – as though there are no bulwarks against dissemination in a graphic culture. Hence writing shares the very open-ended and anarchic tendencies of Plato's vision of democracy. 'One could compare the trial of writing with the trial of democracy outlined in the *Republic*,' says Derrida, as he argues that Plato envisages democratic man as 'wandering like a desire or like a signifier freed from *logos*', an adventurer who, 'like the one in *Phaedrus*, simulates everything at random and is really nothing' (PP, 145).[27] The contest between speech and writing would seem clearly drawn and in consonance with the Platonic view of society in general. Speech can be made to serve a small and worthy elite;

---

[26] Cf. Ben Knights, *The Idea of the Clerisy in the Nineteenth Century* (Cambridge: Cambridge University Press, 1978) for a valuable account of the Romantic and post-Romantic attempt to establish an interpretative elite in English culture.

[27] Derrida uses captivating anthromorphisms which confound writing with the qualities it tends to promote. Rather than allow that writing facilitates democracy, Derrida's characterisation implies that writing, for Plato, is the embodiment of democratic man: 'At the disposal of each and of all, available on the sidewalks, isn't writing thus essentially democratic? One could compare the trial of writing with the trial of democracy outlined in the *Republic*. In a democratic society, there is no concern for competence: responsibilities are given to anyone at all. Magistracies are decided by lots (557a). Equality is dispersed to equal and unequal alike (558e)' (PP, 144).

writing cannot be constrained and will empower the *demos*. Hence no man will write when he is really serious (*spoudē*) (*Seventh Letter*, 344c–e; *Phaedrus*, 276e, 277e–278d).

In many respects, such a response is incontestable. No one will wish to claim that Plato has anything but fearful mistrust of democracy, especially that form of Athenian democracy which condemned to death his friend and master. Likewise, it would be absurd to argue that writing does not in itself tend towards a wider availability of discourses. However, the development of literacy does not consort with democratic reform either *de facto* or *de jure*. So far from existing in any causal relation, systems of communication and systems of political organisation did not fall into any pattern or parallelism in the ancient world.[28] The technology of writing offered itself as much to autocratic fiat as to democratic enfranchisement: the effect of writing in Sumeria, for example, was to freeze the laws for centuries.[29] Given also that the claims of widespread literacy in fifth and fourth century BC Athens have been shown to have little or foundation,[30] the advent of writing would have seemed scarcely propitious to either the political claims of the masses or the reform of political and legal systems.[31] One might wonder, then, whether the class of 'suitable' readers marked out by the *Phaedrus* comprises an elite within an elite – those few of the literate few who are also true philosophers. The possibility of an emergent literate majority (and the political empowerment of the masses which this might entail) is expressed not once in the course of Plato's copious reflections on democracy: one can be sure that if such a prospect were in sight, Plato would have been swift to comment upon its undesirability. So scant, in any case, is Plato's regard for the masses that it seems unlikely he would credit

---

[28] On Thomas's argument, the jagged history of writing's assimilation into Greek culture reveals that '[t]here is no straightforward relationship between political system and the written word.' Rosalind Thomas, *Literacy and Orality in Ancient Greece*, (Cambridge: Cambridge University Press, 1992) p. 149. Against the crude assumption that widespread use of written records is causally related to the development of democratic institutions, she makes the altogether more plausible case that democracy arose 'slowly and in response to specific historical developments' (p. 144).

[29] We must here contest Thomas's claim that Plato came to 'espouse the view that the truly philosophical doctrines should not be written down at all, for fear that they get into the hands of the ignorant multitude' (*ibid.*, p. 126). As Thomas's argument itself shows, the multitude were unlettered (*agrammatoi*), making it altogether likely that the objects of Plato's fears lay not in the masses but in the literate elite.

[30] The thesis of widespread literacy in fifth-century BC Athens has been exhaustively discredited by William V. Harris in *Ancient Literacy* (Cambridge, MA: Harvard University Press, 1989).

[31] 'Written law . . . may be a necessary condition for social justice but it is not a sufficent one. The social and political context determined the efficacy of written law in ancient Greece as elsewhere, and it could equally well have conservative or aristocratic as democratic force.' Thomas, *Literacy and Orality in Ancient Greece*, p. 147. One need only consider its inverse to recognise the redundancy and good sense of this proposition.

them with the capacity to misread a serious discourse. As the *Gorgias* and *Republic* make clear, the masses are always in a state of ignorance (*agnoia*). That Plato *would* strenuously resist writing as a tool of democratic empowerment is beyond doubt; that he *did* remains conjecture.

This is not at all to clear Plato of the charge of elitism: while the same cannot be said of the historical Socrates, Plato's view of discourse is elitist in the extreme.[32] We are only concerned here to note that there is neither internal nor external evidence to suggest that universal discursive enfranchisement was considered a possibility by the Athenians of the late fifth and early fourth centuries BC. Entirely more plausible – and fecund – is the hypothesis that Plato's anxieties are directed towards the already literate classes. Following this intuition, we might turn to the *Republic* not in the tedious expectation of reaffirming the anti-democratic tenor of Plato's thought, but in the hope of finding the class of readers who seem to so trouble Plato and the Socrates of the *Phaedrus*.

Two classes of unsuitable reader are revealed in *Republic* II and *Republic* V respectively: (i) those readers who need to be protected from psychic and moral damage by exposure to material for which they are not psychically prepared; and (ii) those readers who will pervert the discourses which fall into their hands. In the first case the reader is jeopardised by the text; in the second, the text (and by implication, society at large) is threatened by the reader. The former we may regard as passively unsuitable readers; the latter as actively unsuitable readers. Implications of victimisation gather on the one side; villainy on the other. Both categories are of equal importance in ethical terms (and indeed the passively unsuitable reader may evolve into the active case), but it is my contention that the anxieties of the *Phaedrus* focus more towards the latter.

Discourse and its proper bounding is an axial theme not only of the philosophical interrogation of rhetoric but of society itself. The issue of censorship, as it is raised in *Republic* II, will naturally have many affinities with the attempt to contain discourse within dialogic form as elaborated by the closing pages of the *Phaedrus*: in this sense, the aims of both dialogues are consonant. However, though one might read the *Phaedrus* as an act of unilateral censorship, the interdiction of writing is far from asserting itself *tout court*. Several considerations militate against such a reading. First, writing is allowed to elderly philosophers to mitigate their declining memory: although one assumes that this takes the form of a

---

[32] On the anti-elitism of the Socratic practice, see *Apology* 29d; 33a–b; Vlastos, *Socratic Studies*, pp. 87–108.

letter from a present to a potentially future self, its extension beyond this privacy is not actively forbidden. Moreover, as we shall see in the next chapter, the mooting of a tribunal (*Phaedrus*, 278c–d), whose operations will be very different from those of a board of censors, does not work to outlaw writing but productively to cancel certain of its shortcomings.

Indeed, censorship would spare Socrates his considerable labours in the closing section of the *Phaedrus*. The banishment of unsuitable discourses would shortcircuit the need to distinguish between suitable and unsuitable readers. Philosophy could then dispense with the ethical necessity of ensuring that a discourse is signed, whether orally or graphically. Censorship and the signature are institutions hostile to each other: the one affirming the need to monitor discourse before publication, the other accepting a responsibility for the post-publication life of a discourse. The desire to ban a discourse altogether obliterates the ethical necessity of attending to either a text's inception or reception, the past of its writing or the future of its reading. It is not in the *Phaedrus* but in *Republic* II that Socrates speaks in such peremptory tones:

> as to saying that God, who is good, becomes the cause of evil to anyone, we must contend in every way that neither should anyone assert this in his own city if it is to be well governed, nor anyone hear it, neither younger nor older, neither telling a story in meter or without meter, for neither would the saying of such things, if they are said, be holy, nor would they be profitable to us or concordant with themselves. (*Republic*, 380b)

A certain discourse is here deemed to be unspeakable, unreadable in ethical terms. No tribunal, no access to proper intention or exercise of Socratic *elenchus* can redeem discourses that are ethically destructive in and of themselves. Such a position is itself extreme where the *Phaedrus* is discriminating, heavy-handed where the latter is subtle, open-ended, leaden and resigned where the discourse of speech/writing is intelligently festive, light of tongue in its high seriousness.

A little earlier in the *Republic*, however, Socrates distinguished between youth and age in terms of suitable and unsuitable readers. In youth the soul is malleable, corruptible, and its entelechy may be skewed by the intrusion of inappropriate discourse: thus nurses and mothers must be encouraged to cultivate the souls of children by seemly discourse, appropriate and sanctioned use of *muthos* so as to 'shape their souls by these stories far rather than their bodies by their hands' (*Republic*, 377c). Hence the state and its legislators, guardians and *philosophoi* must intervene in the material made available to the fragile, inchoate reading or auditing of the young. In words that might easily be counter-pointed with the wonderfully condensed themes of the *Phaedrus*, 275–8, the *Republic*'s Socrates affirms that while the book cannot select its readers, the young cannot select their reading: 'For the young are not able to distinguish what is and what is not allegory, but whatever opinions are taken into the mind at that age are wont to prove indelible and unalterable' (*Republic*, 378d). We need only think of the example of *graphic* pornography – be it the representation of sex or violence – to see the weighty ethical principles motivating Plato's fears of a technology that cannot monitor its own reception. Something also of the idea of a writing in the soul is picked up negatively here: the very concept of indelibility, similar to Freud's account of unconscious traces, will make us think of those social and psychological theories which insist on the indelible nature of psychic scars inflicted upon the young by exposure to pornography. One will think also – in another key – of the fatal writ against Socrates as a 'corrupter of youth'.

The young are unsuitable readers: discourse in itself, detached from a speaker, from an intention, from the inter-psychic securities of *elenchus*, from a face-to-face meeting of souls, cannot determine if its readership is old or young. Hence the censorship of content (*logoi*) must be accompanied by rigid rules governing style (*lexis*). Prosaic reductions of poetic discourse are to be preferred: metaphor, allegory, tropes in general should be forsworn as dangerous, as misleading and shadowy effects which deprive discourse of its ideal transparency and threaten to obscure a message whose overall intent may well be worthy (*Republic*, 393c–394b).

One may, of course, see the dynamic of suitable/unsuitable readers as trivialised by being grafted onto the opposition adulthood/childhood. However, the *Republic* develops from its concerns with the fragility of the infantile psyche to include young men in the class of ill-equipped readers (388d). Indeed, as the argument proceeds, even the guardians themselves are identified as unsuitable readers, as possessed of insufficient detachment to resist empathising with the speeches and situations of dramatic characters (*Republic*, 395c–dff). Within the entire compass of dialectical education, the opposition youth/age might be usefully appended to those between master and *ephebe*, suitable and unsuitable pupil. In a programme which proceeds – *viva vox* – by a shaping or a leading of the soul (*psuchagōgia*), the responsible dialectician is perfectly placed to determine what mode of discourse, what knowledge, what information will be appropriate to each stage in the development of the *ephebe*'s soul. Thus an *ephebe* may be an unsuitable auditor of certain discourses in the early phase of his novitiate and a suitable auditor or even reader at a later stage.

One and the same individual may be both an unsuitable and a suitable reader along the temporal and educational trajectories of dialectical instruction or *paideia*. When Socrates says that the 'dialectician selects a soul of the right type' (276e) he doubtless means a suitable individual, but he also prescribes a particular state of awareness in that individual. In its ripened state, indeed, the soul may even evolve to a point of wisdom whereby it is fortified against the dangers of writing; in such state, the *philosophos* may utilise the medium as recreation, mnemonic device:

> He will sow his seed in literary gardens . . . and write when he does write by way of pastime, collecting a store of refreshment (*hupomnēmata*) both for his own memory, against the day 'when age oblivious comes,' and for all such as tread in his footsteps (*tauton ikhnos*), and he will take pleasure in watching the tender plants grow up. And when other men resort to other pastimes, regaling themselves with drinking parties and suchlike, he will doubtless prefer to indulge in the recreation I refer to. (*Phaedrus*, 276d)

Republic VII also segregates in similar fashion. Here, the distinction to be made is between suitable and unsuitable novitiates in the art of dialectic. While the issue is once again of maturity, the emphasis is switched. The concern is that dialectical discourse be protected from unsuitable practitioners. Such a position moves somewhat closer to the tenor of the *Phaedrus* which – along with the *Seventh Letter* – is concerned with the contamination of discourse by incompetent or malign readers. However the main contention here is that the discipline rather than society is threatened by its tiros.[33] Having introduced into the *Republic* a discussion of parenting which invites comparison with the *Phaedrus*, Socrates outlines the precautions which must be taken before training disciples in dialectical method:

> And is it not one chief safeguard not to suffer them to taste of it while young? For I fancy you have not failed to observe that lads, when they first get a taste of disputation, misuse it as a form of sport, always employing it contentiously, and, imitating confuters, they themselves confute others. They delight like puppies in pulling about and tearing with words all who approach them . . . And when

---

[33] This is not to suggest that the society constructed in the *Republic* can be dissociated from dialectic. We only wish to draw attention to the difference in emphasis between the *Republic*'s censoring of unsuitable dialecticians (addressed towards maintaining the integrity of the discipline, its purity as discourse) and the *Phaedrus*'s anxieties about protecting society from unsuitable readers. The controlling of entry into dialectic practice is an institutional matter and one whose success is assumed by the *Republic*, whilst the controlling of writing is a social matter and the *Phaedrus* considers it impossible to realise.

they have themselves confuted many and been confuted by many,
they quickly fall into a violent distrust of all that they formerly held
true, and the outcome is that they themselves and the whole business of philosophy are discredited with other men . . . But an older
man will not share this craze . . . but will rather choose to imitate
the one who consents to examine truth dialectically than the one
who makes a jest and a sport of mere contradiction, and so he will
himself be more reasonable and moderate, and bring credit rather
than discredit upon his pursuit. (*Republic*, 539b–d)

Dialectic believes itself to possess the resources to keep the unbefitting,
the impertinent, the headstrong from the gates. The house of writing by
contrast is always open, quietly inviting and unmanned: no one keeps vigil
over its entrants, no one discriminates between guests and interlopers,
between those who will behave once inside and those who will wreak
havoc within its walls. Writing is undefended, without policy or programme in terms of who is admitted and who is refused. In the *Phaedrus*,
Socrates speaks of writing's inability to come to its own assistance
(*boētheia*), to defend or acquit itself, of its helplessness before censure or
abuse. He does so in terms that suggest the plight of one who has not
grown to philosophical maturity, of an infant in the realm of thought;
terms that will recall us to the fact that writing had scarcely entered its
childhood in fifth-century BC Athens. The discourse, rather than its
reader, is in jeopardy, but what is jeopardised may also unwittingly aggress
when inappropriately fostered and Plato's foremost anxiety is that society
at large will be compromised by the misreading of written texts. Which
is to say that the unsuitable readers, in promulgating their own version of
a literally 'speechless' discourse, will become unsuitable authors (whether
of written or spoken compositions). In reading they will rewrite and what
they write will be misreading. They will improvise mixed discourses, creating collages and mosaics, fragments and echoes, shadowy perversions of
the text which has fallen into their hands.

In searching for this active class of unsuitable readers, the argument of
Republic V provides a clarification of who Plato and Socrates have in mind
when they wish to limit discursive circulation. Spurred on by the distinction between three constituents of the individual soul and of society
in general – in a curve that will lead to announcing the philosopher as
ruler of the state – Plato discriminates between two classes of literate
intellectual: lovers of wisdom and lovers of opinion.

The concern to separate the genuine lover of wisdom from the char-
latan is a consistent preoccupation throughout Plato's corpus. Thus the

proponent of eristic is vigorously distinguished from dialecticians, the
sophist from the philosopher, the philosopher from the poet. In the
Phaedo Socrates echoes the mystic aphorism '[m]any bear the emblems,
but the devotees are few' (69c), and in the *Sophist* the distinction between
the philosopher and his shadow is registered in terms that are not only
cognitive but ontological (*Sophist*, 253e–254b). In *Republic* V, however,
when Plato is envisaging the future of society, the task of establishing a
dichotomy between intellectuals will be fundamental to the ethical
ordering of the Ideal State. So many of the major tributaries of Platonism
run through this section of argument (473–480a), which forms the third
wave of response to the objections made to the constitution of the Ideal
State. Pressing a distinction central to the entire Platonic enterprise, and
one in which epistemological and ethical claims work in sublime concert,
Socrates claims that familiarity with particulars of experience will
produce not insight but merely conviction, not knowledge (*epistēmē*) but
opinion (*doxa*). Two cognitive states are thereby delineated which relate
to classes of individual: on the one hand, the *philosophoi* who attain knowledge of the forms; on the other, the *philodoxoi*, sightseers in the world of
appearances, tourists who perceive the beauty of particulars but not
beauty itself. The *philodoxoi* 'delight in beautiful tones and colours and
shapes and in everything that art fashions out of these, but their thought
is incapable of apprehending and taking delight in the nature of the beautiful in itself' (*Republic*, 476b). The distinction derives from Socrates'
definition of the true philosopher at 475b as one who 'desires all wisdom,
not a part and a part not':

> But the one who feels no distaste in sampling every study, and who
> attacks his task of learning gladly and cannot get enough of it, him
> we shall justly pronounce the lover of wisdom, the philosopher, shall
> we not?
>
> To which Glaucon replied, You will then be giving the name to
> a numerous and strange band, for all the lovers of spectacles are what
> they are, I fancy, by virtue of their delight in learning something.
> And those who always want to hear some new thing are a very
> queer lot to be reckoned among philosophers. You couldn't induce
> them to attend a serious debate or any such entertainment, but as if
> they had farmed out their ears to listen to every chorus in the land,
> they run about to all the Dionysiac festivals, never missing one,
> either in the towns or in the country villages. Are we to designate
> all these, then, and similar folk and all the practitioners of the minor
> arts as philosophers? (475c–e)

The doxophilist is a perpetual theatregoer, a *thursus*-bearer rather than a mystic, a dilettante wandering through a pageant of pleasing appearances, one for whom (to adapt our epigraph drawn from that most Platonic of modern poets) 'players and painted stage' occlude those realities they are 'emblems of'. A dreamer so enchanted by his dream he knows not he is dreaming, the doxophilist roams, like writing, like the unreserved sign, like the ungovernable *grammata*, never apprehending 'that essence which is eternal, and is not wandering between the two poles of generation and decay' (485b).

Whilst the depiction of the doxophilist doubtless belongs to Plato's *agon* with the sophists, with Isocrates, with the poets, Socrates' demonstration here displays a disinterested philosophical coherence.[34] The depth of argument becomes clearer when registered in terms of the Form of Justice as well as of Beauty. The perception of many just behaviours do not yield understanding of justice. Like instances of beauty, an example of justice is always subject to compresence of opposites. The doxophilist would say it is just to return that which has been borrowed. However, he would fail to see that in some situations it will be unjust to do so (e.g. when your neighbour asks for the return of a knife in order to slay his family). Similarly, the men of seeming wisdom would fail to see that beauty cannot be determined from an aggregation of experiences of beautiful things. The properties which make a sensible object a thing of beauty may be ugly under other conditions (e.g. atonality may be beautiful in some compositions but not in others). As *eidos*, Beauty is that which can never not be beautiful.[35]

The distinction is itself crucial to that triumphant turning point in the *Republic*, the moment at which the dialogue can assert that philosophers should govern the Ideal State. It will, of course, be reinvoked in the parable of the cave when the same objection will be made to the sophists who remain in a state of conventional wisdom (*doxa*) and mistake observation of the many just actions for knowledge of justice as *eidos*. On the *Republic*'s own terms, the division is achieved with finality: two classes of intellectual are forever set apart:

> Shall we then offend their ears if we call them *doxophilists* rather than philosophers and will they be very angry if we so speak?

---

[34] For an excellent fishing out and analysis of the Socratic/Platonic argument against 'sight lovers', see Terence Irwin, *Plato's Ethics* (New York and London: Oxford University Press, 1995), pp. 264–71. See also Nicholas P. White, *A Companion to Plato's Republic* (Oxford: Basil Blackwell, 1979), pp. 153–62. A suggestive account of the importance of this section of argument to the development of Platonism is also provided by John Gould, *The Development of Plato's Ethics* (Cambridge: Cambridge University Press, 1955), pp. 154–64.

[35] On the issue of compresence of opposites see Irwin, *Plato's Ethics*, pp. 269–70.

> Not if they heed my counsel, he said, for to be angry with truth is not lawful. Then to those who in each and every kind welcome the true being, lovers of wisdom and not lovers of opinion is the name we must give. (*Republic*, 480)

The import of this discrimination, not only for the work of formulating the Ideal State, but also for that whole inauguration of ethics-as-philosophy, is revealed by this transition from the Socratic concern with personal morality to the quest for a properly philosophical ethics; a movement which leads through the *Republic* to the *Statesman* and the *Laws* and one in which Socrates becomes first taciturn, then mute, only to disappear from the stage altogether when Plato turns all his attention to society and law-making. A little earlier, opening the discussion which will separate the rulers from the ruled, the lovers of wisdom from the lovers of sights and sounds, Socrates has announced what we might take as the central tenet of the *Republic*. Nervously marking the moment when morality gives way to ethics, Socrates declares:

> I am on the very verge . . . of what we likened to the greatest wave of paradox. But say it I will, even if, to keep the figure, it is likely to wash us away on billows of laughter and scorn. Listen.
>
> I am all attention, he said.
>
> Unless, said I, either philosophers become kings in our states or those whom we now call our kings and rulers take to the pursuit of philosophy seriously and adequately, and there is a conjunction of these two things, political power and philosophical intelligence, while the motley horde of the natures who at present pursue either apart from the other are compulsorily excluded, there can be no cessation of troubles . . . for our states, nor, I fancy, for the human race either. (473c–e)

Unless philosophy is set up as its ruler, society will always be swamped in evil and suffering. What was true of the individual soul is now true of society as a whole. The turn from morality to ethics is radical, but its groundwork has already been laid in the Socratic theories of personal morality. As one commentator points out, we need only replace 'society' by 'individual' to arrive at a recapitulation of the earlier position. However simple, the shift is immediately effective: 'the one necessary step is taken . . . into the search for the ethical society which occupied the rest of Plato's life.'[36] The first strategy along this road is to distinguish those who are suitable to rule from those unsuited to direct the affairs of state.

---

[36] Gould, *The Development of Plato's Ethics*, p. 155.

It is perhaps not fanciful to see the distinction between those suitable and unsuitable readers in the *Phaedrus* as borne on that same wave of philosophy which sets apart the suitable from unsuitable rulers. Indeed, where the theory of recollection prescribes the necessity of moving from multiplicity to unity, from the variegations of sensible impressions to awareness of the Form which they but adumbrate, the Socrates of the *Phaedrus* makes the same discrimination as that of *Republic* V: 'man must needs understand the language of forms, passing from a plurality of perceptions to a unity gathered together by reasoning . . .' (*Phaedrus*, 249b–c). Only such a passage allows a man to be dignified with the name and soul of a philosopher (249c6). Similarly, the *Republic* will speak of the failure of educators to discriminate between suitable and unsuitable souls in terms which are those of the *Phaedrus*: 'What they aver is that they can put true knowledge into a soul that does not possess it, as if they were inserting vision into blind eyes' (*Republic*, 518b–c). Moreover, *Republic* V is threaded to the discourse on speech and writing by the figure of Isocrates. Although he is not named in *Republic* V, Isocrates stands as an exemplar of the 'humanist fallacy' which consists in asserting that one can derive the idea of beauty from the perception of objects of beauty, perceive the One by means of observing the Many – the very argument of the sight-lovers that Socrates strives so hardily to discredit.[37] The *Phaedrus* itself echoes his work and closes by setting him apart from the true type of the philosopher in a manner that might seem every bit as wry as the depiction of the *philodoxoi*.[38] 'For that mind of his,' it is said towards the close of *Phaedrus*, 'contains an innate tincture of philosophy (*philosophia tis*)' (*Phaedrus* 279a).[39] Furthermore, the *Phaedrus* actually speaks of the unsuitable reader as an ethical menace in so far, precisely, as he is a doxophilist in the making. Rejecting the gift of writing, the king tenders the second objection that it will enlarge incalculably the ranks of sight-lovers, of men of false wisdom:

[37] On the unnamed presence of Isocrates in *Republic* V, see N. R. Murphy, *The Interpretation of Plato's Republic* (Oxford: Clarendon, 1951), pp. 99–104.

[38] Commentators are divided as to whether the evocation of Isocrates at 279a is ironic. Wilamowitz and Hackforth assert that Plato is in very good faith *vis-à-vis* Isocrates, cf. Hackforth, *Plato's Phaedrus*, pp. 167–8. On the echoes of Isocrates in the *Phaedrus* as well as a very strong case for reading the Socratic aside as a 'taunt', see De Vries, *A Commentary on the Phaedrus of Plato*, pp. 15–18. Rowe tends towards the ironic reading: *Plato: Phaedrus*, trans. C. J. Rowe, pp. 315–16. For a fascinating and detailed reading of Isocrates's bearing on the argument of the *Phaedrus*, see Ronna Burger, *Plato's* Phaedrus: *A Defence of a Philosophic Art of Writing* (Alabama: University of Alabama Press, 1980), pp. 115–26.

[39] Rowe's rendering here – 'there is innately a certain philosophical instinct in the man's mind' – might seem to propitiate the non-ironic reading. Nevertheless he is not deterred from affirming that the reference serves to slight Isocrates. See Rowe, *Plato's Phaedrus*, p. 216.

> it is no true wisdom (*alētheian*) that you offer your disciples, but only its semblance (*doxan*), for by telling them of many things without teaching them you will make them seem to know much, while for the most part they know nothing, and as men filled, not with wisdom (*anti sophōn*), but with the conceit of wisdom (*doxosophoi*), they will be a burden to their fellows. (275a–b)

People or citizens, members of the *polis* or more dangerously again 'politicians' who will have become 'appearing-wise' (*doxosophoi*) instead of wise (*philosophoi*), see the forms abound and multiply even as do the sensibles; men possessed of scraps of 'seeming-wisdom' rather than the state of wisdom itself. We note that it is '*for the most part*' that they lack wisdom[40] – like the *philodoxoi* these potential writers are marooned between being and non-being (*Republic*, 479c–d), between nescience and science, between *epistēmē* and *agnoia*, a strange and dangerous band who are 'tumbled about in the mid-region between that which is not and that which is in the true and absolute sense' (*Republic*, 479d).[41] The lover of sights and sounds will discover in writing a means to further the grandiose illusion that they possess knowledge. The illusion will draw succour from both sides of writing's resource. As readers, they will collect shards of insight, which will breed greater confidence that the beliefs they hold are in fact genuine insight; as writers they will inscribe opinion under the sign of knowledge and attract unsuitable readers in their turn. A virtual epidemic would be afoot in the discursive organisation of society: with each new generation of doxographer, thought would spiral further down from truthful discourse (*alēthinos logos*), from *eidos*, and from the king and the throne of Truth.

What applies at the level of reality, of perception, should apply no less when it is a matter of understanding discourse. What goes for misrule may apply also to misreading: certainly, it will be those men of opinion who will pose a threat to the organisation of society both in political and discursive terms. Stranded as they are between *epistēmē* and *agnoia* (*Republic*, 477b), their discourse is neither ignorant nor sapiential, neither fully true nor fully false.[42] Where the judgements of the *philosophoi* will be

---

[40] 'It is discernment and judgment which the pupils are lacking, far more than knowledge'. De Vries, *A Commentary on the Phaedrus of Plato*, p. 250. Such a judgement supports the argument we are pursuing here: to wit, that is the negative ethical effects of unsuitable reading rather than the epistemological issue which animates the *Phaedrus*'s objections to unmonitored circulation.

[41] Cf. also *Sophist* (2543e–254b).

[42] One might also note that the division of society into those who are in states of *epistēmē*, *doxa* and *agnoia* might be appraised in cultural terms as the differences pertaining between (i) those literate who are also philosophers, (ii) the literate who are not yet philosphers (*doxophilists*) and (iii) the illiterate masses.

infallibly true and those of the *demos* invariably false, the *philodoxoi* fabricate a play of truth and falsehood whose bewildering effects would jeopardise not only the ethical and epistemological aims of dialectic but the very fundaments of the society, the city of speech, that it wishes to create as its time-bound testament.

We might then see *Phaedrus*, 273–9 as bound up – whether in a consolidatory or premonitory manner – with the *Republic*'s movement from individual to society, morality to ethics.[43] In the *Phaedrus* the ethical theme of the circulation of discourse is specified, which is to say that *discursive circulation is here specified as an ethical theme*. The link to the *Republic* is arresting. As a programme of social engineering, as a utopia, as the entry of the ultramundane into the construction of the state, the *Republic* is unique in its attention to discourse, to poetry, to distinguishing between proper and improper philosophising. Never since has a work focused itself at such energetic length on the function of discourse within a programmed social order. Everything thereby licenses us to travel with some security (and without preliminary justifications) between these two dialogues, observing the consonances and no less significant discrepancies in their renderings of discursive circulation as a primary ethico-political category. However, it might be well to ask how this transition from the exclusion of the doxophilists from government on ethical and epistemological grounds might translate into the question of reading and writing as it specified in the *Phaedrus*. How, then, might the doxophilists read?

Certainly, there is no reason to suspect that the doxophilists will show themselves any more able to understand the truth to which a discourse aspires than the Forms which precede the multiplicity, the variety of sense impressions. As the *Republic*'s Socrates will go on to say: 'the philosophers are those who are capable of apprehending that which is eternal and unchanging, while those who are incapable of this, but lose themselves and wander amid the multiplicities of multifarious things, are not philosophers' (*Republic*, 484b).

The *philodoxoi* are no more equipped or inclined to understand the truth to which a discourse aspires than the Form which abides at the

---

[43] Encouraged by stylometric analysis, recent scholarship tends to place the *Phaedrus* as belonging to the later phase or the latest phase of the dialogues of Plato's middle period: in both cases, it is thought to succeed the *Republic*. See Nehamas and Woodruff, *Plato: Phaedrus* pp. xii–xii; Rowe, *Plato: Phaedrus*, pp. 13–14. In a detailed analysis, De Vries concludes that the 'evidence points strongly to a date for *Phaedrus* after *Republic*, in the neighbourhood of *Parmenides*'. De Vries, *A Commentary on the Phaedrus of Plato*, pp. 7–11: p. 11. Though such a chronology – one which places the *Phaedrus* after the *Republic* – would harmonise with the current argument, the latter would be substantially unaffected by the anteriority of *Phaedrus*.

unifying level above sensible objects, the Beauty of which the many beautiful objects of perception are a copy. The lover of sights and sounds will
fail to see the wood for the trees, mistaking part for whole, particulars for
the Forms of those particulars. Just so his apprehension of discourse will
be piecemeal, fragmentary, a matter of belief rather than knowledge. The
philodoxoi would wander through a multitude of texts, reassembling the
disjecta membra as material for speeches, written compositions just as they
have roamed in search of each and every Dionysian festival (*Republic*,
475d). The reading of the *philodoxoi* will likewise be fractured: citational
and aphoristic rather than argumentative. Carried away by surface effects,
textual appearances, the sight-lover will not take cognisance of a work's
central truth. Having no more sight of the truth to which a text aspires
than the One which precedes the Multiplicities, he will seize upon
writing's iterability, wrench quotation from one context in which it has
a home to another in which it has no place: the truth of a text will be
twisted, perverted, its overall purpose and aims, its share (*metechein*) in
truth elided by a wilful and ignorant misreading which is scarcely a
reading at all. His mode of existence is one of deracination and diversity.
The metaphors of parent and orphan, home and exile which Plato weaves
through the discussion of speech and writing belong to the same system
which distinguishes the philosopher from the doxophilist. Discourse in
the hands of the *philodoxoi* would float without context, become frag-
mented where it possessed unity, proliferate mindlessly where it might
fructify in the enclosure of the Academy, the dialectical forum. Hence the
Phaedrus counters with an image-system which comprises gardens, suitable soil, boundary, defence, enclosure and cultivation. All the figures
express healthy constraint, controlled growth, supervised development, in
an entire economy of domestication which also defends and nurtures that
which is being tamed – thus the word *boētheia* will be at the centre of a
metaphorics concerning the transmission of *logoi*. Throughout the discussion of the inferiority of the written word, as prevalent in the *oeuvre*
at large, it will orchestrate a whole repertoire of tropes which evoke assistance, succour, help, rescue, support.[44]

Naturally, any discussion of *philodoxoi*, of unsuitable readers, must consider the implication of sophistics in the indictment of writing. One

---

[44] These metaphors of enclosure constitute the favoured half of an image system whose obverse works
around those figures of dissemination and orphanhood that Derrida has taught us to read in the
Phaedrus: 'simulacrum-writing is to what it represents . . . as weak, easily exhausted, superfluous
seeds giving rise to ephemeral produce (floriferous seeds) are to strong, fertile seeds engendering
necessary, lasting, nourishing produce (fluctiferous seeds). On the one hand, we have the patient,
sensible farmer . . . on the other the Sunday gardener, hasty dabbling, and frivolous' (PP, 150).

might simply see sophistics as condemned in the same gesture that condemns writing did Plato's arguments not owe something to the well-developed sophistic injunctions against written speeches.[45] Similarly, the sophist cannot simply be seen as a simple instance of the unsuitable reader or *philodoxus*; the attempt to distinguish the sophist from the genuine lover of wisdom was never to proceed with the assurance by which the *philodoxos* is separated from the *philosophos*. Indeed, Plato devoted much of a lifetime and its genius to distinguishing the sophist from the philosopher, or, one might say, to purging the sophist from philosophy. When Plato dedicates an entire dialogue to the task, it is apparent that the work of *dihairēsis* has an altogether more opaque task before itself. Attempting a similar distinction to the one achieved by *Republic* V, the *Sophist* confronts a more dangerous doubling, a more threatening proximity:

> STRANGER: Dividing according to kinds, not taking the same form for a different one or a different one for the same – is not that the business of the science of dialectic?
>
> THEAETETUS: Yes.
>
> STRANGER: And the man who can do that discerns clearly *one* form everywhere extended throughout many, where each one lies apart, and *many* forms, different from one another, embraced from without by one form, and again *one* form connected in a unity through many wholes, and *many* forms, entirely marked off apart. That means knowing how to distinguish, kind by kind, in what ways the several kinds can or cannot combine . . . And the only person, I imagine, to whom you would allow this mastery of dialectic is the pure and rightful lover of wisdom.
>
> THEAETETUS: To whom else could it be allowed?

[45] Although the Platonic arguments intersect with those of Isocrates, it is important to mark the differences between the Platonic interrogation of writing and sophistic disdain for written speeches. As Derrida observes: 'It is . . . not its pernicious violence but its breathless impotence that the sophists held against writing . . . The dynasty of speech may be just as violent as that of writing, but its infiltration is more profound, more penetrating, more diverse, more assured. The only ones who take refuge in writing are those who are no better speakers than the man in the street. Alcidamas recalls this in his treatise "on those who write speeches" and "on the Sophists". Writing is considered a consolation, a compensation, a remedy for sickly speech. Despite these similarities, the condemnation of writing is not engaged in the same way by the rhetors as its is in the *Phaedrus*. If the written word is scorned, it is not as a *pharmakon* coming to corrupt memory and truth. It is because *logos* is a more effective *pharmakon*' (PP, 115).

STRANGER: It is, then, in some such region as this that we shall
              find the philosopher now or later, if we should look
              for him. He too may be difficult to see clearly, but
              the difficulty in his case is not the same as in the
              Sophist's.

THEAETETUS: What is the difference?

STRANGER: The Sophist takes refuge in the darkness of not-
              being, where he is at home and has the knack of
              feeling his way, and it is the darkness of the place
              that makes him so hard to perceive . . . Whereas the
              philosopher, whose thoughts constantly dwell upon
              the nature of reality, is difficult to see because his
              region is so bright, for the eye of the vulgar soul
              cannot endure to keep its gaze fixed on the divine.
              (*Sophist*, 253d–254b)

Sophistry and philosophy alike make blind. There is the blindness of
the benighted, the blindness of he who has gazed overlong at the sun, a
blindness of non-being, a blindness of excess vision. The metaphors strain
for distinction; in pulling apart they draw close together. Sophistry
belongs to the sun of *alētheia*, if only as its blindspot. Only philosophy, at
its zenith, pushed to the limit, can distinguish sophistry from itself, can
recognise the blood and lineage of the Sophists, can discern 'the conceited
mimicry, of the semblance-making breed, derived from image making,
distinguished as a portion, not divine but human, of production, that presents a shadow play of words . . .' (*Sophist*, 268c–d).

Mimicry, making semblances from images, presenting a shadow play of
words: the depiction suggests that Plato would put sophistry in the place
of a condemned writing. Sophistry is defined as the ghost of dialectical
presence, just as writing is a ghost of speech. Indeed, Plato uses words that
echo the discriminations of the *Phaedrus* when he speaks of the sophist as
the 'mimic of the wise man' (*mimētēs tou sophou*, *Sophist* 268b) in a pronouncement that is an active variant on the king's fear of society being
corrupted by 'men filled with the conceit of wisdom, not men of wisdom
(*anti sophōn*)' (*Phaedrus*, 275b), the sophist being a more self-conscious,
perhaps cleverer, more threatening development from the conceit of the
uninstructed but lettered men of the myth of Theuth.

Yet this search for the other as shadow is indistinguishable from the
dialectical quest of philosophy as substantive. To indict sophistry as
writing is to implicate philosophy along with sophistry, to call attention
to the fact that it is philosophy which creates the penumbra it would

determine as the other. The venture is great, dangerous and complex. For it is philosophy's task to defend itself against misreading – not only of its own works but the misreading that it threatens to execute as philosophy: to guard against the sophist in itself, the sophist who is ever the philosopher's double. Only with the utmost vigilance can the true philosopher tell the two apart, and hence Plato will search ceaselessly for virtually imperceptible points of distinction in his attempt to apprehend this dangerous impostor who is already within the gates of philosophy. Just as sophism rises up against the Socratic–Platonic philosophy, so it rises up within philosophy: the distillation of essence, the quest to distinguish *eidē* from *eidōla*, *epistēmē* from *doxa*, *philosophoi* from *philodoxoi*, suitable from unsuitable readers takes place minute by minute within dialectic itself, as the affair of its self-governance, its very definition.[46] And it does so in the bleak recognition that, of all discourses, a freely circulating dialectical text would itself provide the most dangerous of cultural documents if deflected from the path of truth, turned into its 'opposite', the sophistry that follows philosophy as the shadow does the wanderer. Of this dilemma, this danger posed not only by the sophist outside but the sophist within, Gadamer comments:

> Socrates' question was a new one, i.e., the question of *what* something is. It was based on the suspicion and the experience that he who says something does not always know what he is saying and that it was precisely the art of rhetoric and the general acceptance of mere opinions which made this ignorance dangerous. Thus there had to be a new art which would promise deliverance from this danger and this new art was that of leading a discussion in such a way as to remove the risk that all knowledge and insight would eventually be confounded.[47]

Doubtless this describes perfectly the reasons for dialectic's insistence on an oral method to discriminate between proper and improper understanding on the part of the discourse's recipients. But this exigency might be interpreted somewhat differently if one sees the necessity of the oral

---

[46] Once again an epistemological ideal is also a strenuous ethical principle: the distinction philosopher/sophist is itself explicitly linked to the discrimination statesman/demagogue (*Sophist*, 268b). When this distinction is taken up in own terms, the philosopher will be favoured over the law-bound statesman in terms of an *elenchus* refused: unlike the philosopher, the benighted type of statesman will take as given the judgements of a law which is no more than 'a self-willed, ignorant man who lets no one do anything but what he has ordered and forbids all subsequent questioning of his orders even if the situation has shown some marked improvement on the one for which he originally legislated . . .' (*Statesman*, 294c).

[47] Gadamer, *Dialogue and Dialectic*, pp. 122–3.

method as deriving not only from the deficiencies of the culture at large but also from deficiencies within dialectical philosophy itself. Plato's Socrates acknowledges that undertakings of great moment are always dangerous (*Republic*, 497d), and dialectic itself is the most revolutionary and hence jeopardised of discourses, the most in need of a signature, of an authority, a legacy. The dialectical master must always be at hand, the tribunal in place to judge between faithful and unfaithful practitioners of the method: in this solicitude, the issue of suitable/unsuitable readers becomes indistinct from the insecurities of a method which cannot but fail to govern its own destiny. Under this darker aspect, the dialectical pre-occupation with legacy might suggest an absence at the core of its methodology, deficiency rather than plenitude in its *logos*, one which we shall discuss, *more Aristotelico*, in the next chapter. We must look to the justifications dialectic offers for preferring an oral method, in terms of both legacy and the striking epistemological claims it makes for the dialogic exchange. We must also see this preference as linked to a signatory contract, one drawn against the very author–reader relationship that allows us to raise such a question today, that allows us to know 'Plato' and 'Socrates' at some unknowable point between their antithetical signatures, their refusals fully to sign or consign the work of dialogic philosophy to an uncertain futurity or embrace the only certainty of any theory – i.e. that it can predict everything but its own effects.

3

Signature and Authorship in the
Phaedrus

Living, as we do, deep within a print culture (perhaps even in its twilight) we are at an incalculable remove from the sinister prospects offered by writing in Plato's lifetime. The proprietorial ethic by which he seeks to limit discursive circulation is alien to our temper. Yet with a certain leap of empathy we might see that his concern with discourses being unable to discriminate between suitable and unsuitable readers need not be so remote from our own concerns.

The reception histories of the Hegelian, Marxist, Nietzschean and Freudian discourses, for example, commend themselves to our attention precisely within the ethical problematic demarcated here by Plato. Despite his efforts in setting up the First International, Marx had no means of foreseeing who his readers would be or how they would find themselves stationed. The discursive legacy itself was powerless to stop Marxism becoming the conceptual legitimation of Soviet Communism and – by grotesque extension – the Stalinist regime. Nietzsche, too – who wrote in the knowledge that people would make mischief with his essays, aphorisms, his 'maxims and arrows' – had no way of correcting the National Socialist appropriations of his work. 'The best sense of play is play that is supervised and contained within the safeguards of ethics and politics' (PP, 156), Derrida says of the seeming carceral walls Plato would erect around the discursive space. The dynamic of play and seriousness, of game and gravity, which the *Phaedrus* weaves around the question of writing is motivated by a desire to guard against the game becoming dangerous, the discursive mask masquerading as the man, the ludic being taken for the grave, the playful careening into the heinous, the fatal. It is not for nothing that alongside writing and numbers, the god Theuth is credited with the discovery of games of chance – draughts (*petteia*) and dice (*kubeia*): (*Phaedrus*, 274d). Like gambling, writing is aleatory and like all gaming can be both trivial and deadly, harmless pastime and ruinous irresponsibility.

With writing which bears upon the social construction of justice, political organisation, with nation, state and belief, which discriminates between higher and lower types of humanity, between different classes of men and women and sexual difference within those classes, the gamble extends beyond a lifespan: a loan is taken out on whatever the future may gain or lose to this wanderer who roams without credit or collateral, without accounts, mortal constraints, will and testament. In postmodern terms, the Socrates of the *Phaedrus* affirms that reserve without (mortal) expenditure is always better than expenditure without reserve, that the containment of the system (be it Platonic, Hegelian, Marxist, Darwinian) is ethically preferable to an excess cultivating victims not envisaged by the system, that textual surplus should be countered by authorial scruple.[1]

Derrida was to revisit this issue – without overt recourse to the arguments of the *Phaedrus* – in his reading of the 'destinational structure' of the Nietzschean discourse. In *The Ear of the Other*, Derrida argues that an absolute falsification of Nietzsche's text – or any other for that matter – is not possible and that, at some level and to some extent, Nietzsche's discourse itself cannot be entirely distanced from the monstrous appropriations made of it by the propagandists of National Socialism. Having demonstrated that Nietzsche did little within his texts to discourage aberrant readings, Derrida searches for the principles of reading and writing which gave rise to an appropriation which Nietzsche himself would surely have discountenanced in the strongest terms and yet one for which 'he' or 'his text' (the two becoming virtually indistinguishable in the posthumous estate, and willingly so in a corpus which thematically challenges the borderline between 'life' and 'work', 'biography' and 'logography'). Derrida stresses Nietzsche's responsibility for his misreception and refuses to view the Nazi appropriation of Nietzsche's text as an absolute falsification. Something in Nietzsche's work uniquely opened itself to such propagandist use. Furthermore, the combination of a unique polysemy, an unwillingness to distinguish between proper and improper reading in the composition and construction of the Nietzschean corpus, and the very fact that written works perdure without the assistance of their author in a rescuing or explanatory proximity ensures that the National Socialist incorporation of Nietzschean aphorisms is neither contingent nor vulgar distortion. 'If one refuses the distinction between unconscious and deliberate programs as an absolute criterion,' Derrida observes, 'if one no longer

---

[1] We might note here how Popper's theory that no system can predict its effects would be altogether more relevant to this Platonic case than his specific reading of the Platonic *oeuvre*.

considers only intent – whether conscious or not – when reading a text, then the law that makes the perverting simplification possible must lie in the structure of the text "remaining" ' (EO, 30).

As we shall argue in the next chapter, the worst dreams of Plato's Socrates are recurring in this context of the ethically underdetermined scene of Nietzsche's reception history. As with the work of Marx, we witness writing's inability to sow its 'seeds in suitable soil' (*Phaedrus*, 276b), to 'address the right people, and not address the wrong' (275e), its proclivity for being 'ill-treated and unfairly abused' (275e). The unethical elitism explicit in the *Seventh Letter*'s insistence that 'no serious man will ever think of writing about serious realities for the general public' (*Seventh Letter*, 344c) can seem justified in these particular instances, especially when we rank amongst 'those who have no business with it' (*Phaedrus*, 275e), Lenin, Stalin, Goebbels, Mao, Mussolini and the pedigree of psychopathic murderers who have sought legitimation in Blake or Biblical works, Masonic or mystical esotericism. Mussolini's ignorant synthesis of Nietzsche's 'live dangerously' (GS, 228) with the idea that Marx was the outstanding philosopher of worker-violence is simultaneously a risible and catastrophic example of the unsuitable reader dabbling, to malign ends, with the texts of geniuses who were too preoccupied or aloof to guard against those who have no business with their philosophy.

One might, of course, turn those very strictures against Plato himself, he whose writings have drifted all over the place, he who wrote texts which have *remained* through two-and-a-half millennia and whose effect has been felt in political philosophy through to this day. It would be possible also – along with and against Popper who significantly never thinks of the *Phaedrus*[2] – to consider the deadly bands of revolutionaries-become-politicians who have taken the Platonic testimonies to suit their own ends in totalitarian states. If the Platonic attempt to bring ethics under the sway of the cognitive was to result in the most dangerously aestheticising forms of utopianism, if the frames of the *Republic* were themselves to be misread as utopian, then Plato's fiction inadvertently produced the hazardous inflation of writing and its concrete misreadings that the *Phaedrus* sought to interdict once and for all. The very exclusion of the aesthetic opened fertile

---

[2] Despite making copious references to twenty Platonic dialogues, and notwithstanding the long-standing consensus that the *Phaedrus* juxtaposes productively with the *Republic* (Popper's main focus), the former dialogue is entirely absent from Popper's attack. Where Havelock bypasses the *Phaedrus* for reasons of technological consistency, Popper declines its statement of ethical responsibility in order to further the claim that Plato's *oeuvre* disclaims responsibility for its outcomes. Cf. Karl Popper, *The Open Society and its Enemies*, 2 vols (London: Routledge & Kegan Paul, 1945), especially pp. 345–6 for the conspicuous omission of the *Phaedrus*.

and dangerous possibilities for the recursion of the aesthetic under the guise of the cognitive, possibilities which we might describe as modernity's appropriation of teleology for a godless reckoning. One might wonder, then, why it should have been that Plato fell victim to the very misreception the *Phaedrus* warned against, why his discourse showed itself incapable of distinguishing its good from its bad readers, why it should have wandered into the very legatory abyss against which it sought to provide the most stern bulwarks.

Similarly one could speculate that Plato feared misreception arising from the oral method itself. Just as the venial sin of writing perforce gave way to law-giving, the dangers of misreported 'doctrine' may well have led Plato to inscribe his vision of the legal ordering of society in enduring form (cf. *Laws*, 891a). Along such lines the Socratic caveats might be read as a meta-dialogic recognition of necessary compromise and worth the charge of a performative contradiction which Plato must have perceived in the writing of a text which asks to be read and not to be read. Whatever might have been the (irrecoverable) Socratic position on speech and writing, the dialogues gives us to see a Plato adjudicating between media, between the heterogeneous deficiencies of speech and writing in their attempts to ensure legacy. On the one side, he confronts the inadequacies of word-of-mouth transmission in its loss of the *ipsissima verba*; on the other, the dangerous abandonment of writing, the vulnerability of the written text to abusive and incompetent readers. All of which might be pondered the other way around: in the form of asking why Socrates, he who never sought to preserve a word on any stele more lasting than the psyche of his interlocutor, should have witnessed his oral discourse fall into the hands of the most unsuitable auditors amongst whom there were at least a few who felt that he signed for his teachings with his life. Somewhere between these cultures, between these media, at an indefinite point between 'Plato' and 'Socrates', we find the work of dialogic philosophy falls into our hands, and calls upon us to rise to the challenge of becoming suitable or at least responsible readers.

I: ORAL VERSUS GRAPHIC SIGNATURES

[A]ll the established predicates will hold also for the oral 'signature' that is, or allegedly is, the 'presence' of the 'author' as the 'person who does the uttering', as the 'origin', the source, in the production of the statement.

(Derrida, 'Signature, Event Context')[3]

---

[3] Jacques Derrida, *Margins of Philosophy*, trans. Alan Bass (Chicago: University of Chicago Press, 1978), p. 328.

Someone saw fit to say that 'there is not and will not be any written work of Plato's own', adding that '[w]hat are now called his are the work of a Socrates embellished and modernised' (*Second Letter*, 314c). Whether it was Plato or an impostor who wrote these words, their author recognised how deeply the Platonic signature is split between a Socrates who signed no text which was independent of his life, who left behind not works but pupils and the oral countersignature of the pupil who sought to preserve this oral teaching. The writer of this letter saw a Plato who both abrogated his own authorship and yet fashioned the Socratic discourse to his own signature – one who could neither speak in his own name nor surrender his own subjectivity fully to that of his master. The relationship is not simply one of *prosopopoeia*, nor one of ventriloquism or miming: a unitary subject is not to be found in the dialogic scene of voicing, nor even the *metteur-en-scène* that Bakhtin presupposes at the orchestral centre of the polyphonic novel.[4] We are given neither an authentic Socrates nor an authentic Plato: the Socratic dialogues are caught between the two just as they purport to dwell in a realm that crosses both speech and writing – incorporating both and yet cancelling the deficiencies of either.

The relation between 'Socratic' and 'Platonic' dialogues might well be distributed in terms of the difference between a 'weak' and a 'strong' writing – a distinction which we feel obliged regularly to reinforce and rephrase. By a 'weak' writing we indicate any text which seeks to transcribe or represent a previous oral situation; a 'strong' writing, on the other hand, proceeds directly to the *grammata* without prompting from an oral situation. In the former case writing presents itself as the fixing of the spoken situation; in the latter, the channel flowing from writer to reader flows directly and without reference to a prior event which both parties are summoned to recapture, to assignate within. The movement from a dialogic writing based on a representation of the spoken situation to a philosophical literature which gestures less and less towards any representation of the practice of the historical Socrates is one movement of the Platonic work. The trajectory by which dialogic mimesis gives way to an unmediated writing – writing as the servant of *vox* usurping the oral situation which it sought to fix – is a trajectory parallel to the one witnessed

---

[4] See Mikhail Bakhtin, *Problems of Dostoyevsky's Poetics*, trans. R.W. Rotsel (Ann Arbour, MI: University of Michigan Press, 1973) for an account of novelistic principles of dialogism. The complexities presented by the Platonic *oeuvre*, however, exceed those of the polyphonic novel since even were it possible to locate a controlling voice at the centre of the dialogues that voice would still need to be distributed in terms of its 'Socratic' and 'Platonic' timbres.

in the various mappings of the 'Socratic problem'.[5] As Plato becomes immersed in the writing of his dialogues as opposed to writing dialogues, so the Socratic 'presence' etiolates or is appropriated as a place from which the *Platonic* wisdom speaks. The Socratic voice hollows out as intransitivity comes to dominate the scene of dialogic writing: Plato now *writes* as opposed to *writes down*, and does so with a delicious self-irony by having his Socrates take a swipe at those who twist and paste and pull their words apart (*Phaedrus*, 278e).[6]

Though, when pressed, few if any commentators would dissociate the aporia of 'writing against writing' from the Socratic problem, none makes the connection an explicit theme. Yet the *Phaedrus* can be read as through the competition between the Socratic and Platonic signatures, which is to say between an oral and a graphic signature, between a Socrates who supposedly speaks and a Plato who writes, between a signature in the text which is simultaneously preserved, contradicted and overwritten by the signature outside the text. Given a relatively late dating of the *Phaedrus*, the exchange might seem a swansong to the method of question and answer, the last truly Socratic dialogue, a retrospect which also prospects the form of the treatise whether it was to be embraced overtly as in the *Laws*, or covertly and in dialogic guise as in the *Sophist* and the *Statesman*. One could thus recast the Socratic problem as movement in and through discursive media from *elenchus* to hypothesis. As aporia gives way to euphoria, the *doctra ignoratio* to an increasingly prescriptive tenor, the movement away from Socrates is inseparable from the movement towards writing-as-writing, towards everything that writing as concept seems to embody – not least the shift from the discontinuous mode of conversation (whether as it 'happened' or as it was graphically mimed by Plato) to the composition of continuous treatises which writing fosters. The *Phaedrus* would then be a work at the crossing: a text whose writing, whose art – which defies any record – bids farewell to the Socratic experience. Such would be the opening of an ironic reading, one which

---

[5] For an example of the argument – more popular in the first half of the twentieth century – that everything Plato puts into the mouth of Socrates corresponds to the views of the historical Socrates, see A. E. Taylor, *Socrates* (Edinburgh, 1933), pp. 131–74. Paul Friedländer (*Plato I: An Introduction*, trans. Hans Meyer, London: Routledge & Kegan Paul, 1958, pp. 126–36) offers lively and balanced speculation on the transformation of the historical Socrates into the protagonist of Platonic dialogues.

[6] 'Dionysus of Halicarnassus tells us that Plato continued throughout his life "combing and curling" his dialogues and that at his death a tablet was found with numerous variants of the opening sentence of the *Republic* . . . It is also possible that the present sentence reflects the impatience of Plato the philosopher with Plato the meticulous literary artist.' R. Hackforth, *Plato's Phaedrus* (Cambridge: Cambridge University Press), pp. 165–6.

sees Plato as ironising his own practice of writing through the Socratic objections and yet passing by way of this irony beyond the orality of his master and into a fully formulated, if conditional, acceptance of writing *qua* writing. Are we therefore justified in wondering if Plato wrote his dialogues not so much to preserve and reproduce the discontinuous animations of the Socratic conversations as to edit and refine away their imperfections and to eliminate the attendant risks of irrational identification or pre-critical immersion in the work? The only explicit evidence we have for Platonic endorsement of Socrates' preference for the oral method derives from the testimony of the *Seventh Letter* (whose authenticity as written by Plato is still open to question) and the injunctions of the *Second Letter* (which the majority of scholars believe to be a forgery).

The evidence within the authenticated *oeuvre* is virtually self-cancelling. The *Laws* might be pitted against the *Phaedrus* – as was assayed towards the close of the first chapter of the present work – to argue that writing is appropriate in one medium (law-making) and inappropriate in another (philosophical discourse, especially of a pedagogic nature). Such led us to view oral/graphic questions as subordinate to ethical considerations throughout the Platonic work. When detached from an ethical aspect, however, when taken as the contest of speech and writing *per se*, we are confronted by the endless ambiguity of Plato's text at this borderline between media. What is more, such an ironic reading can only be pursued with vigour by simplifying or neglecting what Plato's Socrates *actually* says about writing in the *Phaedrus*. The impossibility – in practice and in principle – of schematising the layers of irony, of locating a voice at the controlling centre of these reflections on speech and writing, of finding the place of the signature between 'Socrates' and 'Plato' in the Socratic dialogues or of importing tenets from the later work and reading them into earlier works under an authoritative Platonic seal – all and more give us to recall the simple and timeless wisdom of Aristotle's stipulation that we must begin with what is known to us.[7] And this can only consist in weighing the claims made for and against the oral method of dialectic within the terms which authorise us to do so: that is, by weighing the merits of the spoken against the written as they present themselves in Plato's text and within a general ethics of discursive reception. This will involve assessing the claims made for the oral method: first, in terms of the validity of the spoken word as a superior medium for the communication of *logos*, and as the *sine qua non* of responsible legacy:

---

[7] Aristotle, *Nicomachean Ethics*, A2, 1095b3.

secondly, in its claims for the efficacy of the method of *elenchus* as an educational technology which should and must replace the Homeric encyclopaedia or, so to speak, 'Hellenic Bible' as the dominant pedagogic resource; thirdly, the cogency of the apparent Socratic argument for the superior epistemological standing of the interpersonal forum.

Given the prevailingly positive account of the ethical and epistemological aspirations of the dialectico-oral signature in the previous chapters, this assessment will now take a seemingly negative cast, but one which seeks to uphold the foundational ethical values of the *Phaedrus* over and against the literal cast of its argument. To call into question the propriety of the dialectico-oral signature need not neutralise or undermine these Platonic concerns any more than a reopening of this ethical field commits one to a logocentric suspicion of writing. Quite the contrary. Such an interrogation can be conducted to retain and re-mark Plato's ethical concerns through reassessing, revising and, if possible, consolidating the ethical imperatives which drive the distinction between communicative media. The very fact of our existing within a graphic and increasingly digitialised culture, and our placement in the midst of a 'communications revolution' (without having any way of determining whether we are in its early, mid- or latter stages), would recommend a procedure of this kind even were the superiority of the dialectical signature beyond doubt. To attempt such a critique is once again to narrow the gap between the spoken and the written, as has been adumbrated so many times by Plato himself. Given, in any case, that it is not graphicity that Plato objects to in writing but the ethical dangers that writing *qua* writing registers, any mitigation of the dangers of speech via certain unperceived virtues in the written would be consonant with the deepest ethico-discursive aims of the *Phaedrus*.

To make a banal point first, we should note that nothing compels us to assume that the transmission of dialectically articulated truths will be any less insulated against the vicissitudes of posthumous transmission than those announced graphically. If anything, our intuitions would lead in the opposite direction. One might indeed argue with stronger reason that orally transmitted discourse runs the greater risk of perversion in that it does not partake of the condition *scripta manent*. The oral dissemination of discourse is prey to all order of distortions, not least those of mishearing and misremembering. One need only look at the conceptual and historical chaos created by the indirect tradition to see the manner in which trusting to memory is tantamount to an abandonment of the work to chance, hearsay. As the early history of the Academy illustrates, the method of conversation creates all order of confusion in the Platonic legacy, which the very fact of Plato's writing of the dialogues may well have sought to counter. Oral legacy, such as it is, gives rise to dogmatic reconstructions which only the written dialogues have succeeded in challenging. The dialectical insistence on its method as a process which aims at truth is largely lost in an indirect tradition which has insisted on a secret doctrine of Plato's and an unverifiable esotericism in his writings. An indirect, word-of-mouth tradition is itself structurally incapable of carrying forward dialogic philosophy as intricately evolved in the Platonic dialogues. In the counterfactual situation where pupils could retain the Platonic wisdom *expressis verbis*, the act of memorisation would tend to rigidity. The relinquishment of the original words, on the other hand, would sacrifice the method's very template. Were the Socratic dialogues and Plato's teaching at the Academy preserved solely through recall, it is quite possible that the discourses of Socrates and Plato would have become a dogmatic creed, much diluted and of an inflexible and unresponsive cast far in excess of both the concretion of the poetic *paideia* and the putative rigidities of the written word. Furthermore, one might wonder – given all the problems that attend the oral method in its finest flowering with the Socratic life – where hopes might be invested for its post-Socratic future. Does Plato seriously envisage not only *a* future Socrates, but a *megalopsychia* of this rank for every generation? Everything is contingent and depends not only on the competence and sincerity of the audience but also of the dialogic leader himself. To sign dialectico-orally obviously does not commit a subject to discourse responsibly, nor, given that the discourse is conducted responsibly, does it ensure that its contents will not be misprised by the audience, even an audience of one. In many ways, the method is only as good as its participants and one generation of dialecticians can only have the most tenuous hold on the performance of the next. For a method which depends so heavily on the intelligence, open-mindedness and moral probity of its practitioners, the structure of legacy will always be haphazard. Furthermore, there are numerous ways in which the discourse of the historical Socrates in its unfixed and evanescent articulation is vulnerable to abuses which the written word defends (itself) against.

There are numerous hints in the Platonic *oeuvre* that the interpersonal forum presents hazards to rational communication that not even the superhuman type of Socrates is able to circumvent. Face-to-face transmission may promote enchantment by the very same token that it inspires the soul to learning. While Socrates is a gadfly to the Athenian citizens, he can also appear to Meno as a wizard, perplexity or sting-ray. 'I feel,'

Meno protests, 'you are exercising magic and witchcraft upon me and positively laying me under your spell until I am just a mass of helplessness . . .' (*Meno*, 80a). We see Plato here fully aware that the oral method can become a seductive situation altogether closer to the mysteries of poetic enchantment (*ep-aoide*) which the Socratic and Platonic lives have dedicated themselves to dispel. In the *Symposium* the Socratic presence is said to induce transport akin to both the Dionysian experience and the mystical state of intoxication achieved in the *thelxis* of poetic performance:

> For the moment I hear him speak I am smitten with a kind of sacred rage, worse than any Corybant, and my heart jumps into my mouth and the tears start into my eyes – oh, and not only me, but lots of other men. (*Symposium*, 215d–e)

With words and an analogy that cannot but recall the *Ion*, Plato indicates that the very irrationality of poetic identification threatens to become a property of the rationalist forum by which it would be supplanted.

Furthermore, in both his Platonic and historical incarnations, Socrates failed to exercise the caution in selecting his audience which the *Phaedrus* recommends as an edict of responsible communication. The *Apology*, in fact, presents Socrates' practice as quite contrary to the principles of audience selectivity outlined in the *Phaedrus*: 'I shall never stop practising philosophy and exhorting you and *elucidating the truth for everyone that I meet*' (*Apology*, 29d; my emphasis) Socrates declares, almost by way of defiant admission to the Athenian court. So far from choosing a soul of suitable mettle, the Socrates of the *agora* exhibits the very promiscuity, the indiscriminate availability that the *Phaedrus* censures in writing. Socrates in fact articulates the mute principle of writing, the very one that makes it so very dangerous in his view: his discourse is also promiscuous, open to 'young or old, foreigner or fellow citizen . . .' (*Apology*, 30a). Though writing in a largely illiterate culture drew *ispo facto* boundaries in exposing only the educated to its direct influence, the fruits of the Socratic word could be plucked by all and sundry who found themselves attracted to the *agora*. Seemingly 'democratic', the Socratic practice here actually *exceeds* the bounds of the Athenian *demos*: young or old, foreigner or citizen, all are embraced by this radical egalitarianism, this street philosophising which counts nothing human alien to it.[8] This Socrates of the *Apology* would seem to be in stark contradiction with the teacher

---

[8] *Pace* Derrida, the Socratic word does indeed wander in so far as anyone may wander away with their own version of its purport. Derrida neglects this implication of *Apology* 29d–33b when he declares: 'The Socratic word does not wander, stays at home, is closely watched: within autochthony, within the city, within the law, under the surveillance of its mother tongue' (PP, p. 124).

who, in the *Phaedrus*, insists that *logos* must choose a suitable soul for its partner.[9] Indeed, Plato has his Socrates here disclaim responsibility for the ethical effects of his discourse:

> I have never set up as any man's teacher, but if anyone, young or old, is eager to hear me conversing and carrying out my private mission, I never grudge him the opportunity; nor do I charge a fee for talking to him, and refuse to talk without one. I am ready to answer questions for rich and poor alike, and I am equally ready if anyone prefers to listen to me and answer my questions. If any given one of these people becomes a good citizen or a bad one, I cannot fairly be held responsible, since I have never promised or imparted any teaching to anybody, and if anyone asserts that he has ever learned or heard from me privately anything which was not open to everyone else, you may be quite sure that he is not telling the truth.
> (*Apology*, 33a–b)

To disclaim inadvertent audience uptake would seem to fly in the face of everything that the Socratic–Platonic ethic has established. Socrates will heroically accept a death penalty for impieties that neither he nor Plato believed him to have committed, but he distances his own discourse from the negative ethical consequences which he was positioned to foresee as possibility if not as precise form. Thus he will embrace responsibility *de facto* but not *de jure*. The Socratic response to this charge of irresponsibility would, of course, be that his discourse cannot be repeated, reproduced, made into doctrine or dogma. Yet the very situation in which Socrates declares these words shows how easily a discourse may be misconstrued as dogma and as dogma may be misconstrued. Socrates was not only tried for the practice of *elenchus* and for asking questions which undermined the *sensus communis* of the Athenian society. He was also

---

[9] So much so, indeed, that the disparity might be adduced as fresh evidence for the argument that the distance between the historical Socrates and Plato has dwindled to nothing by the dialogues of the middle period. One might, however, preserve a continuity between the practice of the historical Socrates and the recommendations of the *Phaedrus* by distinguishing the elenctic procedure from that kind of discourse in the *Phaedrus* which must delimit its audience. In a more 'constructive' work like the *Republic* which carries propositional or thetic content of sorts, the issue of suitable and unsuitable auditors will be altogether to the fore, given that its discourse provides ample opportunity for irresponsible or incompetent beneficiaries to acquire seeming wisdom. The earlier practice of *elenchus*, however, would not be subject to any such circumspection as its mission is defined as anti-doctrinal. This distinction would, in turn, give rise to a further refinement of the perplexing play of speech and writing in Plato's text. Writing would then be equated with any discourse which carries doctrine; speech with all communications that are neither thetic nor continuous. The Socratic word would then be permitted to wander indeed in so far as its *logoi* are perpetually fluid, intersubjective, purely inquisitive and elenctic. Once more, however, the oral signature would be nothing in itself: the performative function is only required of the thetic text, of the work whose content can be taken as dogma.

charged with failing to worship the city's divinities and of introducing strange and new divinities of his own devising: the latter, at least, must be taken as a form of positive or doctrinal content. That such charges are unsubstantiated alerts us all the more to the hazards of the oral situation, of the difficulties of establishing what one has bequeathed and what has been improperly attributed to a speaker. The untruth of the charges in fact confirms for the oral method the very capacity for falling into the wrong hands which the *Phaedrus* declares as a unique property of the written form. Misreception is doubled in this trial: first, by those Socratic auditors on whose testimony the charges are brought; secondly, by those who listen to the defence. Even in the oral situation of the trial by dicasts, and in spite of disclaiming sophistry and rhetoric in his defence, what Socrates produced was a counter-rhetoric, which was taken by the Athenian court as sophistry. His oral text was misheard, taken as super-subtle evasion.[10] That Plato spent much of his career vindicating his teacher, attempting to ensure that posterity would not take Socrates as a sophist, once again underlines the treacherously thin line which the thinker must walk between philosophy and sophistry. It also shows that an oral signature can be as dangerous to the speaker as the written text to its author (only with increasing literacy does 'libel' overtake 'slander' as an occasion for litigation). The retribution exacted on two great oral teachers of humankind – Socrates and Christ – was never to be exceeded in the realm of written texts. Socrates, as Christ after him, would die in order to uphold his right to sign orally – we will not forget that he refused to allow Lysias to ghost-write his defence.

Socrates is summoned to account for his discourse by the Athenians – summoned on the basis of an oral signature which he insists upon, though he was still able to save his life with its relinquishment. The fact that the Socratic *logoi* were signed in the living present rather than along the relays of writing and brought forth as exhibits through fallible human recall certainly weighs the case here. It is altogether easier to prove that one has not written something than to demonstrate that something was not said. Just as speech cannot be disowned in the time of its articulation, so too it cannot easily be owned in the future. What one has or has not said is subject to the distortions of deficient memory and the impossibility of reconstituting an isomorphic sequence of articulated words. The spoken

---

[10] For a thought-provoking account of the Socratic *apologia pro sua vita* and its possible misinterpretation by the Athenian court, see G. E. Allen, *Socrates and Legal Obligation* (Minneapolis, MN: University of Minnesota Press, 1980), esp. pp. 3–21.

word thus shows itself incapable of defending itself via the supplement of successive spoken words, and obliged Socrates to conduct his defence, his self-vindication, in the form of a magnificent *apologia pro sua vita*. Writing would here serve responsible legacy altogether more efficiently; the supposed non-coincidence of intention and author introduced by the perdurance of the written text is altogether more reliable in the context of any tribunal than the attempt to reconstitute intention from a discourse both spoken and unrecorded.

Even in the actual speech situation, where speaker and auditor are purportedly united in a single act of attention and the question of restoration is not so heavily marked, the oral signature is invaded by possibilities of interruption and displacement. The oral signature ties the speaker to a system of response, elucidation and debate protracted on the assumption of the living crystallisation of a future present in which the subject will be summoned to give account of what she is at the time in the process of articulating. The logic of such a living signature – as the subject, the master, Socrates, or whoever, discourses – is invaded by *différance* in that no future present, that of debate or response, can be absolutely or *a priori* assured. The oral signature therefore still appeals – in the ethico-dialectical sense given it by Plato – to a future in which, as for the written signature, everything is far from certain. Having signed one's discourse in the very act, the very fact, the very performance of articulating it, one may still die, depart, be struck mute or surrender to any other form of dislocative contingency. Death, absence and departure haunt not only the graphic signature but also the 'living' signature of oral discourse. That such a possibility is generally remote would not bear on the transcendental objection which could itself be further refined along the lines Derrida takes in 'Signature, Event, Context', where he argues that the predicates which hold for the oral signature will hold also for its graphic counterpart.[11] Indeed, the very principles of graphicity which introduce lacunae into the oral situation also allow for written signatures to mitigate the breach in presence which they mark and establish structures of legacy altogether more reliable than oral succession.

If the oral method is entirely insufficient to the principle of legacy, it is no less problematic in terms of dialectic's status as a rational mode of inquiry. Dialectic asserts the mode of conversation not only as a means of containing discourse and the appropriate milieu for teaching but as an

---

[11] See Jacques Derrida, 'Signature, Event, Context', pp. 327–31 for his argument that the oral signature is caught up in a play of differences indissociable from the play of writing.

epistemological requirement. Both legacy and pedagogy will in their way imply a theory of knowledge and the *Phaedrus* forces itself to declare that truth is dependent on the co-presence of transmitter and receiver. By thus linking the enterprise of rationalism to the conversational method, Plato severely weakens dialectic's claim to scientificity. His contemporaries were ready to pillory dialectic in precisely those terms. Aristophanes derides dialectic as a 'thinking shop' (*phrontistērion*).[12] Callicles presumably reflects a contemporary prejudice when he caricatures dialectic as 'whispering with three or four boys' in a corner (*Gorgias*, 485d). Aristotle was to inquire more scientifically into this deficiency at the heart of the oral method:

> deception is effected the more readily when we are inquiring into a problem in company with others than when we do so by ourselves (for an inquiry with another person is carried on by means of speech, whereas an inquiry by oneself is carried on quite as much by means of the object itself); secondly a man is liable to be deceived, even when inquiring by himself when he takes speech as the basis of his inquiry. (*De Sophisticis Elenchis*, 169a37–169b2)

Conversation here is more unreliable as a mode of inquiry or teaching, more error-ridden and contingent in its resources than is the written text. The after-effect of conversation can also tend towards opacity rather than clarity in thinking: reconstituting the object of inquiry from an oral forum provides an altogether more fallible basis for solitary reasoning. Aristotle might here be taken as saying that the oral basis of dialectic disqualifies its claim to be a science. A little later in *De Sophisticis Elenchis*, he will specify dialectic in these terms:

> no art that is a method of showing the nature of anything proceeds by asking questions: for it does not permit a man to grant whichever he likes of the two alternatives in the question: for they will not both of them yield a proof. Dialectic, on the other hand, does proceed by questioning, whereas if it were concerned to show things, it would have refrained from putting questions, even if not about everything, at least about the first principles and the special principles that apply to the particular subject in hand. (*De Sophisticis Elenchis*, 172a15–19)

A Socratic dialogue would begin *ex nihilo*: it proceeds towards rather than from first principles. Worked through in the discontinuous mode of conversation and relying solely upon *elenchus* or the positive maieutic process of question and answer, dialectic is unscientific in its programme of

---

[12] Cf. Aristophanes, *Clouds* in *Four Texts on Socrates: Plato's 'Euthyphro', 'Apology' and 'Crito' and Aristophanes' 'Clouds'*, trans. Thomas G. West and Grace Starry West (Ithaca, NY: Cornell University Press, 1984).

enquiry. Refusing to state first principles is disabling in at least two ways. First, it works against the establishment of a due and orderly sequence in discourse. Secondly, it carries the threat that productive enquiry will prove impossible from the outset. Let us suppose, Aristotle continues, that the answerer did not grant the first principles of a discussion: in such circumstance Socrates or the art of dialectic 'would then no longer have had any grounds from which to argue . . . against the objection' (*De Sophisticis Elenchis*, 172a20). The *Gorgias* itself provides the *locus classicus* of such dialogic misfiring: from a fundamental refusal to agree first principles, the gap between Socrates and Callicles enlarges to such an extent that the leader of the discussion resorts to exhortation, while the answerer refuses to reply except '[t]o avoid inconsistency' (*Gorgias*, 495a). Like the *Meno*, by whose conclusion one discerns no 'communion' of souls, the interanimative ideal is in ruins by the close of the *Gorgias*. Callicles quits the conversation altogether, leaving Socrates to assume the role of answerer to his own questioning.[13]

Furthermore, the line between dialectic and sophistics is made faint by the abuses to which the oral method opens itself. As Aristotle observes, drawing one's interlocutor into paradox is 'brought about by a certain manner of questioning, and through the question':

> For to put the question without framing it with reference to any definite subject is a good bait for these purposes: for people are more inclined to make mistakes when they talk at large, and they talk at large when they have no definite subject before them. Also the putting of several questions, even though the position against which one is arguing be quite definite, and the claim that he shall say only what he thinks, create abundant opportunity for drawing him into paradox or fallacy, and also, whether to any of these questions he replies 'Yes', or replies 'No', of leading him on to statements against which one is well off for a line of attack. (*De Sophisticis Elenchis*, 172b12–19)

What applies to sophistics would seem to apply also to certain dangers arising directly from the Socratic *elenchus*. The generality of the Socratic inquiry along with the practice of a relentless questioning which proceeds – counterintuitively, we might think – from teacher to pupil rather than from pupil to teacher might generate its own 'anti-logical' abuses: the perplexity which was so often the fruit of sophistic exchange could easily

---

[13] For an interesting analysis of communicative breakdown in the Socratic dialogues, see Samuel Scolnicov, 'Three Aspects of Plato's Philosophy of Learning and Instruction', *Paideia*, Fifth Annual, Special Plato Issue (1976), pp. 50–62.

be visited on the dialogic answerer, particularly as Socrates often welcomes those with a lack of experience (*Apology*, 30a) and Parmenides chooses the youngest of his company to question as 'likely to give the least trouble and . . . the most ready to say what he thinks . . .' (*Parmenides*, 137b).

Aristotle's specification of the injunction that the learner shall 'say only what he thinks' refers directly to the ground-rule for conversation laid down so often by Socrates.[14] 'Always answer what you think' (*Meno*, 83d), Socrates commands. In the *Crito* he advises his interlocutor: 'Now be careful, Crito, that in making these single admissions you do not end by admitting something contrary to your real beliefs' (49d). On the other hand, the answerer is required to achieve agreement between all his answers and, if he fails to do so, to relinquish one of his beliefs in favour of another with which it is inconsistent.[15] We might see a pedagogical double-bind in the competition between (i) requiring the answerer always to say what he thinks, and (ii) enforcing agreement across propositions generated by this candour. The spontaneity that Socrates calls for precludes the reflection necessary for consistency between responses. The Socratic procedure – '*p* has been affirmed along with the incompatible *q*, therefore not-*p* is true' – is neither logically indubitable, pedagogically sound nor scientifically rigorous. This is presumably the purport of Aristotle's claim that dialectic 'does not permit a man to grant whichever he likes of the two alternatives in the question: for they will not both of them yield a proof . . .' (*De Sophisticis Elenchis*, 172a15). As Gregory Vlastos has succinctly shown, the answerer might well jettison *p* in order to retain his commitment to the *q* with which it is in contradiction: under dialogic scrutiny, the first proposition *p* is invariably thetic and productive while the *q* which Socrates forces as a concession is nugatory or infertile by comparison.[16]

Beyond which neither the *Phaedrus* nor the Platonic text in general provides any epistemological justification for the claim that truths whose original transmission is dialectical can defend themselves once they have departed their subject (*Phaedrus*, 276a). If such 'truths' are 'true', then they will be so regardless of the medium within which they have been articulated: 'If and only if snow is white' is as true in written as in oral media and no worse equipped thereby to defend itself. The claim at 276a is close to proposing *a priori* status for dialectical judgements. When Socrates adds

---

[14] Aristotle also specifies the injunction 'say only what you think' as a feature of dialectic at *Topica*, 160b19–22.

[15] This point has been well made in Richard Robinson, *Plato's Earlier Dialectic* (Ithaca, NY: Cornell University Press, 1941), pp. 82–3.

[16] Cf Vlastos, *Socratic Studies*, pp. 11–29. Vlastos's critique of the *elenchus* is admirably sharp and philosophically technical.

that such truths are fertile and 'contain a seed whence new words grow up in new characters (*en allois ēthesi*)' (*Phaedrus*, 277a), it is not incumbent upon us to take these words in any mystical sense, nor to imbue the inferential process with the epiphanic atmosphere that the *Seventh Letter* evokes as the 'flash of understanding', the moment when the mind is flooded with light (344b). Rather, Socrates' words can be understood quite plausibly as the logical and mathematical process of a pupil or successor extending logical inferences from the axioms of his teacher or precursor.[17] Logical deduction may often be experienced as inter-psychic illumination but its operations are dependent neither on the Socratic procedure of *elenchus*, the dialectical method of question and answer, nor the medium of spoken discourse. Understanding and deduction can equally be achieved in the silent encounter of a pupil with a text whose author is dead or otherwise departed. This is not to say that face-to-face transmission is unpropitious to this process, but it will not assist in all cases and could be required only as a matter of pedagogic efficacy rather than as a *sine qua non* of epistemological inquiry. In response to both assertions, one might simply say that apodeictic truths defend themselves better, whereas speculative thought often stands in need of its author or authorised legatees to correct deliberate or ill-informed misprision and that only logical or demonstrable truths can give rise to fresh truths – whether in other minds or in the mind of their discoverer. The issue of whether such truths announce themselves in conversation or in writing is quite beside this point.

Why, then, should the *Phaedrus* make this pre-philosophical claim that the veracity of a statement depends on the medium through which it is articulated? While it is one thing to assert ethical or pedagogical benefits of the oral method, it is quite another to make an epistemological fiat of conversational transmission. One can only answer such a question by assuming that it is the presence of the speaker that is at issue here. And yet the Platonic text will repudiate the idea that knowledge is author-dependent with great lucidity. In the *Charmides*, Socrates declares that 'the point is not who said the words, but whether they are true or not' (161c). As we shall see, this thought is expressed in many different places throughout the Platonic *oeuvre*, both overtly and as an underlying principle of dialectical epistemology. Why, then, should Plato's text also

---

[17] The translation of *logoi* as 'words' at 276e8 is by no means binding. Hamilton translates *logoi* as 'truth' at this point, a rendering which would clearly support the logical over the mystical interpretation of Socrates' purport here. Nehamas and Woodruff favour 'discourse'. While Rowe offers 'words', he alerts readers to the multivalency of *logos*: 'in the *Phaedrus* as a whole, the term *logos* is thoroughly ambiguous, in a way which cannot be reproduced properly in English . . .' (Rowe, *Plato: Phaedrus*, p. 138).

declare that dialectic can travel only with the master, that it cannot leave to posterity a fixed form of words but must continually reanimate context, intention and understanding in an interpersonal forum? On the one side, Plato's text will describe itself as the discourse of a truth which is properly independent of human agency; on the other, it will protest a complete reliance on an oral/conversational method which ensures the presence of the dialectician. In drawing attention to this dialectical vacillation on the question of agency, one would not simply wish to question the consistency of an *oeuvre* which does not claim a fixed or dogmatic status for itself. Rather, it is to ask how Plato's text sees itself, how it proposes its own legacy. Indeed, it is from within this nexus that one might begin to disentangle Plato's reflections on dialectic, science and ethical responsibility in terms of the relation between subject and system, discourse and signatory. The first step in this process is to address the distinction between discourses which are dependent on presence and those which have no further need of their authors, a distinction which could be crudely registered as that between subjective and objective discourses. Plato would wish this discrimination to distinguish dialectic from all other discourses. What it succeeds in doing, however, is to separate science from non-science through a division which divides dialectic itself. It will also lead us to wonder whether dialectic can any more dispense with a subject than its method can approach, still less achieve scientificity.[18]

II: SCIENCE AND SIGNATURE

The history of philosophy is to a great extent that of a certain clash of human temperaments . . . Of whatever temperament a professional philosopher is, he tries, when philosophising, to sink the fact of his temperament. Temperament is no conventionally recognised reason; so he urges impersonal reasons only for his conclusions. Yet his temperament really gives him a stronger bias than any of his more strictly objective premises. It loads the evidence for him one way or the other, making for a more sentimental or a more hard-hearted view of the universe, just as this fact or that principle would. He *trusts* his temperament. Wanting a universe that suits it, he believes in

---

[18] Which is to say that the dialectical signature must be measured in terms of its aspirations to a scientificity which, until relatively recent times, was thought to submerge its signatories within the discipline. In this classical conception of science, the proper name functions to baptise not an individual, not an agent, not even an *oeuvre*, but a stage in an unfolding series on the path to knowledge. This is not to affirm the model of scientific impersonality: what is at issue here is Plato's construction of such an authorless realm of science and his realisation that dialectic disqualifies itself as science in accordance with such a construction.

any representation of the universe that does suit it. He feels
men of opposite temper to be out of key with the world's
character, and in his heart considers them incompetent and
'not in it' in the philosophic business, even though they may
far excel him in dialectical ability. Yet in the forum he can
make no claim, on the bare ground of his temperament, to
superior discernment or authority. There arises thus a certain
insincerity in our philosophic discussions: *the potentest of all our
premises is never mentioned*. I am sure it would contribute to
clearness if we should break this rule and mention it, and I
accordingly feel free to do so. Of course I am talking here of
very positively marked men, men of radical idiosyncrasy, who
have set their stamp and likeness on philosophy and figure in
its history. Plato, Locke, Hegel, Spencer, are such tempera-
mental thinkers.

(William James)[19]

No method which embraces the ideal of scientific principles will affirm
the concept of an author. Its goal cannot be created, but waits to be discovered much as America was by the first European explorers. To the
extent that his discourse aimed toward *alētheia*, Plato could never lay claim
to the status he so richly deserved as the author of dialectical philosophy.
Nor, however, could he simply desert his discourse: once woven, the web
of dialectical philosophy still claimed the attendance of its weaver. In the
competition between claiming impersonally valid status for his work and
his awareness of the ethical dangers of abandoning that work, Plato's discourse vacillates on the question of signature. These concerns are profoundly exacerbated by the culture of writing in which Plato's text found
itself. In so far as dialectic could be abused as a discourse which lacked scientific principles of self-regulation and remained as writing to be abused,
the questions of signature, of authorship and vigilance over the work's
reception wrote themselves into the discourse on writing. The closing
phase of this chapter will track authorship as the unnameable concept on
which the argument of the *Phaedrus* turns: it will read this concept in its
absence from science, its ambiguous presence in dialectic, its ethical specification in terms of a signatory obligation at the close of the dialogue.

Naturally, the signature could not be declared in name by either the
Phaedrus or the *Seventh Letter*, but it is plainly a concept which is grasped
with uncanny precision in the trial of writing. Just prior to the section
dealing with the inferiority of the written word, Socrates reduces to

---

[19] William James, *Pragmatism: A New Name for some Old Ways of Thinking* (London: Longmans, 1907),
    pp. 6–8.

absurdity the comments in Tisias's manual on the probable. 'Bless my soul!' Socrates declares with what we must take as imperious disdain:[20] 'It appears that he made a brilliant discovery of a buried art, your Tisias, or whoever it really was and whatever he is pleased to be called after' (273c). The inference is clear: as the manual is useless, so too is it useless to inquire into its authorship.[21] The case is trivialised in that Socrates has deemed Tisias's text to be of little ethical and intellectual significance: the judgement is not expansive, still less binding. However, this sardonic and low-case dismissal is to prepare us for the properly dialectical insistence that discourses of *alētheia* dispense with all authorial agency. Immediately upon hearing the myth of writing as a gift refused, Phaedrus raises the questions of its pedigree and authorship. Socrates' reply would seem to decide against the author-function once and for all:

PHAEDRUS: It is easy for you, Socrates, to make up tales from Egypt or anywhere else you fancy.

SOCRATES: Oh, but the authorities of the temple of Zeus at Dodona, my friend, said that the first prophetic utterances came from an oak tree. In fact the people of those days, lacking the wisdom of you young people, were content in their simplicity (*hyp'euētheias*) to listen to trees or rocks, provided these told the truth (*alēthē*). For you apparently it makes a difference who the speaker is, and what country he comes from; you don't merely ask whether what he says is true or false. (*Phaedrus*, 275 b–c)

The truth may spring from trees or rocks, which is to say that it derives from nowhere and no one.[22] An older and more innocent age shows itself scientific in accepting the impersonality of truth: Phaedrus and his peers

---

[20] De Vries comments of this exchange: 'Wilamowitz mistakes the import of the passage. He thinks that the addition does not serve to doubt Tisias' authorship but to mark, in truly Platonic style, that the question of authorship is unimportant compared with the question whether the contention is right or wrong. Of course this is a Platonic thought . . . But in the present passage it is full contempt with which the question of authorship is dismissed: the author may be Tisias or some other fellow of that kind.' G. J. De Vries, *A Commentary on the Phaedrus of Plato* (Amsterdam: Adolf M. Hakkert, 1969), p. 244.

[21] For a substantial discussion of the place of Tisias in the organisation of the *Phaedrus*, see G. R. F. Ferrari, *Listening to the Cicadas: A Study of Plato's 'Phaedrus'* (Cambridge: Cambridge University Press, 1987), pp. 81–5. Ferrari, however, addresses the Socratic remarks in terms of rhetoric rather than authorship.

[22] The collocation 'trees or rocks' had itself atrophied to a proverbial phrase in Greek for that which springs from nowhere – as if not only can we no longer converse directly with oak and rock, we cannot even name these things without trailing indirect associations'. Ferrari, *Listening to the Cicadas*, p. 218. Cf. also De Vries, *A Commentary on the Phaedrus of Plato*, pp. 250–1.

are pseudo-sophisticated pioneers of the genetic fallacy. The rejoinder looks forward and backward: in extolling the simplicity of olden times, Socrates also recommends a disregard for subjective status as central to the future of rational inquiry. The detachment of truth from human and temporal origins is a property of the mythical worldview which should continue to characterise *logos* even as it supplants *muthos*. Two incisions are made in the signature by Socrates here: both the identity and place of origin of the signatory are to be discounted as irrelevant beside the issue of the truth or falsity of a statement.

Why does the issue of authorship bear so strongly on every side of this ostensible demonstration of the inferiority of the written word? On the very same Stephanus page, Socrates insists that the father or author always be at hand to defend discourse against the ill-befitted, against maltreatment of writing when it falls into the wrong hands – those of the unsuitable readers (*Phaedrus*, 275e). An irreconcilable contradiction would seem to emerge between the insistence on authorial auto-attendance and the absolute dismissals of authorship at 273c and 275b–c above. Equally disconcerting is the fact that the contradiction passes without notice not only in the text itself but also in Platonic editions and commentaries.[23] With the one hand, Socrates adduces a discourse which properly transcends all human agency: that of its signatory, its author, its source. With the other, he claims that any written discourse is incapable of acquitting or even articulating itself justly without the perpetual and vigilant presence of its parent or author. How are these claims to be neighboured? Does this dissonance or discordance admit of resolution?

---

[23] Ferrari alone considers the two passages together, but does not register their contradictory force. He is, in fact, concerned to show that the two gestures form a unified Socratic strategy: 'it is proper in our world for the "father" (*patros*) of a written work to come to its defence, because any written work will undoubtedly encounter misunderstanding; but for just the same reason it was *not* proper for the "father" of the act of writing to come to the defence of his creation . . .' Ferrari, *Listening to the Cicadas*, p. 218. Furthermore, Ferrari is concerned with the two passages in their relation to myth and antiquity rather than as statements bearing on discursive epistemology. Burger addresses only the contradiction between 275b and 275e in order to neutralise its effect. In one sentence she brings the two statements into accord on the counterintuitive premise that the dependence of discourse on an author is always a regrettable state of affairs in the world of the *Phaedrus*: 'Socrates' later reproach against the dependence of the written work upon the father who must protect it . . . is foreshadowed by Ammon's censure of the art of writing, misjudged by the father who loves it' (Ronna Burger, *Plato's Phaedrus: A Defence of a Philosophic Art of Writing*, Alabama: University of Alabama Press, 1980, p. 94.) The message to Lysias (278b–d) would indicate quite the opposite – that the best thing is that the father be present; the second best that he be recalled by the tether of a signature. In terms of the seeming acceptance of contradiction in the text itself, we will go on to see the contradiction as displaced by a distinction between scientific and non-scientific discourses. Given that Plato could not formulate the discursive field of authorship which his text seems everywhere to seek, we might plausibly speculate that the contradiction between 275b–c and 275e would not be registered *qua* contradiction.

One might, for example, narrow the gap between these antithetical statements in terms of *when* and *how* one signs, of whether one signs in the present or to a future present within whose possibility the receiver has taken up the discourse and begun to read in the absence of the dialectician; of whether one signs in speaking (for the oral signature is itself a performative as much as it is a performance), or in a present of writing towards a future of reading within which the dialectician will cease to be a dialectician and have become what we today, somewhat too comfortably, call an author. Given a dialectical system of intersubjective transmission, the discourse may proceed without its bearer's mark: it may fructify orally, interpsychically, in the certainty of *alētheia* which dispenses with any historical signature or structure of temporal authorisation. Dialectic might therefore be read as an acutely self-aware species of perlocutionary discourse in seeking to persuade the audience to realise the truth through the illocutionary force of dialogue. Hence Plato's strangely explicit conjunction of the illocutionary effects of signature and the constative realm here: the former becomes the condition for the realisation of the latter.

Dialectical science, on this prospect, would need the oral signature as a first condition of its reception but is then able to develop in the absence of the speaker once the state of *alētheia* has been realised in an apodeictic series of legitimate, necessary and logically irrefragable inferences (*Phaedrus*, 276e–277a).[24] The conflict would then agitate between, on the one side, an oral signature which can disappear once correct audience uptake has been achieved and, on the other, a writing which does not carry a living signature but the dead marks of its logographer's name, a breathless series of letters which do not submit to question and answer, clarification and amplification of the intentions which lay behind its composition. However, even if the two claims were to be brought into harmony in such a radically idealist fashion, one would still be left with the problems of making a pure distinction between oral and graphic signatures which we have specified earlier. Furthermore, the contradiction would not annul itself so much as displace into the definitions of speech and writing. Speech as *logos* would then be seen as the discourse which can dispense with its author or subject (*Phaedrus*, 276a), even though that

---

[24] Thus we might put forward a proposition which rescues Plato from the trap of being hostile to writing in writing: to wit, that *only the highest discourse can be written precisely because it can dispense with a signature.* If we accept this tiering of discourse in the *Phaedrus* (which is easy), the *aporia* would only be apparent in the Platonic system: such a reading would consort well with the ironic view of the *Phaedrus* which sees the text as a defence of Plato's own practice of writing. That such a defence is compromised by dialectic's uncertain sense of itself as 'the highest discourse' would then serve to ironise the ironic reading.

independence is produced by the prior presence of the author in the articulation. Writing as shadow, as *eidōlon*, would thus constitute the discourse that cannot dispense with its author despite separating itself from the author in the very moment of birth or of inscription.

The contradiction needs to be confronted head-on: not as local inconsistency or opposition but as an antinomy itself more robust than the contradictory play of speech and writing. What perplexity is astir here? How can the subject be altogether irrelevant at the same time as its presence is the necessary condition of the proper articulation and reception of any discourse? Why are these discrepant claims registered on the very same Stephanus page? Indeed, given the flagrancy of the contradiction, might we not be justified also in asking if there are two discourses distinguished under this demonstration which claims to be solely concerned with two discursive media: one discourse which is self-sufficient, true in its own terms and impersonal; another which is altogether less assured and defenceless without the presence of its author; an authored discourse and an autonomous discourse; two discourses which the categories of speech and writing overlap? And might we not also wonder where would the dialectical philosophy place itself in terms of this opposition?

The idea that truth is requisitely impersonal will not be new to readers of Plato. In the *Republic*, the disconnection of a truth-claim, discourse or statement from the speaker is recommended as a safeguard against the *argumentum ad verecundiam*: no heed should be taken of the speaker's status regardless of whether he is a reputed man of wisdom, a sophist, a tyrant or 'some other rich man who ha[s] great power in his own conceit' (*Republic*, 336a).[25] The *Symposium* likewise affirms that whilst one may counter Socrates, the truth is beyond contest: 'It's the truth you find unanswerable, not Socrates,' the master declares to Agathon (*Symposium*, 201c). One might argue that the entire programme of dialectic is motivated by the attempt to reach a realm beyond signature, a realm that philosophy and science will hitherto call truth and will see as unauthored, the *logos* of no one. In this realm, quite unlike that of culture, neither an *oeuvre* nor a proper name properly applies: truth is defined as that category which has no need of circumstantial origins, has no author in any principled sense, and at most needs proper names as shorthand

---

[25] One sees in this sense how much closer to modernity is Plato's model of truth than the reliance on authorities and *auctores* in the medieval period. On the latter, see A. J. Minnis, *Medieval Theory of Authorship: Scholastic literary attitudes in the later Middle Ages* (London: Scolar Press, 1984) and A. J. Minnis and A. B. Scott, eds, *Medieval Literary Theory and Criticism c.1100–c.1375* (Oxford: Clarendon, 1988).

marks, indices of the proof or theorem. The absence of an author becomes the condition for the founding of the rational subject whose discourse unfurls in a space without signature, date or place. To the extent that Plato often upholds such a model of *alētheia* as an ideal towards which inquiry should aim, he may well have evolved the model of objectivity from the example of geometry. As the only achieved science in Plato's time, geometry provided a model of apodeictic and universally valid truths that could be added to impersonally and by anyone who productively understood the system. The *Republic* declares that the dialectical pupil must first master all of mathematics (*Republic*, 521d–533a), whilst tradition would have it that an inscription over the door of Plato's Academy read: 'Nobody untrained in geometry may enter my house!'[26]

On the other hand, the *Phaedrus* might be seen to distinguish work that does not unfold in a scientific sphere of self-validation and which therefore shows itself as ethically insecure if not, indeed, troublesome. Agency, recapitulation and authorial testimony will be of the first importance in this case. Taken on these terms, the division in the *Phaedrus* between those discourses that are written in the soul of the learner and can defend themselves (*Phaedrus*, 276a) and those that always need their author to restore context and intention (275e) could be marked as the difference between scientific and non-scientific discourses. In placing dialectical philosophy on the side of scientific discourse in so far as it is the discourse of an ever-renewable *alētheia* (276a), the work of the *Phaedrus* might also be seen to continue Plato's *agon* with the poets in the *Republic* as also with the sophists. Once again, poetry and sophistry would be characterised as lower-order discourses, this time in terms of their inability to help themselves, their dependence on a source or agent.

Along such lines, we might see the epistemic divergence of science and literature in terms of agency as commenced by the Socratic interrogation. Where literature is regarded as in need of an author (for ethical and other reasons), the apodeictic discourses of pure philosophy, physical sciences and mathematics have (during Enlightenment and modernity at least)[27] largely

---

[26] For a perspicuous account of Plato's relationship to the mathematical models of his day, see R. M. Hare, 'Plato and Mathematicians', in Renford Bambrough, ed., *New Essays on Plato and Aristotle* (London: Routledge & Kegan Paul, 1965), pp. 21–38.

[27] Foucault has analysed these modal differences in the nature of authorship by contrasting the contribution of a great scientist to his discipline with the act of founding a discourse or discursivity. See Michel Foucault, 'What is an Author?', in *Language, Counter-Memory, Practice: Selected Essays and Interviews*, trans. Donald F. Bouchard and Sherry Simon (Oxford: Basil Blackwell, 1977), pp. 113–38. One might multiply such discriminations by further delineating the operations of exegetical communities such as those of Judaism and Christianity which operate on the basis of a canon and a collectively assembled theology – a process that differs in essential respects from the

dispensed with an agent, an origin, an author, on the assurance that any discourse tries and tests itself within clear disciplinary parameters which determine its validity or invalidity. Doubtless this dichotomy would have met with Plato's approval given that the canon of scientific and philosophical impersonality is founded in his work. Plato clearly wishes to insist upon agency, signature in discourses without an answerable *logos*: anything which does not admit of rational proof, demonstration, deduction must *eo ipso* be monitored. However, as a discourse which outgrows generic and disciplinary constraints, as a body of work which allows narrative, *muthos*, utopian projection to consort with philosophical demonstration, Platonism runs the risk of calling itself to its own tribunal, of taking its own stand beside the sophists, poets and rhetors. Like the god of writing, Plato cannot deliver his text to impersonality. Nor can he accept dialectical philosophy as the work of his own pen without sacrificing its claims to truth.

III: DIALECTIC AND MATHEMATICS: ITERABILITY
AND THE ETHICS OF WRITING

The twists and turns the *Phaedrus* will make on the issue of agency may well derive from the competition between Plato's desire to model dialectic on the objectivity of mathematical statements and his realisation that philosophical discourse cannot achieve clearly apodeictic status. Faced with such an exigency, Plato had to ensure that the dialectical axioms were not misunderstood by the receiver: the neo–Pythagorean distortion of Plato's discourse in the Academy would have furnished first-hand evidence that this was more than a possibility. Unlike mathematical science, the discipline of dialectical reasoning cannot walk abroad freely, in the knowledge that its axioms will assimilate to the very discipline it strives to institute. Lacking the precision of a rigorous science, it finds itself bound not only to a speaker, a spokesman, an accredited adept in its methods, but also to a small school of auditors judiciously selected and educated. Left to its own devices, the discipline lacks inherent means of distinguishing between its proper and improper uses; which is to say that dialectic cannot dwell with security or independence in the epistemological realm of statements which give rise to judgements of truth and

Footnote 27 (*cont.*)
> founding of a science or a discursivity. Certainly, the relations between scientist and system have been subject to considerable historical variance. Whereas Plato's position founds an impersonal model which is systematically realised in the Enlightenment and modernity, the medieval belief in authority forged a strong link between the scientist's name and the veracity of the statements made under its authority. These transversal patterns in the conceptual and historical connection of subject and work will be dealt with in the next section of this work.

falsity but is always threatened by the pragmatic or rhetorical (and, for Plato, sophistic) realm of discursive acts which test themselves in terms of felicity and infelicity.

Although dialectic may raise the philosopher to apprehension of intuitively given truths such as those of the *eidos* or the *a priori* knowledge rendered through geometry, the statements of dialectic itself are not shielded by the principles of coherence and compulsory agreement sought in Euclidean geometry, Aristotle's syllogisms or the axiomatic structure of the Cartesian *regulae*. That we have recently been tempted to call such compulsory agreement into question does not affect the fact that for a discipline like dialectic – stranded as it is between speculative thought and science – the statements it makes are renewable for an audience at large while mathematical axioms cannot be appropriated outside the system itself (i.e. misapplication may be possible but not productive misinterpretation). Following Parmenides, Plato himself accepts that mathematical entities alone possess the immutable intelligibility required by the objects of a true science. According to the classical model, all inferences made within mathematics will be self-evidently valid and exempt from the evanescence of empirical events. Whilst dialectic and geometry are both concerned with the 'eternally existent' (*Republic,* 527b), the dialectical work that *remains* will always be ethically portentous but epistemologically ambiguous, the consequence, in no small part, of its being articulated in ordinary language, a language whose defects 'Plato–Socrates' sought to assuage by question and answer, by an *elenchus* whose aim was continually to re-establish the speaker's intention and to root out inadvertent significance in his discourse. In this spirit, one could read Platonism tragically, as a movement of thought condemned to pursue the trans-discursive realm of *eidos* in a language whose descent from ideal transparency makes failure inevitable, a language which can only provide approximate and transitory illustrations of the ultimate entities, one which covets but cannot claim the empirically untarnished intelligibility of geometry. The *Seventh Letter* despairs, in its discussion of the five objects/modalities of knowledge:[28]

> For if in the case of any of these a man does not somehow or other get hold of the first four, he will never gain a complete understanding of the fifth (true reality). Furthermore, these four (names, descriptions, bodily forms, concepts) do as much to illustrate the particular quality

---

[28] I adduce the *Seventh Letter* again for its lucidity: in the event that the excursus were to be deemed inauthentic, then *Phaedrus*, 275d, 276c and *Republic*, 527a could be adduced without substantial loss to the argument.

of any object as they do to illustrate its essential reality because of the inadequacy of language. Hence no intelligent man will ever be so bold as to put into language those things which his reason has contemplated, especially not into a form that is unalterable – which must be the case with what is expressed in written symbols. (*Seventh Letter*, 342e–343a)

Here the dual inadequacy of language is stated: (i) language itself cannot convey essential reality; and (ii) the written testaments which its failure leaves behind are mute before questioning, cannot be rephrased and hence open themselves to perversion, to dangerous misprision. Within an emergent graphic culture these problems become graver still and motivate Plato in his drive to establish a structure of legacy to govern the reception of his discourses posthumously above and beyond the wishfully pre-emptive adoption of dialogic form. If the *logoi* of dialectic are vulnerable to misinterpretation in an oral situation, then they will be *a fortiori* so when committed to writing. The ungovernable *logoi* Socrates implicitly condemns in his comparison with the wandering statues of Daedalus in the *Euthyphro* (11c) will wander so much further abroad in a world of freely circulating chirographic signs.

It is towards the principle of iterability that Plato's darkest anxieties are directed. If we take iterability to denote 'that ability of locutions to be separated from the intentional context that gave them birth [whereby] each "repetition" is inevitably a renewal, a rebirth, sucking in the life juices of other contexts and other intentions . . .',[29] then we can see that philosophical statements (logic aside), those of the human sciences or dialectic, are always and everywhere susceptible to iterability whilst mathematical statements do not lend themselves to coherent restatement outside the system or the scientific field of its applications. Intention is far from being a compelling category in mathematical science: the very attempt at a proof establishes an operative intention and the success or failure of the proof determines whether that intention has been achieved. Coherence rather than intention provides the context of a mathematical statement and insulates it from iterability. Divorced from context, from a series of propositions, a mathematical lemma resists appropriation in a heterogeneous series of statements or axioms. Mathematics may indeed offer itself to ethical misapplication if its formulae are used for reprehensible ends, but it does not open itself to misreading or expropriation *per se*: hence responsible reception occurs

---

[29] Zygmunt Bauman, *Postmodern Ethics* (Oxford: Blackwell, 1993), p. 102.

within the disciplinary parameters themselves and independently of *oeuvre* effects, detailed statements of intention, history or surrounding discourses. Even were the texts of mathematics to be incompetently assessed within the discipline, the incommensurability of its language game with the language games of social order, ethics and politics would ensure that any erroneous remainder could never constitute a dangerous excess in the sphere of ethical discourse. Quite in spite of the fact that their application in the realm of physics gave rise to the moral abominations that were Hiroshima and Nagasaki, the mathematical foundation is not open to misinterpretation but rather to heinous incorporation – often the product of political coercion – in the development of lethal technologies. Given the rudimentary point that mathematical formulae cannot be translated into ethical statements, it is only as realisation in invention, as contribution to an occurrence in the world of concrete events, that mathematics can become ethically relevant – which is to say that it is not pure mathematics *qua* mathematics that is ethically questionable but the inventive or innovating discourse – e.g. the political injunction rather than the discipline of physics or the pure mathematical discourse upon which it draws.

In *De Sophisticis Elenchis,* Aristotle was to register the insufficiency of dialectical method as science.[30] He does so in a critique which adduces iterability in everything but name. Comparing malpractice in dialectical argument and geometrical demonstration, Aristotle observes:

> The contentious argument stands in somewhat the same relation to the dialectical as the drawer of false diagrams to the geometrician; for it beguiles by misreasoning from the same principles as dialectic uses, just as the drawer of a false diagram beguiles the geometrician. (*De Sophisticis Elenchis,* 171b35–38)

Dialectical principles may be abused just as geometrical axioms are open to mistaken applications; where there are departures, there must at least be a recognisable method. However, Aristotle goes on to draw the fundamental distinction that dialectical discourse, unlike geometrical law, is vulnerable to iteration:

> But whereas the latter is not a contentious reasoner, because he bases his false diagram on the principles and conclusions that fall

---

[30] References are made to Aristotle, *De Sophisticis Elenchis*, trans. W. A. Pickard-Cambridge, in W. D. Ross, ed., *The Works of Aristotle,* Vol. 1 (Oxford: Clarendon, 1928). The page, letter and line references to *De Sophisticis Elenchis* supplied parenthetically within the text are standardised according to the Berlin Academy edition, *Aristotelis Opera,* ed. Immanuel Bekker, 5 vols (1831–70). Though Aristotle does not specify Platonic dialectic in the analysis which follows, his objections are entirely pertinent.

under the art of geometry, the argument which is subordinate to the principles of dialectic will yet clearly be contentious as regards other subjects. (*De Sophisticis Elenchis*, 171b38–172a2)

We might substitute 'ethically problematic philosopher' for 'contentious reasoner' to render the argument that dialectical philosophy is incapable of containing its misuses within the system itself. This overspill, the excess of the iterable, constitutes an ethical threat, while the making of a false diagram is readily identified as error within the geometrical system. The system of geometry tethers its misapplications to the system itself: hence, as we shall see, the signature functions in a very different ethical context with regard to pure science, both in the Platonic and classical placements.

Furthermore, even if the system were to show itself incapable of detecting certain erroneous practices, those practices themselves are immune from translation into other contexts. Geometrical science is thus incapable of infecting adjacent orders of discourse, of finding its statements reconstituted in any other syntax or system: even seen as a language game, geometry, like chess, exists in a relation of absolute incommensurability with ethically pertinent discourse (even if the contests between Robert Fischer and Boris Spassky were manipulated, like the space race, as emblematic of victory in a supposedly 'Cold' War). Dialectic, on the other hand, carries with it illimitable potential for generating ethically pernicious statements, extrapolations that are foreign to its *ethos* but not to its syntax. In this sense dialectic cannot attain scientificity because the uses made of its own elements are not governed by the systematic interplay of those very elements. Consequently, while a geometrical proposition 'cannot be adapted to any subject except geometry, because it proceeds from principles that are peculiar to geometry', a product of dialectical philosophy 'can be adapted as an argument against all the number of people who do not know what is or is not possible in each particular context: for it will apply to them all' (*De Sophisticis Elenchis*, 172a4ff).

Secondly, and in intimate relation to the iterability of dialectical statements, there is the added danger that the absence of intrinsic disciplinary limits will allow irresponsible, amateurish or sophistic imitators to practise the interrogatory method. Plato is himself continually alert to the danger of eristic and indeed ill-willed attempts to utilise the resources of dialectical philosophy. But once again, competence in the discipline is not made apparent by the *workings* of the discipline itself: hence dialectic's unending attempts to patrol the borderline or fence by which it would separate itself from sophistry. Incompetent mathematical reasoning will reveal itself as the failure to produce intelligible proofs, even as the failure to make mathematical propositions: ethical or dogmatic distortions of philosophical statements, on the other hand, will retain the appearance of statements. As *De Sophisticis Elenchis* assesses the distinction: 'For neither is the art of examination an accomplishment of the same kind as geometry, but one which a man may possess, even though he has not knowledge . . . everybody, including amateurs, makes use in a way of dialectic and the practice of examining . . .' (*De Sophisticis Elenchis*, 172a23–33).

Because dialectic does not possess the intrinsic resources to distinguish between the proper and improper uses to which it is put, legacy must be ensured by the presence of the dialectical master, by an institution which ensures responsible succession. At a crossroads which we will see re-encountered by Marxism and Freudianism in the preoccupation of their founders with forming and presiding over legacies, it is the very insecurity of dialectic as science which dictates that the parent of a discourse be always at hand, keep watch over its effects in a protective, rescuing proximity. Whilst work in a science, in particular mathematics, passes not so much into its author's corpus as into the space, the axiomatic reserve of the discipline itself, discourses such as Marxism and Freudianism must draw a line and a structure of inheritance on the basis of the *oeuvre*. A science will not need an institution in the sense that the First International or Plato's Academy were institutions, since the discipline self-regulates to a far greater extent: for this reason we might wish to distinguish the idea of a scientific community (which refers back to the principles of the discipline) from that of an interpretative institution (which takes its bearings from the overall distribution of forces within the *oeuvre*).

The absence of such disciplinary parameters impels Plato to the establishment of extramural parameters: legacy, constraints on circulation and the formation of an Academy take the place of disciplinary autonomy. The risk of misprision is at the very heart of Platonic rationalism, in its statements, its 'system', its methods and ethos: 'all great things are precarious . . .' (*Republic*, VI, 497d), Socrates declares of dialectic. In *Republic* VII, having approved mathematics and geometry as requisite objects of learning, Socrates will be altogether more circumspect when admitting pupils to the study of dialectic for fear that unsuitable souls will discredit 'the whole business of philosophy' (*Republic*, 539c).

The risk of misprision is at the very heart of Platonic rationalism, in its statements, its 'system', its methods and ethos. Even were dialectic to make good its claim to bring all arts and sciences under its direction (*Philebus*, 16c), if mathematics could be reduced to dialectical synopsis,

Plato would still be left with the ethical remainder of philosophy, the con-
textual mobility of its statements, the very problem of iterability from
which apodeictic science disburdens itself though the narrowness of its
remit.

Because dialectic does not possess the intrinsic resources to distinguish
between the proper and improper uses to which it is put, the text must
set itself the near-impossible task of separating suitable from suitable
readers. The parallel task of discerning suitable and unsuitable practitioners derives from the same deficiency. Since it cannot become an inherent
function of the system, legacy must be ascertained within the mortal
horizons of the dialectical master. When Plato realises that his discursivity does not set its own boundaries, that it cannot determine what is valid
and invalid within its field of application, when he discovers how the
great adventure of dialectic has given birth not to a science but to an ethically problematic *oeuvre*, and that the dialectical wisdom cannot remain
except as written words, the relinquishment of legacy becomes the very
possibility of legacy itself. Thus dialectic contracts itself to an oral method
whilst ensuring it remains as writing. The *Phaedrus* makes this concession
of a most anxious authorship in such a manner that it will travel to every
outpost at which the Platonic work is destined to find itself.

At one and the same time though Plato's colossal corpus creates, out
of this ultimate epistemologico-scientific failure, the textual and cultural
space of a mode of sapiential authorship which continues to shape our
discursive categories, notions of genius and canonicity. This space is
opened in two separate movements which hesitantly – and with all the
necessary precautions in mind – one might characterise as the critical
and constructive, the negative and the positive, the elenchtic and the
assertoric. In the first instance, it follows from the method of *elenchus*,
which demands that a responsible subject emerge from the collective
experience to take responsibility for the words spoken or written in his
or her name. In the second – and this corresponds to the increasing independence of a writerly Plato from the 'presence' of Socrates as oralist precursor – the concept of authorship takes recognisably modern shape
from the production of a vast, interdisciplinary body of work which
treats of so very many aspects of culture under the guidance of a singular oral instruction and the development of an authorial intelligence,
an act of concentration split between the recording of an unprecedented instruction and the construction of dialectical philosophy, a
progress and process spanning some fifty years, and which yet – for all its
divisions between Socratic inspiration and Platonic initiation – emerged

with a sense of continuity only previously attained in the tragic dramas of Aeschylus and Sophocles.

IV: DIALECTIC AND THE (ANXIOUS) ORIGINS OF AUTHORSHIP: TRIBUNAL AND SIGNATURE IN THE *PHAEDRUS*

If Plato created the space of authorship through the sheer force of a copious discourse which exceeded disciplinary and generic boundaries, he did not do so without theoretical reflection on the cultural implications of his prodigy. Whilst the *Phaedrus* must reflect Plato's own status as an author, and therefore cannot be assumed as a deliberate programme of the text, it explicitly addresses the issue of authorship in general. Throughout this section of work, the figures of signature and tribunal have been used to describe Plato's attempts to establish an ethics of discourse. None of these terms is used by Plato in this context, but as concepts they vivify a chain of concerns which run from the first Socratic question through to the work of the *Laws*. Before showing how the *Phaedrus* tethers written discourse to a source, an author or agent through the formation of a discursive tribunal, it is necessary to examine dialectic's construction of itself as a canonising institution. It is from this attempt to bring all discourse under its sway that Plato discovers the concept of authorship as a primary ethical category with a sophistication which has yet to be superseded. We have noted how the question of signature frames the myth of Theuth from which the discussion of writing (re)commences. A little later, it will dominate a cunning epilogue which reverses the priorities it is supposed to confirm.

Issues of authorship and signature dictate and at times seem to confound Socrates' narration of the myth of writing and its rejection by an incorruptible king (of natural memory, of the conservation of wise words for the wise and the wise alone) who would neither barter nor compromise with the minor deity. Immediately upon Theuth's proposal that writing will provide a recipe for wisdom and memory, this narrative – whose authorship or origin is itself to be disputed by Phaedrus in this vertiginous play of signature effects – takes its crucial turn, affirming as originary denial what the text in its very written existence confirms has been accepted:

> the king answered and said, 'O man full of arts (*technikōtate*), to one it is given to create the things of art, and to another to judge what measure of harm and of profit they have for those that shall employ them. And so it is that you, by reason of your tender regard for the writing that is your offspring (*ekgonos*), have declared the very opposite (*tounantion*) of its true effect. (*Phaedrus*, 274e–275a)

Writing is separated from the father at birth: not only as a general condition of inscription but upon its first presentation to the Greek world. Creator and creation are sundered in ethical terms because of the filial bond. Whereas the written word will be censured in terms of the parricide implicit in separating the discourse from its author, and the spoken *logos* will be praised for its affiliation to the philosopher-speaker, writing itself is insufficiently separate from its inventor. The art of writing is defended with altogether too much paternal goodwill by the father of writing (*patēr ōn grammatōn*). Of course, the question of how far one can be said to author an invention, of whether categorical clarity is introduced by analogising the dynamics of invention-as-authorship with textual authorship, of whether the category of authorship broadens to vacuity by incorporating acts of invention – inexhaustibly ponderable matters – are at issue here. But the case is presented as universal: the creator of a work, whatever its nature, will never attest objectively or competently to the ethical value of his creation. Of all people, therefore, the author is the only individual to be *a priori* debarred from the court of judgement. Given Thamus' principle that the creator is incapable of evaluating his work, Theuth is caught in a performative contradiction. Only if his invention were defended by another, by proxy and in the absence of the father, might his art gain a fair hearing. The writing whose great vice consists in separating father and offspring (*erkonos*) is here to be separated from the father. The defender of speech thus introduces the breach for which writing will be condemned. The refusal of authorship might thus be read simultaneously with the myth of writing's degradation.

However, one cannot simply say that, by separating father and offspring and setting himself up as custodian of the god's invention, Thamus pronounces on behalf of the *Phaedrus*. There is the obvious exigency that it is not necessarily Socrates who properly speaks here.[31] Who is the father of our subject (*patēr tou logon*)? Socrates? Plato? Plato's Socrates? Socrates' king, or the king whose myth Plato has Socrates narrate? Who attends these words? Of whom can they claim to be the offspring (*ekgonos*)? Without idiom or inflection, Thamus's voice is audible only as one half of an allegorical structure (the mortal refuser of the gift versus its divine proferrer, the cautious sceptic against an unbridled technological optimism) within a myth whose framing voice itself cannot be registered as

---

[31] Surprisingly, Derrida tends to treat King Thamus as the vehicle for the Platonic judgement: 'It is precisely this ambiguity that Plato, through the mouth of the King, attempts to master, to dominate by inserting its definition into simple, clear-cut oppositions . . .' (PP, 103). Ferrari draws attention to this tendency in Derrida. Cf. Ferrari, *Listening to the Cicadas*, p. 281, n. 25.

a definitive Socratic or Platonic articulation.[32] Whatever the extent to which Socrates or Plato may find themselves in agreement with King Thamus, it is not the purpose of the ensuing dialogue simply to echo the regal judgement. Moreover, though the king wishes to separate work from author in so far as the author is authority or judge *over* the work, he is by no means indifferent to the issues of speaker and origin in the way Socrates will later recommend to Phaedrus. To the contrary, it is on the basis of the speaker's identity and relation to his invention that Thamus commences his repudiation of Theuth's discourse. As the 'negative' image of Phaedrus's susceptibility to the prestige of the speaker, the question 'Who speaks?' is of the first moment for the king even in so far as it is the inventor or father of this *tekhnē* and no one else who speaks. Indeed, the regal gesture which calls the author to the work but denies him any power of judgement over its ethical status functions at a textual level to prefigure the moves by which dialectic establishes itself as a tribunal to whose summons all authors must be alert: it enacts a structure of separation and recall to the work which will characterise the signatory function for both Plato and a great deal of the subsequent history of discursive enquiry.

The myth of writing as a gift refused exercises a vital strategic function which is remarkable and unmarked. It allows the trial of writing to take place. By bringing writing before the court of King Thamus and then detaching it from the judgements of its inventor, the text places writing on trial without explicitly raising its own authorisation to do so. As the *Phaedrus* glides out of the myth – with the discussion of its pedigree – writing has become a defendant without representation or voice at the court not of King Thamus but of dialectical philosophy. The roles of author and ethical judge are deemed by the king to belong to entirely different spheres; whereas, Socrates asserts that any written work cannot be fairly judged without the testimony of its father. A quandary is presented to the dialectician. If the latter position is followed through, then dialectic sacrifices its commitment to the interpersonal ethos; if the former, philosophy cannot establish itself as tribunal unless the author can answer its summons and a dead or departed author would thereby bequeath to posterity a text from which dialectical judgement was itself debarred. We can see this tension at work in the *Theaetetus*, where Socrates

---

[32] Ferrari almost goes so far as to endorse this reversal of the conventional association of King Thamus with the Platonic viewpoint: 'If anything, the philosopher is a combination of Thoth, the inventor, and Ammon, the judge of arts . . . for by attempting to judge the good life, the philosopher brings it into being' (*Listening to the Cicadas*, p. 281).

picks up the pieces and the threads of the Protagorean discourse to ensure
that it receives 'fair play':

SOCRATES: . . . And so no one was left to tell Protagoras' tale
. . . about knowledge and perception being the
same thing.

THEAETETUS: So it appears.

SOCRATES: I fancy it would be very different if the author of
the first story were still alive. He would have put up
a good fight for his offspring. But he is dead, and
here are we trampling on the orphan. Even its
appointed guardians, like Theodorus here, will not
come to the rescue (*boēthein*). However, we will step
into the breach ourselves and see that it has fair play.
(*Theaetetus*, 164d–e)

A good fight or defence: unlike Theueth who is not given voice after
Thamus's judgement, Protagoras would carve out his own space of
boēthein. But Protagoras is dead, indeed his is perhaps the first particular
instance of the general death of the author as theorised in *Phaedrus*.
Dialectic will always negotiate this difficulty in favour of establishing itself
as judge or arbitrator: it is not the decision of the participants in the dialogue to 'step into the breach' and ensure that it has fair play for dialectic, whether putting to the test poetry, sophistics or writing is itself 'fair
play (*boēthein*)'. This is most apparent in the *Sophist*, when the text must
address the Parmenidian thesis that 'all is one'. Courting the idea that the
detachment of the thesis from its progenitor might constitute a kind of
'parricide', the Stranger depicts himself as laying 'unfilial hands on that
pronouncement (*toi patrikōi logōi*)' (*Sophist*, 241e–242a). These words
display Plato acutely aware of the need to examine a thesis, argument or
pronouncement in the absence of its author. Not only the living but also
the dead must be called to the dialectical reckoning. The theme of an
absolute bond between speaker and statement is thus relaxed with the
realisation that commitment to a dialogic method would severely limit
the provenance of dialectical investigation. The notion of fidelity to the
father of the discourse is not jettisoned, however, in this interrogation: by
a connection which resembles a signatory function, the Platonic texts
seek to demonstrate how a discourse which has been abandoned or
orphaned can – if fostered by a responsible audience and tribunal – be
adequately represented in the future.

In this sense, the necessity of dialectic establishing itself as tribunal triumphs in Plato's text over its commitment to dialogic method. One

might even see the vacillation of the *Phaedrus* on the connection of author
to discourse as a working through of this obstacle to dialectic's establishment as the master tribunal before which all discourses must present
themselves, as one might equally argue that the canonising impulse provides a unifying theme throughout the Platonic corpus.[33] Implicit in the
very first Socratic interrogation, the right of dialectic to arbitrate over all
areas of culture is stated more and more explicitly with the *oeuvre's*
growing sense of itself as a discipline. One repeatedly forgets that the
Republic summons the poets to the dialectical tribunal in favour of the
romantic concept of summary banishment from the *polis*: the text does
allow for something like an appeal, albeit whilst casting poetry in preju-
dicially gendered terms and issuing a caveat to the judges to close their
ears to the charms of a virtual Siren's song: 'owing to the love of . . .
poetry inbred in us by our education in these fine polities of ours, [we]
will gladly have the best possible case made out for her goodness and
truth' (*Republic*, 607e–608a). Its cultural and epistemic provenance comes
to encompass not only the discourses of poetry and philosophy, but also
the sciences and making of laws. Long before the attempt to write laws,
the Platonic work had declared: 'the work of the legislator is to give
names, and the dialectician must be his director if the names are to be
rightly given' (*Cratylus*, 390d).

Whilst dialectic will confidently call poetry, law-giving, political discourse, Parmenidean or Protagorean philosophy to its surveillance, it
shifts ground in its attempts to assert authority over scientific productions.
As the text in which philosophy dreams the city as subject to its rule, the
Republic will make the strongest claims: 'we have set dialectic above all
other studies to be as it were the coping stone' (534e). Early and later
Platonic dialogues will affirm philosophy as the supreme court of epistemic judgement. And they will do so according to shifting foci of legitimation. At one time dialectic will see itself as an epistemological tribunal,
the method by which discourses are evaluated in terms of their claims to
truth. At others it will claim the right of ethical adjudication over the
application of scientific discourse. In the *Phaedrus*, as we will see, dialectic will take the significantly more modest step of asserting itself as judge
only over non-scientific work. One might again distribute these modifi-
cations in terms of dialectic's sense of its own interdisciplinarity, the fluidity of boundaries which absorbs and repels poetry and science in a play

---

[33] There are a few dialogues from which the idea of dialectic as rational tribunal is absent – the
Timaeus, for example. However, these works do not concern themselves with assessing the value
of other discourses or the issue of discursive circulation.

of (piecemeal) appropriation and (necessary) incommensurability. In the later *Philebus*, both the insufficiency of dialectic as scientific method and its determination to present itself as the master discourse of culture are registered as Socrates introduces the doctrine of the One and the Many: 'It is a method quite easy to indicate, but very far from easy to employ. It is indeed the instrument through which every discovery ever made in the sphere of the arts and sciences has been brought to light' (*Philebus*, 16c). Just as the *Euthydemus* allots a similar role to philosophy as ethical supervisor and pragmatic adjudicator of legitimate scientific application, here dialectic does not so much assert itself as the discoverer of truth as its facilitator or the tribunal by which discoveries are ratified, communicated and allowed to enter culture at large.

As an overseer of the consequences of his work, the scientist is detached from his discovery or invention by a strategy almost identical to the removal of the father of writing from the dialectical judgement of writing. Dialectic thus sees itself as the supreme council in terms of the ethics of knowledge: scientific expertise does not guarantee ethical vision – only the dialectician can adjudge the proper uses to which scientific findings should be put in a society. Robinson says: 'It is hard to imagine what sort of activity Plato would have classified as a dialectician's use of a mathematical discovery.'[34] However, it is somewhat easier to envisage if we imagine Plato's horizons to be ethical rather than epistemological or methodological here. In the monitoring of science, Plato's concern is not limited to the restriction of discursive circulation, but extends to the overseeing of direct applications. Again, this would seem to reflect the fact that the circulation of scientific discourse is self-limiting through inherent disciplinary parameters: it would also explain why Plato never insists that the scientific parent be at hand to keep watch over his or her *discourse*. Unlike its applications, the scientific text is not placed to disseminate in society and can be ethically pernicious only as discovery or application, not as form of symbols.[35] Given that prior to application the text of mathematical science is *in statu nascendi*, then it is not a text in the sense of an ethically dangerous writing. For these reasons, matters of agency and signature are not raised by the dialectical tribunal

---

[34] Robinson, *Plato's Earlier Dialectic*, p. 78.

[35] If genuine, the *Seventh Letter* (341b–344e) would provide the clearest statement of this distinction, in particular the injunction that 'no serious man will ever think of writing about serious realities *for the general public* so as to make them a prey to envy and perplexity' (344c: my emphasis). Because its language is highly specialised, mathematical formulae are not open to abuse by the general public and hence cannot be ethically pernicious. Only the application of formulae is open to public abuse.

in relation to science. Hence when dialectic comes to proclaim itself in the *Phaedrus* as the tribunal before which the signatory of a discourse must present himself, the scientist will not be called to its reckoning.

Let us draw together these strands of tribunal, signature and agency by considering the concluding section of the *Phaedrus* so as to witness the final move in the sublime orchestration of this piece, the one that has hitherto gone unnoticed.[36] Here the text plays a card that spins the game off in another direction, turns the argument back towards itself and yet forward into what it supposedly repudiates as Socrates carves out the cultural space of authorship from the hollows of the text's condemnation of writing.

The business of the day is ended. Socrates and Phaedrus's pastime is over. The heat has dropped and they will soon return to the city. All that remains, beyond a closing observance, is to compose a message containing the fruits of the exchange. What follows, however, as an account of this exchange, is not a summary or even an amplification so much as a swerve from all that seemed to have been said. The ostensible hostility to writing dissolves; the speech/writing distinction now distinguishes nothing. Or, if it distinguishes anything, it serves only to laud those discourses that answer the summons to the dialectical tribunal and to censure those that do not. The written word can become the word of wisdom; if its author answers lucidly to philosophy, he answers to the name of philosopher. Dialectic offers itself as the supplement through which writing can become *sophia*. In this section which tradition has sundered from the discussion under such trivialising heads as 'Messages to Lysias and Isocrates' or 'Recapitulation', Socrates evolves a paradigm of discursive responsibility which has manifested itself in every corner of western culture to this day:

> SOCRATES: Then we may regard our literary pastime as having reached a satisfactory conclusion (*pepaisthō metriōs*

---

[36] One might even suspect that a force field has built up around these closing words. Even critics such as Ferrari and Burger who present their theses in the form of running commentaries do not register the immense significance of this passage. Despite arguing for the strongest ironic reading which sees Plato as consciously and deliberately defending his practice of philosophical writing, Burger applies these words self-reflexively and thus does not register their import for the practice of writing in general. Cf. Burger, *Plato's Phaedrus*, pp. 105–6. Ferrari says little more of it beyond noting that 'the dangers of the written word are defused by this section: "One who is not reliant on the written word for understanding, who has no false expectations of it, and who is able to supplement its inadequacies in speech may write about what matters to him . . . and yet merit the title "philosopher" . . .' (*Listening to the Cicadas*, pp. 205–6). Furthermore, he declares: 'Socrates brings his own philosophic conversation with Phaedrus to an end with the declaration "let this be the measure of our game" ' (p. 213). The radical gesture by which writing is rescued is not taken into account here, nor is the resonance of admitting the poet to the rank of philosopher.

hēmin). Do you now go and tell Lysias that we two went down to the stream where is the holy place of the nymphs, and there listened to words (*logoi*) which charged us to deliver a message, first to Lysias and all other composers of discourses (*logoi*), secondly to Homer and all others who have written poetry whether to be read or sung, and thirdly to Solon and all such as are authors of political compositions under the name of laws – to wit, that if any of them has done his work with a knowledge of the truth, can defend his statements when challenged, and can demonstrate the inferiority of his writings out of his own mouth, he ought not to be designated by a name drawn from those writings, but by one that indicates his serious pursuit.

PHAEDRUS: Then what names would you assign him?

SOCRATES: To call him wise, Phaedrus, would, I think, be going too far; the epithet is proper only to a god. A name that would fit him better, and have more seemliness, would be 'lover of wisdom', or something similar. (278b–d)[37]

On one level, Socrates outlines a practice that persists today in the form of the *viva*: a proof that you have written the work that bears your name, that you can defend that work, a practice which is also known as a 'defence': both words bear altogether on our purposes – one denoting the medium of speech as a supplement to the written work, the other recalling the play of *boētheia* throughout Plato's reflection on discourse. The *viva* or defence is, of course, a hearing before a tribunal which commissions itself to determine that the writer can rephrase, clarify, explain, expand, justify that work, that he or she can, in a certain fashion, better that work in terms of oral insights, and, no less importantly, prove that the work is the fruit of his or her own labour and composition. On another and intimately connected level, Socrates states the principle that underlies the signatory contract which has governed our culture from the Renaissance onwards. The almost baroque use of proper names alerts us to the importance of authorship in this context as Socrates charges Phaedrus to deliver messages not only to the living but also to the dead: the names 'Homer'

---

[37] Derrida's neglect of this passage is particularly conspicuous: his analysis ceases at precisely 277a. One cannot but suspect that the Derridean reading has no room for such an overt acceptance of writing by Socrates and/or the author of the *Phaedrus*. Cf. PP, pp. 142–71.

and 'Solon' allow Socrates to issue a posthumous summons, just as a signature recalls both the living and the dead in a culture of writing.

The text here reprises the Socratic mission as it is declared in the earlier *Apology*: it draws the force of agency and signature from the reverberations of that first question of *elenchus*. Dialectic establishes itself as the tribunal before which all non-scientific authors must acquit themselves: indeed, we might see our reluctance to name a scientist as an author as stemming from this very discrimination. In the impersonality of his medium, the inability of his text to circulate through society as text, the work of the scientist does not belong to the space of ethically pertinent discourse which is identified here as authorship. The demand made by this tribunal is that the speaker, poet or author must identify and present himself to dialectical interrogation. The statement or intention (*dianoeisthai*) in the text-of-the-text cannot be sufficient: it may be completed only by the necessary supplement of an author entering into discussion and debate of its claims.[38] Agency is not simply assured in the act of composition; it must answer to the afterlife of the text, to the process of its reception. Redoubtably violent, the brackets placed around the speech-writer, poet and law-maker are neither arbitrary nor wilfully agonistic: all three generate discourses – whether for oral declamation or inscription – which purport to have serious ethical content in proposing to human beings the proper manner in which they should live their lives. The orally delivered poem and speech are judged on an equal footing with the text-making of the laws. What Socrates outlines here is an evolved paradigm of authorship which cuts across genres and disciplines, one whose complicity with the process of canonisation is precociously grasped in the gesture of dialectic setting itself up as the canonising tribunal, the discipline which ratifies poet, law-maker, speech-writer in so far as they show themselves sincere and able to justify their claims. In arriving at this space in which the poet is no longer specified as the poet, but within which poet, law-maker and politician may walk abreast as 'lovers of wisdom', the close of this text can only provoke tremors through any reading which sees mutual or symmetrical interdictions at the fore of the *Phaedrus* and the *Republic*, and should also modify the apparent sarcasm with which the

---

[38] This obligation to accept such a summons is modulated in terms of genre even to this day. The author of a non-fictional work will generally accept such a summons while the author of a fictional work might still articulate the right to submerge his agency through appeals to aestheticism in an entirely self-conscious equivalent of the unreflective submergence of poetic personality in the poetic universe. Through statements which carry a freight of assumptions about the supposed 'ontology' of literature, authors – particularly those of the modernist era – make a credo of a depersonalisation which was enforced by memorisation and empathetic performance in oralist cultures.

latter offers poetry a last court of appeal, even should 'she' present herself in the most entrancing garments of the seductress, present her case in the most alluring song of the Sirens (*Republic*, 608a–b). The *Phaedrus* evokes at its close a model of authorship which discriminates neither in terms of genre nor the medium an author chooses. As a lover of wisdom, the poet too can acquit himself at the dialectical tribunal which hears the cases of all who would commit their words to script or memorisation, to all who would speak to the culture at large.

The *Phaedrus* is bound to the transition from a culture of orality to one of writing, but not as an act of retrenchment, a retreat into the oral life-world. The critique of writing is of a piece with the critique of the semi-anonymity of the oral world. An ethical insistence on agency in the bardic tradition consorts with the ethical insistence on signature in a culture of writing to which Plato's work will itself belong. The *Phaedrus* can thus be read as a rehearsal of writing, an ushering in of the new medium, which also warns of its dangers whilst identifying the decisive reconfiguration in discursive categories which the advent of writing promotes. With all modes of communication uprooted from the 'natural' base of their articulation, whether in memorisation and ecstatic performance (poetry), group discussion or seminar (philosophy) and public gathering (political discourse), the new science of writing exerts a gathering force, draws genre together in a space that covers all discursive acts and relieves them of the form to which they were consigned by oral necessity. Hence the serious writer, the one whose text belongs to a broader vision which can be renewed under questioning, should not be 'designated by a name drawn from those writings': i.e. he should not be called a rhetor, a poet or law-maker, but belongs to a larger category of canonised 'lovers of wisdom'.

The cultural space of authorship emerges – if not for the first time, then in its first moment of self-conscious clarity – in the culmination of this dialogue. Nor would it seem unreasonable to suggest that while there is a concept of the text before writing, there is no concept of authorship. In freeing each discourse from its 'natural' forum, writing homogenises the discursive field: Plato's attempt to discriminate via value judgements between the wisely and unwisely written, between that spoken in truth and that spoken in vain, makes of dialectical thought a canonising institution which both attests to this levelling of text and builds hierarchical distinctions in the place of generic differences. Writing further expands the discursive world by serving as a near-guarantee that the work will outlive its subject. It gives birth to a new figure in the field of discourse, a category which is strangely more and less than a person: an ontological reduction and temporal expansion of the individual. It makes of the empirical self a name, a reserve, a boundary that encloses neither life nor death. Where memorisation in/of the epic tradition ensured a certain posthumous continuity, it did so with great uncertainty as to authorial identity and preservation of works *ipsissima verba*. Though writing can never guarantee these functions with absolute certitude, it vastly increases the likelihood that a corpus will survive in the fixed form of words achieved by the author at the moment when s/he determined to complete or abandon the work. Moreover, through the mediation of writing, a life and its thought can speak not to a fellow, a dialectician, but to an unmarked destination, a posterity of which the writer can only have dim outlines. It is into this strange and unmapped country that the writer's work will travel, out of reach and beyond recall of its subject's designs. Before Plato elected to write, the horizons Socrates envisaged were finite, limited by the span and scope of his existence, the sum total of discursive encounters he made. When Plato determined to write, the Socratic discourse – as represented in the dialogues – exceeded the Socratic life: Plato's discourse in turn found its meaning became an intra-textual effect in that he himself would at some time become unavailable for comment, explication, response. The unresponsive nature of the written word brought an author into being, a *savant* whose discourse could be extended beyond the horizons of his lifetime, but only at the cost of sundering his own reading of his discourse from the discourse itself. The Plato of the *Phaedrus* is concerned to grasp, to theorise this new figure emerging on the chirographic horizons. And this figure emerges in the wake of the dialogist, steps out of the departed body of Socrates.

In his very experience of writing, in the inspiration of and eventual liberation from Socrates (which we continue to denote as 'the Socratic problem') and his failure to erect dialectic as a science, Plato has himself (along with certain of his contemporaries, but far outpacing them on this epochal path) conjured the ghost (*eidōlon*) of presence that will henceforth be recognised as the author. It is tempting indeed to see this notion of unmediated authorship as definitively crystallised in the Aristotelian canon, but this would be to ignore the redactory efforts of his pupils in the Lyceum. Just as much of Saussure and Wittgenstein comes to us from lecture notes compiled by their students, so too Aristotle's *Metaphysics* is in no small part the product of transcription, editing and organisation in the absence of the oral teacher. Nevertheless, the emergence of authorship as a strong – if circumstantially contingent–concept derived from the distinct phases of the Socratico-Platonic adventure.

First, authorship emerges as a central property through the process of summoning an individual as rational agent to submit to the method of question and answer, to recognise his or her accountability for the discourse produced and to give a defence and amplification of its truth-claims in the living present. As we have argued, the close of the *Phaedrus* prepares the stage for the entry of this epochal protagonist, one whose boldest features Plato would discern in the mirror: an author who – bearing altogether less resemblance to Pythagoras or Euclid or indeed 'Homer' than to the inventor of dialectic himself – wills to the future not a set of axioms but an *oeuvre*, one whose *logoi* remain in the fixed form of their inscription, however anti-dogmatic, thought-provoking and affectively mobile those words might be.

Secondly, it arises from the colossal task of writing Plato set himself towards the end of the Socratic life and which he continued with ever more distance from the departed dialogic master. In creating a monumental *oeuvre* rather than a science, a body of work so compendious and resonant but bereft of the certainties it everywhere sought, a discourse that is part-philosophy and part-literature, Plato evolved the prototype of a figure who, whilst neither a fictional artificer nor the founder of a science, yet creates an enigmatic structure of thought, a play of protagonists, a space of 'Platonism' to rival any extant genre or discursive space. In this sense Plato in his writings created not only those writings but the cultural space in which they unfolded: a space, an interdisciplinary breadth which will later open itself before Aristotle, Augustine, Hobbes, Rousseau, Kant, Hegel, Marx and Freud, the space of a great author or founder of discourse. Dialectic itself was forged from extant genres, from philosophical debate, Attic tragedy, the narrative resources of myth, as well as at the epistemological boundary that culture constructed between *logos* and *muthos*, science and narrative.[39] It was to give rise to successors who created microcosmic worlds in the spaces between pure philosophy and narrative, between science and literature in the form of discursivities, unratified systems, 'human sciences', confessional works of philosophy,

---

[39] Nietzsche draws attention to the hybridity which resulted in dialectical form. He does not, however, add the impersonalist drives which Plato also wished to add to his new form. Nor, as we have noted, could he precisely state dialectic's liminality with regard to speech and writing: 'If tragedy had absorbed into itself all the earlier types of art, the same might be also said in an eccentric sense of the Platonic dialogue which, a mixture of all extant styles and forms, hovers midway between narrative, lyric and drama, between prose and poetry, and so has also broken the strict old law of the unity of linguistic form' (BT, 90).

philosophical works of confession. Almost against its own wishes, the Platonic work uncovered this realm between two radically antithetical impersonalities: a space of constructive subjectivity which unfurled between the pre-individuation of oral ethos and the impersonality of mathematical demonstration. Defining the poles of pre-rational poetic possession and formal subjectivity, Plato's discourse finds itself most severely in need of the attendance of an author and an author-as-ethical-agent. Having insisted on agency to draw a culture of poetic identification into a *polis* dominated by rational subjectivity, Plato's discourse yet failed to establish itself on the model of *alētheia* by which a science might prescribe what is true and untrue of itself. Which is another way of saying that dialectic itself is in the place of that unassisted, defenceless writing, that discourse in need of its parent to come to the rescue.

One could even see the Socrates of the *Phaedrus* as miming Plato's anxieties about the status of his own work: its future as changeless written words, its expansion into the ethically portentous *oeuvre* that was to be Platonism. When one further takes into account the immense iterability of a corpus which leaves virtually no aspect of knowledge or culture untouched, as also the incalculable scope for iteration offered by the new science of writing, it becomes impossible to dissociate the fear of writing in Plato's text from the very fact that it survives in writing. Whether or not history judges the Platonic writings to have themselves run away with their author, either in terms of the neo-Pythagorean solidifications of Plato's work into a dogma which began in the Academy towards the end of his life, or through the influence of his political philosophy on the totalitarian regimes of modernity, dialectical science nonetheless provides the prototype of the dangerous excess, the destinational uncertainties of a system of thought separated from its speaker. The difficulty which Plato faced was perhaps not so different from the one with which his text confronts us today. For while the gains to Western thought of his text *remaining* are beyond dispute or measure, the ethical balance is no easier to adjudicate now than then.

In exploring further the idea of legacy and the anxiety of authorship outlined above through considering Nietzsche's *Ecce Homo*, we remain resolutely within the framework of Plato's discursive ethics, and closer to the concerns of the *Phaedrus* and *Republic* than if we were to study the 'postal' history of the latter through the theoretical misgivings of the former concerning dissemination, suitable and unsuitable readers and the absence of the author to correct misreading, misappropriation. Nowhere in the history of thought might we bear witness more intimately to an author's terrifying uncertainty as to the status, significance and potentially calamitous nature of the writings he was releasing into the world without their father to come to the rescue.

Despite Nietzsche's career-spanning immersion in the problems of Socratism and Platonism, and the scholarly depth of his knowledge of certain dialogues such as the *Phaedo* (on which he gave numerous lectures in that most drastically truncated of academic careers), there is no evidence of any profound engagement with *Phaedrus*. Indeed, had Nietzsche Plato's text in mind, then it is unlikely that this abyssal meditation on the dangers of writing, of his own writing, and the writing that is *Ecce Homo* would have taken the form it did. Uncannily, the text is poised at exactly the moment of authorial abandonment, of the unleashing of the whole *oeuvre* upon mankind whose history it promises to split into two. Before this unleashing, this great world publicity – his works have not been read, and will not be read for some considerable time to come, he insists – it is necessary to sign the text, to mark its advance with the disclosure of the author of the philosophy of the future. 'Seeing that I must shortly approach mankind with the heaviest demand that has ever been made on it, it seems to me indispensable to say *who I am*' (EH, 3). The title-page aside, the text proper thus begins with a contract that affirms the signature as the *sine qua non* of the transvaluation of all values and an autobiographical or at least self-disclosive pact as absolutely incumbent upon the author. Thus commences perhaps the most unique of signatory contracts in the history of thought: one altogether more intriguing and mysterious that the pseudonymous practices of Kierkegaard, or indeed the wilful or historical contingent absence of a signature that we designate as 'anonymity' or the collection of diverse authors – separated by considerable stretches of time – that have been redacted under names such as 'Isaiah' or 'Homer'.

In the unavoidable paradox of exemplarity, Nietzsche's unique status, his absolutely singular signature, make him the archetypal figure of the ethics of writing as developed in the *Phaedrus*. Many of the other authors of mixed discourses, or discursivities as Foucault called these hybrid systems, from Plato to Marx and Freud, were obsessive about legacy. But whereas Plato oversaw the founding of the Academy, as would his great successor with the Lyceum, as prophets such as Isaiah of Jerusalem gathered together followers (*limmûdîm*) to preserve the truth of his teachings, as Marx sought to make the First and Second International executors of his textual estate, and Freud, through his daughter, sought to shape his legacy through the Institute of Psychoanalysis, Nietzsche wrote in unparalleled isolation, an isolation so intense that it drove him to play out the scene of succession in *Thus Spoke Zarathustra*, and to declare in *Ecce Homo*: 'I do not *want* believers, I think that I am too malicious to believe in myself, I never speak to masses . . .' (EH, 96). Nietzsche too had found – as no doubt did Plato at a certain stage in the composition of the dialogues – that the work amassing under his name did not fall within extant disciplinary parameters: as with Marx and Freud, a new way of looking at the world had come into being primarily through a massive imaginative effort. With the novelty of this way of thinking came its juvescent vulnerability; lacking the intrinsic resources to defend itself, with the passing of the author passed the only guarantee of correct interpretation. A physicist, mathematician or natural scientist may indeed die intestate leaving behind theorems, data or evidence which the respective scientific communities will over time accommodate quite properly into the discipline and its history. With works such as Platonic dialogue, or the array of meditative genres adopted by Nietzsche, in which *muthos* and *logos*, poetry and philosophical analysis coexist in discourses which lend themselves to realisations in the world of politics, wars and revolutions, the obligation to the future is potentially overwhelming. One need only study Darwin's 'Prefaces' from this point of view to place such authors in the position of great tragic protagonists, or the *Utopia* of Sir Thomas More to realise that destinational anxieties resulted in an extraordinarily careful construction of hypothetical frames around the 'constructive' phase of the work.

The choice of Nietzsche is in part governed by convenience, by our greater knowledge of the *res gestae* of his work, of the biographical and medical surrounds, and the fact that his reception history is still so very close to our most deeply felt concerns. It is also driven by a desire to demonstrate the enduring relevance of Socrates' words at *Phaedrus*, 275e, as also by the fact that Nietzsche did not leave behind a system, a model of social organisation, but writings. For all its ostensible drive towards self-revelation, *Ecce Homo* takes writing, writing the future, the past of its writing, Nietzsche's own *oeuvre*, writing on the plane of history, the after-life of the written sign, as its themes in a manner which no work before or since has dared or dreamed to do. The first philosopher actually to make a philosopheme of writing since that moment in the *Phaedrus* which went by and large unnoticed until the middle of the century that succeeded him, Nietzsche tells us contrarily that he is one thing, his writings another, whilst also that he will only be born when his work has been read. Of writing itself, its stirrings, or coming-into-life in his own psyche, he had written (less that three years earlier), in a moment of exquisite reflection on what came to be known in the twentieth century as the Saussurian distinctions between signifier, signified and mental concept; in Popper's three worlds schema as the movement from subjective impression to inscription to effect in the world of concrete events. What Nietzsche here is trying – without the terms – to describe would also become *archē*-writing or the *archē*-trace:

> there is in general good reason to suppose that in several respects the gods could all benefit from instruction by us human beings. We human beings are – more humane . . . Alas, and yet what *are* you, my written and painted thoughts! It is not long ago that you were still so many-coloured, young and malicious, so full of thorns and hidden spices you made me sneeze and laugh – and now? You have already taken off your novelty and some of you, I fear, are on the point of becoming truths: they already look so immortal, so pathetically righteous, so boring! And has it ever been otherwise? For what things do we write and paint, we mandarins with Chinese brushes, we immortalizers of things which *let* themselves be written, what alone are we capable of painting? Alas, only that which is about to wither and is beginning to lose its fragrance! Alas, only storms departing exhausted and feelings grown old and yellow! Alas, only birds strayed and grown weary in flight who now let themselves be caught in the hand – in *our* hand! We immortalize that which cannot live and fly much longer, weary and mellow things alone! And it is only your *afternoon*, my written and painted thoughts, for which alone I have the colours, many colours perhaps, many many-coloured tendernesses and fifty yellows and browns and greens and reds: – but no one will divine from these how you looked in your morning, you sudden sparks and wonders of my solitude, you my old beloved – *wicked* thoughts! (BGE, 201–2)

In the succeeding chapter we might allow these words to hover over many of the pronouncements of *Ecce Homo* – 'I am one thing, my writings are another' (EH, 39) – as but the most striking and textually contradictory of the 'signatory' and 'autobiographical' claims of this last work that cannot ever permit itself to be 'the last word'. In addressing 'the case of Nietzsche' we will continue, less directly but we hope with no less resonance, to explore further the ever-expanding rather than diminishing relevance of the *Phaedrus* as modernity advances into postmodernity. In the absence of any discernible influence, the work of *Ecce Homo* writes the thematic of writing into its very performance, and continues to advance the anxieties spoken through Socrates about legacy and posthumous destination into the twenty-first century. To this extent, just as *Phaedrus* reads and decisively critiques the work of Havelock, so, even more uncannily, will it postdate Nietzsche's *oeuvre* as the dialogue's explicit anxieties about the uncertain legacy of the written word reassess *Ecce Homo* from the vantage of an intensely ethicised, postmodern hermeneutic of reception.

4

The Textual Estate: Nietzsche and Authorial Responsibility

one will guess why I bring out this book beforehand; it is
intended to prevent people making mischief with me [*dass
man Unfug mit mir treibt*].

(Ecce Homo, 96)

mischief, thou art afoot
Take thou what course thou wilt!

(Julius Caesar III.ii)

Ecce Homo is the strange summation of the strangest *oeuvre* in modernity. Not looking back from any vantage of supposed or assumed maturity, it inscribes itself within an unfolding project. The text heralds the work, not only that of the promised revaluation but the corpus, the textual phenomenon that is 'Nietzsche' seen *sub specie futuris*. That the work has not been *read* is due, Nietzsche contends, to 'the disparity between the greatness of [his] task and the *smallness* of [his] contemporaries' (EH, 3). Nor indeed could those texts have been read if one sees writing as *potentia* to be realised on the plane of history. History itself awaits 'Nietzsche'. For all its Christian connotations, Nietzsche's posthumous birth is a trope for an overwhelming concern with legacy. Perhaps impelled by a sense that his creative life was drawing to a close, or by the painful realisation that he was unequal to the grandiloquent project of 'the revaluation of all values', Nietzsche purports to teach us how to read his work.[1]

The supposed revaluation is presented as self-revelation: 'it seems indispensable to me to say *who I am*' (EH, 3); 'the self-overcoming of morality through truthfulness; the self-overcoming of the moralist, into his opposite – *into me*' (EH, 98). Yet the self revealed is unsure who or what it is,

---

[1] Nietzsche often claims that the truth or significance of a text necessarily eludes its author, a claim in which his own texts will necessarily be implicated. See, for example, BGE, 18–20, 201–2.

quite apart from what it is to become. In the insistent refrain '[h]ave I been understood?', the emphasis might fall equally upon the first-person pronoun since the failure to construct a coherent philosophy is one with the failure to gather up the self.

'I am one thing, my writings are another' (EH, 39), he says. Often lazily taken as a conundrum in the author–text relationship, this statement in fact precisely states the condition of authorship in its separation of subject and sign that calls for such vigilance in the *Phaedrus*. The idea of the 'posthumous birth', carried over from *The Antichrist*, expresses a wish to defy the laws of time and writing so that 'Nietzsche' will preside over the interpretation of texts whose truth eluded him at the time of writing, the time of living. Hence Nietzsche is fully alert to tense in announcing not 'why I *will be*' but 'why I *am* a Destiny', for a Destiny must precede its realisation, its moment of self-reflexive *anagnorisis*. The 'I am' is deferred to that futurity in which destiny will realise itself *qua* destiny. The Nietzschean 'I' is to become what it is at the hour of understanding when the mendaciousness of millennia has come to see itself as such in the full assimilation of his nihilistic teaching. Embodied in a monstrous trope, not only the Coriolanean name remains but also a 'Nietzsche' (re)incarnate.

Nietzsche dreamt of being his own successor (*'yo me sucedo a mi mismo'*, in the words of Lope de Vega: TI, 75) but the idea that he will be born posthumously in his writings is a baroque conceit, a reversal of the commonplace textual estate in which only the proper name will inherit from the flesh. He will not exercise a posthumous paternity; his texts will always need their father to come to their rescue. One senses in *Ecce Homo* the desperation of an author – virtually unread, as he was – realising what danger and ungovernable potency he is unleashing: 'one will guess why I bring out this book *beforehand*: it is intended to prevent people from making mischief with me [*dass man Unfug mit mir treibt*],' he writes (EH, 96). Of course it did no such thing, nor could it given that *Ecce Homo* is more a prospect than retrospect, an exercise in self-promotion rather than a clarification or critique (as had been the impressive 'Attempt at a Self-Criticism' of 1886). Moreover, all bombast aside, *Ecce Homo* lacks confidence in itself and the corpus it represents. The revaluation, upon which he staked his overweening claim to be the thinker who had split history in two, amounted to no more than a single atheistic tract. Though the critical aspect of his thought (*disputatio*) was without precedent in its bravery, its unmasking of formerly sacred values, the constructive phase (*speculatio*) could seem only trivial when set against the metaphysical tradition it sought to supplant. The advent of the *Übermensch* and a Zarathustran tragic age were at best speculations. The eternal return remained philosophically unintelligible unless taken as a dramatised moral imperative and Nietzsche's attempts to find scientific groundings for this concept were in vain.[2] Of the constructive doctrines, only will-to-power, as Heidegger was first to demonstrate, survives prosaic translation to constitute a significant entry in the philosophical encyclopedia. Yet Nietzsche had not devoted more than half-a-dozen continuous pages to its elaboration.[3]

Moreover, his corpus had evolved no intrinsic criteria whereby a 'correct' reading of his work could be distinguished from an 'incorrect', a 'positive' from a 'negative' interpretation. Nietzsche constantly raised the issue of demarcating suitable from unsuitable readers, but *worried* rather than addressed the issue in a manner confirmatory of his discourse's inability to legislate towards its reception.[4] He writes so as not to be understood by the unworthy (WS, 327–8), distinguishes between those who do not know and live in simple faith in their environment as though it were an *aeterna vertitas* and an 'elect of knowledge' who will read with judgement, finesse, revisionary acuity. *The Gay Science* will joyously affirm this insecure and unsystematic discrimination:

> One does not only wish to be understood when one writes; one wishes just as surely *not* to be understood. It is not by any means necessarily an objection to a book when anyone finds it impossible to understand: perhaps that was part of the author's intention – he did not want to be understood by just 'anybody'. All the nobler spirits and tastes select their audience when they wish to communicate; and choosing that, one at the same time erects barriers against 'the others.' (GS, 343)

Against which *Ecce Homo*'s question 'Have I been understood?' and injunction to '*not, above all, confound me with what I am not!*' (EH, 3) seem at best

---

[2] 'So act (or so be) so that you would be willing to act exactly the same way (or be exactly the same thing) an infinite number of times over. Heeding this, men might stop feeling *ressentiment*. In existentialist terms, it is a plea for authenticity.' Arthur C. Danto, *Nietzsche as Philosopher* (New York: Columbia University Press, 1965), p. 212. On Nietzsche's attempts to find scientific support for eternal return see pp. 201–13.

[3] The *Nachlass* aside, *Beyond Good and Evil* (sections 9, 22, 23, 36) is the only text in which will-to-power is consistently discussed. See Maudemaire Clark, *Nietzsche on Truth and Philosophy* (Cambridge: Cambridge University Press, 1990), pp. 212–18 for an account of the 'published argument for the will to power'.

[4] A preoccupation of *Human, All-Too-Human* and *Thus Spoke Zarathustra*, textual legacy is arguably *the* theme of *Ecce Homo*. *Beyond Good and Evil*'s promotion of the mysterious 'philosophers of the future' (who will carry forward the Nietzschean inheritance) again reflects this concern with readership and legacy.

ironic, at worst enounced in bad faith. Yet, *Ecce Homo* again shows an eerie prescience. Nietzsche would be intestate, leaving behind neither a coherent body of concepts, a settled corpus, a system of intentions nor instructions as to his work's interpretation. Unable to categorise his flood of often contradictory insights, his legacy raised the question as to whether he, 'Nietzsche', was *sui generis* in the history of discourse, possessing only what Derrida calls 'the unity of his uniqueness, his singularity'.[5] Not for him, in any case, an Academy, a Lyceum, a First International or Institute of Psychoanalysis. A handful of competent readers aside, he found his executrix in the unscrupulous figure of his sister. It became the task of the twentieth century to find the homeland of his thought, to debate around the tacit question as to whether 'Nietzsche' was not indeed his own genre.[6]

I: COUNTER-PHILOSOPHY

[I]f Nietzsche does not belong to philosophy, it is perhaps because he was the first to conceive of another kind of discourse as counter-philosophy. This discourse is above all nomadic; its statements can be conceived as the products of a mobile war machine and not the utterances of a rational, administrative machinery, whose philosophers would be bureaucrats of pure reason.

(Giles Deleuze, 'Nomad Thought')[7]

Deleuze sought to maintain Nietzsche's thought in its nomadism, its danger, but his position is not as 'new' as he and others would have us believe. His is the 'Nietzsche' of a Lawrence, D'Annunzio, Apollinaire or the young Musil, the vitalist philosopher of extremes whose super-abundant flow of insight and intuition cannot be reduced to disciplinary parameters; an infinitely appropriable Nietzsche, a thinker and corpus without limits. What 'newness' Deleuze's 'nomadism' possesses is garnered from the attempts to find a habitation for Nietzsche's thought in the post-war era.

---

[5] Jacques Derrida, 'Interpreting Signatures (Nietzsche/Heidegger): Two Questions', trans. Diane Michelfelder and Richard E. Palmer, in Peter R. Sedgwick, ed., *Nietzsche: A Critical Reader* (Oxford: Blackwell, 1995), pp. 53–68; p. 54.

[6] That Nietzsche is his own 'genre' is implicit in much counter-philosophical criticism that celebrates the singularity of his *oeuvre*. Foucault, for example, writes: 'I do not believe there is a single Nietzscheanism. There are no grounds for believing that there is a true Nietzscheanism, or that ours is any truer than others.' Michel Foucault, 'Critical Theory/Intellectual History', in Lawrence D. Kritzman, ed., *Michel Foucault: Politics, Philosophy, Culture. Interviews and Other Writings 1977–1984* (New York: Routledge, 1988), pp. 17–46: p. 45.

[7] Giles Deleuze, 'Nomad Thought', in David B. Allison, ed., *The New Nietzsche: Contemporary Styles of Interpretation* (Cambridge, MA and London: MIT Press, 1985), pp. 142–9: p. 149. On Nietzsche's influence on twentieth-century French thought, see Alan D. Schrift, *Nietzsche's French Legacy: A Genealogy of Poststructuralism* (New York and London: Routledge, 1995).

Kaufmann sought to unify Nietzsche's thought by affirming its supposed commitment to empirical truths, whilst Heidegger reconfigured Nietzsche as a philosopher with a mission to promulgate a single, controlling idea, that of will-to-power:

> for a long time it has been declaimed from chairs of philosophy in Germany that Nietzsche is not a rigorous thinker but a 'poet-philosopher'. Nietzsche does not belong among the philosophers, who think only about abstract, shadowy affairs, far removed from life . . . The error will be recognized only when a confrontation with him is at the same time conjoined to a confrontation in the realm of the grounding question of philosophy.[8]

What emerges, however, is a sanitised, even castrated Nietzsche, who is ultimately subsumed within Heidegger's own grounding question, that of the 'essence of Being'. Richard Schacht simply excises 'Nietzsche's frequent rhetorical excesses' as blemishes and mars on the surface of his thought and filters 'them out as so much unfortunate static' in order to 'get down to matters of philosophical moment'.[9] Ethically sensitive though such a position may be, it possesses all the textual violence of a radical abridgement. Danto, for his part, seeks to pare down Nietzsche's thought to a series of stark, even skeletal philosophical positions which can be taken on their own terms, a conceptual reduction that is however virtually overwhelmed by a writer who is 'distrustful and almost officially defiant of philosophic rigour . . . the thinker *de choix* of men who find academic and professional philosophy too circumspect or meticulous for their bold and bohemian tastes'.[10] Absent of necessity from such recuperations is the 'Nietzsche' who turned philosophy into performance, in a hybrid, dangerous art of persuasion.

Between the two readings lies an interesting contrast: one seeking to rehabilitate Nietzsche for philosophy, another (then largely comprising young French philosophers) seeing in Nietzsche a means to rejuvenate philosophy. Given a choice between taking all the 'danger' out of Nietzsche's thought or celebrating that 'danger' in a romantic and pre-critical fashion, between the polarities of a 'responsible' neutralisation and 'irresponsible' mobilisation of the fragmentary and hazardous, we are not obliged to choose. One reading ignores excess; the other, in its pragmatic concern as to what to *do* with Nietzsche, disrespects an ethics of intention. Both centre on the issue of what is 'properly' philosophical in

---

[8] Martin Heidegger, *Nietzsche: Volume I: The Will to Power as Art*, trans. David Farrell Krell (London and Henley: Routledge & Kegan Paul, 1981), p. 5.
[9] Richard Schacht, *Nietzsche* (Boston, MA: Routledge & Kegan Paul, 1983), xv.
[10] Arthur C. Danto, *Nietzsche as Philosopher* (New York: Columbia University Press, 1965), p. 13.

the formulation of an ethics of reading: this is no less the case with Foucault's observation that '[i]n relation to academic philosophical discourse . . . Nietzsche represents the outer frontier' than in Heidegger's presentation of Nietzsche as the last metaphysician.[11] Neither 'construction' examines Nietzsche in terms of an ethics of writing or considers that textual mischief is practised as much by the producer as by consumers of his text. To insist that we 'settle' Nietzsche as a philosopher or that we refuse to domesticate his 'thought' are contrary ways of failing to address the question of his propriety in constructing a canon that uses and abuses the philosophical frames of its choice. Nietzsche as mobile 'war machine' is no less insulated from ethical interrogation than Nietzsche as pure philosopher of perspectivism, empirical truth or will-to-power.

Certainly, the new Nietzscheans are right to insist that Nietzsche's texts are signed to more than one concept, but we cannot take his plurality, his styles, his masks and nomadism to imply an unselving 'innocence of becoming'. Nothing, it is true, seems more foreign to this writer than the stoic injunction *idemque inter diversa*, yet it is only against the backdrop of the name, of the presumption of a unitary selfhood, that the dissolution of the self can be enacted. Nietzsche's styles are remarkable only in so far as they are *Nietzsche's* styles and not those of James Joyce or Louis Ferdinand Céline. Even were the self a fictional construct, an ethical imperative would remain. 'I can say this because it is not I that speaks' may convince a theorist of language, but can only be fatuous under an ethical consideration. Even though the self may never arrive on time, never be fully present to itself or put a halt to discourse, an ethics of writing obliges the writer to act as though there is a self.

Nietzsche lives and thinks within this oscillation. At times he writes with faith in continuous selfhood; at others, he dismisses his existence as mere prejudice or melds his identity with proxies such as Zarathustra or Dionysus. Certainly, '[n]o one is accountable for existing at all, or for being constituted as he is, or for living in the circumstances and surroundings in which he lives' (TI, 54). But this does not render the subject unaccountable for what he or she writes. 'To trace something unknown back to something known' is doubtless 'alleviating, soothing, gratifying and gives moreover a feeling of power' (TI, 51), but to collapse the desire for attribution and cause into psychological assuagement is to declare oneself oblivious to the ethical sphere. Nietzsche's works may not

---

[11] Michel Foucault, 'The Functions of Literature', in Kritzman, ed., *Michel Foucault*, pp. 307–13: p. 312.

comprise a textual system, but the texts therein bear his name and do so in the manner of a contract, a structure of accountability. However strange the corpus might be, the act of signature remains both freely chosen and contractual in taking the form of a commitment to certain generic expectation. To write is still today to enter into a contract. Mystical discourses announce themselves as such: the product of a vision, of a visitation, the reader is free to take the discourse as revealed theology, fantasy or even a species of mental illness. But Nietzsche appeals to our reason, our truthfulness, in recognising illusions as illusions, debased coinage as debased. At the same time, he allows himself the Whitmanesque luxury ('I contradict myself? Very well I contradict myself') of inconsistency and celebrates the Dionysian nature of writing as excess and radical dispossession. To assess the ethical composition of this signature that simultaneously erases itself requires us to ask what it means to write 'counter-philosophy' from behind the mask of philosophy.

II: MIXED GENRES

The mixed genres – The mixed genres in art bear witness to the mistrust their originators felt towards their own powers; they sought assistants, advocates, hiding-places – for example, the poet who calls on philosophy for aid, the composer who calls on the drama, the thinker who calls on rhetoric. (AOM, 245)

Vincent Descombes charges the 'new Nietzscheans' with failing to distinguish between sound and unsound arguments.[12] Cavalier in political and moral terms, their attempts to 'radicalise' Nietzsche are prosecuted at the cost of confusing philosophy and rhetoric, *logos* and *pathos* in argument. In what is his own defence of 'Nietzsche as philosopher', Descombes repeats the contemporary insistence on an ethics of reading without acknowledging the extent to which the failings of the French Nietzscheans receive ample authorisation in the Nietzschean text. If the French Nietzscheans are indeed guilty of elevating the persuasive over the logical force of argument, then they do no more than reflect the influence of a philosopher who counted no suasive device alien to the promulgation of his teaching.

Autobiography, poetry, dithyramb, satyr play, music, mock-biblical, hyperbole, invective, intimacies, classical or gothic figures, homily, parable, lyrical tenderness, parody, sarcasm, buffoonery, prophesy, and so on, are used here to cajole, there to seduce the reader into accepting the truth of

---

[12] Vincent Descombes, 'La moment français de Nietzsche', in Alan Boyer et al., *Pourquoi nous ne sommes pas nietzscheans* (Paris: Éditions Grasset et Fasquelle, 1991), pp. 99–128.

his discourse. The youthful idealist who with Wagner dreamt of a total art-form went on to reject his mentor but also to construct an *oeuvre* which consistently subordinated the epistemological to the aesthetic in seeking the most arresting form of expression for its ideas. Metaphor inevitably invades the text of philosophy, but it is too easy merely to instantiate Nietzsche in this eventuality. A matter of degree can become so pronounced as to provoke a question of kind. There is a world of difference between Kant's recourse to mechanical metaphors and the overwhelming effect of artistic devices in Nietzsche. What, for example, would be left of the formulation of eternal return without the Gothic setting of its dwarf, gateway into past and future, its spider and moonlight? Would it not be like a face, never handsome, which has lost the first flush of youth; or that poem without the carriage of rhythm which was for Nietzsche a cripple in the realm of thought?[13]

Nietzsche declares that 'Plato mixes together all forms of style; he is therewith in the matter of style a *first décadent*' (TI, 106).[14] Nietzsche himself would not be long in adverting to his possession of 'altogether the most manifold art of style any man has ever had at his disposal' (EH, 44) and must have been aware that his own writing far exceeded that of Plato in its stylistic trespasses. Yet the comparison is apt. Plato certainly used myth against mythical thinking, poetry against a poetic worldview. Moreover, his discourse obsessed about its legacy, distinguished its worthy recipients (*philosophy*) from those tourists in the realm of thought that he calls *philodoxoi*, and Nietzsche deplores as 'plundering troops', those who 'take away a few things they can use, dirty and confound the remainder, and revile the whole' (AOM, 245).

Indeed, the founder of logocentrism and the so-called 'counter-philosopher' implicate themselves in the problems of any mixed discourse (and here we might add, at the very least, the names of Hegel, Marx and Freud). By opening their enterprises to other genres, they allowed for the most expansive discursive economy, but thereby increased the hazards of misreception. Both Plato and Nietzsche hint at a secret teaching, the very notion of which sets up a paradox in terms of an ethics of reception for just as encryption keeps barbarians at the gates, its requisite lack of clarity

---

[13] Nietzsche's view of poetry sometimes echoes that of Plato (*Republic*, 601c): 'The poet conducts his thoughts along festively, in the carriage of rhythm: usually because they are incapable of walking on foot' (HH, 93).

[14] This late judgement negatively echoes Nietzsche's observation in *The Birth of Tragedy* that 'the Platonic dialogue which, a mixture of all extant styles and forms, hovers midway between narrative, lyric, and drama, prose and poetry' is a very distant predecessor of the 'philosophical novel' (BT, 90).

facilitates barbarously incompetent readings. Here, an overt concern with legacy betrays a cognitive deficiency within the discourse itself. A philosopher who wrote within strictly disciplinary limits would have no need to guard against unsuitable readers. One cannot imagine catastrophic readings of 'Quine' or 'Strawson' precisely because such philosophers respect genre and do their very best to stay at the level of the apodeictic, the thetic, the hypothetical or provisional. On an intentional and disciplinary level, rigorous philosophers pre-programme discourse in such a way that misreception can only arise as a failure to comprehend the system, to think within its logic as within an extended mathematical demonstration.

Catastrophic philosophy arises only when philosophy has somehow overreached itself, stepped beyond the gates or breached the walls of its own vigilance. Yet, while this propensity for danger is strenuously guarded against in Plato, it is wantonly celebrated by Nietzsche. One needs no grounding in philosophy to follow either Plato or Nietzsche, but serious engagement is required by dialectic. Rung by rung, the *ephebe* is led up to the Ideas; attempts at shortcuts issue in a Plato unread rather than misread. Nietzsche, on the other hand, is entirely hospitable to the 'plundering troops' he professes to revile. As his signature mode, the aphorism is the iterable mode *par excellence* and one that as such would have earned Plato's most virulent disapproval. Derived from the Greek *horus*, denoting a boundary or activity which encloses, limits, defines, the aphorism is a virtual *enantioseme*: entirely conducive to uncouth repetition, independent of any broader context of meaning, incapable of simply replicating an intention, it sets no limits upon its interpretability.[15] Perversely enough, it belongs with the a priori (and, indeed, the haiku) as a form of self-sufficient statement. Yet whilst the haiku is an aesthetic delectation, and the *a priori* as well-defended as it is redundant, the aphorism is unprotected when offered up to the unsuitable reader. What Plato's Socrates said of the written word can only be *a fortiori* the case with the aphorism.

The aphoristic impulse is itself a formal analogue of a general tendency in Nietzsche to refuse the challenge of imposing interpretative constraints upon his discourse. We are presented with a corpus that admits of incalculable and contradictory readings. As with a grand, tempestuous poetic corpus (comparison with Shakespeare is not hyperbolic), each new act of

---

[15] Of course, any statement can lend itself to aphoristic appropriation: 'the starry heavens above and the moral law within' belonged to a structure of argument in a way that many of Nietzsche's aphorisms did not. The aphorism is therefore that mode that overtly frames itself according to an iterability to which all written and memorised texts are subject.

reading seems to produce a distinctive reconfiguration not possible with the works of an Aristotle, Descartes, Russell or even Kierkegaard. In the history of philosophy, perhaps only Plato has produced a corpus of such 'infinite variety', but the dialogic movement provides interpretative guidance for the reader. With the exception of *The Genealogy of Morals*, Nietzsche's post-*Zarathustran* texts refuse to incorporate intention at the level of discursive structure. Nehamas describes *Beyond Good and Evil* as a work of 'dazzling obscurity' which does not permit us to understand 'its structure, its narrative line',[16] and most of Nietzsche's other works leave the reader to become, if not the producer, then the *bricoleur* or configurater of their aims, arguments, coherences and harmonies. Many will, of course, argue that this is a positive step in terms of the ethics of discourse because it grants freedom to the reader. Nietzsche himself did not elevate the reader to an ideal figure who cannot make ethically grievous errors of an unconscious or voluntary order. Nonetheless, through impatience or electively patrician disdain, he left the *reconfiguration* of his work to those who came afterwards.

Careful attention to *dispositio* is not a sufficient condition of philosophical discourses: many thoroughly intelligible arguments proceed without transitional conclusions, signposts between phases of argument, statements of what remains to be achieved, adjudicated and considered. *The World as Will and Representation*, for example, proceeds as an argument without formally highlighting its moves and premises; the *Meditations* of Descartes unfold with a fluency that need not bludgeon home their deep structure. But Nietzsche strives to perform the anti-conceptuality he promotes in a supra-mimesis, a performance of the ungraspable, unstable flow of becoming. As Michael Harr says:

> While the dominant words of Nietzsche's discourse . . . are meant to subvert, fracture, and dismiss concepts, his overall effort is one aiming to set the entire logical, semantic, and grammatical apparatus (in which the philosophical tradition had naively taken up its abode) to moving in a direction contrary to its constant tendency: namely, toward the assignment of proper nouns, the reduction to identity, and the passage to the universal . . . (Nietzsche's discourse) wills to rock, to topple, to dissociate, to disperse all conformity. With its various games of irony, parody, interrogation, innuendo – but especially with its ruptures, shifts, displacements and the like . . . Nietzsche's style

---

[16] Alexander Nehamas, *Nietzsche: Life as Literature* (Cambridge, MA: Havard University Press, 1985), p. 6.

aims finally at destroying, or at least checkmating, all logical and, especially, dialectical 'seriousness', the goal of which is always to establish
identities or to reveal the one absolute Identity.[17]
Nietzsche thus becomes a Heraclitean poet of flux, a Dionysus of the
written word. But what might it mean to write philosophy beyond philosophy? Why articulate anti-conceptuality in the first place? Why present
as philosophy this refusal of all conceptuality? Why use language – whose
genius is to discover the one amongst the many, to impose a clarity,
however illusory, upon the river of becoming – to undo conceptual language? Why does this end of philosophy need a philosophy of its own,
and to whom is it addressed?

The argument is not consolidated by its performative supplement. The
illusory nature of the concept cannot be argued without invoking
counter-concepts: one might as well write, in the manner of the metaphysicians of Tlön, without proper nouns, without presupposing identity.
Construed as such, Nietzsche's project is doomed from the outset to write
itself into the *aporia* between attempting 'an exit and a deconstruction
without changing terrain . . . by using against the edifice the instruments
or stones available in the house, that is, equally, in language' and changing
'terrain, in a discontinuous and irruptive fashion . . . by affirming an
absolute break and difference'.[18] This latter way madness or at least an utter
failure of communication lies; according to the former, one is always recu-
perable for the tradition as a critical philosopher. 'Nietzsche's styles' thus
beg the question of his belonging to philosophy: either he steps outside in
a language beyond identity (an as yet unwritten poetry) or he resigns
himself to the role of sceptic rather than liberator, iconoclast or 'dynamite'.

III: THE WILL-TO-POWER AS WORK OF ART
no one [but I] has ever had more of the new, the unheard-of,
the really new-created in artistic means to squander. (EH, 44)

The aesthetic becomes Nietzsche's desperate endgame – just as, in *The
Birth of Tragedy*, it was his opening gambit. By sheer artistry, the philosophy of the future can write itself beyond metaphysics and into the coming
(Nietzschean) epoch. Once the critical labours are completed, creativity
must fill the void opened by a vanquished conceptuality. Nietzsche's view
of the philosopher's role in this constructive phase (which once again

---

[17] Michael Harr, 'Nietzsche and Metaphysical Language', in Allison, ed., *The New Nietzsche*, pp. 5–36:
pp. 6–7.
[18] Jacques Derrida, *Margins of Philosophy*, trans. Alan Bass (Brighton: Harvester Press, 1982), p. 135.

reveals its paucity beside all that it would supplant) becomes apparent when he envisages the heirs of his discourse. Projecting *from* the self as much as *into* the future, Nietzsche declares that his philosophers of the future will be 'legislators of new values'. As distinct from Plato's philosopher-king as are Zarathustra's figs from the Socratic 'seeds of wisdom', the new philosopher 'lives "unphilosophically" and "unwisely", above all *imprudently*, and bears the burden and duty of a hundred attempts and temptations of life – he risks *himself* constantly, he plays *the* dangerous game' (BGE, 113). Analysis, debate, questioning, duties such public responsibility, accountability, etc., have no place beside the qualities of heroism, courage, creative defiance of epistemological concerns that Nietzsche requires of his phantasmal legatees. For the philosophers of the future,' "knowing" is *creating* . . . creating is a law-giving . . . will to truth is – *will-to-power*' (BGE, 123). Further still, they will be men 'of the most comprehensive responsibility' who have 'the conscience for the collective evolution of mankind' (BGE, 67–8). This nomothetic depiction is perfectly suspended between the chilling and the bathetic. The trope is stale by the time it gets into Nietzsche's hands. Thomas Carlyle had fancied the poet was the type of a legislator, and before him Percy Bysshe Shelley had declared: 'They measure the circumference and sound the depths of human nature with a comprehensive and all-penetrating spirit . . . Poets are the hierophants of an unapprehended inspiration, the mirrors of the gigantic shadows which futurity casts upon the present . . .'[19]

Trusting not to critical faculties but to imagination's transformative powers, the philosophers of the future are poets in all but verse. Shelley had similarly expanded the demesne of the poetic or aesthetic to encompass untimely men, men of genius, regardless of whether they be artists, politicians or scientists. But the legislation of the poets is unacknowledged and one cannot know if Shelley wished his poets to become actual legislators, or if he was content to point out their subtle, elevating, invisible influence on the souls of individual readers. Nietzsche, though, wishes to write his vision on the plane of history; masquerading as philosophers, his emissaries, his hallucinatory successors will write up the new tablets of the law. As creators of values, as self-overcomers, as *soi-disant*, they are related to the overmen. Their ability to stamp upon the process of becoming the character of being remains a Dionysian creativity, a romantic self-fashioning rather than an epistemological foundation for agency

---

[19] Percy Bysshe Shelley, *Shelley's Poetry and Prose*, ed. Donald Reiman and Sharon B. Powers (New York and London: Norton, 1977), p. 508.

and selfhood: the philosopher 'would even determine value and rank according to how much and how many things one could endure and take upon oneself' (BGE, 124). This proposed 'philosophical' manner of ordering experience is akin to the artistic rather than Kantian imagination, a poetic or esemplastic function whereby the self is aesthetically unified. The 'philosophers of the future' salvage the place left vacant by 'the primordial artist of the world' in Nietzsche's first work.[20] It is not only the Nietzsche of *The Birth of Tragedy* who romantically decides the quarrel between poetry and philosophy in favour of the former.

Indeed, it is tempting to look backwards rather than forwards, to see not the future of a philosophy beyond good and evil, *archē* and *telos* in the Nietzschean text, but rather a crisis statement in the romantic subordination of the cognitive and ethical to the aesthetic. We can read that most famous passage in *The Gay Science* in this context:

> At long last the horizon appears free to us again, even if it should not be bright; at long last our ships may venture out . . . to face any danger; all the daring of the lover of knowledge is permitted again; the sea, *our* sea, lies open again; perhaps there has never yet been such an 'open sea'. (GS, 280)

The sea is open to those who would create values in the wake of religious belief and to those others who would explore the free play of signifier upon the collapse of meaning. But it is also the 'open sea' of genre, of a writing in which 'once again' (as in pre-Socratic Greece) there are no demarcations between what is poetic, philosophical and scientific. In the tradition of German Romanticism which shaped Nietzsche as much if not more than the world of classical Greece, philosophy had become answerable to imagination and creativity rather than analytic precision. Novalis and Schelling had called for poetry to rejuvenate philosophy, and Nietzsche had embraced this challenge from his first work onward. *Zarathustra* may have implicated itself in the performative contradiction of poetry repudiating poetry (Z, 149–52), but Nietzsche never ceased from extolling creativity or poetry in its radically expanded, Shelleyean provenance. Where the critical project ends in Nietzsche, there his work becomes the last great visionary statement of Romanticism. Collapsing boundaries between creation and knowledge, will and reason, he responded to the challenge to compose the grand mythological poem of modernity. But the ethical risks of this undertaking were exponentiated by the fact that he supposedly wrote

---

[20] An interesting argument for continuity between the late and early representations of 'Dionysus' in Nietzsche's work is made in Bruce Detwiler, *Nietzsche and the Politics of Aristocratic Radicalism* (Chicago: University of Chicago Press, 1990), pp. 162–8.

under the aegis of philosophy. As the twentieth century has taught us, it is altogether less dangerous when poetry philosophises than when philosophy takes up the lyre. In the freedom and loneliness of the post-patronage writer, Nietzsche 'danced with the pen', wrote 'unwisely' and 'imprudently', unravelled his discourse with the abandon of the abandoned, with the coeval loss and liberation of one who, under the approximate simultaneity of one and the same cover, declares himself a destiny who split the history of Europe in two but will also, absolutely irreconcilably, and wilfully remain 'non *legor*, non *legar*' (EH, 40). Hence the tangible fear of *Ecce Homo* as it embraces both the descent from neglect to oblivion at the same time as premoniting the catastrophic outcome of the *oeuvre*; the disappearance and calamitous apotheosis of the signature, the proper name, the textual estate of 'Friedrich Nietzsche'. Having played the dangerous game to its limits and without a stirring of public or academic interest, Nietzsche had little choice but to affirm himself as 'necessarily a man of fatality' (EH, 97) and to recast philosophy itself as danger. As Gödel shows in the hard case of pure mathematics, unintended outcomes are the hazard of any form of thought. But Nietzsche courted this risk. Like Blake's Isaiah, he 'cared not for consequences, but wrote'.[21]

Nietzsche looked to the future for his texts' historical supplementation. Mountingly hysterical, his later works have little of the calm he attributes to Bizet and everything of (imputed) Wagnerian *sirocco* (CW, 157). The judgement made as early in his career as the essay 'Schopenhauer as Educator', that 'every word behind which there does not stand such a challenge to action to have been written in vain' (SE, 184), prefigured Nietzsche's increasing militancy in his post-Zarathustran work. Zarathustra talks chillingly of writing in blood, and the Nietzsche of *The Antichrist* promises that '[w]herever there are walls' he will 'inscribe this eternal accusation against Christianity . . . in letters which make even the blind see' (AC, 186). We might also look to the Lutheran 'Decree Against Christianity' – intended as a flysheet in the text of *The Antichrist* – to see that his notion of himself as 'dynamite' was not entirely tropological.[22] His writings would indeed be 'dangerous tinder for sensitive and susceptible souls' (BT, 89) even if only offered up to the idle hours of a psychologist. But when we further consider that his discourse was written as 'a pledge across the centuries to an unknown posterity, a promise to be

---

[21] William Blake, *The Marriage of Heaven and Hell* in *William Blake's Writings: Volume I*, ed. G. E. Bentley Jr. (Oxford: Clarendon, 1978), p. 86.

[22] For a translation and discussion of 'The Decree Against Christianity', see Gary Shapiro, *Nietzschean Narratives* (Bloomington, IN: Indiana University Press, 1989), pp. 146–7.

fulfilled only by the posthumous birth of Nietzsche', then the ethical stakes of the gamble become ingravescent.[23] *Ecce Homo* only underwrites a point made earlier: 'The time for petty politics is past: the very next century will bring with it the struggle for mastery over the whole earth – the *compulsion* to grand politics' (BGE, 119). From this perspective, Derrida is correct to say that what 'Nietzsche willed in his name resembles . . . poisoned milk' and that it did not by accident get mixed up with 'the worst of our times' (EO, 7).

As Derrida explicates, 'the signature is not only a word, or a proper name at the end of a text, but the operation as a whole, the text as a whole, the whole of the active interpretation which has left a trace or a remainder' (EO, 52). There is, he says, 'nothing absolutely contingent about the fact that the only political regimen to have *effectively* brandished his name as a major and official banner was Nazi' (EO, 31). The Platonic register of Derrida's tones here will only surprise the reader who assumed that Derrida was ever in the first place arguing with or against the *Phaedrus*:

> I do not aim to 'clear' its 'author' and neutralize or defuse either what might be troublesome in it for demagogic pedagogy or 'leftist' politics, or what served as 'language' for the most sinister rallying cries of National Socialism. On the contrary, the greatest indecency is *de rigueur* in this place . . . One may wonder how and why what is so naively called a falsification was possible (one can't falsify just anything), how and why the 'same' words and the 'same' statements – if they are indeed the same – might several times be made to serve certain meanings, and certain contexts that are said to be different, even incompatible. (EO, 23–4)

Derrida stops short of talking of the attendance of the father of *logos*, and *logoi* needing their author to come to their rescue if unfairly treated or abused, but the Socratic caveat at *Phaedrus* 275e, that words can wander into different contexts and take on different meanings, could not have been far from his mind. If anything, *The Ear of the Other* is somewhat sterner than the *Phaedrus* in saying that these (Nietzschean) words carry a weight of responsibility even in seemingly the most abusive of cases. And he implies, still further, that there is something in the quality of the Nietzschean 'words', the Nietzschean 'statements', that open themselves, over and above the common run of discursive or authorial acts, to an

---

[23] Daniel C. Conway, *Nietzsche's Dangerous Game: Philosophy in the Twilight of the Idols* (Cambridge: Cambridge University Press, 1997), p. 226. This fine book identifies 'parastrategesis' as a generic term which embraces the range of esoteric (and generally inadequate) devices by which an author attempts to preprogramme posthumous reception.

iterability not only through a cultivated polysemy but also by the refusal of a programme. This ethical recursion, from use and abuse to text itself, is not only beyond erasure or absolution because of the most multifarious art of style, or indeed the dance with the pen. It is incorporated within the very structure of the signature itself: 'this testamentary structure doesn't befall a text as if by accident, but constructs it' (EO, 51).

Nietzsche signs in such a manner that his signature is unprecedented and, as such, opens the signatory question to clearer view than would the more conventional contract drawn up between author and readership. Indeed, Derrida goes so far as to assert, with an exorbitant logic which in terms of Nietzsche's self-proclamation is nonetheless logical, that the author of the *oeuvre* signs on the back of the eternal return. In order to appraise the singularity of this signature, we will need to place it beside less exorbitant signatory modes, those which, at the very least, do not imply that their author will come into recognisable being over a century after the text's composition, or con-sign themselves to eternal return. In total contrast, the signature of the scientist will only have a proprietory or historical and classificatory value: it may serve to patent a discovery for financial reward or to identify a theorem or theory within the history of the discipline. This is also the status to which pseudo-scientific discourses aspire in a deceptively self-effacing signature – that *Geist* rather than Hegel signs the *Phenomenology*, or the inevitable unfolding of the dialectic signs the Marxist *oeuvre* is integral to the presumption of impersonal truth as expressed – authorlessly – in these works. Furthermore, the signatures of authors who, like Plato, Aristotle, Marx and Freud, are actively in search of the counter-signatures of guardians, followers (tried and trusted during the author's lifetime) or admitted members of authorised interpretative institutions such as the Academy, Lyceum, First International and Institute of Psychoanalysis contrast most revealingly with the singularity of the Nietzschean paraph. In an incomparable solitude, Nietzsche declares that he spent the best part of two decades casting a line only to find there were no fish in the waters. His sole, defended consolation? 'I do not *want* 'believers', I think I am too malicious to believe in myself, I never speak to masses . . .' (EH, 96).

In the following section, we will be concerned with the signature as a *meditatio generis futuri* and as a contract drawn up with readers present, readers future and readers who will read the work of a dead or otherwise unresponsive author (the Nietzsche of the last decade of his life falling into this category). We will then turn to the generic problematics of the signatory contact an author draws up with his near-contemporaneous audience and the textual estate that was formerly known as posterity. Prime among the many 'laws' (or we prefer here to say 'ethics') of genre is the decision whether one signs as a scientific, philosophical or literary author – an issue that is perhaps forever beyond resolution in epistemological terms, but one that must be tabled among the opening ethical questions put to speculative philosophy.

IV: SIGNATURE AND THE ETHICAL FUTURE

Any onymous or signatory discourse accepts that the bearer(s) of its name is ethically answerable to whatever tribunal may be instituted on its account. The degree of self-consciousness with which a discourse will take account of this ethical future is, however, subject to enormous variation and relates to the author's mode of signing. That is to say, the signature outside the text binds the author *ipso facto* to a system of ethical trackback whether or not the author is conscious of this contract, whereas the signature inside the text, or, more accurately, inside the *oeuvre*, signals a more sophisticated, responsible and ardent acceptance of ethical responsibility in addressing itself directly to the ethical future.

The majority of texts are signed on the covers alone and the ethical contracts consciously entered into remain within the domain of legalities: the avoidance – or, in exceptional cases, the promotion – of charges of plagiarism, slander, racism, blasphemy, obscenity, and so on. Such signatures thereby address themselves only to a destination which does not transgress extant legalities and do not anticipate any significant involvement in the broader ethical future. Another form of signature accepts that the text may become ethically problematic, but refuses to accept responsibility for the text's effects. Such is generally the signature of the *avant-garde* which invests in the reader the freedom to construe, receive and reread the text unreservedly and without recall or recourse to any putative structure of intention instituted within the text. Implicit in such signatures is a naïve faith in something like a textual ontology; just as the poem should not mean but be, the existence of the work in the world signals an ethico–interpretative breach between text and producer.

At the furthest remove from such self-dispossessing signatures are those which sign within the text in an attempt to govern and delimit the ethical field of its reception. The signatures of writers such as Freud and Marx alert their audiences to potential readings of their texts that they were not prepared to countersign: readings that is, from which their paraph was to be erased, readings that were forbidden *in nomine auctoris*. This concern also directed itself to the posthumous destinies of their work in that both Marx and Freud struggled to authorise and institute executors of the textual estate. Marx's justly famous refusal to participate in the conversion of his proper name into a collective noun served – all too vainly when we consider the mixture of high-mindedness and vanity with which his name was to be taken – to alert ensuing generations to the necessity of monitoring very carefully those readings that his *corpus* would discountenance, readings which signed themselves *with* but not *in* his name. Freud's *oeuvre* too unfolds as in an almost obsessive codicillary quest – largely executed by his relentless training of his daughter, Anna – to preserve the purity of the signature and the governing intentions established in its name. The Freudian and Marxist texts thus – to a different degree and in unique fashions – incorporate within themselves both the possibilities of their own misreading and certain protective strategies to preserve the authentic signature and the intentions guaranteed by its seal. The nature of such signatures is to sign not just for the text's immediate future but for its every foreseeable consequence and to assign to the authorised legatees, *ephebe* or *limmŭdĭm* an absolute vigilance in upholding original authorial intent. When such an author signs, he or she demands a counter-signature ensuring more than adequate comprehension and absolute protection of the progenitors' legacy. Similarly, though without such institutional determination, Darwin's numerous 'Prefaces' to *The Origin of Species* amount to so many precautionary, premonitory signatures (the ethical in-working from the outwork into the scientific legacy) and testify to the highest degree of responsibility in that evolutionary biology awaited (and has achieved) scientific validation, but not without its originator foreseeing potential distortion and the ethical abuse to which it might be vulnerable, if undefended. Fortunately for such a troubled soul, Darwin was to die a considerably long time before the chilling Nazi experiments and obsession with eugenics came into worldview. With a comparable sense of responsibility to the future, Kant made every effort – in this case through a signature within the text rather than in the outwork – to ensure rigour and exactitude in argument would not lead to epistemological confusion or ethical distortion. Nonetheless, his work would play its own part in the bright dawn and darkest recesses of the Romantic imagination along a chain that one could conceivably trace between German Idealism, English Romanticism, French decadence, surrealism and the founding of psychoanalysis as a 'science'.

Between irresponsible or self-effacing signatures and those that assume the full weight of monitoring their ethical future, there is another type of signature, one that is heresiarchal in that it calls upon itself the burden of misreading and thus declines to bound the ethical category of accountability by that of intention. The structure of such signatures, however, is double and contradictory. Whilst such a signature is a gesture of considerable ethical responsibility in that it assumes the full weight of the text's reception history, it simultaneously affirms a certain irresponsibility in that the author therein ceases to insist – in whatever vain valiance – on preserving an ethical standard in the reading of his or her text. Such maverick signatures accept full responsibility for the text but refuse to delineate patterns of authorised reading. This is indeed a rare mode of signing but one we certainly witness in its exceptional nature – with de Sade, with Huysmans – but most especially in the both cavalier and heroic way in which Nietzsche staked his life with his writings in the form of the most defiant paraph.

Nietzsche does not append his name in such a way as to establish the passage of original, pure or proper intentions. He (con)signed his text to uncertainty, to a future in which his proper intentions would be discovered by a certain projected class of elect readers. His texts are therefore signed but unaddressed or rather addressed to the hazards of unmarked destination; that is, he left it to history to determine his intentions, a history within which he would not be at hand to expiate or repay that which fell to his name's account. Nietzsche defied the ethical constraints put in place by a signature and put his name to this transgression. The fact that he acknowledged his irresponsibility and signed his name to it is precisely why we have always had some difficulty in finding him entirely innocent of the most pernicious readings of his work. In this regard, Nietzsche's signature is heroic in the tragic sense of making an ethically responsible acknowledgement of an ethically irresponsible act.

The peculiarity of such a signature can be registered via the traditional philosophical distinction between deontological and teleological ethics, terms which translate approximately into literary theory as 'intentions' and 'consequences'. Macbeth illustrates the tragic lacuna between deed and outcome when wishing that the act could trammel up the consequence in prospect of murdering Duncan; more prosaically, Popper insists that a theory can envelop all but its consequences. The Nietzschean signature, however, entertains a unique relation to the issue of intended and unintended consequences. In playing fast and loose with intention, the signature leaves the space of deontological judgement undefended, open to invasion and restructuration by its consequences. Freud and (to a greater extent) Marx drew enormous lines of credit on the consequential, looked to the future for the decisive interpretation, *summum bonum* and apotheosis of their work, but left behind clearer instructions, guidelines as to how they should be read, what uptakes would fall within and outwith a sedulous – if imperfectly defined – set of intentions. They attempted to pre-programme interpretation; first, at the level of textual organisation and discursive proprieties; secondly, through authorised interpretative institutions roughly equivalent to the ancient Academy of Plato, the Lyceum of Aristotle, the apostolic succession of Jesus Christ. That such signatures, both oral and written, achieved anything but safe succession does not alter the signatory mode, but rather reflects the ungovernable space open by the science, system or structure of belief to which the instituting signature signed itself.

With Nietzsche, though, the only sustained attempt at shaping his legacy – apart from the ineffectual esotericism by which he sought to address his true teaching only to an elect of knowledge, and prefaces of uneven quality – takes the form of *Ecce Homo*. Here, though, we behold not so much the man as a confusing summation of his writings and an auto-canonical labour. Bizarre chapters on how to read his previous work build not towards a conclusion or set of parameters, but to an invocation, an impassioned, creative admission that he does not know what he means or how we should read him. Not for nothing is the ultimate chapter entitled 'Why I am a Destiny' for it is the work of the future to make his meanings cohere as intention and significance, his writing life having been a provocation rather than a programme, a performance rather than a project. Thus he tells us and himself that he is a violent transformative destiny who cannot be read until he – in his textual afterlife – has become what he is. The text gives us to wonder whether he knew how to read himself. The question 'Have I been understood?' (EH, 101, 103, 104) – both aloof and pleading in its repetition – reverts, Lear-like, upon its poser. Self-assessments of his previous publications – so different in every respect from the entirely clear-headed, courageous and enlightening 'Attempt at a Self-Criticism' which had prefaced the 1886 edition of *The Birth of Tragedy* – read as last-ditch attempts to divine an intentional structure beneath so many diverse, brilliant and stormy inspirations.

A search for coherence in his *oeuvre* is better rewarded by the failure to cohere than some such homogenising concept as will-to-power or the Dionysian; the grand plan is best discerned in the refusal of a plan; the governing intent in the abandonment of intent to infinite variety, discursive fecundity. The relations between the deontological and the consequential undergo a peculiar reversal because the former has little to work upon other than an authorial recklessness. The concept of 'play' further complicates this signature in that the (im)properly appended name does not establish a generic contract with his projected readerships. The names 'Immanuel Kant' and 'Charles Dickens' sign to generic expectations, whilst that of Friedrich Nietzsche signs to a discursive freedom and a bountiful, uncertain space of authorship. 'Play' may be more candid than 'the risk of reason' or the pious Marxian renunciation of the hermeneu-tic project, but it refuses outright the duty to establish a generic contract with his projected readerships or even the duty to attempt to maintain a consistent moral selfhood over and against its (Heraclitean/Humean) epistemological scepticism as to whether the man of Monday would be the man of Tuesday, as to whether 'the self' can ever coincide with 'itself' over inevitable temporal dislocations. Nietzsche himself acknowledges and even celebrates this indeterminacy. 'Supposing,' he says, not without a self-congratulation in terms of his most multifarious art of style, 'I had baptized my Zarthustra with another name, for example with the name of Richard Wagner, the perspicuity of two millennia would not have sufficed to divine that the author of "Human, All Too Human", is the visionary of Zarathustra' (EH, 29: sic).

At the most conspicuous level, Nietzsche's absolute insistence that the revaluation is an act of self-revelation and that he must sign to his phi-losophy and its future is motivated by the understandable need for genius to see itself recognised. Indeed, he concedes as much in the opening para-graph. On the other hand, Nietzsche's philosophy has consistently sought to unmask the notion of a disinterested 'will-to-truth' as a pernicious fiction concealing a more fundamental and intensely personal will to self-expression – 'the *hidden* history of the philosophers, the psychology of their great names' (EH, 4). *Beyond Good and Evil* had already denounced the attitude of impersonal reason, of transcendent neutrality as dishonest, immoral: philosophers 'pose as having discovered and attained their real opinions through the self-evolution of a cold, pure, divinely unperturbed dialectic . . . while what happens at bottom is that a prejudice, a notion, an inspiration, generally a desire of the heart sifted and made abstract, is defended by them with reasons sought after the event . . .' (BGE, 18). Nietzsche remained loyal to the conviction, formed early in his author-ial career, that philosophical works constitute a circuitous path to self-expression: 'Whither does this whole philosophy, with all its circuitous paths, want to go? Does it do more than translate . . . a strong and con-stant drive, a drive for all those things which are most endurable precisely to me? A philosophy which is at bottom the instinct for personal diet?

An instinct which seeks my own air, my own heights, my own kind of health and weather, by the circuitous paths of my head?' (D, 223).

There *is* a realm of scientific truth (no right-minded person disputes the life-saving properties of penicillin); in philosophy, there is a small range of valid propositions (those which are a priori or tautologically true, and those which are empirically verifiable). All else is the product of a certain perspective as cultivated by and/or channelled through an authorial psyche. Just as it is fundamentally dishonest to suppress the personal wellsprings of philosophical writing in order to confer the appearance of disinterested truth upon one's discourse, so an ethics of philosophical writing would require that authors sign their discourses in the sense of acknowledging their human-all-too-human provenance. 'In the philosopher,' Nietzsche had written, 'there is nothing whatever impersonal; and, above all, his morality bears decided and decisive witness to *who he is* . . .' (BGE, 19–20). Consequently, as part of Nietzsche's general demystification of the will-to-truth, and as an ethical demand, it is encumbent on the good reader to rediscover the pyschobiographical drive behind a philosopher's 'most remote metaphysical assertions', to return the subject to the system, and the author to the text he or she would depart so as to give it the appearance of 'objective truth' (BGE, 19). As the great psychologist himself, as he who unmasks the impersonal ruses of idealist philosophers, it therefore falls most emphatically to Nietzsche to sign for his philosophy in *Ecce Homo*. To absent himself would be to refuse the first question of conscience for a philosophical author as unmasked by the author of *Beyond Good and Evil*. It is for this reason, too, indispensable to say *who he is*. Whilst it is his responsibility to sign, though, it is also a matter of integrity to register the illusory nature of the notion of continuous selfhood. Already, the paradoxical play of being and becoming, of the self as a goal and process of self-creation, has been registered in the subtitle 'How One Becomes What One Is'.

Nor will Nietzsche's habit of donning masks, of adopting pseudonyms, cease in this work. How to sign remains a problem through to the end, when, on Derrida's reading, Nietzsche signs off '*Dionysus against the Crucified* . . .' (EH, 104), and perhaps even signs, as Derrida cannily points out, neither as Christ nor Dionysus, but 'in the name of the versus, the adverse or countername, the combat called between the two names' (EO, 11). The name of 'Zarathustra' dominates the text, as the one which bears the most profound insights and lessons of the Nietzschean philosophy. Moreover, Nietzsche also implies that the names of others are on occasion vehicles for his own signature. 'I am all the great names in history', he writes; adding elsewhere that when he has used the name Schopenhauer, he has in fact been naming himself: 'in "Schopenhauer as Educator" it is my innermost history, my *evolution* that is inscribed' (EH, 57) – all of which could be evidenced as symptomatic of an extreme narcissism were psychoanalytic reading our concern. As if perversely to undermine the great adventure of the name and its textual destiny, he begins the chapter entitled 'Why I Write Such Good Books' by declaring the aforementioned breach between self and text (EH, 39). To sign fully in *Ecce Homo* is not simply to sign. The works that bear his name overreach the field of coherence and continuity that is delimited by an authorial canon.

With a corpus such as Nietzsche's, the term signature is altogether more enabling than that of author in allowing for the specificity and unique nature of each authorial act to be most visibly registered. This is further apposite in that the name Friedrich Nietzsche does not establish a generic contract between text and reader in the manner that 'Charles Sanders Peirce' signs in the name of a relatively bountiful pragmatic philosophy and 'August Strindberg' with the morbid flourish of a misanthropic playwright. The name attached to Zarathustra, as Nietzsche indicates, signs as a visionary. In this sense, Nietzsche's mode of signing could be seen as a gesture at least towards generic responsibility in terms of marking radically different operations in a realm of discursive freedom and a bountifully open space of authorship. Subtitles such as *A Book for Free Spirits, with a Prelude in Rhymes and an Appendix of Songs* show a concern to identify suitable readerships by stipulating that *The Gay Science* is not written within recognisable disciplinary constraints and is not directed towards those who expect clear demarcation of genres. The charge made by Popper against Plato, Hegel and Marx is essentially that of covering over purely speculative claims arrived at through narrative or metaphoric means under the guise of objective knowledge with disregard as to the human cost of implanting such fictions as 'truths' within the minds of state architects. Rather than deploying imaginative and aesthetic strategies in the promulgation of discourses that spoke from within philosophy or even a scientific determination of history, Nietzsche's admission that his discourse was the product not of a disinterested will-to-truth but of a passionate desire to create values could be seen as a comparatively responsible gesture in terms of the contract established between author and reader.

This was certainly the view taken by Rudolf Carnap, perhaps the most committed and productive member of the movement against speculative thought which, emerging from the Vienna Circle as the logical positivist or logical empiricist movement, had an analogous influence on twentieth-century philosophy to that of Russian Formalism and the New Criticism in literary studies. In 'The Elimination of Metaphysics', a significant essay whose general target is discourses which speak beyond the bounds of verifiability whilst using the vocabulary and resources of philosophy and which specifically instantiates Heidegger's *Was Ist Metaphysik?*, Carnap concludes by upholding Nietzsche's attention to generic contracts as candid and ethically responsible:

> Our conjecture that metaphysics is a substitute, albeit an inadequate one, for art, seems to be further confirmed by the fact that the metaphysician who perhaps had artistic talent to the highest degree, viz. Nietzsche, *almost entirely avoided the error* of that confusion. A large part of his work has predominantly empirical content. We find there, for instance, historical analyses of specific artistic phenomena, or a historical-psychological analysis of morals. In the work, however, in which he expresses most strongly that which others express through metaphysics or ethics, in *Thus Spake Zarathustra*, he does not choose the misleading theoretical form, but openly the form of art, of poetry.[24] (my emphasis)

Between a careless discursive libertarianism and a parsimonious insistence upon writerly responsibility for outcomes, Carnap's position would seem to be dis-entropic in suggesting that the exorbitant work has a rightful place in culture providing its author frames the work according to a responsible horizon of disciplinary and generic expectation. *Entre deux guerres*, Schlick, Russell and Carnap saw the speculative metaphysics of Bergson and Heidegger as altogether more threatening to the disciplinary coherence of philosophy than Nietzsche's most multifarious art of style. One way, indeed, of viewing Nietzsche's attempted deconstruction of the will-to-truth in terms of a more fundamental will-to-power is through the demand that philosophy declare itself as the expression of attitude, prejudice, temperament, outlook on life (*lebenseinstellung, lebensgefühl*), as an unconscious memoir of their megalopsychic signatories (EH, 4). Carnap works from the same presumption but towards a reclassification whereby discourses such as those of Hegel and Heidegger are indexed as curious (and failed) artistic projects.[25] Allied to the ambiguity of the

---

[24] Rudolf Carnap, 'The Elimination of Metaphysics Through Logical Analysis of Language', trans. Arthur Pap, in A. J. Ayer, ed., *Logical Positivism* (New York: Macmillan, 1959), pp. 60–82: p. 80. The article was originally published as 'Überwindung der Metaphysik durch Logische Analyse der Sprache', in *Erkenninis* Vol. II (1932).

frame which can at one and the same time seem both mock-Biblical and yet designed to propose *Zarathustra* as a work more authoritative than the New Testament, the assumption made by Carnap that Nietzsche's 'analytic' works – *The Birth of Tragedy* and *The Genealogy of Morals* would appear to be indicated above – are secure in their 'theoretical form' is misguided, as history and indeed the liminality of Nietzsche's so-called 'philosophical works' attest. Indeed, Carnap fails to recognise both *oeuvre* effects and the insecurity of the ostensibly poetic Zarathustran frames. Nor is his position helped by Nietzsche's insistence that *Zarathustra* was the *secretum arcanum*, the esoteric repository of his most profound teaching. In *The Twilight of the Idols*, Nietzsche announces the end of philosophy and the beginning of creative thinking with the words 'zenith of mankind; INCIPIT ZARATHUSTRA' (TwI, 41). *Ecce Homo* is rarely more than a few pages away from either a citation from *Zarathustra* or a proclamation that the kernel of his thought has been distilled into this hybrid text. Carnap need not have had access to Nietzsche's letters in order to divine that metaphor is the abiding strategy in this uncanny discourses which straddles so very many disciplines: Nietzsche proclaims as much in the section 'Why I Write Such Good Books' (EH, 39–47).

Two years prior to writing his last work, Nietzsche had written to Jacob Burckhardt on 22 September 1886 declaring that an essentially poetic or musical impetus opened the most glorious word-shrines – of which Zarathustra was the epitome – but that articulating such inspiration 'may well be the most dangerous venture there is, not for the one who dares to express it but for the one to whom it is addressed'.[26] Numerous other testaments, inflections and statements from 1883 to 1889 could be invoked to demonstrate that Nietzsche believed *Zarathustra* to be an altogether more profound philosophical work than any other in his *oeuvre*; similarly, from the prophetic vision on Sils Maria in the summer of 1883 his published work resonates with the idea of writing as danger, one which makes its first appearance in his first book (BT, 89). Moreover, Carnap misjudges the insecurity of the poetico-Biblical frames in which *Zarathustra* is superficially enclosed. So much within this work, as with the Psalms, gives itself to aphoristic extraction and the inevitable risk of malign or ignorant appropriation. Rather like the *Republic*, the frame does not hold, nor does the implied author wish

[25] *Ibid.*, p. 80.
[26] As cited in Allison, ed., *The New Nietzsche*, xx.

it to do so: Socrates'city in words' is an *en passant* apologia for a discourse which would write a totalitarian philosophy onto the ethico-political order; Nietzsche's *Zarathustra* is closer to the Nietzsche of *Beyond Good and Evil* than to the author of *Untimely Meditations* or *Human, All Too Human*. As in the *Republic*, there is not the slightest indication of any ironic distance between 'author' and 'speaker' of metatextual reflection.[27] The added naïveté involved in Carnap's failure to recognise that whilst Nietzsche did not make Bergson and Heidegger possible, their thought took significant orientations from his work is not without significance to a general critique of post-Kantian metaphysics. Primarily, though, Carnap neglects the interrelated issues of the generic contract instituted by the signature and what – for want of a better expression – we are confined to describing as the '*oeuvre* effect'. No matter how much he toyed with, cajoled and criticised the *logos*, Nietzsche wrote in the name of philosophy, and as such each succeeding generation of readers have approached his *Zarathustra* with a certain horizon of generic (i.e. philosophical) expectation. We need not look so far afield as Plato or even Thomas More to see how arbitrary this expectation is when attempting to draw the line between philosophical expression of a fundamental attitude to life and its literary 'equivalent'.

Indeed, the Dostoyevsky so much admired by Nietzsche provides a perfect counterpoint in his elaboration of the morbid 'philosophy of the underground'. The underground discourse is without constraints: spite, invective, sarcasm, violent opinion can be articulated without the constraints of evidence, reference, philosophical architectonics, rational coherence. Commentators have noted that here Dostoyevsky gave us his most 'naked pages', access to 'the inmost recesses, unmeant for display of his heart . . .'.[28] The transition from underground discourse to narrative is artistically clumsy, crudely appended to the subterranean meditation. One can see a simple principle of textual economy at work. Realising that the callow misanthropy of the underground philosophy would not do as a discourse in itself, Dostoyevsky provided a hesitant fictional surround and a sociological justification so as to ironise the meditation, irony being that most saving figure which allows one to own whilst disowning

---

[27] This is apparent not only at the level of textual organisation but also in extratextual reflections, in particular Nietzsche's letters of 1883–4 as also in *Ecce Homo* which continually insists that 'Zarathustra' is not only expressive of Nietzsche's deepest philosophical convictions but that he has put more of his genius into the mouth of the prophet than into his other works which, with the exception of the Dionysian Dithyrambs, do not speak through a figurative or dramatic personae.

[28] 'Translator's Introduction', Fyodor Dostoyevsky, *Notes from Underground/The Double*, trans. Jessie Coulson (Harmondsworth: Penguin Books, 1972), p. 10.

the articulation.[29] The following passage could so easily belong to the Nietzsche of *Beyond Good and Evil*. And in Nietzsche's text, it would not be enounced *oratio obliqua*:

> a man, whoever he is, always and everywhere likes to act as he chooses, and not at all according to the dictates of reason and self-interest; it is indeed possible, and sometimes *positively imperative* (in my view) to act directly contrary to one's own best interests. One's own free and unfettered volition, one's own caprice, however wild, one's own fancy, inflamed sometimes to the point of madness – that is the one best and greatest good, which is never taken into consideration because it will not fit into any classification, and the omission of which always sends all systems and theories to the devil. Where did all the sages get the idea that a man's desires must be normal and virtuous? Why did they imagine that he must inevitably will what is reasonable and profitable? What a man needs is simply and solely *independent* volition, whatever that independence may cost and wherever it may lead. Well but the devil only knows what volition . . .[30]

A 'sick man', 'an unattractive man' who has 'something wrong with [his] liver' and who will make a pitiful fool of himself among his peers and a callous fool before an innocent prostitute – such a man might even be the implied author of the Nietzschean work. But the explicit provision of fictional frames allows the underground discourse to unfold while serving as a protective guardrail by which Dostoyevsky is not accountable for the underground philosophy. The discourse itself is hybrid but the sphere of the fictional (here at its most fragile) functions disentropically to gather all (hatred of life, of women, intemperate 'philosophising') within itself. Dostoyevsky may well have written the underground philosophy initially in all seriousness. But the aesthetic frame ensures that *Notes from*

---

[29] Nietzsche, of course, abounds in irony and is not above moments of self-deprecating humour but such tempering (para)strategies are not incorporated at the level of discursive framing. Passing witticisms enliven rather than structure a discourse. Similarly, the 'epode' that closes *Beyond Good and Evil* and the poems bookending *The Gay Science* scarcely deters us from taking the texts with a seriousness or levity that is so often deadly in its designs. Against this threat, Deleuze recommends a way of avoiding the ethico-political hazards of reading Nietzsche which is insecure at best: 'If Nietzsche does admit of a legitimate misinterpretation, there are also completely illegitimate misinterpretations – all those that spring from the spirit of seriousness, the spirit of gravity, Zarathustra's ape . . .' Giles Deleuze, 'Nomad Thought', p. 147. Central to the theoretical construction of a 'new Nietzsche', Deleuze's position is not nearly as new or anti-traditional as much commentary would have us believe. It belongs to what we might call a romantic reading of Nietzsche, one which extolled the vitality and vitalism of his thought over any Alexandrian attempts at systematisation.

[30] Dostoyevsky, *Notes from Underground*, pp. 33–4.

Underground is classified under 'literature' while the equally diseased and dangerous text of *The Antichrist* reposes in the seeming calm of the philosophy sections of libraries or bookshops.

One can also read the comparison transversally. In his discovery of Dostoyevsky and his reading of passages such as the above, Nietzsche himself may well have found inspiration towards a discursive freedom by freeing himself from the protocols of philosophical presentation, questions of method, continuity and all 'the imperatives of classical pedagogy'. In this inter-generic space which he was already beginning to open, this prized encounter doubtless encouraged the freewheeling, tempestuous economy which allowed Nietzsche to write so wide-rangingly, so quickly, and so copiously in the last five years of his productive life. And that very determination urged him not to waste time on pretending that the wild, brilliant, vehement and 'wicked thoughts' that found their way onto his pages were those of any other than the self-proclaimed poet-philosopher-prophet of Sils Maria himself.

V: THE ESTATE SETTLED?

It is common knowledge that nomads fare miserably under our kinds of regime: we will go to any lengths in order to settle them . . .

(Giles Deleuze, 'Nomad Thought')[31]

Some one hundred years after the death of its author – aided and abetted by sponsorial academic philosophers and theorists – Nietzsche's work is more settled now than it was during its author's lifetime or in the first half of the previous century. Attendant upon the growing breach between non-specialist intellectual culture and the academy, Nietzsche's 'philosophers of the future' manifested themselves as critical theorists whose works are unread outwith the university. The still-to-be-discovered Nietzscheanism revealed itself as a matter of scholarly interpretation, an activity Nietzsche himself thought fit only for oxen. Whether this curtailment of the reach of discourse and the retreat from mythopoeia and grand narrativising would have occurred without Nietzsche is impossible to determine, but for many Nietzsche has shaped the philosophy of the future as negative exemplar. Without heirs or imitators – for even Heidegger, despite his dependence on Nietzsche's reading of philosophy during the tragic age of the Greeks, appends nothing resembling a counter-signature to this incredible, perhaps inimitable corpus – he is not

---

[31] Deleuze, 'Nomad Thought', p. 149.

the last metaphysician so much as the last Romantic philosopher for a
Western intellectual culture sedulously reshaping its discursive boundaries in the twilight of the idols. It is *just* possible, as Derrida suggests, that
the 'great' Nietzschean politics 'is still to come in the wake of a seismic
convulsion of which National Socialism or fascism will turn out to have
been mere episodes' (EO, 31), but a chair put aside for the interpretation
of his *Zarathustra* (EH, 39) seems to us altogether more likely than the
realisation of the noontide of its prophesies. The stage is not set for 'Incipit
Zarathustra', nor does the dawning of a post-Christian Dionysian age
suggest itself as the likely outcome for Western culture: indeed, the
death of the Christian God is by no means overwhelmingly accepted.
Nonetheless, the vast majority of Nietzsche's *oeuvre* belongs with the very
best that has ever been thought or written. 'We would,' writes Richard
Rorty,

> like . . . to admire both Blake and Arnold, both Nietzsche and Mill,
> both Marx and Baudelaire, both Trotsky and Eliot, both Nabokov
> and Orwell. So we hope some critic will show how to put together
> . . . a beautiful mosaic. We hope that critics can redescribe these
> people in ways which will enlarge the canon, and give us a set of
> classical texts as rich and diverse as possible. This task of enlarging
> the canon takes the place, for the ironist, of the attempt by moral
> philosophers to bring commonly accepted moral intuitions about
> particular cases into equilibrium with commonly accepted moral
> principles.[32]

In a sense, few activities are more common among dedicated readers than
the formation of a canonical mosaic which is often not only constructed
through a canon of authors but cuts across works or indeed moments in
an individual author's corpus. One can admire Hegel's analysis of the
master–slave dialectic whilst dismissing outright the notion of the World
Spirit returning to itself, as also Marx's critique of capital whilst abhor-
ring notions such as historical inevitability and the violent dictatorship of
the proletariat. Similarly, one and the same reader may find Nietzsche's
diagnosis of the slave morality thoroughly enlightening without assent-
ing to the notion of higher types, the *Übermensch* or eternal return. In such
fashion do we, as good liberals, assume the position of the 'suitable' readers
marked by the *Phaedrus*. However, such discrimination – of an ethical or
aesthetic cast – proves impossible to formalise. Furthermore, even the

---

[32] Richard Rorty, *Contingency, Irony and Solidarity* (Cambridge and New York: Cambridge University
Press, 1989), p. 81.

benefit of the most well-developed liberal educational curriculum cannot protect against the emergence of the renegade or reckless reader. As the twentieth century has taught us, at an incalculable cost, only a very small percentage of unsuitable readers need arise in circumstances propitious to their ambitions in order to produce drastic consequences on the politico-historical plane. Hence, from Deleuze's intractable libertarianism, through the wistful Arnoldianism expressed by Rorty above, to the unsparing acuity of a more harassing master such as the Derrida of *The Ear of the Other*, we are confronted with the problem of writing falling into the wrong hands. Stranded between useless decrees such as 'Nietzsche should not have written at all' or 'no one should again be allowed to write with the recklessness of the prophet of Sils Maria', and an unethical refusal to countenance his catastrophic reception history, we must find a place between textual parsimony and profligacy. Under the provisional heading 'Creativity versus Containment' we will consider this ethical aporia by way of conclusion before taking it up in the second volume of this project on the ethics of writing, where we will argue for a certain mode of Derridean deconstruction as a disentropic manner of allowing the coruscating brilliance of much speculative thought to preserve itself in culture whilst protecting against its abuses in the social order when its essentially tropological asseverations are taken for genuine truth-claims. In what follows immediately, we will consider the fictional or poetic frame as an essential aesthetic defence against the dangerous discourses which, beginning with the very *Republic* of Plato, flourished in the 'open sea' of loss and liberation that we now name as modernity, then again as the romanticisation of philosophy.

Conclusion: Creativity versus Containment: The Aesthetic Defence

It is, of course, too late in any case: just as Hegel did not preface his *Phenomenology* with the words 'this is all a thought-experiment', so history will not permit us to read Nietzsche with the codicil: 'To be read as if spoken by a character in a novel'.[1] But the case of Nietzsche does point towards an ethic of discourse that began to take shape with the formation of the Vienna Circle, the logical positivist movement and which, after Auschwitz and Stalinism has never been far from the thoughts of responsible authors. Hence, the import and purport of the epigraph at the very front of this work.

Uncannily, the *Phaedrus* foresaw precisely the Nietzschean predicament. Every destinational problematic in the Nietzschean *oeuvre* (as its fissiparous potential gathered force between the writing of *Thus Spoke Zarathustra* in 1883 and the completion of the cavalier, bombastic, humorous but profoundly unsettled and unsettling *Ecce Homo*) is given through the persona of Socrates at 275d–e. Such prescience, we have argued, derives from the fact that dialectic covertly is also in the place of that defenceless writing, that discourse in need of its parent to come to the rescue.

Plato evolved the most succinct (if not, indeed, the most sophisticated) account of discursive ethics that we have as reference, even today. On the other hand, he transgresses the terms of his ethic by the very fact that the *Phaedrus* is a written work, a work which *eo ipso* takes its chances with uncertain destination, with unsuitable readings. The Platonic philosophy

---

[1] Kierkegaard declared that had Hegel announced at the opening of his *Science of Logic* that it was 'all just a thought-experiment' his thought would be peerless in the history of philosophy. Søren Kierkegaard, *Concluding Unscientific Postscript*, trans. David Swenson and Walter Lowrie (Princeton, NJ: Princeton University Press, 1968), p. 558. With greater scruples, and yet in an altogether less ethically problematic context, Roland Barthes asks that we read his autobiographical *récit* 'as if spoken by a character in a novel'. See *Roland Barthes by Roland Barthes*, trans. Richard Miller (London: Cape, 1977).

is thereby summoned to its own tribunal, as a dangerous instance of the general dangers of writing. The work of the *Republic* in particular falls under the censure of so many of the discursive judgements that were entirely original and new with his writing and the teaching of his master. Plato identified literary adornment as alien to *logos* yet metaphor carries much of his discourse, most marvellously in the striking metaphor *contra* metaphor in which he declares that stripped of tropes, 'the sayings of the poets . . . resemble the faces of adolescents, young but not really beautiful, when the bloom of youth abandons them' (*Republic*, 601b) and it befell Aristotle to develop the ostensibly more reputable concept (and operations) of *analogia*. Plato's banishment of myth and metaphorics from the text of philosophy makes an exception of his own work, particularly as the most powerful statement of the necessity of emerging from the shadowy unreality of *muthos* into the light of dialectical reasoning is presented – as one famous movement of a pervasively heliocentric metaphorics which for Nietzsche and Derrida has carried an optimistic western metaphysics[2] – as the myth or parable of the cave. More significantly, Plato has called himself before his own tribunal in producing a writing that was not able to defend itself against mistranslation onto the plane of history. Homer has not had a more dangerous effect upon society than Plato; indeed, no work of literature has affected the political organisation of nations in anything like the manner of the *Republic*; the only rival candidates in this respect are the works of Marx. Plato's text did not distinguish between its suitable and unsuitable readers. Moreover, it influenced the development of speculative philosophy which – at least from Rousseau to Marx – has proved the dangerous discourse *par excellence*. We might here hold Plato both 'responsible' and 'irresponsible', terms that are interchangeable in any context in which a text turns out to have dangerous effects – here the category of intention perforce gives way to outcomes – in serving to legitimate violent regimes. That his *Republic* should have provided a blueprint for every subsequent projection of an ideal order onto the plane of history is doubtless an accident that he could never have foreseen. In his view of writing as blind consignment, however, he condemns himself by letting loose his words in the

---

[2] The myth of Er that closes the *Republic* and that of Atlantis that opens the *Timaeus* are particularly resonant in that Plato here again feels that unadorned prose and propositional language will not prove adequate to the communication of the higher truths: at the close of the *Republic* one is left unsure whether a battle has been fought by philosophy with poetry or if Plato has proposed himself as the superior poet and mythologiser, and one who can, to boot, produce rational arguments. On the heliocentric metaphor, see Jacques Derrida, 'White Mythology', in Jacques Derrida, *Margins of Philosophy*, trans. Alan Bass (Brighton: Harvester Press, 1982), pp. 207–71: 245–57.

knowledge of their uncertain destination, in the knowledge that no text could ever defend itself against unsuitable readers.

Should, Plato have left his dream of the ideal commonwealth un-recorded and unwritten? Should Nietzsche have remained a classical scholar and not written inspirationally of the ends of man from the heights of Sils Maria? Would the world have been a worse place without *The Communist Manifesto* or *The Social Contract*? After all, the climate of imaginative freedom which gave us *The Prelude, The Rights of Man, A Vindication of the Rights of Woman, Prometheus Unbound, Les Fleurs du Mal, Tristan und Isolde* and Joyce's *Ulysses* also gave us *Mein Kampf,* Mussolini's *The Garden of Fascism,* Auschwitz, Treblinka and the Soviet Gulags.

'All great things are precarious,' says Socrates (*Republic,* 497d) and those who feel they are on the verge of a momentous discovery or an unprece-dented cultural achievement cannot but proceed with a sense of freedom and danger, a mixture of obsession, awe and recklessness. Marx wrote from a passionate conviction that the interests of social justice and human wants would forever be served by his work; Freud believed that culture needed the concept of the unconscious to heal the wounds of the civilised psyche; William Blake knew that the world would be incomplete without his elaborate mythologies; and John Milton that Genesis had to be rewrit-ten in the form of classical epic. Darwin's devout Christianity could not deter him from the great adventure of evolutionary biology; Socrates drank hemlock rather than recant his relentless interrogation of cultural and intellectual presuppositions. What applies here to artists and intellec-tuals naturally applies also to great scientists. If something radically new is to come into the world, it is essential that a leap of the imagination be made, one which generally makes profound connections between orders of knowledge where none had previously been perceived. Without risk, knowledge and creativity ossify as they did under the long and vigilant authority of the Church prior to the Renaissance. There must be in every great poet, philosopher or scientist something of the spirit of the William Blake who declared, 'I must Create a System, or be enslav'd by another Man's'.

How to find a balance, a middle path between creativity and contain-ment, imagination and ethics? This question can be answered in terms of textual frames, of a work's capacity to prescribe the boundaries of its own legitimate influence. It is also a question of the frames provided by the distinction between *muthos* and *logos* and of the dangers of mixed dis-courses which combine aesthetic strategies with seemingly scientific assertions. Plato succeeded in showing how poetry should not be taken as a discourse of truth, but he could not foresee the extent to which philosophy would covertly appropriate literary devices in the propagation of deterministic theories of history. Although Socrates referred to the Ideal State as a 'city in words', the *Republic*, the reference is brief, as ineffective as Zarathustra's beguiling presentation as 'poetry' (and one which, as we have noted above, is altogether contradicted by Nietzsche's unrelenting insistence that the core of his philosophy is encrypted in this work). The *Republic* does not reinforce its fictional or *ex hypothesi* frames in anything like the manner of Thomas More's *Utopia* or William Morris's *News From Nowhere*. The dialogic presentation is entirely superficial: what emerges from the 'persona' of Socrates is less a procedure of question and answer with sceptical interlocutors, and more a hollowly formal interruption in what issues as an essentially uninterrupted thesis of vast and revolutionary scope. Nor does the dialogue discourage the idea that its vision might be realised on the plane of human history. Were the ethical issue purely dependent upon content, More's *Utopia* would belong alongside the works of Rousseau, Hegel, Marx and Nietzsche as a text which lent itself to violent (mis)appropriation. But by refracting the political content through an imaginary scenario, More established a contract with his readerships – then, now and to come – that the text is to be taken as a 'philosophy of as if', a potential world with no necessary purchase on or connection with the world as it does or should stand.

Such a precedent might well have been followed by the authors of the grand narratives of modernity. Marx, for instance, could have presented his critique of capital as political philosophy and have abandoned the mythical notion of historical inevitability altogether, or presented it as a vision or fanciful hypothesis; Hegel could have catalogued his analysis of the master–slave relationship with other philosophical passages in his work and redrafted his *Phenomenology* as a curious novel centred on a mysterious and imaginary concept called the World Spirit (*Geist*), or as an epic poem charting the soul's return to itself in the manner, say, of Wordsworth's *Prelude*. As it was, Hegel proffered his mythological narrative of human history as absolute truth; Marx claimed scientific status for his story of class conflict and its utopian resolution at the end of history. The twentieth century – which is still, in its way, only now becoming *our* century – gives us to wonder what would have been the effect of the *Communist Manifesto* had Marx and Engels written a novel around its convictions, had it all been articulated by, say, Levin in Tolstoy's *Anna Karenina*, or had Nietzsche distilled *all* his wondrous and stormy insights through the medium of verse.

Plato thus prefigured the realm in which speculative philosophy would unfold and yet provided the most systematic exposition of the dangers of utilising aesthetic strategies towards cognitive ends. In this sense Popper is *partly* correct in linking Platonic dialectic and the dialectical philosophies of Hegel and Marx, but egregiously one-sided in neglecting Plato's insistence on responsible legacy and the principle of dialogue. Popper may be correct in his extreme stance on the Socratic problem in seeing the monologic strictures of the *Republic* as an arrant betrayal of the oral dialogism of his teacher, but suppresses the *Phaedrus* (in a manner which, though driven towards virtually antithetical ends, is strangely analogous with the Havelockian suppression) which serves at least as a dialogic counterbalance.[3] No such counter-balance is to be found within the two towering nineteenth-century dialecticians. What 'dialogue' there is in the Hegelian or Marxist system occurs only within the system itself. The movement from thesis to antithesis may mimic a dialogue within history, but the very idea of historical inevitability is monologic in denying people the right to be in dialogue with the history in which they live. Moreover, their capacity for generating memorable, aphoristically extractable, often self-aggrandising statements reaches the pinnacle of authorial irresponsibility. Let for the moment the very famous statements serve: 'The real is the rational, the rational is the real.' 'Workers of the world unite!' 'Hitherto philosophers have only sought to interpret the world when the point is to change it.' On a different level of irresponsibility, we might look at the opening line of the *Communist Manifesto* as literally dishonest, the ignoble lie if the noble variant could ever be ethically or philosophically upheld. The spectre of communism was not haunting Europe in the late 1840s; rather it was taking shape in the imagination – if not the DNA – of Marx himself.

Furthermore, speculative philosophy developed in the wake of religious belief as a culturally unifying force. Mobilised by a newly secularised *telos*, philosophy is now borne on the back of history, whose course

---

[3] That Popper finds himself bound to repress the *Phaedrus* in his hostile focus on the totalitarian monologism of the *Republic*, and Havelock to do likewise in advancing his altogether different thesis that the exclusion of poetry was inspired by a commitment to the written word, suggests that a forcefield emerges between these two dialogues in the elaboration of grand theories about the Platonic estate. Concerning the Socratic problem, Havelock casually treats the *Republic* as a Platonic work whose articulation through the persona of Socrates is unproblematic. Popper, on the other hand, proposes the most radical of all possible positions: i.e. that Plato actively, consciously and malignly betrayed the critically dialogic principes of his master. For Popper, the Socratic spirit and the Platonic work are entirely antagonistic. See Karl Popper, *The Open Society and its Enemies*, Volume I: *The Spell of Plato*, Volume II: *The High Tide of Prophecy: Hegel, Marx, and the Aftermath* (London: Routledge & Kegan Paul, 1945).

the speculative text partly directs. Quasi–religious providentialism is disguised as scientific process: thus the socialism of Marx and Engels will cover over its own fictionality by claiming scientific status for the narrative of conflict and resolution by which its utopian ends were to be achieved. This simultaneous deployment and occultation of aesthetic devices allows speculative philosophy to exceed the frames imposed by philosophical discipline: latent appeals to mythic and soteriological patterns of history extend the influence of nineteenth–century dialectic beyond its texts. Attempting to pattern the very fabric of a history which it can at best study, speculative philosophy further advances its influence through self-promoting, insupportable and circular dicta, which tell us that the point of philosophy is not to interpret but to change the world, or that the rational is the real. Reflection on history is construed as historical substance; mentalistic events are confused with physical events; concepts mistake themselves for the concrete. An instrument for *approaching* history presumes to determine historical reality. It is as if the map of a river's course were to alter the course of that river itself. The boundaries that separate the fictional and the cognitive are breached as the text of speculative philosophy writes itself as the future.

In 'Tlön, Uqbar, Orbis, Tertius' Jorge Luis Borges tells of how a utopia in which material objects do not exist becomes a dystopia when it connects with the real world. In Tlön, 'every philosophy is a dialectical game', its 'metaphysicians do not seek for the truth or even for verisimilitude, but rather for the astounding' and even 'judge that metaphysics is a branch of fantastic literature'.[4] The shape of the story makes it clear that speculative philosophy is benign activity whilst it remains an object of aesthetic pleasure rather than an impetus to social and political change, a stimulus to abstract contemplation rather than a seismic event in the destinies of nations. Written during the Second World War, the story was for a long time seen as an escapist fantasy or written *au dessus de la mêlée*. However, towards its close, when Tlön is engulfing the real world, the narrator writes: '[R]eality yielded on more than one account. The truth is that it longed to yield. Ten years ago any symmetry with a semblance of order – dialectical materialism, anti–Semitism, Nazism – was sufficient to entrance the minds of men.' 'Tlön', the narrator continues, 'is surely a labyrinth, but it is a labyrinth devised by men, destined to be deciphered by men.'[5] Thus does idealist thought write itself on the plane of history;

---

[4] Jorge Luis Borges, *Labyrinths* (Harmondsworth: Penguin Books, 1970), p. 34.
[5] *Ibid.*, p. 42.

the failure of mankind is to take its own imaginings for reality, to take fiction for truth. Idealist thought belongs with art, literature and music; when the Idea begins to direct the real, catastrophe ensues. Thus must humanity constantly remind itself that a compelling text is not a discourse of truth simply because it has been classified under a non-fictional category. Respect of the role and rule of genre is hence a matter of grave ethical responsibility, particularly in the writing and reading of works whose construction of historical change is fissiparous.

Here Plato's subordination of literature to philosophical analysis undergoes a curious reversal in that philosophy of a speculative cast can learn rules of prudence from poets, novelists and dramatists. The movement towards self-consciousness in literature can be read as the retreat of the work from its world. However, such an inward turn also defends literature against misreading as dogma or constructive myth. A literary work will insist on a hypothetical frame, on the fact that it is articulated 'as if'. Yet the work inhabits conditionality perpetually rather than provisionally: unlike the scientific hypothesis, it never aspires to shuffle off the hypothetical frame. A hypothesis wishes to become a demonstrable truth; a poem dreams only of being a poem. We have seen how the work of pure mathematics exists within clear disciplinary parameters. Indeed, Frege provides an exemplary historical counterpoint to Heidegger and Nietzsche in that nothing within 'his' logic is contaminated by the immorality of its author's political views. As a discourse which can defend itself, formal logic neither needs the assistance of nor can be corrupted by the attendance of the father. Analytic philosophy of the kind practised in the Anglo-American tradition also insulates itself against spectacular misreading: in these instances we encounter cognitive discourses without negative ethical overspill. Might we make any such case for the literature of modernity, in particular for the status of poetry in our world? The movement towards self-consciousness in poetry, pronounced since at least the Romantic era, can be read as a retreat of the work from its world. However, such an inward turn also defends poetry against misreading as dogma or constructive myth. As Hans Vaihinger argued in the 1920s, a poem will insist on a hypothetical frame, on the fact that it is articulated 'as if . . .'.[6] Yet the poem inhabits conditionality perpetually rather than provisionally: unlike the scientific hypothesis, it never aspires to shuffle off the hypothetical frame. A hypothesis wishes

---

[6] Hans Vaihinger, *The Philosophy of As If: A System of the Theoretical, Practical and Religious Fictions of Mankind*, trans. C. K. Ogden (London: Routledge & Kegan Paul, 1924).

to become a demonstrable truth; a poem dreams only of being a poem. As Wallace Stevens writes in 'An Ordinary Evening in New Haven': 'The poem is the cry of its occasion / Part of the res itself and not about it.' Self-conscious uses of aesthetic strategies, the reminder to the reader that what is being read exists within the realm of the imagined, the capacity of literature to be in dialogue with itself – all these meta-fictional cues do the serious work of reminding us that literary events are not to be construed as imperatives in the broader ethical realm. This is not naïvely to build up a force field between the poetic and the real, the fictive and the lived, but to commend the sense of ethical responsibility assumed in a poem drawing attention to its existence *qua* poem, a novel reminding us of its status as novel. The framing 'What would it be like if . . .?' is sanctified by the modern poet, just as it is suppressed by the speculative philosopher. In 'Of Modern Poetry', Stevens tells us that the modern poem:

> . . . has
> To construct a new stage. It has to be on that stage
> And, like an insatiable actor, slowly and
> With meditation, speak words that in the ear,
> In the delicatest ear of the mind, repeat,
> Exactly, that which it wants to hear . . . [7]

This insistence on poetry finding its own realm is not an evasion of responsibility: it resists the solidification of the work into dogma or myth, prevents it from invading the political order. On this stage, the aesthetic contains all mutinies within itself. The poetry of Keats, for example, is altogether enriched by the treacheries of his language: these treacheries feed back into the enclosed labyrinth of the work. Nor again is this to deny the power of literature to allow us to reflect critically on ethical issues: indeed, as Martha Nussbaum might argue, the novel provides a splendid forum for the consideration of social, moral and ethical dilemmas, but does so within the splendidly elaborate yet consequence-free setting of a hypothetical situation.[8] Similarly, Balzac and Dickens invite us to pass judgement on a significant moment in history but in novels which seek to understand rather than to drive history. These containments seem essential if we are not to allow fictions to masquerade as truth, to become myths which people refuse to recognise as such. As Kermode a good while back reminded us: 'If we forget that fictions are

---

[7] Wallace Stevens, *Collected Poems* (London: Faber and Faber, 1955), p. 473; p. 240.
[8] See Martha C. Nussbaum, *Love's Knowledge: Essays on Philosophy and Literature* (New York and Oxford: Oxford University Press, 1990).

fictive we regress to myth . . . "making human sense" is something that literature achieves only so long as we remember the status of fictions'. Kermode adds: 'World history, the imposition of a plot on time, is a substitute for myth.'[9] Anticipating by a long time Lyotard's call for a war on totality, Popper too teaches us that History is an unjustifiable abstraction from the many and real histories through which people live. The genius of literature is to remind us of these resonant singularities even as speculative philosophy worked to deprive thought of this meagre but invaluable knowledge.

The same critical eye which resists totalisations is today most acutely trained on the claims of contemporary science. No doubt scientific investigation can and should continue to develop along objective lines; but it can and must submit to both epistemological scepticism and ethical scrutiny. This is not to say that scientific work should be limited, only that discoveries should be passed through a tribunal similar to the one which the Socratic–Platonic philosophy hoped to make of itself some 2,500 years ago. As that philosophy said, in words that would still have relevance to contemporary debates in the ethics of science:

> when they have captured what they hunted . . . huntsmen and fishermen hand over to the cooks. Geometers and astronomers and calculators – for these are a sort of hunters too, since they are not mere makers of diagrams, but they try to find out the real meanings – so because they do not know how to use them, but only how to hunt, they hand over their discoveries, I take it, to the dialecticians to use up, at least all of them hand over who are not quite without sense.
> (*Euthydemus*, 290b–c)

The twentieth century affords us grotesque examples of the inadequacy of politicians or law-makers to intervene or arbitrate in the uses to which scientific discoveries are put. In Plato's scheme, the scientist would not be charged with responsibility as an ethical being, but neither would scientific discovery be independent of ethical judgement. That judgement would be provided not by those with an interest in political expediency, but by the dialectician or philosopher: all products of science, like those of discourse, would then be subject to philosophical and ethical interrogation before being allowed to circulate as discoveries in society at large.

---

[9] Frank Kermode, *The Sense of an Ending: Studies in the Theory of Fiction* (London and Oxford: Oxford University Press, 1966), p. 41; p. 43. For contrasting but illuminating studies of romantic self-consciousness, see David Simpson, *Irony and Authority in Romantic Poetry* (Totowa, NJ: Rowman and Littlefield, 1979); Michael O'Neill, *Romanticism and the Self-Conscious Poem* (Oxford: Clarendon, 1997).

Here again we arrive at a model of criticism in the most expansive sense – criticism as a regulative rather than constitutive practice, as an interrogatory activity governed by ethical considerations.

As we see all around us, there is once again a crisis in our distinctions between the realms of the aesthetic, cognitive and the ethical. We have witnessed the aestheticisation of science; we have also encountered the doomed project to make a science of the aesthetic; we have seen the lethal consequences of aestheticising the political. We are currently seeking to bridge the cultural divisions between cultures in which the word should only ever be the word of *logos*, and cultures for which fictional frames are sufficient to insulate the discourse against charges of racism and blasphemy. A resurgence of various forms of Christian and Islamic fundamentalism has arisen within – and perhaps in reaction to – a supposedly postmodern age in which the concept of mediation is central to cultural reception. At the same time, the synthesising temperament of a Romantic modernity has been rejected as grand narrativising. Poetry repudiated the mythopoeic and has taken cautious refuge in a parochial, demotic shelter. Philosophy in its analytic mode has preoccupied itself with technical issues or ('the end of history' hypothesis aside) has engaged with political issues only in a communitarian prudence, Aristotelian virtue or *civitas*. If we are witnessing an upheaval in epistemological categories, and should discourse become answerable to any of these three categories, then it must be the ethical that is established as the highest tribunal. And for us, as for Socrates, there is no other forum for an ethics of discourse than that of dialogue or multilogue. We can never fully recapture the culture of spoken discourse, but criticism provides its closest approximation. Criticism dialogises, it forces the work to keep answering for itself, enacts across temporal chasms what spoken dialogue achieved in the animate present. It supplements the mortality of the author and finds its own unique way of eliciting responses from the changeless form of the written, as registered in the perennial phrase *scripta manent*. While criticism produces misreadings of its own, it also produces challenges to those misreadings in a continuous exchange which defends the text from ossification within one particular structure of misreading. It enacts its own *ekphrasis* by generating movement in the static object that is a sequence of written words.

Perhaps this is why criticism in its gentlest, its most gentlepersonly form manifests itself as literary criticism because great works of art are always already in critical discussion with themselves: the experience, for example, of reading one of Keats's great odes is that the poetic movement undoes itself as dogma, subsumes every seemingly constative statement in an endless spiral of reflection. Following that experience, opening it up to new readers, allowing the poem to 'speak to the delicatest ear of the mind', is the very fine business of the literary critic. Something else again is asked of the philosophical critic: the philosopher-critic is called to challenge every truth-claim she encounters. It is her no less august calling to ask: 'What does that mean?' 'How can you claim X when Y has been assumed?' It is her duty to carry forward the relentless task of refutation begun by Plato's Socrates, to work towards a society in which nothing can be claimed until everything has been asked. Hopefully, criticism can continue to develop upon the dialogic principle which Plato visibly enshrined *within* his work.

Criticism derives etymologically from 'crisis'. This alerts us to its enduring function, for the deep structures of our ethical contracts manifest themselves with clarity only during times of crisis. Our era faces crises in knowledge which only ethical discourse seems capable of addressing. In a theocratic or properly monarchic society, the realms of the aesthetic and cognitive and ethical were subject to the constraints of power. With the demise of such cultural authority, the ethical asserts its independent claim upon thought. Perhaps this is what Kant envisaged some two centuries ago when he declared that of pure reason, aesthetic judgement and practical reason, the last deserves first rank in our thought. Criticism interposes practical reason between the claims of the aesthetic and the cognitive. As activity, it does not derive from an impulse to create but from an impulse to intervene between a text and its reception. If we were to seek the source of this interventionist imperative, we would not find it in the aesthetic or cognitive realms. For these reasons, criticism is neither an art nor a science but an ethical realm and a realm of the ethical.

Separating out what is philosophical in a 'philosophy' from what is poetic, what is narrative in a social 'science' from what is scientific, should have been the responsibility of authors in the first place but can now only fall to us in our attempts to be good readers. W. H. Auden famously wrote 'poetry makes nothing happen', a phrase which can be taken to indicate either poetry's ineffectuality or its power to give life to the void. 'No more poetry after Auschwitz,' the slogan imposed on Adorno, seemingly says quite the opposite.[10] Yet, if we take Adorno – against the grain – to mean that never again should discourses mix truth-claims with aesthetic effects, we do fullest justice to his concerns by reversing the manifest sense of the

[10] See Theodor W. Adorno, *Negative Dialectics*, trans. E. B. Ashton (London: Routledge & Kegan Paul, 1973). Adorno's actual statements on 'poetry after Auschwitz' will be discussed in the succeeding work.

slogan. 'More poetry after Auschwitz' he is best taken as saying. 'More poetry' would then mean not the proliferation of new discourses but the reclamation by literature from philosophy of all that properly belongs within its sphere, its domain. On this account alone, the responsibilities of the writer extend beyond the writing of ethical works to an ethics of writing in general.

The forthcoming companion work will consolidate this critical impulse in the ethical phonocentrism of Emmanuel Levinas and a covert ethical drive it detects behind Derrida's work on speech and writing of the 1960s. Driving further into the dilemma which the present work has only begun to open, we will explore in detail critical (dis)positions – from the Vienna Circle to the Derridean critique – which protect against the dangerous discourses of modernity as a prelude to confronting the challenges still facing criticism 'after Auschwitz', thus returning at the close to the issues raised in the opening of the present work, in both its epigraph and the ensuing critical parable. We will also continue to read the *Phaedrus* and the *Republic* as they write themselves into Levinas's ideal of face-to-face communication and his post-war antipathy to the artwork. Hence we will conjoin the irenic aims of Levinas's mission to restore ethics as 'first philosophy' with the most profound reawakening of the Socratic spirit in the Derridean critique.

Our times need the *Phaedrus* more than the *Republic* but cannot dispense with the 'good beyond being' (*epekeina tês ousias*) proposed by the latter. The importance of the *epekeina tês ousias* does not reside in its reality as an ultramundane realm: indeed, the highest ethical character may be expressed by those who do not believe that God exists but act in the world as if He did. The ethical is not a realm which surrenders answers but the imperative which summons us to our duty as to seek ways of redirecting, rephrasing and critically revising the question 'What is the Good?' If the tentative suggestions made here and in the succeeding volume towards an authorial ethics of writing make only the slightest contribution to the rethinking of this question from within what is but a minor area of literary theory, this project will have achieved its highest aspiration.

Bibliography

The reader is also referred to the 'Key to References and Abbreviations' section at the opening of this book in which publication details of the primary texts under consideration are provided.

Adkins, Arthur W. H., 'Orality and Philosophy', in Kevin Robb, ed., *Language and Thought in Early Greek Philosophy* (La Salle, IL: The Monist Library/The Hegeler Institute, 1989), pp. 207–27.

Adorno, Theodor W., *Negative Dialectics*, trans. E. B. Ashton (London: Routledge & Kegan Paul, 1973).

Allen, G. E., *Socrates and Legal Obligation* (Minneapolis, MN: University of Minnesota Press, 1980).

Allison, David B., ed., *The New Nietzsche: Contemporary Styles of Interpretation* (Cambridge, MA and London: MIT Press, 1985).

Arnold, Matthew, *Lectures and Essays in Criticism: Complete Words, Volume III*, ed. R. H. Supir (Ann Arbor, MI: University of Michigan Press, 1962).

Augustine, *Confessions*, trans. Henry Chadwick (Oxford: Oxford University Press, 1991).

Bakhtin, Mikhail, *Problems of Dostoyevsky's Poetics*, trans. R. W. Rotsel (Ann Arbour, MI: University of Michigan Press, 1973).

Barthes, Roland, *Image-Music-Text*, trans. and ed. Stephen Heath (London: Fontana, 1977).

Barthes, Roland, *Roland Barthes by Roland Barthes*, trans. Richard Miller (London: Cape, 1977).

Bauman, Zygmunt, *Postmodern Ethics* (Oxford: Blackwell, 1993).

Bernasconi, Robert and Critchley, Simon, eds, *Re-Reading Levinas* (London: Athlone, 1991).

Bernstein, Jay, *The New Constellation: The Ethical-Political Horizons of Modernity/Postmodernity* (Cambridge: Polity Press, 1991).

Blake, William, *The Marriage of Heaven and Hell* in *William Blake's Writings: Volume I*, ed. G. E. Bentley Jr. (Oxford: Clarendon, 1978).

Bluck, Richard Stanley Harold, *Plato's Life and Thought* (London: Routledge & Kegan Paul, 1949).

Bowie, Andrew, *Aesthetics and Subjectivity from Kant to Nietzsche* (Manchester and New York: Manchester University Press, 1990).

Burger, Ronna, *Plato's* Phaedrus: *A Defence of a Philosophic Art of Writing* (Alabama: University of Alabama Press, 1980).

Carnap, Rudolf, 'The Elimination of Metaphysics Through Logical Analysis of Language', trans. Arthur Pap, in A. J. Ayer, ed., *Logical Positivism* (New York: Macmillan, 1959), pp. 60–82.

Clark, Maudemaire, *Nietzsche on Truth and Philosophy* (Cambridge: Cambridge University Press, 1990).

Clark, Timothy, *The Theory of Inspiration: Composition as a Crisis of Subjectivity in Romantic and post-Romantic Writing* (Manchester: Manchester University Press, 1997).

Clement of Alexandria, *The Writings of Clement of Alexandria*, trans. Rev. William Wilson, Ante-Nicene Christian Library: Translations of the Church Fathers, Down to A.D. 325, eds Rev. Alexander Roberts and James Donaldson, vol. 4 (Edinburgh: T. and T. Clark, 1867).

Colli, Giorgio and Montinari, Mazzino, eds, *Kritische Gesamtaugabe, Werke* (Berlin and New York: Walter de Gruyter, 1967).

Conway, Daniel, *Nietzsche's Dangerous Game: Philosophy in the 'Twilight of the Idols'* (Cambridge: Cambridge University Press, 1997).

Critchley, Simon, *The Ethics of Deconstruction: Derrida and Levinas* (London: Blackwell, 1992).

Cushman, Robert, *Therapeia: Plato's Conception of Philosophy* (Chapel Hill, NC: University of North Carolina Press, 1958).

Danto, Arthur C., *Nietzsche as Philosopher* (New York: Columbia University Press, 1965).

Darwin, Charles, *On the Origin of Species by Means of Natural Selection or the Preservation of Favoured Races in the Struggle for Life*, sixth edition (London: John Murray, 1872).

Derrida, Jacques, 'Violence et métaphysique: essai sur la pensée d'Emmanuel Levinas', *Revue de Métaphysique et de Morale*, 1964, no. 3 (pp. 322–54) and 4 (pp. 425–73).

Derrida, Jacques, *Writing and Difference*, trans. Alan Bass (Chicago: University of Chicago Press, 1978).

Derrida, Jacques, *Margins of Philosophy*, trans. Alan Bass (Brighton: Harvester Press, 1982).

Derrida, Jacques, *Spectres of Marx*, trans. Peggy Kamuf (London: Routledge, 1994).

Derrida, Jacques, *Points . . .: Interviews, 1974–1994*, ed. Elisabeth Weber, trans. Peggy Kamuf et al. (Stanford, CA: Stanford University Press, 1995).

Detwiler, Bruce, *Nietzsche and the Politics of Aristocratic Radicalism* (Chicago: University of Chicago Press, 1990).

De Vries, G. J., *A Commentary on the 'Phaedrus' of Plato* (Amsterdam: Adolf M. Hakkert, 1969).

Dillon, John, *The Middle Platonists: A Study of Platonism 80 B.C. to A.D. 220* (London: Duckworth, 1977).

Dostoyevsky, Fyodor, *Notes from Underground / The Double*, trans. Jessie Coulson (Harmondsworth: Penguin Books, 1972).

Eaglestone, Robert, *Ethical Criticism: Reading after Levinas* (Edinburgh: Edinburgh University Press, 1997).

Edelstein, Ludwig, *Plato's Seventh Letter, Philosophia Antiqua*, vol. XIV (Leiden: E. J. Brill, 1966).

Edmundson, Mark, *Literature against Philosophy, Plato to Derrida: A Defence of Poetry* (New York: Cambridge University Press, 1995).

Ferrari, G. R. F., *Listening to the Cicadas: A Study of Plato's 'Phaedrus'* (Cambridge: Cambridge University Press, 1987).

Fish, Stanley, *Self-Consuming Artifacts: The Experience of Seventeenth-Century Literature* (Los Angeles and London: University of California Press, 1972).

Foucault, Michel, 'What is an Author?' *Language, Counter-Memory, Practice: Selected Essays and Interviews*, ed. Donald Bouchard, trans. Donald Bouchard and Sherry Simon (Ithaca, NY: Cornell University Press, 1977), pp. 113–38.

Friedländer, Paul, *Plato 1: An Introduction*, 3 vols, trans. Hans Meyerhoff (London: Routledge & Kegan Paul, 1958).

Friedman, F. R., *Who Wrote the Bible?* (London: Jonathan Cape, 1988).

Gadamer, Hans Georg, *Hegel's Dialectic* (New Haven, CT: Yale University Press, 1976).

Gadamer, Hans-Georg, *Dialogue and Dialectic: Eight Hermeneutical Studies on Plato*, trans.
P. Christopher Smith (New Haven, CT and London:Yale University Press, 1980).

Golomb, Jacob and Wistrich, Robert S., eds, *Nietzsche, Godfather of Fascism?: On the Uses
and Abuses of a Philosophy* (Princeton, NJ and Oxford: Princeton University Press,
2002).

Gould, John, *The Development of Plato's Ethics* (Cambridge: Cambridge University Press,
1955).

Graziosi, Barbara, *Inventing Homer:The Early Reception of Epic*, Cambridge Classical
Studies (Cambridge: Cambridge University Press, 2002).

Gulley, Norman, *The Philosophy of Socrates* (London: Macmillan, 1968).

Habermas, Jürgen, *Theory of Communicative Action* (Boston, MA: Beacon Press, 1984).

Hackforth, R., *The Authorship of the Platonic Epistles* (Manchester: Manchester University
Press, 1913).

Hackforth, R., *Plato's Phaedrus*, ed. with an intro. and commentary R. Hackforth
(Cambridge: Cambridge University Press, 1952).

Hamilton, Walter, trans., *Phaedrus and the Seventh and Eighth Letters* (Harmondsworth:
Penguin Books, 1973).

Hare, R. M., 'Plato and Mathematicians', in Renford Bambrough, ed., *New Essays on
Plato and Aristotle* (London: Routledge & Kegan Paul, 1965), pp. 21–38.

Härltle, Heinrich, *Nietzsche und der Nationalsozialismus* (Munich, Eher: Zentralverlag der
NSDAP, 1937).

Harris, William V., *Ancient Literacy* (Cambridge, MA: Harvard University Press, 1989).

Havelock, Eric A., *The Literate Revolution in Greece and its Cultural Consequences*
(Princeton, NJ: Princeton University Press, 1982).

Havelock, Eric A., 'The Orality of Socrates and the Literacy of Plato:With Some
Reflections on the Historical Origins of Moral Philosophy in Europe', in Eugene
Kelly, ed., *New Essays on Socrates* (Boston, MA: University Press of America, 1984),
pp. 67–93.

Havelock, Eric A., *The Muse Learns to Write: Reflections on Orality and Literacy from
Antiquity to the Present* (New Haven, CT and London:Yale University Press,
1986).

Heidegger, Martin, *The Question Concerning Technology and Other Essays*, ed. and trans.
William Lovitt (New York: Harper & Row, 1977).

Heidegger, Martin, *Nietzsche: Volume I: The Will to Power as Art*, trans. David Farrell Krell
(London and Henley: Routledge & Kegan Paul, 1981).

Irwin, Terence, *Plato's Moral Theory* (Oxford: Clarendon Press, 1977), pp. 39–40.

Irwin, Terence, *Plato's Ethics* (New York and London: Oxford University Press, 1995).

Isocrates, 'Letter to Philip', trans. George Norlin, in *Isocrates I*, Loeb Classical Library
(London:William Heinemann, 1928), pp. 262–3.

Jaeger, Werner, *Aristotle: Fundamentals of the History of his Development*, second edition,
trans. Richard Robinson (Oxford: Clarendon Press, 1948).

James, William, *Pragmatism: A New Name for Some Old Ways of Thinking* (London:
Longmans, 1907).

Jay, Martin, *Fin de Siècle Socialism* (New York: Routledge, 1988).

Kermode, Frank, *The Sense of an Ending: Studies in the Theory of Fiction* (London and
Oxford: Oxford University Press, 1966).

Kierkegaard, Søren, *The Journals of Søren Kierkegaard*, No. 5777 (1846), trans. Alexander
Dru (London: Fontana/Collins, 1958).

Kierkegaard, Søren, *Concluding Unscientific Postscript*, trans. David Swenson and Walter
Lowrie (Princeton, NJ: Princeton University Press, 1968).

Knights, Ben, *The Idea of the Clerisy in the Nineteenth Century* (Cambridge: Cambridge
University Press, 1978).

Kritzman, Lawrence D., ed., *Michel Foucault: Politics, Philosophy, Culture. Interviews and Other Writings 1977–1984* (New York: Routledge, 1988).

Lang, Berel, *Act and Idea in the Nazi Genocide* (Chicago: University of Chicago Press, 1990).

Leavis, F. R., *The Common Pursuit* (London: Chatto and Windus, 1952).

Leavis, F. R., *The Critic as Anti-Philosopher: Essays and Papers*, ed. G. Singh (London: Chatto and Windus, 1982).

Levinas, Emmanuel, *Totalité et infini: Essai sur l'extériorité* (The Hague: Martinus Nijhoff, 1961).

Levinas, Emmanuel, 'La trace de l'autre', *Tijdschrift vour Philosophie* (September 1963), pp. 605–23.

Levinas, Emmanuel, *Totality and Infinity: an Essay on Exteriority*, trans. Alphonso Lingis (The Hague: Martinus Nijhoff, 1969).

Llewelyn, John, *Appositions of Jacques Derrida and Emmanuel Levinas* (Bloomington and Indianapolis, IN: Indiana University Press, 1995).

Lord, Alfred B., *The Singer of Tales* (Cambridge, MA: Harvard University Press, 1960).

McDonald, Christie and Gary Wihl, eds, *Tranformations in Personhood and Culture after Theory: The Languages of History, Aesthetics and Ethics* (University Park, PN: The Pennsylvania State University Press, 1994).

Mackenzie, Mary Margaret, 'Paradox in Plato's *Phaedrus*', *Proceedings of the Cambridge Philological Society* XXVIII (1982), pp. 64–76.

McLuhan, Marhall, *The Guttenberg Galaxy: The Making of Typographic Man* (London and Toronto: Routledge, 1962).

Man, Paul de, *Allegories of Reading: Figural Language in Rousseau, Nietzsche, Rilke and Proust* (New Haven, CT: Yale University Press, 1979).

Margolis, Joseph, 'The Emergence of Philosophy', in Kevin Robb, ed., *Language and Thought in Early Greek Philosophy* (La Salle, IL: The Monist Library/The Hegeler Institute, 1989), pp. 228–43.

Marx, Karl, and Engels, Friedrich, *The Communist Manifesto*, intro. and notes A. J. P. Taylor, trans. Samuel Moore (Harmondsworth: Penguin Books, 1967).

Megill, Alan, *Prophets of Extremity: Nietzsche, Heidegger, Foucault, Derrida* (Berkeley and Los Angeles: University of California Press, 1985).

Miller, J. Hillis, *The Ethics of Reading* (New York: Columbia University Press, 1987).

Minnis, A. J., *Medieval Theory of Authorship: Scholastic Literary Attitudes in the Later Middle Ages* (London: Scolar Press, 1984).

Minnis, A. J. and Scott, A. B., eds, *Medieval Literary Theory and Criticism c. 1100–c.1375* (Oxford: Clarendon, 1988).

More, Thomas, *Utopia* (Cambridge: Cambridge University Press, 1989).

Murphy, N. R., *The Interpretation of Plato's Republic* (Oxford: Clarendon Press, 1951).

Nehamas, Alexander, *Nietzsche: Life as Literature* (Cambridge, MA: Harvard University Press, 1985).

Nehamas, Alexander and Woodruff, Paul, trans., *Plato: Phaedrus* (Indianapolis, IN and Cambridge: Hackett, 1995).

Nietzsche, Friedrich, *Socrates und die Griechische Tragödie: Ursprüngliche Fassung der Geburt der Tragödie aus dem Geiste der Musik*, ed. H. J. Mette (Munich: Beck, 1933).

Nussbaum, Martha, *The Fragility of Goodness: Luck and Ethics in Greek Tragedy and Philosophy* (Cambridge: Cambridge University Press, 1986).

Nussbaum, Martha, *Love's Knowledge: Essays on Philosophy and Literature* (Oxford: Oxford University Press, 1990).

O'Neill, Michael, *Romanticism and the Self-Conscious Poem* (Oxford: Clarendon, 1997).

Ong, Walter J., SJ, *The Presence of the Word: Some Prolegomena for Cultural and Religious History* (New Haven, CT and London: Yale University Press, 1967).

Ong, Walter J., SJ, *Orality and Literacy: The Technologizing of the Word* (London: Methuen, 1982).

Ophir, Adir, *Plato's Invisible Cities: Discourse and Power in the Republic* (London: Routledge, 1991).

Owens, Joseph, *The Doctrine of Being in the Aristotelian Metaphysics*, second edition (Toronto: Institute of Medieval Studies, 1963).

Pappas, Nickolas, 'Socrates' Charitable Treatment of Poetry', *Philosophy and Literature*, vol. 13, no. 2 (1982), pp. 248–61.

Parry, Milman, *l'Epithète traditionelle dans Homère* (Paris: Société d'Éditions 'Belle Lettres', 1928).

Parry, Milman, *The Making of Homeric Verse: The Collected Papers of Milman Parry*, ed. Adam Parry (Oxford: Oxford University Press, 1970).

Pickstock, Catherine, *After Writing: On the Liturgical Consummation of Philosophy* (Oxford: Blackwell, 1998).

Popper, Karl, *The Open Society and its Enemies*, Volume I: *The Spell of Plato*, Volume II: *The High Tide of Prophecy: Hegel, Marx, and the Aftermath* (London: Routledge & Kegan Paul, 1945).

Robinson, Richard, *Plato's Earlier Dialectic* (Ithaca, NY: Cornell University Press, 1941).

Rorty, Richard, *Contingency, Irony and Solidarity* (Cambridge: Cambridge University Press, 1989).

Rosen, Stanley, *Nihilism: A Philosophical Essay* (New Haven, CT: Yale University Press, 1969).

Rowe, C. J., *Plato: Phaedrus, with Translation and Commentary* (Warminster: Aris and Phillips, 1886).

Ruthven, Malise, *A Satanic Affair: Salman Rushdie and the Wrath of Islam* (London: The Hogarth Press, 1991).

Schacht, Richard, *Nietzsche* (Boston, MA: Routledge & Kegan Paul, 1983).

Schrift, Alan D., *Nietzsche's French Legacy: A Genealogy of Poststructuralism* (New York and London: Routledge, 1995).

Scolnicov, Samuel, 'Three Aspects of Plato's Philosophy of Learning and Instruction', *Paideia*, Fifth Annual, Special Plato Issue (1976), pp. 50–62.

Scully, Stephen, *Plato's Phaedrus: A Translation with Notes, Glossary, Appendices, Interpretative Essay and Introduction* (Newburyport, MA: Focus Philosophical Library, 2003).

Sedgwick, Peter R., *Nietzsche: A Critical Reader* (Oxford: Blackwell, 1995).

Shapiro, Gary, *Nietzschean Narratives* (Bloomington, IN: Indiana University Press, 1989).

Shelley, Percy Bysshe, *Shelley's Poetry and Prose*, ed. Donald Reiman and Sharon B. Powers (New York and London: Norton, 1977).

Simpson, David, *Irony and Authority in Romantic Poetry* (Totowa, NJ: Rowman and Littlefield, 1979).

Solmsen, Friedrich, Review of *Preface to Plato*, *American Journal of Philology*, vol. LXXXVII, no. 1 (1966), pp. 99–105.

Sprague, R. P., ed., *The Older Sophists* (Columbia: University of South Carolina Press, 1972).

Stevens, Wallace, *Collected Poems* (London: Faber and Faber, 1955).

Taylor, A. E., *Socrates* (Edinburgh: Edinburgh University Press, 1933).

Thomas, Rosalind, *Literacy and Orality in Ancient Greece* (Cambridge: Cambridge University Press, 1992).

Vaihinger, Hans, *The Philosophy of As If: A System of the Theoretical, Practical and Religious Fictions of Mankind*, trans. C. K. Ogden (London: Routledge & Kegan Paul, 1924).

Vlastos, Gregory, *Socratic Studies* (Cambridge and New York: Cambridge University Press, 1994).

Waite, Geoff, *Nietzsche's Corps/e: Aesthetics, Politics, Prophecy, or the Spectacular Technoculture of Everyday Life* (Durham, NC: Duke University Press, 1995).

West, Thomas G. and West, Grace Starry, trans. *Four Texts on Socrates: Plato's 'Euthyphro', 'Apology' and 'Crito' and Aristophanes' 'Clouds'* (Ithaca, NY: Cornell University Press, 1984).

White, Nicholas P., *A Companion to Plato's Republic* (Oxford: Blackwell, 1979).

Wiesel, Elie, *Night* (London: Penguin Books, 1981).

Wihl, Gary and Williams, David, eds, *Literature and Ethics: Essays Presented to A. E. Malloch* (Kingston and Montreal: McGill-Queen's University Press, 1988).

Willard, Dallas, 'Concerning the "Knowledge" of the Pre-Platonic Greeks', in Kevin Robb, ed., *Language and Thought in Early Greek Philosophy* (La Salle, IL: The Monist Library/The Hegeler Institute, 1989), pp. 244–53.

Williams, Bernard, *Moral Luck* (Cambridge: Cambridge University Press, 1981).

Williams, Bernard, *Ethics and the Limit of Philosophy* (London: Fontana, 1985).

Yack, Bernard, *The Longing for Total Revolution: Philosophical Sources of Discontent from Rousseau to Marx and Nietzsche* (Berkeley and Los Angeles: University of California Press, 1992).

Zeller, B., ed., *Marbacher Kataloge: 'Das 20. Jahrhundert. Von Nietzsche bis zur Gruppe 47'* (Deutsche Schillergesellschaft Marbach a. N., 1980).

Index of Names